THE URBAN STARS IN THE TEXAS CROWN

by

Delbert R. Ward

A Hearthstone Book

Carlton Press, Inc. New York, N.Y.

Manufactured in the United States of America
ISBN 0-8062-3831-3

CONTENTS

FOREWORD

The towns and cities of Texas are young and still growing. The oldest town is approximately 166 years old. Stephen F. Austin was one of the earliest colonizers. He received his grant from the Mexican Republic in 1822. He wisely chose the fertile, well watered, temperate area between the Colorado and the Brazos River for his colony.

Colonists came to Texas to secure large tracts of cheap land. The desire to own land and to be independent were inbred characteristics of these colonists. Many of them were poor share-croppers, with little chance of ever acquiring their own farm or ranch in their present location. All of history shows us that people are willing to fight and suffer when they truly want something. These colonists would endure great hardships to obtain the land and independence they wanted.

During the Texas War for Independence from Mexico, these colonists were willing to fight and die for the lands they had gained or the lands they were promised. Without their willingness to fight against great odds, Texas could never have defeated Mexico.

Once Texas won its independence, the new nation was anxious to have as many immigrants as possible. Settlers were offered 320 acres of land for $0.50 per acre. Thousands of settlers flocked in and took land in the river bottoms of the San Antonio, Guadalupe, Colorado, Brazos and San Jacinto Rivers. And, unlike the people who later joined the California Gold Rush, these seekers brought their families with them. This made it easier to form good communities.

From 1836-1845 people flocked to Texas. The entry of Texas into the Union in 1845 and the ensuing war with Mexico temporarily slowed the immigration. However, the offer of land still brought the settlers to Texas.

Many ethnic groups migrated to Texas, and we are richer for it. Thousands of German immigrants settled in the New Braunfels, Sequin, Fredericksburg, and Kerrville areas. There were also Czech, Polish, French, Irish, and English settlements.

Prior to 1875 the area west of a line from San Antonio north to Wichita Falls was still Indian country. The Apaches, Kiowas and Comanches vigorously contested all settler encroachment. After the Civil War the federal government finally established an army post along this frontier, and by 1880 had pushed the Indians onto reservations. We modern Texans are sometimes prone to discount the threat and danger that the Indians had on the colonization of Texas. The Indians fought ferociously to hold onto the land they claimed as theirs (true, they had no title to the land, but it was theirs by right of first possession). The Spanish had brought horses which the Indians captured and bred. This gave the Texas Indians great mobility and greatly increased their ability to wage effective war against the settlers. This threat retarded the western movement of the settlers for about 60 years.

In addition to fighting the Indians, Texans have fought in many wars: the War for Independence against Mexico in 1836, the U.S. war with Mexico in 1845-46, the Spanish-American War in 1898, World War I in 1917-19, World War II in 1941-45, the War in Korea in 1950-53, and the War in Vietnam from 1961-75. All of these wars have had a major impact not only on the people of Texas, but also on the growth of Texas towns and cities.

From the start of Texas colonization in 1822 until the vigorous entry of the railroads in 1872, there was only very primitive transportation. The foreign immigrants landing at undeveloped Texas ports and the settlers from other states all travelled overland by horseback, wagons or ox carts. There were few roads and fewer bridges. Until about 1855 there were no shallow-draft steamboats to ply the navigable stretches of the large Texas rivers. During this 33-year period the settlers had a tendency to settle along the few roads and trails, and at fords and mule-powered ferries on the rivers.

Several famous dirt roads developed, and these also had a great impact on the location of settlements. The Opelousas Road from Louisiana through Nacogdoches and on into the interior of Texas was well travelled. And, in early years, the Camino Real from San Antonio to Mexico was heavily travelled.

Prior to the coming of the railroads, the ranchers had to drive their cattle to Kansas to the nearest railheads. There were several well-known cattle trails, such as the Dodge Trail and the Chisholm Trail. The push to build railroads in Texas was strong. A railroad could transport cattle, cotton, lumber, hides, and grain for about 10% what it cost to transport these products by wagon train and ox cart. The Texas and US governments offered lucrative land bonuses to the railroads. The great railroad construction boom in Texas lasted from 1875-1925. This 50-year period greatly accelerated the entry of colonists into Texas. The path of the railroads also dictated the location of towns.

The formation and location of Texas towns were the result of many factors, as you will see in this book. The largest factor in the location of the early towns was the availability of dependable water and adequate rainfall. This dictated the location along rivers, streams and at springs. In addition to a water supply the river valleys invariably had the most fertile land. Access to water and fertile soil caused the earliest settlers to favor land east of San Antonio.

Later, with the great railroad construction boom, hundreds of towns sprung up along the railroads where the railway companies established water supply points, depots, and terminals. Some towns grew up at natural ports. Towns grew up around fords on the rivers and at points where ferries had been established. A number of towns were located by major oil strikes. In the cotton belt, towns grew up around cotton gins. Some towns grew up around army posts. Several towns were started as trading posts along the trans-Texas roads and trails where wagon traffic was heavy. When they established new counties, the Texas legislature dictated the location of many towns as county seats. Many towns bloomed for a while and then died. Underlying the development of practically every town and city is the economic reason that made it possible for them to exist and produce employment for their citizens.

There are about 1900 incorporated towns in Texas. Of these, 295 have populations over 3,000. These are the towns selected for inclusion in this book.

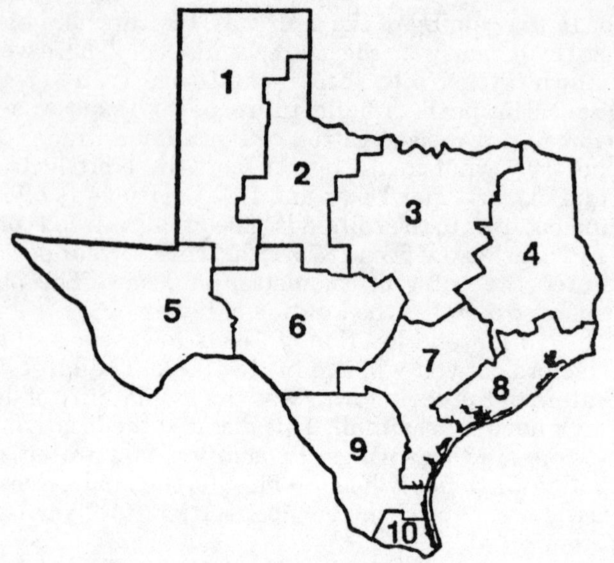

REGIONS

1. High Plains
2. Low Rolling Plains
3. North Central
4. East Texas (Piney Woods)
5. Trans-Pecos
6. Edwards Plateau
7. South Central
8. Upper Coast
9. South Texas Plains
10. Lower Valley

ABILENE

This prosperous city is near the geographical center of Texas. It is accessible by Interstate Highways 20 and 80 east-west and Highways 83, 84, and 277 north-south. It is located on the Missouri Pacific Railroad, the successor of the Texas and Pacific Railroad, which was completed through Abilene in 1881. It was at that time that the county seat was moved from Buffalo Gap to the newly formed town of Abilene.

Colonel C. W. Merchant and John Simpson were prominent Texans who had induced the Texas and Pacific Railway to route the railroad through the location of what came to be named Abilene. These two men named the town "Abilene" after the famous Kansas cattle shipping point of the same name, in hopes that Abilene, Texas would become even more important than Abilene, Kansas.

It was on the 15th day of March 1881 that the city of Abilene was "born" upon the completion of the railroad.

Settlers had began to move into this part of the country in 1875, after the Comanche Indians had been pushed to the west.

The United States Armed Forces began their long relationship with West Texas in 1852 with the building of Fort Phantom. This fort is no longer in existence. Today Dyess Air Force Base houses the 96th Strategic Bombardment Wing. During WW II, Camp Barkely, the training center which housed in excess of 60,000

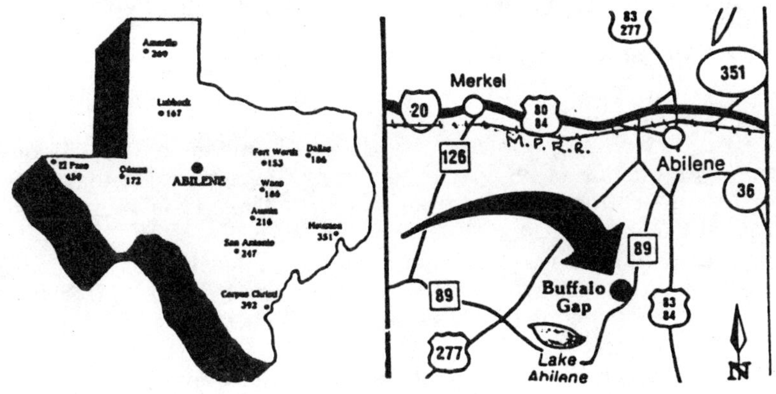

men, was located there. A large prisoner of war camp was also located there.

Abilene Christian University, Hardin-Simmons University, and McMurry College are located at Abilene.

Abilene Metropolitan Service Area, which encompasses Taylor County, has a population of 118,600.

ALBANY

Albany is 35 miles northeast of Abilene. It is the county seat of Shackleford County. It is served by U.S. Highways 285, 180 and 283, and S.H.- 6 and FM 1084 and 601.

There is no railroad at Albany or in Shackleford County. The nearest commercial airport is Abilene.

The altitude of Albany is approximately 1200 ft. above sea level. The annual rainfall is 26.5 inches, which is ample rain for growing cotton, milo maize, and wheat. The area around Albany raises cattle, sheep, and hogs.

The terrain in Shackleford County is hilly with a considerable amount of relief. The elevation ranges from 1200 to 2000 feet. The land that has not been cleared is covered with mesquite and cedar.

The annual agricultural income of the county is $12,000,000, which is less than 4% of the average income for Texas counties.

Albany was named for Albany, Georgia, which was the hometown of one of the co-founders of the town.

The population of the city is 3,100.

Albany has a council-mayor/city manager form of city government.

The economy is based on oil, gas and agriculture.

ALICE

Alice is a young, vibrant city. It was founded in 1904. It now has a population of 28,400. It serves as the regional trade center for a multi-county population of 130,000. The city is 44 miles due west of Corpus Christi.

From a barren wasteland stretching endlessly west from the Gulf Coast, where wild cattle wandered and drank water from stagnant pools formed from some past rainfall, has sprung a modern thriving city.

Shortly after 1850, a few settlers came in ox-carts and wagons, bringing with them only the barest of necessities, to a trading center just east of the present town of Alice. This friendly and progressive community was to bear the name "Collins," named after N. G. Collins, an owner of extensive land in this section. In 1877, the Texas-Mexican Railroad laid rails through Collins on its erratic course toward Mexico, thereby giving Collins a transportation connection.

The town of Collins was shortlived, about 30 years, and was soon to become a ghost town, just a name to remember.

The San Antonio and Aransas Pass Railroad, wishing to push their rails south from San Antonio toward the Rio Grande, attempted to buy right-of-way through the village of Collins and was refused by several of the landowners. They then secured right-of-way some two miles to the west. In 1886, their line was completed to intersect the Tex-Mex tracks.

As a result of this, a new town was started at the point where the two railroads meet. The new town was first named "Bandana," because of a presidential election in which the red bandana was a symbol.

The name Bandana was soon discarded in favor of the new name, "Kleberg," honoring Robert J. Kleberg, son-in-law of the famous Capt. Richard King, who was active in developing the area. The postal authorities refused to sanction the name of "Kleberg" because another community already bore the name. At the suggestion of Mr. Kleberg, the little town was named "Alice" in honor of his wife, Alice King, the daughter of Captain Richard King.

With so many settlers moving into the western part of Nueces County, it became necessary to organize a separate county to serve the area. Jim Wells County was carved out of Nueces County in 1911. The Texas Legislature created Jim Wells County. The county was named in honor of Judge James B. Wells, a statesman and jurist of the area.

The town of Alice was incorporated in 1904, while still located in Nueces County. It became the county seat of Jim Wells County.

At one time, Alice shipped more cattle by rail than any other railpoint in the world. Prior to the coming of the railroads, the Chisholm Trail passed through Jim Wells County.

During the period of 1890-1900, Alice was nicknamed "the

Windmill City," because there were so many windmills in the immediate vicinity.

The rich history of Alice is interesting. It is a city formed by active, strong people. It owes a lot to its Hispanic heritage.

ALPINE

Alpine is a beautiful town situated at the foot of the picturesque Davis Mountains. It has an elevation of 4,484 ft. Twenty-four miles to the northwest is the Old Fort Davis, which was established by the U.S. Army in 1854. Fort Davis is called the "Mile High City of Texas." Fort Davis National Historic site is owned and operated by the National Park Service, U.S. Department of the Interior.

Alpine has a city-council form of government with a mayor and city manager.

Alpine is located 356 miles west of San Antonio on U.S. 90 and 210 miles east of El Paso.

The first name of Alpine was Osborne, which was given to the water-stop station by the Southern Pacific Railroad. The railroad was experiencing difficulty in getting good water for their steam locomotives, and they found that there was a clear spring stream adjacent to the railroad on property owned by Thomas O. Murphy. They negotiated with Mr. Murphy to get this water, and in the trade he got the railroad to name the town Murphyville. This was done in 1882, shortly after the Southern Pacific Railroad reached Alpine. Murphyville was designated as the county seat of Brewster County when it was carved out of Presidio County in 1888. Just prior to the formation of Brewster County, the people had become dissatisfied with the name of Murphyville for their town, and at a special election in 1888 the citizens voted to change the name to Alpine. The name Alpine was selected by a committee because the mountainous scenery around the area was somewhat similar to that in Switzerland. The town was aptly named.

Alpine is located in a mountainous region of West Texas. The Davis Mountains are located to the west and north of the city. The Glass Mountains lay to the east. The Santiago Mountains, Chalk Mountains, Christmas Mountains and Chisos Mountains of Big Bend National Park are south of Alpine.

Alpine is located at the junction of the Southern Pacific Railroad and the Sante Fe Railroad. The Southern Pacific runs east and west and the Santa Fe comes in from the northeast. Alpine is a regular AMTRAK stop. Alpine is also well served by major highways. The U.S. Hwy. 90, which runs from San Antonio to El Paso, goes through Alpine. U.S. Hwy. 67 goes north from Alpine to Fort Stockton. State Hwy. 118 goes northwest to Fort Davis and south through the Big Bend National Park to the town of Terlingua and to Santa Elena Canyon on the Rio Grande River.

Brewster is the largest county in Texas, and the primary industry is ranching, followed by tourism. Some mining is still carried on, but the larger operations are not active. It has more area than the state of Connecticut and Rhode Island combined. The county has an area of 6,169 sq. miles.

Alpine is the home of Sul Ross State University which was established at Alpine in 1919. This was a great help in insuring the steady growth of Alpine. Alpine's Municipal Airport has a 6,000 foot runway capable of handling most aircraft and heavy loads. Recreation includes hunting for mule and white-tail deer, javelina, quail, and dove, as well as hiking, camping, river running, rock hounding, photography, four-wheel driving and horseback trips.

Alpine has a population of 6,575, its elevation is 3800 feet. It is at the center of a great ranching country of West Texas. There is scenery all around Alpine that is fantastic. Other attractions include the Woodward Agate Ranch, Big Bend National Park, Terlingua, Lajitos on the Rio Grande, the Gage Hotel in Marathon, the Museum of the Big Bend, and the Marfa Lights near Marfa to the west of Alpine. There are very few people in Texas who know of the beautiful mountains of this area. Alpine is the gateway to the Big Bend National Park, as well as Marathon, which is located to the east of U.S. 90.

ALVIN

Alvin is located in the northeast part of Brazoria County. It is 25 miles N-NW of Galveston and 26 miles SE of Houston.

State Highway 6 runs through Alvin in a NW-SE direction. The Santa Fe Railroad parallels Highway 6 on the south side. State Highway 35 runs almost due south from Houston to Alvin, then turns to the southwest and parallels the Gulf Coast.

Alvin is one of the several towns in Texas built for, and because of, the cattle industry. During the 1800's the Santa Fe Railroad constructed cattle holding and loading pens along the banks of Mustang Bayou. At the same time they built a large water storage tank, in the vincinity of what is now the Santa Fe Depot, for the purpose of storing water for the livestock. These two facilities were the very beginning of what is currently Alvin. During those years cattle were driven to the pens and shipped to the central and eastern markets of the United States by railroad. This particular business increased to such an extent, it became necessary to employ an overseer for the loading and shipping. The man they hired in 1872 was Alvin Morgan. In 1879 Morgan built the first house in Alvin on Mustang Bayou.

When settlers began building homes across the prairies, Morgan built a general store and saloon on his property. He obtained a used boxcar, placed it next to the Santa Fe tracks and established the first post office in Alvin.

The community was incorporated in 1881 with the official census figure at 49. The people of the community felt obligated to Alvin Morgan and decided to name the town in his honor. For a brief period the community was known, unofficially, as Morgan. However, research proved a town using that name was in existence in Texas. The citizens still felt that the town should be named in honor of its founder, so the name selected was Alvin.

Cattle raising in the area continued to dominate the economy, however, in the early days of the 20th Century, the production and shipping of other commodities supplemented the income of many Gulf Coast residents. Alvin was at one time, recognized as one of the leading producers of strawberries. The fruit could not be shipped great distances because of spoilage.

C. W. and "Ole" Benson, brothers, were the owners of a firm that bought and shipped produce. The brothers persuaded the Santa Fe Railroad to consider the idea of refrigerating railroad cars. In 1895, the first refrigerated railroad car left Alvin with its load of fresh strawberries. Ice for the cars was shipped in by freight from northern states. The ice was cut in large blocks, shipped to Alvin and stored in a special icehouse until used to refrigerate the cars. The first icehouse was built on what is now the present location of the Magnolia Bulk Warehouse on Santa Fe Avenue.

In subsequent years, pears, oranges, and other fruits were grown for markets. The raising of figs and The Alvin Fig plant became one of the leading moneymakers for many people and a leading industrial concern for many years. The plant still stands and is currently being used for storage purposes by the Gulf Furniture Co.

Rice became one of the major factors of the economy in the early 1930's. This particular agricultural product still remains one of the "big four" in the Gulf Coast country. Three rice dryers and one mill are located in Alvin, all active in this particular operation, proving the importance of the industry.

Oil was discovered in eastern Brazoria County in the early 1930's. Production of oil and gas related products is currently the number one economical aspect of the county.

Alvin has continued to progress at a steady pace through the years. Tropical hurricanes, fires, depressions, mosquitos, storms, feuds, and three wars, have failed to daunt the spirit of these sons of Texas. Located "deep in the heart of Texas' Golden Crescent," Alvin is an area on the threshold of industrial greatness and expansion.

AMARILLO

Amarillo is the dominant city of the Texas Panhandle. It is the county seat of Potter County, and has a population of 149,500. It has an altitude of 3400 feet and an annual rainfall of 20 inches.

Amarillo is the Spanish word for "yellow." The town received its name from a nearby creek, with many yellow cliffs and breaks. Yellow flowers also line the banks in the spring.

Amarillo is served by two railroads, the Atchison, Topeka and Santa Fe Railroad, and the Burlington Northern Railroad. The city is served by U.S. Highway 87, and 287 running north and south, U.S. Highway 40 running east and west and by U.S. Highway 60 running northeast and southwest.

Amarillo is located on the high plains. It is on the north edge of the Ogallala water aquifer. Ground water pumped from this aquifer has made it possible for the area from Lubbock north to Amarillo to become one of the richest agricultural areas in Texas.

One of the main tourist attractions in the panhandle area is the Palo Duro Canyon located just south of Amarillo.

Amarillo is a medical and educational center for the High Plains region. Amarillo College is a comprehensive community college.

Amarillo is a rich area as a result of its agricultural income and the income from oil and gas. Its manufacturing industry employs 12,600 people and has a payroll of $95,600,000. The value of manufactured shipments was $2,250,000,000 in 1988. Amarillo had a personal per capita income of $12,500 in 1988.

The city is rapidly growing and progressing economically.

ANDREWS

Andrews is the county seat of Andrews County. It is located in extreme West Texas. It is 62 miles west of Big Springs and 35 miles N-NW of Odessa. Andrews has a population of 11,200. The city has an altitude of 3200 ft. The rainfall is 14 inches annually.

The town is served by U.S. Highway 385, which runs north to south and SH 376 running east to west and SH-115 running northeast to southwest.

The City of Andrews is truly an offspring of the oil business. Starting about 1908, and prior to the first oil well that blew in on December 27, 1929, the town was just a group of houses, one store and a schoolhouse. There was very little city government until 1937, when the people incorporated the city. One of the reasons the local people were so slow in incorporating the city, was that very few people lived in the city limits. Most people lived in oil camps located in the area where oil was produced.

The county has been the largest oil producer in the state. More than one billion barrels of oil have been produced from 7,000 wells. More than one-thirtieth of all proven oil reserves in the United States are said to be located beneath the prairie grass and mesquite of Andrews County.

Andrews County was organized in June, 1910. The new county was named "Andrews" in honor of Richard Andrews, the first hero to fall in the war for Texas Independence, on October 28, 1835. The town took the same name.

Comanche Indians ruled this area of West Texas for more than 400 years, successfully repelling all invaders. This Comanche era ended shortly after 1845 when the State of Texas was admitted to the Union, and when the Gold Rush to California got underway in 1849. These two events touched off a large scale migration to the west, and the Indians were driven from their lands.

When you are in Andrews, Texas, you are truly in West Texas.

ANGLETON

Angleton is the county seat of Brazoria County. It has a population of 14,100. Again, like many other Texas towns, a railroad created what is now Angleton. In 1890 two men, Faustino Kiber and Lewis R. Bryan, decided to build a railroad from Velasco to what is now Angleton. The new town was christened May 10, 1892. It was named after Mrs. George Angle, wife of the general manager of the new railroad.

Angleton was incorporated in 1912. The cotton gin's generators supplied the town's first electricity, illuminating the houses from 6 to 11:30 p.m. Industrialization began as a result of sulphur production; the discovery of oil bolstered the economy. These two industries, however, had little direct impact on Angleton and it was not until the coming of Dow Chemical Company that the town received an influx of population. The coming of Dow did more to change the county and Angleton than any other thing since Lincoln freed the slaves. Since then Dow has been joined by Monsanto, Phillips Petroleum, BASF, Amoco and Intermedics, Inc.

Angleton has access to six railroads: the Missouri-Pacific; Southern Pacific; Union-Pacific; Missouri, Kansas, Texas; Atchison, Topeka, and Santa Fe; and the Burlington Northern.

The port of Freeport serves Angleton. Freeport has a new 38 ft. deep channel, which is currently being deepened to 45 ft. The port is less than 20 minutes away from Angleton.

Angleton is served by U.S. Highway 288 which runs from Houston to Freeport.

Angleton is truly a city in the right place at the right time.

ARANSAS PASS

Aransas Pass was named for the pass between Mustang and St. Joseph's Islands. It is located partially in Aransas County and partially in the southeast part of San Patricio County. It is connected by a causeway with Port Aransas.

The town site was laid out in 1885 with construction of the San Antonio and Aransas Pass Railroad. At that time the town was called Aransas Harbor. The name was changed in 1891, when the Aransas Harbor Terminal Rail was built to connect the town and the harbor. The town was incorporated in 1910.

During the period of 1910-1913 the channel was deepened. In 1915 the first cotton was shipped from the port.

The population in 1910 was 1800 when iron foundries, boat building and cotton compressing were the chief industries. Discovery of oil in the 1920's and the development of the Sinton, McCampbell and Aransas Pass oil fields in 1935 and 1936 increased industry and population.

Eight commercial seafood companies located in Aransas Pass, operate fishing fleets. Approximately 300 shrimp boats use Aransas Pass as their home port. The town has come to be known as the "Shrimp Capital of Texas." More than 1300 people are employed by the commercial fishing industry.

Aransas Pass is served by the Aransas Harbor Terminal Railroad and the Texas and New Orleans Railroad.

Aransas Pass is served by SH-35, which terminates at Ingleside and Aransas Pass and runs northeast to Houston. SH-361 runs from Sinton through Aransas Pass and terminates at Port Aransas on Padre Island.

The island that lies just offshore from Aransas Pass is St. Joseph Island. There is a lot of Texas lore about this island. It was the headquarters for the pirate LaFitte in the mid 1850's. Oil tycoon Sid Richardson bought the island in the 1940's and built a mansion on the island.

The famous Aransas National Wildlife Refuge is located 35 miles north-northeast in Aransas County on the west side of San Antonio Bay.

The city has a population of 7,200. The population is employed in the fishing and seafood industry, in oil, farming, ranching and shipping.

ATHENS

Athens is the county seat of Henderson County and is located squarely in the center of the county. The city has a population of 14,200. It is 65 miles southeast of Dallas. The city was named for Athens, Greece. The group that selected the name wanted the city to be the cultural center of Texas.

It is located in rolling, sandy clay country, and is on the western edge of the great East Texas pine country. The city was organized in 1851. The city is governed by a mayor, a city council and a city manager.

It is on U.S. Highway 175 which starts at Dallas and runs southeast through Athens and ends at Jacksonville and State Highway 19, which runs north and south. State Highway 19 runs from Paris, near the Oklahoma border, then south through Athens to Huntsville, and State Hwy 31, running from Waco to Athens then east to Longview.

It is served by the Southern Pacific Railroad going northwest to Dallas and the St. Louis Southwestern Railroad running southwest to northeast through Athens.

Athens has considerable industry, including plants that manufacture TV sets, mobile homes, and clay products.

Trinity Valley Community College is located in Athens. The football team won the 1988 national championship for junior colleges.

ATLANTA

Atlanta had two beginnings in two separate locations, both starts generated by the railroad. The first Atlanta was started in 1862 by the Rev. Jesse Dodd. He brought his wife Martha from Georgia to a place in Texas about two miles from where Atlanta is now and named it Atlanta for the Georgia city. A railroad was going to be built near the Dodd home so people moved there and began a town. There were several stores, a post office, a school and a church.

Railroad officials then changed their plans about the location and moved it to where Atlanta is now. This land belonged to Capt. Preston Rose Scott. He gave 111 acres for a town.

In 1872 the land was surveyed by the railroad and the town of Atlanta was platted. The new town was called Atlanta to make those in the old town happy. Scott did not draw the plat for the town, but he did reserve the right to name some of the streets. His three sons Hiram, William, and Buckner, had streets named for them as did his daughter, Louisa, later called Louise. More and more people moved in and built businesses. "Old Atlanta" died out. The Dodd house is now the oldest house in Atlanta.

Atlanta has a population of 6,300. It is located in the northeast part of Texas, not far from the Arkansas border. It is 24 miles south-southwest of Texarkana.

The town is served by U. S. Highway 59, which begins at Laredo and goes northeast through Victoria, Wharton, Houston, Lufkin,

Marshall, Atlanta and Texarkana. It is also served by six other state highways which run through Atlanta in all directions.

Atlanta is served by the Union Pacific Railroad which runs northeast-southwest through Atlanta.

This is a rich agricultural and timber area, receiving 46 inches of rainfall annually. It is located in the pine timber belt of Texas. The principal products are beef cattle, hogs, hay, watermelons, fruits, vegetables and timber. It is in the Sulphur River watershed.

There is a considerable amount of industry in Atlanta. There are numerous plants located there, manufacturing paper, wood, steel, and agricultural products.

AUSTIN

In 1839, five mounted scouts ranged over a broad area of wilderness seeking a site for a new capital city for the Republic of Texas. A site was chosen on the north bank of the Colorado River. The river flowed through the Balcones Fault at this location. The site was occupied at the time by the small settlement of Waterloo, consisting of four families. About September 1, 1839, the archives and furniture of the Texas government were trasported from near Houston to Austin by 50 ox-drawn wagons. The city was named after Stephen F. Austin, "the Father of Texas."

Austin is located in the very heart of Texas on highways Interstate 35, US 290, US 183 and Texas Highway 71. Austin, in addition to being the capital of Texas, is the county seat of Travis County—named after the hero of the Alamo, Colonel William B. Travis. It was incorporated in 1840 and has a council-manager form of government. This beautiful city is one of the fastest growing research and development, high-technology centers in the southwest.

The hilly limestone terrain begins on the north and west side of the city with the blacklands to the east and south. The population of the city of Austin is 495,900 (MSA is 755,000—1989 est.). The altitude ranges from 400 ft. on the east side to over 1000 ft. in the hills to the west and north. These scenic hills are broken by a series of dams on the Colorado River, creating the spectacular Highland Lakes which wind for 150 miles to Austin. The terrain is covered by cedar and pecan trees in the creek bottoms and a variety of oak trees.

The economy is supported primarily by the state, local and federal government which employs in excess of 100,000 people. In the industry sector, the Austin area has more than 700 manufacturing plants employing more than 40,000 people, with an annual payroll of over $900,000,000 and gross sales of $1.8 billion. Over 60% of manufacturing is high technology-related.

The city's municipal airport is served by ten major airlines. Railroads for the area include the Southern Pacific and Union Pacific/Missouri Pacific.

With more than 30% of the area adults having college degrees, Austin has long been an intellectual oasis. At the center is the University of Texas, ranking second only to Harvard in endowed faculty positions and third nationally among state-supported universities. Enrollment exceeds 50,000 students. Also located in the area is Austin Community College (20,000), St. Edward's University (2600), Corcordia Lutheran College, Huston-Tillotson College with Southwestern University (the oldest in the state) and Southwest Texas State University close by.

Noteworthy things for Texans and tourists to see in Austin are:

Austin Children's Museum
Austin Nature Center
Barton Springs
Daughters of Confederacy and Daughters of Republic of Texas Museums
Elisabet Ney Museum
French Legation
George Washington Carver Museum
Governor's Mansion
Harry Ransom Center (UT)
Huntington Art Gallery (UT)
LBJ Presidential Library
Laguna Gloria Art Museum
Sixth Street, with live music clubs, restaurants
State Capitol Building
Texas Memorial Museum
10,000 acre Zilker Park

AZLE

The town was informally organized in 1881 when the first post office was established. The community had several earlier names, such as Elizabeth Town, Marysville, Mooresville, and O'Bar. In November 1883, Dr. Azle Stewart told the people that if they would name the town after him, he would deed them enough land for a townsite. This he did and the name became "Azle."

Azle is located on the Tarrant and Parker County lines along

State Highway 199. It is surrounded by hills and trees and is nestled on the shores of Eagle Mountain Lake, just 16 miles from metropolitan Fort Worth. In Azle, you have the best of both worlds: friendly country living, plus city culture and conveniences. Azle is known as the "Gateway to Eagle Mountain Lake."

The 1988-89 population was 8,200. The population is projected to double in the next five to seven years due to the Alliance Airport just North of Azle and the expansion of industry into northwest Tarrant County. The average annual rainfall is 32.5 inches with moderate humidity.

Azle has a council-manager form of government. The city owns three public parks, one of which is 33 acres and presently under construction. This park is located right on Eagle Mountain Lake.

The nearest railroad is the Weatherford, Mineral Wells and Northwestern and the Texas & Pacific Railroad which goes through Weatherford, 17 miles to the southwest.

Azle has a diversified industrial base. Several small industries employ many of the citizens of Azle. Tandy Corporation also has an industrial plant in Azle. Many people in the community are also employed in Fort Worth by Carswell Air Force Base and General Dynamics.

Lake Weatherford on the Clear Fork of the Trinity River is a major recreation area.

BALLINGER

Ballinger is the county seat of Runnels County and is located 36 miles northeast of San Angelo and about 57 miles south of Abilene. The Colorado River is just south of the city. Ballinger can be reached by U.S. Highways 67 and 83 and State Highway 158. Its 1980 population was 4,207.

Like many West Texas towns, Ballinger came into being as a result of the building of the railroad. The city is named for William Pitts Ballinger, an attorney for the Santa Fe Railroad.

The Atchison, Topeka & Santa Fe Railroad built a passenger and railway express terminal in 1911 in Ballinger. After passenger service was discontinued in 1965 and freight service in 1983, the railroad donated the building to the City of Ballinger. After restoration and modifications, the old railroad terminal became the new City Hall for Ballinger.

The Runnels County Courthouse was built in 1888 of stone

quarried on the south side of the Colorado River. The building was remodeled in 1941 and wings were added, and it is still in use today.

Ballinger City Lake, completed in 1983, is five miles northwest of Ballinger and is used for camping, swimming, fishing and boating.

BASTROP

Bastrop is the county seat of Bastrop County. It is located on the Colorado River 35 miles southeast of Austin, Texas. The area was first settled in 1829. The county was created in 1836.

The city has a population of 4,200. It has a mayor-council form of city government. The annual rainfall is 36.8 inches, which is ample rain for all kinds of agriculture. The county income from agriculture is average for Texas counties, being $28 million; 90% of the income is from beef, dairy cattle, hogs and poultry. The crops include sorghum, pecans, corn, wheat, oats, and fruit.

Bastrop has some industry. It is a well supply center. There are several agribusinesses. There is a furniture manufacturing plant.

The University of Texas Cancer Research Center is located in Bastrop. The Federal Correctional Center is located at Bastrop.

The city is served by the Missouri Kansas-Texas Railroad. The nearest commercial airport is at Austin, 32 miles northwest. It is served by State Highways 21, 71 and 95 and Farm-to-Market Highways 304 and 1441.

The proximity to Austin is a great asset. The citizens have access to the University of Texas and the other outstanding universities and colleges located there.

The minerals in the area are clay, oil, gas, and lignite coal.

Bastrop is one of Texas' oldest settlements, first called Mina. The town's name was changed about 1837 to honor a man of fame and influence in early Texas. The man was Felipe Enrique Nen, Baron des Bastrop, a prominent Dutch nobleman.

Bastrop is located 80 miles west of the north-south line in Texas that separates the pine timber belt from the oak timber land, but a beautiful pine grove of several hundred acres is located near Bastrop. It is called the "Lost Pines."

BAY CITY

In 1894 the Bay City Townsite Company was formed by G. M. Magill, N. M. Vogelsang, N. King and David Swickheimer. They bought 640 acres 20 miles from the coast (Matagorda Bay was right in Matagorda at that time—about where the Intercoastal Canal is now—and near the Colorado River) from D. P. Moore at $1.00 an acre with some lots as collateral. These men had some rather grandiose plans to build a new city on that site in northern Bay Prairie and had even chosen a name for this proposed town—electing to call it "Bay City." Mr. Magil and Mr. Vogelsang were resident managers and laid out a model townsite exactly one mile square including plans for a courthouse in the center of a 300-foot block in the center of town.

Bay City is the county seat of Matagorda County. Bay City is located in the lush green delta along the banks of the Lower Colorado River. Century-old oak trees, beautifully restored antebellum homes, and expansive parks give the city an atmosphere of quiet tranquility.

In addition to the city's historic beauty and serenity, there is an underlying current of growth and prosperity. An aggressive business spirit is building Bay City into one of the fastest growing trade centers along the Texas Coast.

Bay City had a 1985 population of 23,964. Bay City is within 80 miles of Houston and 133 miles of Corpus Christi.

In addition to the area's rich and fascinating heritage, it is also an area high in natural resources. Fertile farmland, abundant water supply, and extensive oil resources combine to make this a vibrant center of activity for the Coastal Area.

Bay City is served by the Santa Fe Railroad, originally called the Cane Belt Railroad. The famous Texas rancher Shanghai Pierce was instrumental in having the railroad built through Bay City in 1901. The Southern Pacific came to Bay City in 1902. The St. Louis, Brownsville, and Mexico Railway (later the Missouri-Pacific) was built through Bay City in 1903.

In the early days the Colorado River flooded frequently. In 1913 the dam at Austin broke and the town was flooded. A major flood occurred in 1922. Shortly after this, levees were built along the banks of the river, ending the flood menace.

Bay City is served by State Highway 35, which parallels the Gulf Coast and State Highway 60 which generally follows the Colorado River.

BAYTOWN

Baytown is truly an industrialized city. The city is situated on the northwest side of Trinity Bay and the east bank of the San Jacinto River. It is 30 miles east of Houston and can be reached by Interstate 10 and State Highway 146. It acquired its name by virtue of it being located on Trinity Bay.

The site of present-day Baytown was inhabited by Indians for hundreds of years. The Karankawas, the last of the tribes known to be in the area, did not leave until the late 1830's.

In 1821, a surveyor, E. J. Rider, built a home at Morgan's Point. About the same time, Nathaniel Lynch established a trading post at the site he called Lynchberg. By 1822, his Lynchberg Ferry was in operation. Other settlers soon moved to Lynchberg and the Cedar Bayou area. Dr. Ashbel Smith arrived in 1937 and built a home overlooking Tabbs Bay.

Residents of the area played a major role in the Battle of San Jacinto. Afterwards, David G. Burnet, a Lynchberg resident, was appointed interim President of Texas; and General Sam Houston built a summer home at Cedar Point.

The Lynchberg crossing was an important trading post before the Civil War, when the new trading post of "Baytown" was established on the site of what is now the Baytown Country Club.

The name of Governor Ross S. Sterling is very important to Baytown's history. Gov. Sterling laid out the townsite of what is now Baytown, founded the Dayton-Goose Creek Railroad (whose rail lines served the area), and organized the Humble Co.

Early settlers in the area were mainly farmers. However, when storms destroyed most of the crops in 1915, many of the farmers took employment in the newly-developing oil fields. Then, in 1918 just as drilling was declining, Humble Oil & Refining Company located its largest plant in Baytown, and the city's future was secure. Humble began production of toluene to be used in TNT during World War II; nearly all of the TNT used by the Allies came from Baytown.

The present city of Baytown was formed in 1948 when Pelly, Goose Creek, and Baytown consolidated. In 1953, the Baytown-LaPorte Tunnel of State Highway 146 (under the Houston Ship Channel) was opened, replacing a ferry.

Baytown's 1989 population was 62,500. It has a city manager-council form of municipal government. Lee College, with an enrollment of 7,200, is located there. The average rainfall is 45.4 inches. The area of the city is 29.5 square miles. Its tax rate is $0.605 per $100 of assessment.

Although agricultural crops are grown and cattle are raised in adjacent areas, Baytown today is primarily an industrial city. Oil refining, rubber, chemicals, and carbon black are the industrial base of Baytown's economy. The Southern Pacific and the Union Pacific Railroads serve the city. Baytown is 44 miles from Intercontinental Airport. It has one private airport.

The following State agencies have facilities in Baytown:

Texas Rehabilitation Commission
Texas Department of Safety
Texas Alcoholic Beverage Commission
Texas Department of Human Resources
Texas Department of Highways
and Public Transportation.

The principal manufacturers located in Baytown are:

Name	*Product*
Baytown Olefins Plant	Petro Chemicals
Exxon Chemical Americas	Chemical Products
Exxon Company USA	Oil Refining
Gulf Oil Chemicals	Poly/Olefins
Helmerich & Payne	Natural gas odorizing
Hoesch Tubular Prod.	Pipe
J. M. Huber Corp.	Synthetic inks
Mobay Chemical Co.	Chemicals
Stauffer Chemical Co.	Sulfuric Acid
Amoco	Polypropylene
Chevron Chemical Co.	Polyethylene
Other Exxons	

The total labor force is 183,300. Industries draw labor from a radius of 30 miles. The city of Baytown is in the Goose Creek Consolidated Independent School District, accredited since 1921, and has 13 elementary schools, five junior schools, two high-schools, one special education school, one alternative school, and one Vocational Center. Baytown has seven private schools. Total school enrollment is over 16,800.

Baytown has the usual ethnic mix of population. It is 77% White, 14% Hispanic, 8% Black and 1% Asian.

The large steel mill previously owned by the U.S. Steel Corporation, and located about ten miles north of Baytown, has been closed for several years.

Of special interest in the area are the Baytown Historical Museum which features artifacts and memorabilia of local and pioneer history; the Republic of Texas Plaza with a statue of Ashbel Smith; Wallisville Heritage Park with displays and artifacts of Spanish Mission Nuestra Senora de la Luz and Presidio San Augustin de Ahumada; and the Lynchberg Ferry (in operation since 1822) for a trip to LaPorte across the San Jacinto River, and a visit to the San Jacinto Battleground.

BEAUMONT

Beaumont is located approximately 90 miles east of Houston and 30 miles west of the Texas-Louisiana state line on Interstate 10. U.S. Highways 90 and 96 and State Highways 105 and 347 also lead to the city.

Beaumont is the county seat of Jefferson County and has a current population of 120,000.

Beaumont was chartered in 1838 by the Third Congress of the Republic of Texas and consisted of 200 acres and less than 100 people.

There is disagreement as to the origin of the name of the city—some claim the city was named for Jefferson Beaumont; others say it was named for another pioneer family in the area named Beaumont; and others claim it is just a descriptive French name meaning "beautiful knoll, hill or mountain." (The city is located on the Neches River at a place formerly known as Tevis Bluff.)

Beaumont is perhaps best-known as the home of the Spindletop oil field. In 1901, the Anthony F. Lucas Well blew in and changed Beaumont forever. Within thirty days of the oil discovery, Beaumont's population surged from 8,500 to 30,000. Six major refineries were built in the Beaumont area.

Shipyards were constructed in Beaumont during World War I, and synthetic rubber and petrochemical plants were built during World War II. Although Beaumont is 20 air miles from the Gulf of Mexico, it is situated on the Neches deep ship channel. The Port of Beaumont ranks second among Texas ports in total ship tonnage handled.

Petroleum, natural gas, petrochemicals and shipyards continue to be important factors in Beaumont's economy, as are rice and timber production.

Railroads serving Beaumont are the Southern Pacific, the Atchison, Topeka & Santa Fe and Kansas City Southern.

Beaumont is the home of Lamar University.

Babe Didrickson Zaharias, considered the world's greatest woman athlete, was a Beaumont native.

BEDFORD

Bedford is located in Tarrant County, 24 miles northeast of Fort Worth. It is located on State Highways 26 and 183 and U.S. Highway 30. The nearest railroad is the SLSW, 10 miles to the northwest.

The population of Bedford is 44,700. The population is increasing at a compound rate of 10%. The average annual rainfall is 32.3 inches. The altitude is 750 feet. The Dallas-Ft. Worth International Airport is only seven miles to the northeast.

The Bedford unemployment rate is 3.6%, which is very low. Bedford is part of the tri-city complex of Hurst, Euless-Bedford. These three cities have a common Chamber of Commerce.

Twenty-eight years ago, Bell Helicopter announced the coming installation of its $3,000,000 plant in Bedford area. This industry has grown into a huge industrialized plant. It has contributed greatly to the growth of Bedford and Hurst. Bell Helicopter Company is the principal employer in the area.

Hurst-Euless-Bedford have a school district that serves all three cities.

Bedford is only eight miles from the Dallas-Ft. Worth International Airport. The city is served by the St. Louis & Southwest Railroad, by the Chicago, Rock Island and Pacific Railroad, the TNO, and the Santa Fe Railroads.

BEEVILLE

Beeville is located on U.S. Highways 181 and 59 in South Texas. It is about 60 miles northwest of Corpus Christi and about 90 miles southeast of San Antonio. Its current population is about 15,000.

Irish settlers arrived by boat in 1834 and some settled on the East side of Paesta (Poesta) creek, the site on which the city of Beeville would later be built.

When Bee County was organized in 1858, its county seat was Marysville, seven miles east of present-day Beeville. In 1860, after 2,000 acres of land for a townsite were donated by Mrs. Anna Burke, the town was moved. Because there was already a town called Marysville, the name was changed to Beeville.

Beeville, as well as Bee County, was named for Bernard C. Bee, a colonel in the Texas Army, Secretary of War under President Houston, and Secretary of State under President Lamar.

Local townspeople were influential in persuading the San Antonio & Aransas Railroad to build its line through Beeville. Capt. A. C. Jones became known as the "Father of Beeville" for his efforts on behalf of the railroad.

In 1929, the first oil well in the area was brought in near Pettus, about 15 miles north of Beeville. New residents were attracted to the area, and oil companies headquartered in Beeville.

In 1943, the Beeville municipal airport was commissioned as Chase Field, a Naval Auxiliary Air Station, to train Navy pilots for World War II. After the war, the airport reverted to the city, but was later sold to the government for use in training jet pilots.

Nine official historical medallions have been erected in Beeville to designate historical sites.

Texas Agricultural Experiment Substation No. 1, operated by Texas A & M University, is located five miles east of the city. The Substation was started in 1894 and is the oldest station operated by A & M.

BELLAIRE

Bellaire is a residential city located in Harris County. It is surrounded by the city of Houston and is located in the outer southwest part of Houston. Loop 610 bisects the city.

The city has a mayor-council-manager form of government. The city had a population of 15,300 in 1989. The city is the location of a number of office buildings, and there are several small manufacturing plants within the city limits.

The city's population is sustained by being a bedroom city to Houston. Houston has a number of these cities similar to Bellaire within its borders.

BELTON

Belton is located eight miles west of Temple and halfway between Austin and Waco. It can be reached by Interstate 35, U.S. Highway 190, and State Highway 317.

In 1849, the state legislature carved three counties from giant Milam County. One of the three counties, "Bell," was named for Peter Hansborough Bell who was the governor of Texas from 1848 through 1853.

The county seat was formed in 1850. The 120-acre townsite was donated by Mrs. Matilda (Connell) Allen and named Nolandville for nearby Nolan Creek. In December of 1851 the county seat name was changed to Belton. The county seat town name was probably a contraction of the words Bell-town.

Belton's council-manager form of municipal government serves over 14,000 citizens with four public parks, an 18-hole public golf course, 20 tennis courts, two libraries, and a youth center.

The people of Belton are proud of their 30-plus historical markers, including National Register of Historic Places, Registered Texas Historic Landmarks, 1936 Texas Centennial Markers, and Texas Historical Commission Markers.

Belton was the site of Bell County's first chartered national bank in 1882, first town to operate under the independent school system, first public library (the historic Carnegie Library is now being remodeled to house a museum) and the county's first newspaper.

The Bell County Courthouse, built in 1884, is a source of great pride. Its exterior remains much the same as it was at its construction; however, extensive renovation occurred inside the building. The original dome, and its clock, were removed in 1950.

Belton's city population has grown from 1,000 in 1875 to an estimated 14,000 people in 1989. Belton's rural growth has always been, and is today, dependent upon its abundant agricultural and livestock industry. In 1988/89 the industrial growth of Belton has included a new 120-bed facility nursing home, custom printing manufacturing plant, and a 48-bed psychiatric hospital for adolescents. UPS located their Central Texas distribution center in Belton's Industrial Park, and Capitol Seating (school furniture) expanded their plant. The Bid Resource Center opened to assist businesses obtain government jobs. The Bell County Expo Center opened its 9,500-seat facility. Summer Fun USA, a new swim center park, on the Leon River is to be opened in 1989, and Loop 121 was extended from Highway 190 to Lake Road.

Many of Belton's residents are employed at the United States' largest military facility, Fort Hood, which is located 10 miles west of Belton. Belton is a favorite shopping stop for Fort Hood military personnel.

Belton's 5,000 school students can commute to one of the following schools of higher education: the University of Mary Hardin-Baylor in Belton, Temple Junior College, eight miles to the east, Central Texas College in Killeen, fifteen miles to the west, Baylor University in Waco or Austin's University of Texas, each being 45 miles from Belton.

Belton borders on Lake Belton and Stillhouse Hollow Lake. Water Sports are enjoyed at these two U.S. Army Corps of Engineers operated facilities.

Community sponsored golf, tennis and basketball tournaments are held yearly. The Independence Day Celebration is city sponsored and includes rides, a shoot-out on the courthouse lawn, a God and Country concert, a parade and a rodeo.

The Bell County Livestock Show is in February every year. The "Outstanding Farmer" award is presented in May, while April is set aside for Belton's Historic Home Tour and a Belton merchant fashion show for ladies in the area.

Every month of the year is busy at The Bell County Expo Center, Central Texas' newest and best entertainment complex located in Belton. The large center includes a Main Arena, Special Events Room, Assembly Hall, Exposition Building and Horse Barn. Annual events at the Expo are the Arts and Crafts Show, Gun and Knife Exhibit and Sale, Shrine Circus, Circus Vargas, Killeen's New Car Show, Temple's New Car Show, the 4th of July Rodeo and many others. A sampling of the 1989/90 concerts booked at the Expo Center are George Strait, Kenny Rogers, Ray Price, and Ronnie Milsap.

BIG SPRING

Big Spring is located at the junction of Interstate 20 and U.S. Highway 87. State Highways 176 and 350 also lead to the city. It is located in West Texas, 110 miles west of Abilene and 105 miles south of Lubbock. It is the county seat of Howard County and has a population of approximately 25,000.

Big Spring is named for a naturally-occurring large spring of water. Although Indians and buffalo apparently had known of and used the spring for many years, it was 1849 before the spring was discovered by white men. The spring and its fifty-foot deep reservoir became a campsite on the Overland and Santa Fe Trails. A tent city was established at the site to provide services to travelers and trail drivers.

Big Spring remained a tent city until 1881 when the Texas and Pacific Railroad arrived. The railroad remained the principal industry until 1925 when oil was discovered nearby. Oil is still important in Big Spring's economy.

Big Spring is home to Howard County Junior College, a two-year accredited community college, as well as the Southwest Collegiate Institute for the Deaf and Veterans Hospital.

Points of interest in or near Big Spring include: Comanche Trail Park (a city park with the historic "Big Spring"); Big Spring State Park (featuring a prairie dog town); Scenic Mountain Drive, Moss Creek Lake (a recreational site for fishing, boating, and camping); Natural Dam Lake (a salt lake that furnishes winter refuge for sandhill cranes); Big Spring State Hospital; U.S. Agriculture Experimental Station; and Signal Mountain (used long ago by Indians to send smoke signals).

BISHOP

Bishop is located in Nueces County. It is 33 miles southwest of Corpus Christi. It is located in the semi-tropical Coastal Bend of South Texas. It has an elevation of 59 feet above sea level. The prevailing "Mari-Time Weather" produces a favorable variety of mild winters and breezy summers.

Bishop is served by the Missouri Pacific Railroad which is now owned and operated by the Union Pacific Railroad Co.

The town has good highways. U.S. Highway 77 runs north and south through Bishop and State Highway 70 runs east and west.

Bishop has an interesting and dynamic history. It was incorporated in April 1912. Bishop did not grow up gradually; it sprang into existence almost fully developed in 1910 as the fulfillment of a young insurance agent's dreams.

F. Z. Bishop, the young insurance man-promoter, figured the blackland prairies of South Texas was "mighty good cotton and corn land," and envisioned a model town, surrounded by farm tracts. He made a deal with the Driscoll Ranch for 2,300 acres, bisected by the new rails of the St. Louis, Brownsville and Mexico Railroad which had been extended to the Rio Grande Valley four years earlier.

The developer brought in 20 steam plows to turn under the waist high grass and laid out his farmland in mile-square tracts, linking the sections with 120 miles of improved roads.

Some of the farmland was sold as soon as it was broken, but before Bishop put a single town lot on the market, he laid out a zoned business district, designated industrial and residential districts, drilled three artesian wells, put in a water system and built an electric light and power plant.

By the end of 1912, Bishop and his chief assistant, D. W. Taylor, had sold more than 40,000 acres of farmland and the town had grown to 1,200 inhabitants. When Bishop closed operations just as World War I started in Europe, he had opened for settlement more than 80,000 acres of land and had seen the city well established and looking towards a prosperous future.

Bishop today is a far-cry from the city that suddenly sprouted from the coastal prairie in 1910. Agriculture, the community's sole reason for existence in those early days, is still a mainstay of the local economy. But the ensuing years have brought the discovery of oil and gas in the area, and the resulting development of the growing chemical industry.

Bishop's biggest boost came in 1945 when the Celanese Corporation of America entered the chemical field with the opening of its Bishop plant. Today, the big Celanese plant sprawls out along Highway 77, south of Bishop, and is one of the largest and fastest growing chemical complexes in Texas. In 1988, a German Company bought the plant, and it is now referred to as: Hoechst-Celanese. The company has now expanded to include pharmaceuticals.

So with the coming industrial expansion, the years since World War II have been Bishop's period of great growth. With its solid industrial and agricultural base, Bishop reversed the trend of population decreases shown by many small towns. Bishop's population passed 2,700 in 1950 and the 1980 census showed 3,706 residents.

BOERNE

The site for Boerne was selected and established in 1849 for a farm settlement by an intellectual group, the Latin Settlement, a branch of the Adelsverein. The farming settlement was not successful because the settlers had no farming knowledge. The land was sold to Gustav Theissen and John James, a surveyor, who platted the town of Boerne in 1851. The town was named in honor of Ludwig Boerne, a German publicist.

Boerne is known as the "Key To The Hills" of the Texas Hill Country. It is a historical delight to visit the town's beautiful setting along Cibolo Creek. The town is located 28 miles northwest of San Antonio in Kendall County. It is located on Interstate 10 and on State Highway 46 which runs east and west, starting at Seguin on the east and running in a big loop through the Hill Country to New Braunfels, then to Boerne, and on west to Bandera. The town is well served by farm-to-market paved roads, 474 and 1376.

The town is served by the Southern Pacific Railroad and the Union Pacific Railroad which have sidings within eight miles of Boerne.

Boerne is famous for the wild game that abounds in the area. There are a large number of turkey and white-tailed deer.

This is a great agricultural area. Crops of corn, wheat, rye, barley, tobacco, sorghum, cotton, and potatoes are grown. Fruit trees thrive in this area. It is famous for the peaches grown here.

The old stagecoach route to the West passed through Boerne. In 1856, the first post office and stage stop was operated by August Staffel. The first business was a sawmill and a grist mill established by William Dietert on Cibolo Creek near the dam.

Boerne is located in the heart of the several German settlements that were located in the Hill County. It has a population of 3,400 and is a thriving, beautiful town, steeped in Texas history.

For the past two years Boerne has been chosen as a site for the Tour of Texas Olympic-Class Bike Race. A World Cup Event was held during 1989. Bikers from 27 different countries participated in this event.

There are three caverns in the surrounding area of Boerne: Natural Bridge Caverns—Texas largest, Cascade Caverns—which has a beautiful waterfall which plunges almost a 100 feet and a cave known as "The Cave-Without-A-Name."

BONHAM

Bonham was named after James Butler Bonham, the famous hero of the Alamo. In 1837 Bonham was called Fort Inglish. In 1838 it was changed to Bois d'Arc, after the trees that are plentiful in the area. In 1843 the Congress of Texas changed the name to Bonham to honor the hero.

Bonham is the county seat of Fannin County. The Red River is the north boundary of the County. It had a population of 7,700 in 1988. It is served by U.S. Highway 82 and State Highways 78, and 121. It is 65 miles north-northeast of Dallas.

Bonham is served by the Missouri Pacific Railroad, which is now owned and operated by the Union Pacific Railroad.

Bonham is famous for being the hometown of the Honorable and cherished Sam Rayburn. Serving during four presidencies, he was Speaker of the U.S. House of Representatives for 17 years, a record. He was an honorable, clean, admirable man; there was never anything that remotely indicated dishonesty or any immoral conduct on his part.

Bonham has a city council-manager form of government.

The area receives an average of 43.6 inches of rainfall. The town has an elevation of about 600 feet.

The country is a rolling prairie, drained by the Red River and Bois d'Arc Creek. The soil is mostly blacksand.

This is a rich agricultural area. Some land is irrigated, (about 3900 acres). The area raises beef cattle, hogs, sorghum, maize, soybeans, peanuts, hay, cotton and grapes.

There are a considerable number of manufacturing plants in the town. Products are mostly related to electrical cable, gasoline pumps and ferti-lome, fertilizer products and clothing.

Bonham has four primary tourist attractions: the Sam Rayburn Library, Sam Rayburn House, Fort Inglish and the Depot Museum. They have two excellent small lakes that offer good fishing, boating, camping and skiing.

They have some twenty historical markers within the city limits and over 100 in Fannin County.

BORGER

The city of Borger is located in the southern part of Hutchinson County. It is 42 miles northeast of Amarillo, and 162 miles north of Lubbock. State Highway 136 runs north-northeast from Amarillo and terminates at Borger. State Highway 207 starts at Conway and run north through Borger and thence north, terminating at Spearman. State Highway 152 runs east to Pampa. Borger is 93 miles east of the New Mexico line, 78 miles west of the Oklahoma boundary and 62 miles south of the north-end of the Panhandle. The city is located on the "High Plains."

The city of Borger has a council-manager form of government. It has a fire rating of $0.27. The tax rate is on the high side, being $2.0966 per $100 of assessment. A rate over $1.75 is considered high.

Borger is served by the Santa Fe Railway. Air transportation is available at Amarillo, 42 miles to the south. There American, Delta, Southwest, United and Continental Airlines offer daily flights.

Frank Phillips College is located at Borger. Borger has one newspaper, the *Borger News Herald*. The city has four channels of TV available from Amarillo.

The city has an elevation of 3,050 ft. The average rainfall is 20.7 inches. Part of the area surrounding Borger is underlaid by the Ogallala Aquifier and irrigation is available from wells. Borger draws its water from Lake Merdith and underground wells. The average humidity is 42%.

Borger is the home of the world's largest inland petrochemical complex. Phillips Petroleum Co. is involved in the processing of crude oil, natural gas liquids, various specialty chemicals, and is also the sole manufacturer in the world of RYTON plastic. Borger has the Sid Richardson and J. M. Huber carbon black plants as well as the Cominco Fertilizer Plant.

Borger has a very interesting history. In 1925 A. P. Borger, a promoter from Carthage, Missouri, heard of the oil boom in the Texas Panhandle and came to take advantage of the opportunities. He bought 240 acres of land for $6,000, formed a private corporation, the Borger Townsite Corporation, and proceeded to lay out a town.

The sale of lots opened on May 8, 1926, and on the first day of the sale Borger Corporation netted $100,000. Within six months, Borger sold out. His gross sales aggregated over $1,000,000. People flocked from everywhere to "make it rich" in the new town, and in eight month's time, the population was 15,000.

The Santa Fe Railroad laid tracks to serve the new booming town. Their freight traffic revenue from the Borger Station was in excess of $1,000,000 per month.

Borger was incorporated on October 18, 1926, It has a mayor-commission form of government.

The oil boom brought many rough characters to the city; and there was much vice. Dixon Street was notorious for its dance halls and red-light district. A young district attorney, John A. Holmes, was determined to get rid of the lawlessness and vice. He began gathering evidence to indict some of the worst known criminals; but before he could bring them to trial, he was murdered in his own garage on September 13, 1929.

On September 21, Frank Hamer of the Texas Rangers was sent to investigate, followed by Brigadier General Jacob F. Walters. As a result of the investigations, Governor Dan Moody sent 84 National Guardsmen with 14 officers on September 29. Though this quieted things down, the murderer of District Attorney Holmes was never apprehended.

The old residents of Borger tell about the rough elements who were being arrested and chained to large logs along the main street and to telephone posts. The little jail would not hold them all.

Considering the chaotic conditions existing in those early days, modern-day Borger can well be proud of its many attainments, achieved in less than sixty years of history. The highlight of the city came when the National Municipal League, *Look* magazine, and the Conference of Government declared Borger an All-American City.

The famous Alibates Flint Quarries and the Texas Panhandle Pueblo Indian Ruins are located on the Bivins Cattle Ranch on the shores of Lake Meredith. The sites are about thirty-five miles north of Amarillo. There are 550 quarries that pockmark this area. Paleolithic man fashioned weapons and tools from this flint as long as 23,000 years before Christ, and 10,000 years before the Great Pyramids of Egypt were built.

Lake Meredith, a large lake on the Canadian River ten miles west of Borger, is a popular spot for fishermen and water sportsmen.

BOWIE

Bowie, with a population of 5,610, is located in Montague County, midway between Wichita Falls and Dallas-Fort Worth. It can be reached by US 81, U.S. 287, SH 59 or SH 101.

Bowie was founded in 1882, and was named for Jim Bowie, one of the heroes of the Alamo. Its settlers needed the same pioneering spirit, courage, bravery, and faith to sustain them in frontier living.

Bowie's actual location came about because of a delay in building the Fort Worth & Denver Railway. Workers erected a tent city at the site when earth-moving for the roadbed took more time than expected. The community grew when it was designated as a railhead for supplies and construction until the railroad was completed to Wichita Falls. Then, when the merchants of Queen's Peak, a small town four miles north, learned the railroad would bypass their town, they, too, moved their businesses to Bowie.

The Rock Island Railroad arrived in Bowie in 1892, its track crossing that of the Fort Worth & Denver Railway at the location of the original railhead.

In 1893, when Bowie was incorporated with a population of 1,100, it came to be known as the "One Year Wonder of the West."

Later, it became known as the "Chicken & Bread Town" because of small boys selling chicken and bread to the passengers of trains stopping at Bowie. The town at that time was home to Johnson's Chicken Ranch, the world's largest producer of White Leghorn chickens.

The nearby Queen's Peak had been a favorite place for Indians to camp and observe the area. In 1936, the State of Texas erected a monument at the site dedicated to the memory of pioneer women.

Modern-day Bowie is an agribusiness center and is noted for livestock sales as well as being the manufacturer of apparel, boats, farm equipment, insulation and metal products.

"Trades Day," is held on the weekend prior to the second Monday of each month. Trades Day began in 1890, primarily for horse and mule trading, and has continued ever since, evolving into one of the oldest continuing flea markets in the country.

Fishing, camping, and boating are available at nearby Bowie Lake and Lake Amon G. Carter.

BRADY

Back in 1831 one of the bloodiest Indian fights in Texas history took place at Calf Creek southwest of Brady. James Bowie and ten other men were attacked while en route to the old Spanish presidio in Menard. They were outnumbered fifteen to one, and the Indians kept them pinned down for eight days before giving up and allowing them to return to San Antonio.

The first move to colonize this area came in 1847 when John O. Meusebach, founder of Fredericksburg, met with the Comanche Indian chiefs at Camp San Saba. Giving them $3,000 in presents, he extracted a promise that they would not harm his colonists.

Later in 1847, a survey party headed by J. J. Giddings arrived, and in the crew was Peter Brady. Finding a small stream here, Brady insisted it was the Concho River. It wasn't, and for want of a better name it became "Brady's Creek." When the town was established, it became "Brady City" and eventually just "Brady."

During the Civil War, a troop of Rangers was stationed on the San Saba River to protect the frontier from Indian raids after the state's western settlements were left defenseless by the withdrawal of U.S. troops. Around the camp grew up the community of Camp San Saba, largest in the county at that time.

Brady became the county seat of McCulloch County in 1876. It is on the edge of the "Hill Country" and was located on the Dodge Cattle Trail. It is almost at the geographical center of Texas. It is approximately 430 miles to the Rio Grande River at El Paso and 400 miles to the Rio Grande at Brownsville, 412 miles to the Panhandle north border and 341 miles to the Sabine River near Burkeville.

The longest fenced cattle trail in the world once extended from a Brady railhead to Sonora, Texas.

Brady is located at or near the intersection of four U.S. Highways: 87, 190, 283 and 377. It is on Brady Creek, which is a tributary to the San Saba River to the south. It is 135 miles north-northwest of San Antonio and 125 miles west northwest of Austin.

The terrain in the Brady area is hilly and rolling, and drains to the Colorado River, Brady Creek and the San Saba River. The soil grades from black loams to sandy soils. The trees are mesquite, cedar and oak. The elevation of Brady is 1250 feet. The average annual rainfall is 23.4 inches. Brady is in the heart of the ranch country. The rainfall is sufficient for native grasses, but is not quite enough for most crops without irrigation. Only 2,000 acres are irrigated.

Brady is served by the Santa Fe Railroad, which runs from Brady to the northeast.

The agricultural income of McCulloch County is $21 million,

which is about 60% of the average Texas county income. 80% of the income is from beef cattle, sheep, goats and hogs. The crops include oats, wheat, sorghum, cotton, peanuts and hay.

Lake Brady is located three miles west of Brady. It is a popular recreation spot.

The population of Brady is 7,200. The city has a mayor-council form of city government.

Brady will soon have G. Rollie White Downs, in operation. This will be the first track to kick off parimutuel horse racing in Texas, when it opens in October 1989. Racing will be held from October 1989 until January 28, 1990.

Brady has a number of points and events of interest. Some of them are: The Kenneth Memorial Range at Brady Lake (this has been the headquarters for the Texas Muzzle Loaders shooting matches); Miss Heart of Texas Pageant, Tennis Tournament, Heart of Texas Bicycle Classic, and Old Fashion County Fair.

BRAZORIA

In 1826, Brazoria was settled one-half mile from present-day Brazoria. The town is located on the Brazos River, from which its name is derived. The Brazos River was the reason for Brazoria's birth. The river was the main artery for transportation serving the Stephen F. Austin Colony. Brazoria was established as a port in 1828.

After the Texas Revolution, Brazoria became the county seat of Brazos County and remained an active river port for many years, seeing many boats such as the Yellow Stone, Brazos Laura, and Alice Blair come and go through the years. With the decline of river traffic and lack of rail service, commercial interest in the town declined. The county seat was moved to Angleton.

Anson Jones was a Brazoria physician and plantation owner. He served as the last President of the Republic of Texas and handed Texas over to the United States, completing annexation in February, 1844.

In 1906, the St. Louis, Brownsville and Mexico Railroad came through Brazoria and the town rebuilt along its tracks.

In 1932 a very severe hurricane almost destroyed the town, but it rebuilt and grew to become a healthy, vibrant town.

In 1945, Brazoria incorporated. It has a population of 3,200. It is served by the Missouri-Pacific Railroad, now owned and operated by the Union Pacific Railroad.

It is located on State Highways 521, 36, and 332. It is located 38 miles southwest of Houston and 17 miles northwest of Freeport.

The annual rainfall is 52 inches. It is located in an extremely fertile area. The agricultural products are rice, soybeans, maize, cotton, and livestock.

BRAZOSPORT

Brazosport is a most unusual community of nine cities, situated at the mouth of the Brazos River. Each city is separate, but they are joined by a similar outlook and destiny. These cities are Freeport, Clute, Lake Jackson, Brazoria, Jones Creek, Quintana, Richwood, Oyster Creek and Surfside. Brazosport is located in Brazoria County. The population is 54,000.

Brazosport is located on the Gulf Intracoastal waterway. It is served by State Highways 36, 288 and 332, and by farm-to-market highways, 521, 523, 1495, 2004 and 2611.

BRECKENRIDGE

The Texas Legislative Act of 1858 designated the boundaries of a county to be named Buchanan (for President James Buchanan) and a county seat to be named Breckinridge (for John C. Breckinridge, who was James Buchanan's Vice-President and was later a Major General in the Confederacy). However, because of the Civil War and Indian problems, it was not until the late 1870's that numbers of settlers entered the area. The county was officially reorganized as Stephens County (for Alexander H. Stephens, Vice-President of the Confederacy), and the City of Breckenridge was founded. At about that time, the name of "Breckinridge" was misspelled as "Breckenridge," and that misspelling has been retained to this day. Breckenridge is the county seat of Stephens County.

By 1900, Breckenridge was a thriving community. When oil was discovered in the area in 1918, the population of Breckenridge increased from 1,590 to over 20,000 in one year. Many oil companies, including the Texas Company (later known as Texaco), maintained "oil camps" in the area for their workers.

Breckenridge is supported by oil, gas, small manufacturing, ranching and, in recent years, more and more by the vacation industry. Cattle and oil were important in the early days of Breckenridge and have continued to contribute to the prosperity of the city. More recently, manufacturers of clothing, petrochemicals, furniture, oil field equipment, and aircraft parts have located here. Stephens County is basically cattle country with very little agriculture of other types in the county.

Breckenridge's population in 1989 was estimated to be 7,600. The city is located at the intersection of U.S. Highways 180 and 183 is about 100 miles due west of Fort Worth and about 65 miles northeast of Abilene. Breckenridge has a commission-manager form of government. There is no railroad in Stephens County. The nearest airport is at Abilene.

Attractions in the area include:

a) Swenson Memorial Museum, a historical oriented museum featuring an excellent collection of local historical data, with several changes in exhibits during each year.
b) Sandefer Oil Museum Annex, an addition to the Swenson Museum which features a collection of oil industry history and equipment as well as the Area Hall of Fame exhibit.
c) Breckenridge Aviation Museum, featuring a collection of World War II Aircraft and other World War II memorabilia. There are some 20 aircraft permanently stationed at the airport and part of the museum which is headquarters for the Big Iron Squadron of the West Texas Wing of the Confederate Air Force.
d) Breckenridge Library and Fine Arts Center, a beautiful new center with large exhibit hall, meeting rooms, special workshops in painting, sculpture, music, special story telling and numerous programs in the Arts.
e) Kuhn's Exotic Animal Farm, an outstanding collection of exotic animals.

Two special events held in the City of Breckenridge are: the Breckenridge Air Show (held in May of each year) and the Annual Breckenridge Big Bass Bonanza (held in June of each year).

Possum Kingdom Lake, Lake Daniel, and Hubbard Creek Lake are all nearby, and furnish water for the city as well as recreational opportunities.

BRENHAM

Brenham is the county seat of Washington County. It is located on U.S. Highway 290 and State Highway 36. It is 72 miles west-northwest of Houston, 83 miles east of Austin, and 40 miles south of College Station. The average elevation is 350 feet. The average annual rainfall is 38.9 inches, which is nearly an ideal amount for nearly all crops.

The city was founded as the county seat in 1844 and named for Richard Fox Brenham, a hero of the ill-fated Mier Expedition. The city was incorporated in 1858. During and after the Civil War, Brenham was occupied by federal troops, who partially burned the city in 1867 following a confrontation with the local citizens.

German immigration began in 1850 and increased after the Civil War. Polish immigrants followed in the 1870's. The plantation-agrarian economy was greatly disrupted by the war. Most of the large farms in the area were divided into smaller ones and taken up by the German immigrants. In 1890 a yellow fever epidemic wiped out a third of the county population.

Brenham is located in the heart of Stephen F. Austin's first colony. Two of Austin's original 300 colonist's homes are still standing in the county today. The area was opened to settlers in 1821. Pioneers from all parts of the United States and immigrants from Western Europe flocked to Austin's Colony and its liberal land grants.

The city of Washington was started in 1821 and developed and flourished with the steamboat navigation on the Brazos River until the coming of the railroads in 1860-1880.

The topography of the country surrounding Brenham is rolling to gently rolling. It is in the post oak belt and the blacklands of the Gulf Coastal Plain.

The population of Brenham in 1989 was 14,000. The city has a mayor-commission-manager form of government.

The taxes of Brenham are very reasonable compared to urban areas in Texas. These taxes are:

State	$0.0000
County	$0.3500 per $100 assessment
City	$0.3502 per $100 assessment

Blinn College	$0.0372 per $100 assessment
Brenham School	$0.6065 per $100 assessment
	$1.3439 per $100 assessment

The city is served by the Atchison, Topeka & Santa Fe Railroad.

Brenham is the home of Blinn College, which is a two-year liberal arts college with an enrollment of 6,090. There are 2,500 students on the Brenham Campus. College Station and Bryan also have campuses.

The area around Brenham is still principally agricultural, producing mainly beef, dairy, horses, swine, poultry, horticulture and forage. There has been a renewed interest in horticulture such as home gardens, pecans, peaches, plums, pears, grapes and landscaping. Also gaining national attention is the area's horse operations. It is now one of the top horse-producing centers in the United States. The area now has a reputation as the "Horse Capital of Texas."

Leading manufacturers include Blue Bell Creameries; Brentex Mills; Gates Molded Products; Valmont/A.L.S.; TFE Company, Inc., Steadley Co., Inc.; Sealy Mattress Co.; Continental Carbon Paper Manufacturing Co.; Cleaners Hangar Co.; Magnetic Instruments Co.; Texas Fibers, Inc.; and Ellison's Greenhouses; HDL Research Lab, Inc., and Brenham Broom & Mop.

BRIDGE CITY

Bridge City is located in the southern part of East Texas in Orange County, 20 miles east of Beaumont and just a few miles west of the Texas-Louisiana stateline. The city is located on State Highway 87 at the foot of Rainbow Bridge which spans the Neches River. Rainbow Bridge, the tallest bridge in the South, was completed in 1938 at a cost of $3 million.

The community was originally called "Prairieview" (because the surrounding area looked like prairie). Then, in 1946, residents were asked to suggest possible new names for the town. The winning name of "Bridge City" was submitted by Winnie Fontenot Lormand who pointed out, "There is a bridge everywhere you go to get out of Prairieview."

In the early 1930's, the economy of the area was dependent on cotton and rice farms. Many former rice farmers are now raising crawfish, a growing industry for the area. Bridge City, with a large Cajun population, holds a Crawfish and Crab Festival each March.

Bridge City's population is now estimated at 8,000. The city has a home rule charter form of municipal government. Gulf States Utilities, which services the entire southern part of the state of Texas, is the community's largest industry.

Bridge City's assets include its bayous and Lake Sabine to the south. Not generally known is that Monarch butterflies, while migrating south for the winter, stop at Bailey's Fish Camp on nearby Lake Sabine. About October or November, the trees are covered with butterflies.

Another annual event, "Bridge City Days," is held in the Fall.

BRIDGEPORT

Bridgeport is located in Wise County on the west fork of the Trinity River. It is 45 miles northwest of Fort Worth and 38 miles west of Denton, and is on U.S. Highway 380 and State Highway 114.

Bridgeport had its origins back in 1860 when a toll bridge was built across the Trinity River to provide a crossing for the Butterfield Stage on its St. Louis to San Francisco route. After the completion of the bridge, settlers began arriving, attracted by the water, timber, grass, wild game and rich soil. The new town took its name from the bridge.

Bridgeport's population is now about 3,700. Livestock and dairying are principal industries. The area has natural gas and petroleum deposits and the state's largest limestone mining operation.

Every July, Bridgeport celebrates Butterfield Stage Days with a rodeo, parade, street dance and barbeque.

BROWNFIELD

Brownfield became the county seat of Terry County in 1904. Brownfield won out over the thriving little village of Gomez by five votes in an election.

In 1920, Brownfield was incorporated. The city was named for Dick Ray and M. V. Brownfield, prominent pioneer settlers. The 1988 population was 11,850.

The town is located on U.S. Highway 385 running generally south to north, and on U.S. Highway 380 running due east-west, and U.S. Highways 82 and 62 running to the northeast. It is 35 miles southwest of Lubbock and 116 miles due south of Amarillo. It is in the middle of the Texas High Plains.

The town has an excellent climate. The elevation is 3,312 feet. The mean temperature is 58.1 degrees. The mean annual rainfall is 17.4 inches. Because of the rather low rainfall, the country is mostly devoted to raising livestock; however, there is a considerable amount of wheat, maize, cotton and corn where it can be irrigated.

The Santa Fe Railroad came to Brownfield in 1917. The coming of the railroad insured the healthy growth of the area.

Irrigation is now used extensively by the farmers. They pump water from the Ogallala Aquifier. Terry County is in the middle of this aquifier.

Oil was discovered in Terry County in the early 1940's. Brownfield is near the geographic center of the oil field activity on the Texas High Plains.

BROWNSVILLE

Brownsville was incorporated in 1850. It has a commission/manager form of city government. It was named in honor of Major Jacob Brown of the U.S. Army, who commanded the U.S. Army Post, located at what was to be called Brownsville. Major Brown lost his life defending the post during the Mexican War with the United States.

Brownsville is located at the extreme southern tip of Texas, on the north banks of the Rio Grande River. It is located at the same latitude as Miami, Florida. The population is 110,000. It is the largest city in the Lower Rio Grande Valley, which has a population of 625,000.

Brownsville is the county seat of Cameron County. The county is one of the richest agricultural areas in Texas. The average income from agriculture and livestock for a Texas County is approximately $35 million. Cameron County has an agricultural income of $91 million. The main crops are citrus, cotton, corn, maize, and vegetables. Fishing and port activities are becoming more and more important.

Brownsville has been called by many leading Texas historians "the second most important city, historically, in Texas." Visitors to Brownsville have added their names to a long list of national and international historic figures: Jose Escandon, Robert E. Lee,

Phillip Sheridan, Braxton Bragg, Don Buell, George Meade, George H. Thomas, George McClelland, Thomas "Stonewall" Jackson, U. S. Grant, Jefferson Davis, Lew Wallace, Edmund Davis, Juan Cortina, Richard King, Mifflin Kenedy, Francisco Yturria, Charles Stillman, Jose San Ramon, Henrietta King, Dr. William Gorgas, Abner Doubleday, Amelia Earhart, Charles Lindbergh, and many others.

At the end of the Mexican War, Charles Stillman, a young merchant from New England, purchased land to establish a townsite, where Brownsville is today. Construction of the first building started in 1846. Because of the unsettled condition in Matamoros and northern Mexico, large numbers of French, German, Spanish and North American businessmen moved their operations to Brownsville. In addition to establishing the city, Stillman purchased steamboats that had been used by General Taylor to ply the Rio Grande River from its mouth to Camargo, Mexico to supply his troops. Stillman formed a steamship company with Mifflin Kenedy and Richard King; men who would play a major role in the development of South Texas. The trio soon obtained a monopoly on river trade. The venture was assured financial success with the outbreak of the American Civil War. The Brownsville-Matamoros connection soon resulted with this area being the largest exporter of Confederate cotton. This was referred to as the "Backdoor of the Confederacy."

Brownsville is elbow-to-elbow with Ol' Mexico. The sights, sounds, and flavors of a foreign land are five minutes away. Matamoros, a city of over 300,000 population, has been catering to U.S visitors for three-quarters of a century. It abounds with fine restaurants, night clubs, shops and markets stocked with the exotic goods of Latin America. There's a constant exchange of people, trade and culture. More than thirty million crossings a year are recorded at the two international bridges. Brownsville has valued the tourist trade at $135 million dollars.

Brownsville has a fine deep water port. The channel to the turning basin was dredged from the Gulf of Mexico.

Brownsville is served by U.S. Highways 77 and 281, and Texas farm to market highways 1419, 3069 and 511.

Two railroads come into Brownsville, the Union Pacific (formerly the Missouri Pacific) and the Southern Pacific.

Brownsville is nationally known as a fine winter haven. Its climate is unparalleled.

BROWNWOOD

Brownwood is the county seat of Brown county. Located near the geographic center of the state, Brownwood lies only 161 miles southwest of Dallas, 120 miles southwest of Ft. Worth, 191 miles north of San Antonio and 290 miles from Houston.

Brownwood has a population of 19,800, and has an annual rainfall of 27.2 inches. The altitude at the Brownwood Municipal Airport is 1,380 feet. U.S. Highways 67, 377, 84 and 183 connect with the High Plains, East Texas, West Texas and the Gulf Coast.

The first Anglo-Americans to enter the country were under the leadership of Capt. Henry S. Brown, for whom the county was named. He and his men were there in 1828 as they sought to recover horses stolen by the Indians. In August of 1856 the Texas state legislature created Brown County. Brownwood was settled in 1867.

Today, Brownwood features an impressive industrial park with several large manufacturing plants situated on land that was once home of the Texas National Guard, 36th Division. Howard Payne University campus, featuring the Douglas MacArthur Academy of Freedom, is located in Brownwood. Lake Brownwood supplies water for the surrounding residents and offers many West Texans a summertime playground.

BRYAN

Bryan and College Station are twin cities with a common midpoint city limit. The cities are served by State Highways 6, 21, and 30, as well as Interstate 190.

William Joel Bryan, grandson of Moses Austin and nephew of Stephen F. Austin, gave a right-of-way to the Houston & Texas Central Railroad and, in 1859, laid out, surveyed, and platted a townsite of 640 acres along the route of the railroad. The townsite was then named Bryan in his honor.

In 1866, the county seat was moved from Boonville to Bryan, although Bryan was not formally incorporated until 1872. Bryan was one of the first cities in Texas to adopt a "Common Council" form of government, which, at that time, consisted of a mayor, five aldermen and a city marshall.

Modern-day Bryan is an agribusiness center and is the home of manufacturers of business forms, defense electronics, aluminum buildings, furniture and shoe products.

The citizens of Brazos County donated land in 1871 for the establishment of the Agricultural & Mechanical College of Texas. The college opened in 1876 and, since 1963, has been known as Texas A&M University.

The city of College Station was not incorporated until 1938. Its 1980 population was 37,272. Besides being the home of Texas A&M University, College Station is a center for mini-computers, offshore technology, and research and development.

BURKBURNETT

Burkburnett is located in North Texas about 15 miles north of Wichita Falls and just south of the Red River, which serves as a boundary between Texas and Oklahoma. The city is located on State Highway 240 just west of Interstate 40. It is in Wichita County and has a population of approximately 10,000.

Burkburnett had its beginnings on the 6666 Ranch owned by Samual Burk Burnett. In 1856, Mabel Gilbert and his family rafted up the Red River and settled at the site of the present-day Burkburnett—a spot where a fresh water creek emptied into the Red River, where there was spring water, grass, and wild game.

Wagon trains passed through the area, with some settlers staying; other settlers rafted up the river and decided to stay. Cowboys referred to the little community as Nesterville, but the settlers called it Gilbert in honor of the first settler.

When the federal government announced that Indian Territory (Oklahoma) would be opened to white settlers, Samuel Burnett invited President Theodore Roosevelt to attend a wolf hunt on his ranch. In 1905, Burnett sold some of his land to two men from Wichita Falls who were building a railroad through the property. In 1907, a town lot sale was held. President Roosevelt suggested the new town be named for his friend, Samual Burk Burnett. Since there was already a town called Burnet, it was decided to combine Burnett's middle name and last name—hence, Burkburnett.

Cattle and agriculture were the mainstay of the community. Principal crops were corn, cotton, and watermelons.

Oil was first discovered in the area in 1912, but it wasn't until

1918 when the oil boom began. Almost overnight the population exploded from 1,500 to 15,000. Nearly 200 oil companies were operating. Burkburnett was referred to as "Boomtown"; oilmen claimed the oil derricks were so close together you could walk across town from derrick to derrick without touching the ground. Then, almost as quickly as it started, the oil boom was over.

Oil is still important to Burkburnett, but in reduced quantities. Farming and ranching also continue to be important. The area is served by the Missouri-Kansas-Texas Railroad.

BURLESON

Burleson was founded in 1881 as a result of the construction of the M-K-T Railway. It was incorporated in 1912, and became a "home-rule" city in 1969.

It is located 12 miles south of Fort Worth and 35 miles southwest of Dallas on I-35 (U.S. 81) and SH 174. It lies in both Johnson and Tarrant Counties. According to 1985 estimates, the population was 16,400.

Burleson was named in honor of Dr. Rufus C. Burleson, a pioneer educator and preacher, who later became President of Baylor University.

Prior to the coming of the railroad, the area was open range country. A village known as Red Oak Academy was built up around a Presbyterian school of that name. However, after an outbreak of typhoid fever, the village was abandoned in favor of nearby Burleson, already a thriving town.

Burleson has a council-manager type of government.

Two annual events in Burleson are the Burleson Good Life Days Celebration (held one full week in mid-April) and the Annual Texas Heritage Trail Ride (held the second Saturday in October).

In its early days, Burleson was the center of a large livestock raising area; it later became a prosperous farming community, and finally evolved into its present country-city mix, serving commerce and industry as well as farming.

BURNET

The county was created in 1854. The county was named for David G. Burnet, the provisional President of the Texas Republic. The county seat took the same name.

Burnet is the county seat of Burnet County. It is located in the

Hill Country, 55 miles northwest of Austin, 110 miles north of San Antonio, and 190 miles southwest of Dallas.

The population of the City is 3,650. The average annual rainfall is 30.2 inches, which is adequate for most crops. The city has a council-mayor-manager form of government. The tax structure is:

City	$0.36	per $100 assessment
County	0.31	per $100 assessment
School	0.97	per $100 assessment
	$1.64	per $100 of assessment.

The highways serving the city are U.S. Highway 281 and State Highway 29. The city is served by the Austin-Northwestern Railroad Co.

The major employers are:

Burnet Construction Co.
Shepperd Hospital
Sure Cast Co.
Pioneer Rock Crushing Co.
Dean Word, Contractors
Billbrough Marble Co.
Delta Materials
Hoover Building Co.

The seven Highland Lakes in Central Texas have over 450 miles of shoreline and are the largest concentration of lakes in Texas. The Hill Country is the winter home of the American Bald Eagle, which can be seen along the lakes and rivers.

Some of the places of great beauty and interest to the tourists and visitors are:

1. Enchanted Rock State Park—on Hwy. 16, 16 miles south of Llano
2. Inks Lake State Park—On Park Road 4, between Burnet and Marble Falls
3. Inks Dam National Fish Hatchery—On Park Road 4
4. Longhorn Cavern State Park, on Park Road 4
5. Packsaddle Mountain, Kingsland. Site of last Indian battle, on FM 1431 just west of Kingsland
6. Granite Mountain, Marble Falls—Just west of Marble Falls, off FM 1431

7. LBJ National Historic Park—Former President Johnson's Ranch

8. Lake Buchanan—Highest of the Lakes, Buchanan Dam is 250 ft. tall, and the lake is 8 miles wide, and 32 miles long

9. Lake LBJ—on FM 1431

Burnet is referred to as the Bluebonnet Capitol of Texas.

CALDWELL

In 1840, the Congress of the Republic of Texas designated Caldwell as the county seat of a new county to be formed. The proposed town was named for Mathew "Old Paint" Caldwell, an Indian fighter, Texas patriot, and signer of the Texas Declaration of Independence.

The site selected for the new town was the same location as an earlier trading and settlement founded by Lewis Chiles at the crossing of the Old San Antonio Road on Davidson Creek.

In 1880, the Gulf, Colorado & Santa Fe Railway built its main line through Caldwell; and in 1912, the Houston & Texas Central Railroad extended a line from Hearne through Caldwell to Flatonia where it joined the Southern Pacific Railroad to the West Coast. Caldwell is still served by these two railroads.

Caldwell is the county seat of Burleson County and is located 25 miles southwest of Bryan/College Station. It can be reached by State Highways 21 and 36. Present population is 2,953.

CAMERON

Cameron is located on U.S. Highways 77 and 190, and State Highway 36. It is 53 miles south of Waco, 78 miles northeast of Austin, and 137 miles northwest of Houston.

It was named for Capt. Ewen Cameron, a member of the Mier expedition during the war with Mexico.

Cameron was established as the county seat of Milam County by the first State Legislature in 1846. It has a home rule government, consisting of a mayor and city council.

In 1881, the Gulf, Colorado & Santa Fe Railroad built a line through Cameron, connecting the Gulf Coast with Fort Worth. Then, in 1890, the San Antonio & Aransas Pass Railroad also built a line to Cameron.

A jail, built in 1895, is now the Milam County Museum.

Cameron has a diverse economy—primarily agricultural and light industry. Its current population is 5,817.

CANADIAN

Situated in the scenic Canadian River Valley, surrounded by colorful mesas and hills, the town of Canadian is a welcoming oasis where transcontinental U.S. Highway 60 and 83 meet, merge briefly, then go their separate ways, near the top of the Texas Panhandle.

Built on hills overlooking the confluence of the Canadian River and Red Deer Creek, Canadian was created when the pioneering Kansas & Southern (now the Atcheson, Topeka and Santa Fe Railway) extended its main-line rails across the Canadian River en route from Chicago to the West Coast, bridging the broad sandy reaches of this western stream for the first time.

Beginning as "Hogg Town," a construction camp on the railroad in 1887, it shifted location to the south bank of the river as the crossing was completed in 1888. Canadian quickly developed as a cattle shipping center of the Panhandle ranching empire, and it won the name of "Rodeo Town" with one of the first-ever organized rodeos on the Fourth of July in 1888, and continues the tradition into modern times with the annual event.

The townspeople began referring to their community as Canadian after the Canadian River, which passed through town. The railroad officials who named the town first, agreed, and the town officially became Canadian.

Capitalizing in post World War II years on its proximity to Lake Marvin and the abundance of white-tailed deer, wild turkey and bob white quail in the wooded areas along the river, Canadian became known as "The Playground of the Panhandle," and promoted its popular Fall Foliage Tours when neighbors from the treeless plains were invited to drive to Canadian to view the colorful cottonwoods, wild grape, soapberry and other plants in their autumn glory. This tradition continues.

In more recent times Canadian has become a center for oil and gas development in the mineral-rich Anadarko Basin of the northeast Panhandle. A broadened tax base has allowed city, county and school officials to aggressively meet the needs of growing population while keeping tax rates low. Recently constructed were the new Canadian Elementary School, the expanded Hemphill

County Library and the Hemphill County Law Enforcement Center. A modern 26-bed hospital was built in 1976.

In the way of transportation, Canadian has the Santa Fe serving the city with thirty trains daily. The Amarillo International Airport offers facilities, 101 miles away.

The city has a city manager, mayor-council form of government.

The altitude of Canadian is 2500 feet which accounts for its pleasant climate. The rainfall is 21 inches a year, which is just barely enough for some crops like wheat. Hemphill County has an average agricultural income compared to other Texas counties. It is the center for the oil and gas industry in the northeast corner of the Panhandle. The income from beef cattle and hogs is considerable. The crops are wheat, hay, sorghum, and grain.

Canadian has a population of 4,000 people and is growing.

CANTON

Canton is the county seat of Van Zandt County. It has a population of 3,100. It is the farming and livestock marketing center of Van Zandt County. The area terrain consists of rolling hills, of which over 70% is forested. The city is on the extreme western edge of the piney woods country of Texas.

The city is 55 miles east of Dallas on U.S. Highway 20. State Highways 19, 64, 198 and 243 serve the city as well as FM 859 and 1255. It is the highway hub of that part of the state. In that area, nearly all roads lead to Canton.

The area around Canton is a rich agricultural area. The county has an annual agricultural income of $51 million; 70% of the income is from cattle, hogs and dairy products. It is the leading county in producing beef cows and calves. The crops include nursery stock, vegetables, grain, cotton and hay.

The annual rainfall is 43.1 inches. The altitude of the city is 500 feet. The nearest railroad is the Union Pacific, 10 miles to the north at Edgewood. The nearest commercial airport is Love Field in Dallas, 55 miles to the west and the Dallas-Ft. Worth International Airport, 68 miles away.

The city is noted for the "First Monday Trades Day," held on the first Monday of each month and the first Friday, Saturday and Sunday preceding; 100 acres of antiques and handmade articles are on display for sale. This is one of the largest, best-known and most interesting flea markets in the nation.

An attraction in the area is Brewer's Belle Museum. This is a collection of Belle Brewer and contains some 3,200 bells, many rare and exotic.

Canton has some manufacturing industry. There is an apparel factory and a plant which manufactures trailers. Minerals in the area are oil, gas, salt and clay.

CANYON

Canyon is located in the Texas Panhandle 16 miles due south of Amarillo. Interstate 27, U.S. Highway 60, and State Highway 217 all serve Canyon.

The town was laid out by Mr. and Mrs. L. G. Conner who wanted to have a town of law-abiding, religious, educated people. Rather than name the town for themselves, the name of Canyon City (for the canyon in the eastern part of the county) was chosen.

The first elections in Randall County were held in 1889 and 45 votes were cast for county offices.

In 1906, the Commercial Club of Canyon was formed to try to get Palo Duro declared a national park. Palo Duro Canyon is now a state park and is located just east of the city.

The Santa Fe Railroad serves the city.

West Texas State Normal College (now West Texas State University) was organized in 1909.

Wheat and grain sorghum are the principal grain crops of the county.

Current population is about 12,201.

CARRIZO SPRINGS

Carrizo Springs is located in South Texas on State Highways 83, 85, and 277, and Farm-to-Market Road 2644. It is 80 miles northwest of Laredo and 115 miles southwest of San Antonio.

Carrizo Springs is the county seat of Dimmit County, with a population of 6,886.

"Carrizo" is the Spanish name for the cane which grew along the creeks and was often used to thatch roofs. Fresh-water springs ran through the townsite area. The town's name combined the two and became Carrizo Springs.

Industries in the community include a feedlot, food processing, garment manufacturing, oil and gas processing, and a pecan shelling plant.

CARTHAGE

Carthage is the county seat of Panola County. Panola is an Indian word meaning "cotton." Carthage was formed in 1848 when 100 acres were donated for the townsite. Today, it is a center for gas and oil processing, petrochemicals, lumber mills, chicken processing and small industries. It is the home of Panola County Junior College.

Carthage is located in the very northeast corner of Texas, deep in the piney woods belt. Its population today is 7,100. Carthage has a mayor-commissioner-city manager form of government. Carthage is located on U.S. Highways 59 and 79 and on Texas Highways 10, 149 and 315.

Carthage is served by the Santa Fe Railroad. The nearest airport with regular airline passenger service is Shreveport, Louisiana, which is 44 miles to the east-northeast.

One of the objects of interest in the Carthage area is the boundary marker that was installed to mark the boundary between the Republic of Texas and the United States. It is located 30 miles southeast of Carthage on FM 31. This granite marker was erected in 1840 by surveyors, and is the only boundary of its kind in the world. It was placed by representatives of the United States of America and the Republic of Texas. It marks the borderline between two countries that now lie within the United States. In 1941, the U.S. Geological Survey Team proceeded to check the accuracy of this location. They placed a hole in the top of the shaft which confirms the accuracy of the original survey made one hundred years earlier by members of the joint commission.

The Jim Reeves Memorial is located 3 miles east of Carthage on Highway 79. Jim Reeves was born August 20, 1923 at his family home in Panola County. Jim Reeves is remembered as an American singer who pioneered the musical crossover between country and pop music. In 1946, "Gentleman Jim" Reeves, a soft-spoken East Texan, began presenting country songs, performed in his special style, to audiences throughout the area. The number of his devoted fans increased dramatically following his appearance on Shreveport's "Louisiana Hayride." He died in a plane crash near Nashville, Tennessee on July 31, 1964. His lifesize statue stands sentry over his grave beneath a huge oak tree.

Carthage has a rather high ad valorem tax structure. The tax rates are:

City	.7800
County	.3540
School	.8900
	$2.0240 per $100 per assessment

This is high, in that the average Texas city tax rate is approximately $1.75 per assessed value.

Carthage has several sizable manufacturing facilities in the general area of the city. They are as follows:

Louisiana-Pacific	Lumber
Tyson Foods	Chicken
Drew Woods, Inc.	Contractor
United Gas Pipeline	Gas Processing
Champlin	Gas Processing
Texas Utilities Mining Co. (Largest Employer)	Lignite Coal
Carthage Cup	Plastic Cups

CEDAR HILL

Cedar Hill is located in the extreme southwest corner of Dallas County. Downtown Dallas is sixteen miles to the northeast. The altitude of Cedar Hill is 841 feet. The area of Cedar Hill is 33 square miles. The average annual rainfall is 34.5 inches. The population is 18,500 people.

Dallas-Fort Worth Regional Airport is located approximately 25 miles to the north. The Santa Fe Railroad serves the area with four to six trains daily.

Cedar Hill was named after a stand of cedar brakes in Mountain Creek. Cedar Hill is a fast-growing city which enjoys a magnificent setting of tree-studded rolling hills covered with massive stands of stately cedars, oaks, and native trees.

Cedar Hill was settled in the 1840's and is the second oldest city in Dallas County. Settlers found a beautiful hilly area with fertile fields and abundant wildlife. They built log cabins from the wood in the timber hills and set them in closely arranged pattern as a precaution against the Caddo Indian raids. In the 1860's, the city flourished as a stop on the old Chisholm Trail. This path led the great herds of cattle through the south part of the city to cattle markets in Kansas.

Cedar Hill combines an old west past with a modern present. Well situated in the Dallas-Fort Worth Metroplex, Cedar Hill is easily accessible; a network of super freeways and highways link the city to communities in the metroplex and beyond, including the Dallas/Fort Worth Regional Airport. Highway 67 makes downtown Dallas a quick 20-minute ride away. The final portion of Interstate 635 is located just north of Cedar Hill. Highway 1382 provides easy access to the mid-cities and links the new Interstate 20 to Loop 12.

Cedar Hill is known as "The Tower City of the Southwest" due to a concentration within the city limits of radio, television, and other communications towers. It is the highest point in the metroplex; with an elevation of 841 feet. On clear days you can stand on any hilltop and view downtown Dallas skyscrapers to the north and the Fort Worth skyline to the west.

Cedar Hill has a home rule form of government. It has six councilmen, one mayor, one city manager, and one assistant city-manager.

The soon-to-be completed Joe Pool Lake is located one and a half miles from the town square, making Cedar Hill ideal for fishing, boating, and peaceful lake living.

CENTER

Center is the county seat of Shelby County. The city had a population of 6,100 in 1988. The county borders on Louisiana's west boundary. The boundary is the center of the huge Toledo Bend Reservoir on the Sabine River. This lake is 70 miles long and 15 miles wide.

The large Sabine National Forest is on the west side of the Toledo Bend Reservoir and extends along the reservoir for approximately 50 miles. The width of the national forest averages approximately fourteen miles. The lower part is in St. Augustine County.

Center is located on U.S. Highway 96, running north and south, and on State Highways 7, 87, 699, and 138. The city is 118 miles due north to Beaumont.

The city is served by the Atchison, Topeka and Santa Fe Railroad.

Center got its name in a rather bizarre manner. One night in 1866, following a hotly-contested election, R. L. Parker, with the help of two Negro servants, stole the records from the courthouse and moved them to a cabin he had built at the geographical center of Shelby County; in that way, "Center" was born. The following morning, trackers found Parker seated by the door of the log cabin with his rifle; and he informed them that court was open for business.

The courthouse and all records were destroyed by fire in June, 1882. The present courthouse was designed and built by J. J. E. Gibson, an Irishman, from the plans of an Irish castle in his native Ireland. The unique structure is still in service and dispensing justice. The courthouse displays the Texas Medallion and a U.S. Historical marker and is the only one of its kind in the United States.

In 1946, the broiler industry was born in Shelby County, and the farmers changed from cotton and corn row crops to raising poultry. By using fertilizer byproducts of the poultry production, they fertilized the old cotton and corn fields to establish excellent pasture grasses; and where cotton and corn once grew, large herds of beef cattle now graze. Also, because of the good management of their forest lands, they grow large amounts of forest products. Center is deep in the beautiful piney woods of East Texas. The area has an annual rainfall of 49.2 inches.

Shelby County has an area of 791 square miles. Part of this is taken up by the Sabine National Forest and Toledo Bend Reservoir. Even with the production lost from these areas, the county has an annual $49 million agricultural income, which is over twice the average for Texas counties.

Toledo Bend Reservoir is bringing in thousands of fishermen and tourists to further diversity the local economy of "Beautiful East Texas."

CHILDRESS

Childress is located 110 miles west of Wichita Falls. It is located at the base of the eastern panhandle line, south of the corner with Oklahoma. The city was named after George C. Childress, a member of the 1836 convention and co-author of the Texas Declaration of Independence.

Ranching and farming has also played a huge part in the Childress Story, as many years ago, this was nature's wilderness, inhabited only by the native Indian and the wild animals of the great plains. But where buffalo and antelope thrived, cattle too would flourish. This brought the early rancher and his longhorn cattle to the area. Childress County was occupied by four large cattle companies: the Mill Iron, the Diamond Tail, the Shoe Nail, and the O-X, which was organized in 1880. At that time, land here could be bought for fifty cents an acre, some even cheaper. As one old timer explained, "We didn't buy it from nobody, it was out-side land and we jest took it!" Today, cotton and wheat are the principal crops. Generally 60,000 acres of cotton are planted in Childress County; 6,000 acres are irrigated.

Childress is at the crossroad of two U.S. highways. U.S. Highway 62 and 83 runs north and south. U.S. Highway 287 crosses at Childress and runs east and west. It is the road from Amarillo to Wichita Falls and Fort Worth. The population of Childress is 5,970. It has a fair ad valorem tax rate, a total of $1.844 per $100 of assessment. The elevation of Childress is 1,877 feet. The average rainfall is 21.03 inches per year. This amount of rainfall is inadequate for the raising of most crops, such as cotton and feed grains.

Childress is the county seat of Childress County. Childress has a mayor-council form of city government. It is served by the Burlington Northern Railroad which runs both east and west through the city. The nearest airport is Wichita Falls, 110 miles to the east.

Lake Childress is located five miles west of Childress. The city is unique in that there are not any organized unions in the area.

During the period of 1865-1885, the Goodnight-Loving trail passed through Childress. Many thousand head of cattle were driven over this trail to market annually.

CISCO

Eastland is the county seat of Eastland. Cisco is on U.S. Highway-183 and is just two miles north of IH-20. It is on SH-6 and 206. It is 44 miles east of Abilene and 182 miles west of Fort Worth. It is the hub of SH 6, 206, U.S 80, 183 and FM 2945.

The city was named for John J. Cisco who financed the construction of the Katy Railroad. The city was located at the rail crossing of the Texas Pacific and Katy Railroad.

The city has a mayor-council, city manager type of government.

The terrain around Cisco is hilly, and rolling with sandy loam soils to the south and clay soils to the north. It is in the Leon River water shed. The altitude is 1900 ft. The average annual rainfall is 27.1 inches.

Cisco has a population of 4,700. It is the home of the Cisco Junior College.

Cisco was established in 1881. The community was needed to serve as a marketing and distribution center for the large cattle and agricultural area.

In 1917 the economy was stimulated by the discovery of the Ranger oil pool. It continues as the center for oil and gas production.

It is served by the Union Pacific Railroad.

Eastland County has an average annual agricultural income of $28 million; 60% of its income is from beef cattle, sheep, and horses. The crops are peanuts, wheat and milo maize.

Cisco has some industry. It has plants manufacturing clothing, building stores, steel tanks, oil field equipment, and other products.

A point of interest in the area is the Mobley Hotel. It was bought by Conrad Hilton in 1919, when that was the only way he could get a place to sleep. The hotel became the first in the Hilton chain. The hotel has been restored and serves as the Chamber of Commerce office and a Community Center.

Lake Leon is 10 miles to the southeast of Cisco and Lake Cisco is four miles to the north, offering fishing and recreation and providing a water supply to the town.

CLARENDON

Clarendon is the county seat of Donley County. It is located 55 miles east of Amarillo on U.S. Highway 282.

The town was founded by Henry Lewis Carhart, a young Methodist preacher. He took a two-year leave from his church and procured 343 sections of West Texas land just below the Caprock east of Amarillo. This land extended from the JA Ranch to McClellan Creek, eight miles west of the present town of Clarendon and east to Lelia Lake. All of the acreage was located just below the Caprock and it has no Aquifer under it for irrigation. On this large tract of land he established the Carhart Christian Colony. He named the Colony Clarendon, for his wife Clara. That is the way the town got its name.

The population of the town is approximately 3,100 as of 1989. The Burlington Northern Railroad runs through the city and it is served by U.S. Highway 287 and by State Highway 70 and by farm to market roads 2362 and 262.

The rainfall in the area is 20.7 inches per year. This is just barely enough to have a good agricultural industry. The dry land crops are sorghum, maize, wheat, cotton, alfalfa, and cotton. Corn is raised where irrigation is available. There are 12,000 acres of land irrigated in the county. The livestock are beef cattle, hogs, horses and sheep. The Greenbelt Dam and Reservoir located on the Salt Fork of the Red River is located about six and a half miles northwest of Clarendon.

Carhart's Colony was often called the Prohibition Colony and it was referred to by a lot of the local people as "Saint's Roost." The town of Clarendon was organized in 1879 and Donley County was organized in 1882.

Clarendon is strictly a ranching and farming area. The only reason for its existence is to serve as a trading center for the ranches and farmers in the region.

CLEBURNE

The county seat of Johnson County was moved to Cleburne (then Camp Henderson) in 1867.

Cleburne was incorporated in 1871, and was named for Gen. Patrick Ronayne Cleburne, a Confederate Army officer.

The city is located 17 miles south of Fort Worth at the junction of U.S. Highway 67 and State Highways 171 and 174. Population has grown from 683 in 1870 to 16,015 in 1970 to approximately 22,500 in 1987.

Rail service was constructed to Cleburne in 1881 by the Gulf, Colorado & Santa Fe Railroad.

Today Cleburne is a dairy center and rail shipping terminal. Local manufacturing includes wall components, detention hardware, prefab siding, and trusses.

Lake Pat Cleburne is located nearby.

CLEVELAND

Cleveland is located 40 miles north of Houston on U.S. Highway 59 and State Highway 105. It is in Liberty County and its population is approximately 5,977.

The city was named for Charles Lander Cleveland (a Kentucky native, lawyer, and judge) who, in 1878, deeded a 63.6-acre townsite to the Houston East-West Railroad, provided that the town bear his name.

The city grew as a result of natural resources, such as oil, timber, iron ore, gravel, and sand. Major employers in Cleveland are Kirby Forest, Inc.; Union Tank Car Co.; Charter Memorial Hospital; and Campbell's Ready Mix.

Sam Houston National Forest and the San Jacinto River are nearby.

CLIFTON

Clifton is located in Bosque County. It is 44 miles northwest of Waco on State Highway 6. It is almost 115 miles south of Ft. Worth. The highways serving Clifton are Highway 6 running north to northwesterly and FM- Road 219, which runs west-southwest out of town, FM-709 and FM-199.

The city has a population of 3,300. It has a very low tax rate. The city has an ad valorem tax rate of $.9900 per $100 of evaluation. This is broken down as follows:

County	.22
City	.25
School	.52
	.99

This is just a little over half of the average tax rate of Texas cities. The city government consists of a mayor and six councilmen.

As to the name source of Clifton, the best explanation for this is that when the town was being organized and they were looking for a name, they decided to name it after the chalk cliffs, located near the city, and so they came up with the name Clifton.

The Santa Fe Railroad serves the city. The nearest commercial air service is at Waco, Texas.

Bosque County is of average size, having 989 square miles. The County has an agricultural income of $33,000,000 which is slightly over the average for Texas Counties. Nearly all of the income is from cattle, goats, sheep, poultry and hogs. The crops raised are peanuts, cotton, pecans, wheat, sorghum and oats.

Some of the recreation spots in the vicinity are Lake Whitney, which is located some 19 miles to the northeast, the Meridian State Park, north of the city and the Bosque Memorial Museum at Clifton. One of the attractions in the area is the Texas Safari, located about five miles southwest of Clifton. This is the world's largest exotic animal drive-through park.

COLEMAN

Coleman is the county seat of Coleman County. Both the city and the county were named for Robert M. Coleman, an aide-de-camp to Gen. Sam Houston.

Coleman is located in Central Texas on U.S. Highways 84 and 283 and State Highway 206, 52 miles southeast of Abilene and 74 miles northwest of San Angelo. Its 1987 estimated population was 6,400.

The area has abundant deposits of silica sand and a known reserve of 15 million tons of bituminous coal. Its economy is based on farming (cotton, wheat, oats, barley, and grain sorghums); ranching (beef and dairy cattle, sheep, and quarter horses); oil; brick and building tile; and light industry.

The city is on the main line of the Atchison, Topeka & Santa Fe Railroad.

Coleman County has been featured in most major sporting magazines, and sporting information describes Coleman County as one of the "Hunting Capitals of the World."

Coleman County, land of the lakes, is surrounded by enormous amounts of lake waters. Nearby are Hords Lake, Lake San Tana, Memory Lake, Lake Scarborough, Lake Coleman and Stacy Reservoir with 20,000 surface acres and 200 miles of shoreline. All of these are available for camping, boating, fishing, and water sports. Stacy Reservoir completion date is scheduled for Spring 1990.

Coleman has a council-manager form of government.

COLLEGE STATION

The City of College Station was incorporated in 1938. It now has a population of 52,900 and is growing rapidly. It has a common boundary with Bryan on one side. It has a mayor and council form of city government.

It was named for the railroad stations located on both the Southern Pacific Railroad and the Missouri Pacific Railroad. The Missouri Pacific is now the Union Pacific Railroad.

College Station is located in Brazos County, and it is 90 miles northwest of Houston and 80 miles southeast of Waco.

The citizens of Brazos County donated land in 1871 for the establishment of The Agricultural & Mechanical College of Texas. The college opened in 1876 and, since 1963, has been known as Texas A & M University. Serving and supporting the University is the main economic function of the city.

Texas A & M University now has an enrollment of 39,500. The University operates the Texas Extension Service which is a major organization by itself.

College Station is served by State Highway 6 running northwest/southeast and by State Highways 60 and 30 and Farm-to-Market Roads 2154 and 2818.

COLLEYVILLE

The settlement in the area that is now the city of Colleyville began over 100 years ago. Texas, as a young republic and as a state, used its vast lands holdings to entice settlers to populate its territory. One means of granting land was to issue certificates entitling the holder to patent (locate and claim) a specific allotment of public land. Since the law did not require that the original grantee locate and claim the land, these certificates could be sold, and many changed hands several times before a patent was applied for.

Some settlements were made in the pre-Colleyville area by the mid-1800's, but most of the land remained in the public domain until the 1870's when free land became available for homesteading. Under the Homestead Act, citizens who promised to cultivate, improve, and make their homes on the land were issued certificates that would allow them to claim title to their homesteads after they had lived on them for three years. The citizen had to pay for having the land surveyed and a small fee for paperwork, but the land itself was a gift from the state.

As pioneers pushed the western frontier of the United States into northeast Tarrant County, the fertile land between the creeks provided farmers from the older eastern states the opportunity to acquire large land holdings. Some would be land owners for the first time, while others left their holdings in the east to seek better opportunities in a new land. The threat of civil war and later the aftermath of that war influenced many families to head west to begin a new life. In the same way, the political unrest in Europe brought immigrants to the area. However, by 1898 free land had been depleted, and these new Texans had to purchase their property.

The name Colleyville first applied to a small crossroads town on the main road between Fort Worth and Grapevine. Dr. Colley owned a building containing the Couch Store, Dr. Colley's office and a sub-post office. Needing a name for this settlement, the citizens selected the name Colleyville, which was named after the first doctor in the area, Dr. Colley.

Colleyville was incorporated as a village in January 1956 with an area of less than two square miles and a population of approximately 250. Today Colleyville has a population of over 10,000. Colleyville is located on State Highway 26, 25 miles northeast of Fort Worth and Dallas. Colleyville does not have a railroad. The main reason for its existence is that it is primarily a residential settlement serving Fort Worth. The farmland that surrounds Colleyville has now been put into residential development.

Colleyville offers country living in the heart of a major metropolitan area due to its location in the north-central section of the Metroplex, approximately 30 minutes from Dallas, 20 minutes from Fort Worth and 7 miles west of D/FW International Airport.

COLORADO CITY

Colorado City is the county seat of Mitchell County. In 1877 a Texas Ranger Camp on the present townsite was the first known Anglo-American Settlement. The county seat of Mitchell County did not come into existence until the Texas and Pacific Railroad reached the vicinity in 1881. With the advent of the railroad construction, cities sprang up along the line and Colorado, named for the river, was one of these boom towns. Headquarters of the construction were located in this new townsite.

The Colorado River flows just west of the city limits of the city. This river forms a major drainage system of central Texas. It rises at the edge of the staked plains and flows southeast 840 miles into the Gulf of Mexico at Matagorda Bay. The river drains 42,444 square miles as measured by length and drainage area.

"Colorado" is one of the Texas names that tells the story of Anglo-American influence overcoming the earlier Spanish culture. The larger rivers in Texas carry Spanish names, such as Rio Grande, Nueces, Brazos and Colorado. The Spanish name Colorado means red, or more precisely "reddish." There is evidence that the name Colorado was given originally by Spanish explorers for the reddish color of the water in the river.

Colorado City's government is administered by a city manager, mayor, and city council.

Colorado City is served by two highways. The main east-west highway is Interstate 20, which is also U.S. Highway 80. The north-south highway is State Highway 208 and State Highway 163 which leads southwest.

The Missouri Pacific Railroad now serves the city. It is now owned and operated by the Union Pacific Railway System. The Missouri Pacific is the successor to the first railroad, the Texas and Pacific Railroad.

The area has an average annual rainfall of 19.7 inches. This is barely sufficient to produce a limited agricultural income. Unfortunately, Mitchell County is east of the Ogallala Aquifier.

Colorado City has an altitude of 1950 feet. It has a population of approximately 5500.

The below average agricultural income of the area is produced from raising beef cattle, hogs, sheep, and horses, and from producing dairy products, poultry, cotton, sorghum, and small grains.

This area affords a lot of game for the hunter. There is an abundance of wildgame population such as antelope, deer, quail, and turkey. There are two sizeable lakes in the county that afford good fishing. These lakes are Lake Colorado City, located eleven miles southwest of the city, and Champion Creek Lake, located fourteen miles south of the city.

COLUMBUS

Columbus is the oldest surveyed town in Texas. The first pioneers settled there on the west bank of the Colorado River in 1821, in the vicinity of old Indian campgrounds. It was on the route of the Mexico-to-Sabine River trail. The settlement was first known as Montezuma, then Beasons Crossing, where there was a grist mill and a ferry across the Colorado River.

The Texas Army burned the town in 1835 to keep the buildings out of the hands of Santa Anna. After the war was over in 1836, Columbus rose again. The new town was platted in 1837 by W. B. DeWees. It was located on the west bank of the Colorado River. The settlers were part of Austin's first Colony, known as the "Old Three Hundred." Surveyor DeWees gave the town the name of Columbus on the town plat because he was from Columbus, Georgia. Columbus is located on IH-10. It is served by State Highways 71, 109, 1890 and 806.

Columbus is 71 miles west of Houston. It is the county seat of Colorado County. It has a population of 4,100. The area is an agricultural center and produces sand, gravel, oil, gas, oil field servicing and clothing.

The Colorado River played an important role in the development of Columbus. Rafts and barges were floated downstream from Bastrop to Columbus carrying pine lumber. There were four paddle wheelers that plied the Colorado—the Moccasin Belle, the Flying Jenny, the Kate Ward and the Buffalo Bayou.

The Southern Pacific Railroad (originally called Galveston, Harrisburg & San Antonio Railway) goes through Columbus. It runs from New Orleans to Houston to Columbus, San Antonio and El Paso.

Columbus was incorporated in 1927. The Buffalo Bayou, Brazos and Colorado Railroad was completed to Alleyton, three miles east of Columbus. During the Civil War 48,000 bales of cotton came to this railroad terminus, and were hauled by oxen and mule teams to Mexico for shipment to England.

Columbus is blessed with the rich alluvial soil of the Colorado River Valley. The average annual rainfall is 41 inches. The huge live oak trees are beautiful. Many of the old ante-bellum homes in Columbus have been preserved. There are many historical markers in the area.

COMANCHE

Comanche is the county seat of Comanche County. It is near the geographical center of Texas. The town is located on U.S. Highway 67/377 and State Highways 36 and 16. Comanche is the crossroads of Texas. Comanche is 100 miles southwest of Ft. Worth, 130 miles north of Austin, and 80 miles southeast of Abilene.

Comanche was named for the savage Comanche Indians. The 1989 population is estimated to be 4,400. The annual average rainfall is 28.4 inches. The elevation is approximately 1050 ft.

Late in 1851, freight wagons travelling the Fort Gates to Fort Phantom Hill Road, passed through the area where Comanche is located. The first permanent settlers arrived in December of 1854. The settlers were mainly from the southern states. During the Civil War, a number of settlers enlisted in the Confederate Army. However, a small number remained at home to serve in the Frontier Guard Companies to defend against the Indians who were attempting to drive the pioneers from their land. Between 1857 and 1870 this area of Central Texas suffered a number of Indian depredations.

The country surrounding Comanche is a prosperous farming and ranching area. The largest crop is peanuts. Comanche County is one of the leading peanut producing counties in the United States. The other major crops are melons, grain sorghum, peaches, maize and pecans. Ranches have always yielded assorted types of livestock, with the dairy industry ranking among the top in the state in milk production. The total income from farms and ranches in the county in 1988 was $64,300,000.

In the area, manufacturing consists of leather goods, wholesale drugs, roasted peanuts, shelled pecans, fertilizer, insecticides, pottery, livestock feeds, minerals and concentrates, cement, and all types of trailers.

The Santa Fe Railroad runs through Comanche and goes direct to Fort Worth.

The town has a mayor, city council and city secretary.

Comanche offers something for everyone. Located in Central Texas, Comanche is home of the oldest original existing courthouse in Texas. Named "Old Cora," it sits on the southwest corner of the courthouse square next to the legendary "Fleming Oak."

The Comanche County Museum is open Sundays from 2:00-4:00 p.m.

The city park provides sports fields, swimming pool, jogging trail, covered pavilion and picnic sites for unlimited outdoor fun. The Comanche Community Center is located near the entrance to the city park and houses the Chamber of Commerce office.

There is an annual Rodeo in July. Every September the Comanche County Pow-Wow festivities are held.

Located eight miles northeast of Comanche, beautiful Lake Proctor attracts visitors from across the nation with its 4,000 acres of prime public hunting and fishing. Plentiful fish include hybrid striped bass, catfish and crappie. Over 250 campsites from primitive to group shelters provide for relaxation and enjoyment. Picnicking and water sports are fun for all. There are over 30 historical markers in the Comanche area.

COMMERCE

Commerce is in Hunt County about halfway between Dallas and Paris and is located on State Highways 11 and 24. Its current population is 8,136.

The city was originally known as Cow Hill because of the cattle herds in the area. Newcomers originally settled north of the current city limits around a store opened in 1864 by J. H. "Si" Jackson. Later, one of the local farmers and store owners, William Jernigan, donated a section of his land for a town square. The community was unnamed, so when Jernigan ordered merchandise for his store, he asked that it be shipped to "Commerce."

The community was incorporated in 1885 with a population of 145. Its growth was encouraged by the St. Louis Southwestern Railroad which completed its rail lines into Commerce in 1887.

East Texas State University, begun in 1894 as the Mayo School, is located in Commerce.

A historical marker has been placed on the house in which General Claire Chennault, leader of the Flying Tiger Squadron in World War II, was born.

CONROE

Conroe, the county seat of Montgomery County, is located in the beautiful rolling forested acres of southeast Texas. It lies at the crossroads of Interstate 45 and State Highway 105—37 miles north of Houston on the Houston-Dallas Interstate.

Conroe was incorporated as a city in 1885. The city was named for Isaac Conroe who was interested in operating a lumber business; he decided that the site where Conroe is now located would be a suitable location for loading logs and lumber on the railroad. Mr. Conroe established "Conroe's Switch" about 1881.

The city and county depended upon timber, lumber, and limited agriculture until oil was discovered in 1932 by George Strake. This changed the economy of the area. The Conroe Oil Field is one of the major producing fields in Texas with 10 to 12 million barrels a year being produced.

Timber, clay, oil, and gas are natural resources available in Montgomery County. The timber products include pine, oak, magnolia, ash, and gum. Agriculture products include beef and dairy cattle, feed for livestock, and poultry.

The city has a mayor-council type of city government. In 1989, the city's population was approximately 18,950.

Conroe is well served by a fine network of highways. U.S. Highway 75/45 runs north and south through Conroe and goes from Galveston to Houston to Conroe to Huntsville to Corsicana to Dallas. Loop 336 encircles the city. State Highway 105 runs east and west through Conroe.

The city has two railroads; the Santa Fe goes east and west and crosses the Missouri Pacific Railroad (now the Union Pacific) in the north edge of the city.

The area around Conroe has only a limited amount of agriculture. The agricultural income of Montgomery County is $18 million which is about half the average income of the Texas counties.

The Spanish explorers arrived in the latter half of the 17th century. They attempted to convert the heathen savages. The Spanish monks built stone missions. The priests and monks tried to overcome the barriers of the strange languages and customs. They toiled in this foreign land, setting examples of poverty, chastity, and reverence. The Indians' reactions were mixed.

The Spanish from the southwest were soon joined by the French from the east. For decades, dominance of the area vacillated between the Spanish and the French, with neither very successful in gaining control of the nomadic Indians.

Gradually the Indian population thinned; many of their number succumbed to the white man's diseases such as smallpox, measles, and typhoid fever.

The Indian inhabitants that had populated the area included the Bidai, the Attacapans, the Coushatta, and the Kickapoo. They were nomadic and primitive people. They alternated between living on the bounties of the sea along the Gulf of Mexico and the inland forests and streams.

Just to the north of Conroe lies the Alabama-Coushatta Indian Reservation where the descendants of their respective tribes remain today.

The population of Conroe is 27,000.

The proximity of Conroe to Houston is a tremendous asset to Conroe. Many people live in Conroe and work in Houston, which has many facilities that the people of Conroe can enjoy and from which they receive benefits.

Conroe is the southern gateway to the piney woods of deep East Texas. Within the county, lies the Sam Houston National Forest and the W. G. Jones State Forest, each with hiking and biking trails, birdwatching, fishing, camping & picnicking. The recreation mecca has over 200 holes of golf, and beautiful 22,000 acre Lake Conroe boasts fantastic water sports, including fishing, sailing, and swimming.

COOPER

Cooper is the county seat of Delta County. It was founded in 1874, by an Act of the Texas Senate. It is located in a rich farming area between the north and south Sulphur Rivers. The city is a principal commercial center in that area. It is located at the intersection of Texas Highways 19 and 24. It is 84 miles northeast of Dallas. Delta County is said to be the smallest county in Texas. It has 278 square miles of area, which is about ⅓ the size of the average Texas county.

The nearest railroad is the Santa Fe at Ben Franklin, 14 miles to the northwest. The population of Cooper is 3,000. It was named after L. W. Cooper, a well known Texas senator of that time.

The site was initially referred to as Yates' Prarie. The average rainfall of Cooper is 44.3 inches, which is sufficient to raise all types of crops. The main crops in the county are cotton, milo maize and corn.

The city has a mayor-council form of city government.

Cooper has a high tax rate. It is broken down as follows:

Delta County	.67800 Per $100 Assessment
City of Cooper	.75547 " " "
Cooper ISD	.80000 " " "
Municipal Utility Dist.	.12000 " " "
	2.35387 Per $100 Assessment

Cooper has a large lake south of the city. This is Cooper Lake. Big Creek Lake lies immediately northwest of town.

Cooper is in the center of a productive agricultural area. Cooper serves as the marketing center for the ranchers and farmers in the area.

COPPERAS COVE

Copperas Cove, a city nestled in a circle of hills, had an estimated 1989 population of 27,500 people. Sitting next door to Ft. Hood, the largest armored military establishment in the free world, Copperas Cove is a part of one of the fastest growing areas in Texas, the Central Texas Region.

Copperas Cove gained its name from the early years of settlement because of the coppery taste of the water along with the stories of cattle movers holding their cattle in the natural cove basin.

The railroad came to Copperas Cove in 1882 and the town began to boom. Jesse Clements is credited with founding Copperas Cove. When the railroad came to Copperas Cove, Clements sold land rights to 1,136 acres to Gulf Colorado and Santa Fe Railroad for $196.00. The Santa Fe Railroad continues to serve Copperas Cove today.

Copperas Cove was incorporated as a city on July 5, 1913. At that time the city comprised 590 acres. It is almost ten times that size today.

Today, Copperas Cove continues to grow. The city was developed as a service and retail area adjacent to Ft. Hood. Civil service jobs on Ft. Hood are a mainstay of the community. Ft. Hood sits between Copperas Cove and Killeen with the northern boundary close to Gatesville.

Central Texas College and the American Technological University are located on common ground just east of Copperas Cove. The Metroplex Hospital and Greenleaf Center are also located in this area along with many medical office complexes as well as service agencies for the medical industry.

The KC's host a big three-day Oktoberfest each fall, attracting thousands of visitors. Adding these festivals to opportunities to drive through Ft. Hood as well as visit the two museums on Post that are open to the public, provides an ongoing opportunity for good times in the Cove.

A concerted effort to develop business and industry is well underway with the Copperas Cove Industrial Foundation and city fathers working hand-in-hand to promote four business and industry parks in the city.

Copperas Cove is located on Highway 190, 24 miles west of I-35. It is located within 60 minutes of Austin on one side and Waco on the other. San Antonio is approximately 126 miles south.

Copperas Cove has an average annual rainfall of 32.5 inches. It has an elevation of approximately 1050 feet.

Copperas Cove's surrounding areas are full of deer and wild turkey. A pleasant year-round climate, along with access to several lakes and hunting areas, make it a very enjoyable place to be.

CORPUS CHRISTI

Long before there was a settlement at Corpus Christi, seafaring Conquistadors plied the waters of the Gulf of Mexico, and according to legend, it was one of them, Alvarez Alonzo de Pineda, who discovered the blue waters of Corpus Christi Bay on the Festival Day of Corpus Christi in the year 1519. It is said that the Bay was named to fit the occasion, and Corpus Christi later derived its name from this bay.

The Spanish, the Portuguese, the English and the French alternated in making port in Corpus Christi Bay and in visiting the coastal islands, the most famous of which is the 110-mile long Padre Island. The galleons of Hernando Cortes appeared here, as did the vessels of Jean Lafitte's free-booting band. At one time, the buccaneers held such sway in the area that Padre and Mustang Islands are said to have become mines of buried treasure, and even today a pleasant pastime is the search for pirate gold in the island sand.

Reminiscent of the days of the roving raiders is the annual Buccaneer Days celebration, usually held in late April or early

May, when citizen buccaneers control Corpus Christi once again and blithely force the mayor to walk a plank.

The city of Corpus Christi began as a frontier trading post, founded in 1838-1839 by Colonel Henry Lawrence Kinney, adventurer-impresario-colonizer. The small settlement, hardbitten and lawless, was called Kinney's Trading Post or Kinney's Ranch. Kinney's partner was William Aubrey, for whom Aubrey Street is named.

The Trading Post remained an obscure settlement until July 1845, when United States troops under General Zachry Taylor arrived on the local scene. Troops, horses and equipment were lightered ashore. The army remained until March, 1846, when it left to march southward to the Rio Grande, as the beginning of the Mexican War was near.

A year or so later, the city took the name of Corpus Christi from the bay as one resident put it, ". . . so as to have a more definite postmark for letters." Nueces County, of which Corpus Christi is the county seat, was formed in January, 1847. The county originally extended to the Rio Grande. Sixteen South Texas counties and parts of several others have been carved from its original confines.

The Nueces River, from which Corpus Christi derives its water, empties into Nueces Bay northeast of the city. In early days this river was lined with pecan trees. The word Nueces is a Spanish word meaning "nuts."

Corpus Christi had some semblance of a deep-water port as early as 1848, when steamship service to New Orleans was offered. In 1862, during the Civil War, Corpus Christi and the Port were blockaded by federal gunboats. Two attempts to occupy the city were successfully resisted, but the city finally fell to federal troops in 1864.

The modern port of Corpus Christi opened on September 14, 1926, and is one of the leading and most modern in America.

The first gas well in this immediate area was discovered on September 14, 1913. It was located in White Point on the north shore of Nueces Bay, and it was uncontrollable. Today, there are approximately 700 oil and gas fields within five minutes to three hours ride of Corpus Christi, and they contain 20,000 producing wells.

The Corpus Christi Naval Air Training Station, one of the largest in the world, was commissioned on March 12, 1941. During World War II, the station trained more than 40,000 Naval fliers. Since then an average of 500 Naval pilots each year receive training at the station. The Corpus Christi Army Depot, in operation since 1961, is the city's largest employer with 3,000 civilian workers.

The completion of the city's stout seawall in 1940 saw the birth of a new civic consciousness, and today, Corpus Christi, a city of more than 230,000, is known as one of the most beautiful and industrious on the coastline of the country.

The city of Corpus Christi was incorporated in 1852. The first railroad built was the Corpus Christi, San Diego & Rio Grande. It later became the Texas-Mexican Railroad. The second railroad, the San Antonio and Aransas Pass, was constructed in 1886. In September, 1926 the Port of Corpus Christi was opened. In 1930 the ship channel was deepened from 25 feet to 30 feet and in 1935, the Del Mar Junior College was created. In 1940 the Bayfront seawall, T-Heads and L-Heads were completed. In 1945 the city manager form of government was established. In 1951 Reynolds Aluminum Plant started; it is one of the areas largest employers. In 1959 the Harbor Bridge was completed. In 1960 the Corpus Christi International Airport was completed and opened. In 1961 the Army established ARADMAC. In 1973 Texas A & I University was established at Corpus Christi and the following year Texas A & M University Research and Extension Center was opened in February. In 1982 the Choke Canyon Dam was completed and the gates were closed to create a new reservoir. This is one of the city's sources of water.

Corpus Christi is the sixth largest city in Texas. It stands at an altitude of 35 feet above sea level and is located on the same parallel as Tampa, Florida. It has a year-round average temperature of 71.2 degrees. It has eight basic industries: oil, tourism, agriculture, fishing, manufacturing, port, ranching, and the military.

The Port of Corpus Christi is the ninth largest deepwater port in the United States. Access from the east is over the huge high bridge over the harbor entrance. It was completed in 1959 at a cost of more than $18 million and is 235 feet high with a span across the channel, and is 640 feet in length.

Corpus Christi is a building, growing city and has a most promising future.

CORSICANA

Corsicana is 53 miles south of Dallas on Interstate 45. U.S. Highway 287 and State Highways 22 and 31 also lead to the city.

Corsicana currently has a population of 26,000 and is the county seat of Navarro County. Navarro County was named for Jose Antonio Navarro, one of the signers of the Texas Declaration of Independence. When asked to suggest a name for the new community, Navarro suggested naming it for his father's birthplace, Corsica, Spain. Corsicana has the distinction of a unique name—there is no other Corsicana in the world.

Mobil Oil (as Magnolia Oil) and Texaco had their beginnings here. "Derrick Days" is a week-long celebration of Corsicana's oil heritage each spring.

Wolf Brand Chili originated in Corsicana, as did Mellorine and coffee creamer.

Corsicana's past is still alive. Pioneer Village is a reconstructed village of historical structures from Navarro County. The Carriage District is an area of homes built around the turn of the century. Corsicana was the first city to have natural gas streetlights.

Temple Beth-El, built in 1892, is listed on the state and national registers of historic places. It is Texas' only onion-domed synagogue.

The Collin Street Bakery, established in 1896, is world-famous for its fruitcakes. Navarro Pecan is the largest pecan processor in the world.

Navarro College is a fully-accredited two-year college and is located here.

Corsicana is serviced by three railroads—Burlington Northern, Southern Pacific, and St. Louis Southwestern. AMTRAK provides daily passenger service on the route between Dallas and Houston.

Lake Halbert, Richland-Chambers Lake, and Cedar Creek Lake are all nearby for recreational use. Richland-Chamber has 400 miles of shoreline.

Native sons include Beauford Jester (Texas governor) and Lefty Frizzell (of the County and Western Hall of Fame).

COTULLA

Cotulla is the county seat of La Salle County. It is located on Interstate Highway-35, halfway between San Antonio and Laredo. It is 85 miles south-southwest of San Antonio and 70 miles north of Laredo, which is located on the Texas-Mexican Border. State Highway 97 leads due east and Farm-to-Market 624 leads southeast. Farm-to-Market 460 runs northwest from Cotulla. The population of Cotulla is 4,200.

The Union Pacific Railroad runs through the city enroute from San Antonio to Laredo.

The annual rainfall is 20.7 inches, which is not quite enough rainfall to raise most crops. The altitude is approximately 450 feet. The area around Cotulla is primarily devoted to cattle raising. About 90% of the agricultural income is derived from raising beef cattle. The crops include guar, sorghum, cotton, wheat, oats, peanuts, vegetables and melons. Approximately 4,000 acres of farmland in the general area is irrigated.

The first industry in Cotulla was a "brick kiln" which furnished brick for all of the early brick buildings of the town. The kilns were located on Mustang Creek. In the early days of Cotulla, there was no bank of any sort, so people took their money to M. J. Barlow, as he did have a small safe, or they hid it at home. L. A. Kerr later had a large safe. He and T. R. Keck built a small vault and started keeping money for the residents of the town. Eventually Kerr and Keck opened a national bank in Cotulla. Kerr did not stay with the venture long and Keck became the sole owner of the bank, which was named Stockmens National Bank. The bank was continuously operated by members of the Keck family, until a few years ago when they sold the controlling interest.

As soon as the settlers began to arrive in Cotulla, a school was established. In 1883, there was a large group attending school. As a rule, the pioneers and settlers of Cotulla had limited education or none at all. However, they wanted a good education for their children and realized the importance of schools. Today's air-conditioned schools are a far cry from the "out houses" and wood heat of the early day schools.

The city water well was drilled in 1915 and a deep, pure strata of artesian water was found, and Cotulla soon became known as the "best watered" small town in Texas.

In December of 1909, an election was held to incorporate the city of Cotulla, and in January 1910, it was incorporated. The first city election was held in 1910 to elect a mayor and aldermen.

In 1881, Joseph Cotulla gave a townsite of 120 acres and called the newly created town Cotulla. Lots were sold at an auction.

The auction brochure describes Cotulla as being situated on a high rolling prairie, three quarters of a mile from the Nueces River. The soil was described as red sandy loam. There were wells with good water in the surrounding country at depths of 25 to 35 feet, and it was believed there would be no trouble in securing an abundance of water. The Nueces River, as well as three lakes which never dried up, was situated within one mile of the townsite. The railroad had been extended to Cotulla and on to Twohig Station and soon would be completed all the way to Laredo. Plans were underway to make Cotulla the shipping point of a large area. New roads were being opened to Tilden, Fort Ewell, Carrizo Springs and Cotulla.

So ends the story of Cotulla, which is a most interesting Texas town in deep South Texas.

CRANE

Crane is the county seat of Crane County. In fact, it is the only town in the county. The town has a population of 3,650 in a county having a total population of approximately 5,000.

Crane is located in deep west Texas. It is 58 miles southeast of the southeast corner of New Mexico, and it is 33 miles south of Odessa.

Crane County does not have a railroad. The town of Crane has two highways serving it, U.S. Highway 385 runs north and south. It starts at McCamey to the south and runs north through Crane to Odessa, Seminole, Brownfield and Lubbock. State Highway 329 runs east and west through the town.

This is a sparsely populated area of Texas. There are less than seven people per square mile. The average density of U.S. population is 60.40 per sq. mile. The average annual rainfall is 13.0 inches. This is not enough rainfall to sustain agriculture, so Crane county only has an annual agricultural income of 2.5 million.

This is less than 10% of the annual average agricultural income per county.

Crane is in the area of west Texas that is broken by canyons and deep valleys of the Pecos River and its tributaries. Crane is located at the southern portion of the western High Plains. The city has an altitude of 2555 feet above sea level. The soils in the area are light sandy to gravel, red and chocolate loams. The prairie surface has coverings of mesquite and greasewood.

The city was established in 1926 and organized in September 1927. The town serves a territory rich in oil, gas and sulphur. A plant for producing sulphur from sour gas and numerous plants and facilities used in manufacturing, processing and distributing oil, gas and their by-products are located in the area.

It was on February 26, 1887, that the Texas legislature approved an act dividing Tom Green County into six new counties. The 796 square miles just east of the Pecos River came to be known as Crane County. It was named in honor of Dr. William Carey Crane, a native Virginian, Baptist minister, author of *The Life of General Sam Houston,* and president of Baylor University for 25 years.

Looking out across the sun-baked, mesquite-covered terrain, one can't help but wonder what induced the first settlers to remain in the area. By 1920, a total of only 37 people inhabited the lonesome, barren prairie of Crane County.

Suddenly in 1925, all that changed. For years men had searched and dug around Castle Gap for the legendary gold of Maximilian, but none even dreamed of the countless wealth of "black gold" lying much deeper in the layers of rock and sand. Oil prospectors struck oil in the spring of 1926 when an oil well was brought in. It proved a vast oil and gas field which is still booming. In 1972 Crane County distinguished itself by becoming the third county in Texas and the fourth in the nation to produce one billion barrels of oil.

The oil activity brought great prosperity to Crane. The tract of land for the townsite known as "Crane" was deeded to the general public by Mrs. M. F. Stephens in March 1937. The town of Crane was duly incorporated on July 25, 1933. The town has a mayor/alderman form of city government.

Some things haven't changed. The area is still rugged, desolate, hot, dry, isolated and covered with mesquite and caliche dust. The citizens of Crane give full credit to the oil industry that has brought prosperity to their town. The industry payrolls provide one of the highest per capita incomes in the state.

CROCKETT

Crockett is the county seat of Houston County. It is 103 miles due north of Houston. It has a population of 7,600. It is among the oldest towns in Texas and the site of many historic structures.

The coming of the railroad in 1872 brought community development. Up and down the tracks, every 5-6 miles, small communities were built. The railroad is now the Missouri Pacific, which is owned by the Union Pacific Railroad.

The area around Crockett is heavily devoted to agriculture. About 80% of the income is derived from cattle, poultry, crops (including cotton, peanuts, coastal hay), and timber sales.

The county has 41 plants, employing 1200 with a payroll of $20,300,000. The manufacturing production has a value of $135,000,000.

Crockett is located on U.S. Highway 287. It is served by State Highways 21, 19 and 7. It has farm to market road 2022. Crockett is 133 miles southeast of Dallas, and 110 miles east of Waco.

The western 25% of the county is included in the Davy Crockett National Forest. The eastern boundary of the forest is the Neches River.

Crockett and Houston County have a lot of Texas history. Crockett moves toward 1990 and the recognition of the tricentennial of the establishment of the Mission San Francisco de los Tejas in May 1690, located some 20 miles east of Crockett on El Camino Road, now SH-21.

Though the first Spanish Mission was abandoned in 1693, Christianity had begun in East Texas and the X in Texas came from the Tejas Indians for whom the Mission was built.

Some 130 years later, around 1820, the area west of Nacogdoches County, along the Neches River and over to the Trinity River, attracted settlers. The Mexican Government awarded many of the pioneers land grants. Others who fought in the War for Texas Independence received land. Those settlers of the area petitioned the Congress of the Republic of Texas on April 22, 1837, asking that a county be created. Some 110 names were signed to this petition, which was approved on June 12, 1837, and signed by President Sam Houston. This county was the first created under the new Republic of Texas and named for its first President. The size of the county was three times that of the present, as Trinity, Anderson and Henderson Counties have been carved out of it.

Crockett was selected as a county seat and incorporated by an Act of the Republic of Texas on December 29, 1837. The town was named for the Tennessee Scout, David Crockett, who camped near the area enroute to the Alamo and his death in 1836. While camped, he discovered that a former Tennessee neighbor, Elijah Gossett and family, had a homestead nearby. Elijah Gossett's son, Andrew Edwards Gossett, gave the township of Crockett, so he and his father Elijah were given the privilege of naming the town and the county. The town they named for Elijah's old friend, David Crockett; they named the county for their former commander at the Battle of San Jacinto and the first President of the Republic of Texas, Sam Houston.

The Indians were much in evidence in the county during the 1830s through the 1850s. Several massacres of families are known.

The Neches & Trinity Rivers contributed much to the county's development, providing natural boundaries, a means of transportation and business as ferries were established along both of them.

The famous link between the rivers, joining east and west, was El Camino Real (The King's Highway), which transverses the county. Stage stops were common along this route, the best known being the residences of Jacob Masters and Joseph Redmond Rice.

Cotton was a big crop from the 1840s through 1900. Farmers would move their crops to the river and flatboat it down the Trinity to Galveston for sale and export to New Orleans. The cotton was grown with slave labor. With the Civil War, this was changed, and the virgin pine timberlands of eastern Houston County gained recognition.

One of the largest sawmilling operations of all time (the Four C Mill) was established in the Ratcliff area during the 1900s and ran for nearly 20 years or until the 120,000 acres of virgin pine timber were cut over. Following the Civil War, the county's economy changed more to lumbering and cattle, production of hay and small grains. The economy remains basically agricultural, lumbering and ranching today.

CROSBY/HUFFMAN

Crosby is located 24 miles east of Houston on Farm-to-Market Road 2100 and 2 miles north of U.S. Highway 90. It is east of the San Jacinto River and approximately three miles southeast of the Lake Houston dam on the San Jacinto River.

Crosby is an unincorporated town and has a population of 16,000. Its area is the same as that of the Crosby Independent School District.

In 1974, the towns of Crosby and Huffman decided to form a joint Chamber of Commerce. Huffman is located 8 miles north of Crosby at the intersection of Farm-to-Market Roads 2100 and 1960. It, too, is unincorporated, and it has a population of 10,000 people. Its area is the same as that of the Huffman Independent School district. The two school districts and town areas meet about midway between Crosby and Huffman. The two combined towns have an area of 150 sq. miles.

In 1861, the Sabine and Galveston Bay Railroad built a railroad into the area and the town was named Crosby after one of the railroad surveying engineers, G. J. Crosby. Later, in 1903, the Texas and New Orleans Railroad built a line through Crosby.

In the railroad's wake came the major influx of Czechs and Swedes from Nebraskan settlements. By the early 1900's, Crosby was known as Little Czechoslovakia.

About 1860, Harrison Barrett, a black native of Louisiana, was sold as a slave to the Barrett family of Goose Creek. He used the earnings he saved from cutting wood to purchase 400 acres of land (at 50 cents per acre) on the site now known as Barrett's Station, just south of Crosby. The community that grew around him, originally settled by his relatives, remains largely black today.

Prior to the coming of the railroads, the large quantity of cotton and rice that were produced in the area were hauled by mule and ox teams to the port of Lynchburg.

Huffman was named after the pioneer family of Abb Huffman who moved to the area from Louisiana about 1832. He was one of Stephen F. Austin's original 300 families.

The Crosby-Huffman town areas are today thriving urban communities. There is a considerable amount of oil production in the area. There are many thousands of acres in the area devoted to the growing of rice, corn, cotton, maize, and soybeans. The area is also a large producer of cattle.

The Southern Pacific Railroad (formerly the Texas & New Orleans) serves Crosby, and the Union Pacific (formerly the Missouri Pacific) serves Huffman.

One of the major factors in the growth of these two towns is their proximity to Houston and to the Intercontinental Airport.

CROWLEY

Crowley is in Tarrant County, a few miles south of Fort Worth on FM 1187, just west of Interstate 35.

The city was founded in 1881 as a stop on the Santa Fe Railroad and was named for a foreman with the railroad.

Much of Crowley is still rolling farm land but subdivision development is becoming more important. Population has increased from less than 500 in the early 1960's to 6,700 today.

CRYSTAL CITY

Crystal City is the county seat of Zavala County. In 1989, it had a population of 8,800. Crystal City is a home-rule city with a mayor, city-council, and city manager. It is 114 miles to San Antonio, Texas on U.S. Highway-83. Eagle Pass is 45 miles due west on the Mexican Border. Uvalde is 48 miles due north on U.S. Highway-83. Crystal City is located in the Nueces and Leona River Valleys.

The area around Crystal City is irrigated from artesian wells, which flow from the strong Carrizo Wilcox Aquifer. The water is crystal clear, and that is how the City got its name. The area around Crystal City was explored by the Spanish in the late seventeenth century. The Old San Antonio Road traversed the area and was the major eighteenth century transportation route between San Antonio and Monterrey. The county was created in 1858 but did not receive its first Anglo colony until the late 1860's. Today, 89% of the population of Crystal City is of Spanish origin. The first county seat was established at Batesville in 1884. When this community was bypassed by the railroad in 1928 a new county seat was established in Crystal City.

The area around Crystal City is rolling hills, brush country and plains enhanced by the fertile Nueces and Leona river basins. The area was primarily used for cattle ranching until 1907, when artesian water was discovered. The land rapidly developed into farms and became known as the "Winter Garden" because of its ability to produce winter vegetable crops. Farming remains very productive in Zavala County with 63,822 acres in cultivation and annual agricultural income of $42 million primarily from spinach, onions, grains, pecans, cotton and cattle. Crystal City is known as the "Spinach Capital of the World" and the "Home of Popeye." There is a statue of Popeye located in the center of Crystal City on the City Square and is a favorite place for tourists to take snapshots. The average rainfall is 21.5 inches with a 280 day growing season and a mild climate year round. Oil and natural gas production have also become a significant sector in the area's economy. Oil production was valued at $23 million in 1984. Many services and supply businesses have developed to meet the needs of the agricultural and oil production industries.

An abundance of wild game makes the Crystal City area a favorite with hunters and sportsmen. Especially popular is the hunting of whitetail deer, quail and whitewing dove. Several large private hunting preserves are established in the county. Fishing and swimming in the clear water of the Nueces river is another favorite recreation activity.

The Union Pacific Railroad serves the City.

CUERO

Cuero is the county seat of DeWitt County. It is located almost in the exact center of the county. Highways radiate from the city in all directions. These highways are U.S. Highways 77-A, 87 and 183 and State Highway 72, and farm to market roads 236, 1447, and 766. The city is located 80 miles east-southeast of San Antonio on Highway 87.

The population is 7,463. The city is served by the Southern Pacific Railroad. The annual rainfall is 33.4 inches. Cuero has a council/manager form of city government.

DeWitt County, in South Central Texas, was created and organized from Gonzales and Victoria Counties in 1846 and named for Green C. DeWitt, who led the early colonists.

The DeWitt area was probably on Cebeza de Vaca's route across Texas in 1528. In 1689 Aloso de Leon, Jr. led an expedition through the region in search of LaSalle's settlement—Fort St. Louis. Other explorers crossed the region in 1718 and 1727. The area was inhabited by Karankawan Indians when James Kerr, as DeWitt's agent, brought the first settlers to Green DeWitt's grant in 1825.

In those early days many cattle bogged down in a creek about five miles north of Cuero; many died. Skinners made good money off the hides. The origin of the name Cuero is Indian. When the Spanish came to the area and questioned the Indians as to the name of this creek, they replied "rawhide" or "greenhide"—this translated from Karankawan to Spanish "cuero." When the town was settled, it was named after the creek. Stagecoaches and wagon trains crossed the county as it lay between Indianola on the Texas Coast and San Antonio. By 1861 railroad construction was being urged; however, the War Between the States delayed that project. In 1873 the Gulf Western Texas, and Pacific Railroad line reached Texas. As terminus, Cuero experienced a frontier boom and reputation, until the line was extended to San Antonio in 1906. Cuero was founded in 1872 with the arrival of the railroad and the population grew after the coastal storms of 1875 and 1886 which destroyed Indianola, and refugees from there made a new start here.

Pecan producers sold approximately one million pounds of pecans in 1988, representing about one-half of the county's potential. Peaches, apples and various vegetables are increasing in importance in the county. DeWitt County is in the top third portion of the state's oil and gas production.

Cuero has two banks, two savings and loan offices: a bi-weekly newspaper; AM radio station; and cable television. Cuero community Hospital, a major employer, is listed as one of the best in the area for a town of its size. Other major medical facilities are as close as Victoria.

Other major employers are Cuero Independent School District, Brentex Mill (textile), Gulf Coast Wood Products (millwork and casework). TIMCO (plastic laminate doors), Allied Feed, City of Cuero, Wal-Mart, Crossroad Canning (soft drinks), and several others.

One of the most successful volunteer-run Farmers' Markets in the state is in Cuero. The Texas Department of Agricultural uses it as an example of how to organize and operate a market for local small farmers and backyard gardeners.

The National Register of Historic Places and the Texas Historical Commission list 195 homes and buildings located in three historical districts within the city. The structures have been recognized for their architectural and historic significances and were among 1,179 surveyed through the Cuero Main Street project. The Cuero Commercial District contains an extremely cohesive collection of late 19th and early 20th century commercial structures which retain a significant degree of their architectural integrity. The survey noted that many of the structures were relocated in Cuero after the seaport town of Indianola was devastated in 1875 and 1986 by hurricanes. The city's greatest period of economic prosperity occurred in the late 19th and early 20th centuries, as the city developed into an important regional center for banking, commercial and agricultural interests. Many of the buildings and homes erected in those years have been restored and provide a real link to the boom era.

Today Cuero no longer produces the turkeys for market as it once did. The fame Cuero enjoys for its Turkey Trots and the TurkeyFest is worldwide. The events were so unusual because the turkeys were driven to market much as a cattle drive. It became such a spectacle people came from miles around to witness it. By word of mouth, the fame of these drives spread and each year more and more out-of-town visitors came to watch. In 1912, an organized celebration was held, and the citizens came up with the name "Turkey Trot," the most popular dance of the time. The name caught on and remained that until 1973 when it was reorganized and renamed the TurkeyFest.

Commercial progress and modern methods have made inevitable changes in turkey production in DeWitt County. The range turkey of 1908 no longer has a place in modern production. Cuero is no longer listed as a major turkey producing county. Cueroites celebrate the memory each fall in October with the "Turkeyfest." The major event of this celebration is a turkey race between two world famous turkeys: Ruby Begonia of Cuero and Paycheck of Worthington, Minnesota. Ruby travels to Worthington in mid-September for the first heat of the race and Paycheck comes to Cuero in October for the final test. The average of the two races determines the winner. The prize is a four-foot trophy: "The Traveling Turkey Trophy of Tumultuous Triumph" as well as the title "World's Fastest Turkey." The city is called "The Turkey Capital of the World." The race is known as the Great Gobbler Gallop.

Cuero is on the beautiful Guadalupe River, a popular fisherman's haven. Canoeists are discovering its natural beauty and are attracted to it from around the state. Hunters find the area a paradise with dove, quail, squirrel, turkey and deer available. Cuero was named an All-America City in 1975, a Texas Historical Main Street City in 1985, and won the Keep Texas Beautiful Governor's Achievement Award in 1987.

Cuero was chosen for the second year in a row, as the site for the Texas Babe Ruth Baseball Tournament. Cuero athletes are legendary for their accomplishments. The Cuero High School athletes are named the Cuero Gobblers, of course.

DAINGERFIELD

Daingerfield is the fourth oldest town in Texas. It is the county seat of Morris County, which is the smallest county in Texas, having an area of only 256 sq. miles. The Sulphur River is its northern boundary.

Daingerfield is on U.S. Highway 259 and State Highways 11, 49, 130 and 400.

It is served by the Kansas City Southern Railroad.

Daingerfield is 38 miles due north of Longview and 130 miles east of Dallas. It is deep in East Texas in the Pine Timber Belt.

The town was named in honor of Captain L. Daingerfield. He came from Nova Scotia to Texas with 100 followers in 1830, with the avowed purpose of driving the Indians out of East Texas. He landed in Arkansas and crossed the Red River and went to Lanes Port, a town near Jefferson. He and his small band camped near the foothills and encountered Indians in a bloody battle in 1830. The Captain was killed in this engagement, but his men were successful in driving the Indians away.

Daingerfield has an elevation of 400 ft. It had a population of 3400 in 1988. The annual rainfall is 46.1 inches. It is just north of the Lake of the Pines, which is a famous fishing place.

There is a considerable amount of industry in the area. There are plants manufacturing chemicals, clothing, roofing products, process pipe, and steel production.

This is a rich agricultural area. About 20% of the income is from beef cattle. The crops include peanuts, sweet potatoes, corn, sorghum and vegetables. There are several sawmills producing pine and hardwood lumber.

DALHART

Dalhart is located in the Texas Panhandle on U.S. Highways 54 and 87; 31 miles due north is the Texas-Oklahoma state line, and less than 30 miles due west is the Texas-New Mexico state line. Amarillo is 88 miles southeast of Dalhart.

Dalhart is the county seat of Dallam County, but it is located in both Dallam and Hartley Counties. Its population is 6,840.

A tent city for section hands was established on the prairie where the Fort Worth & Denver Railroad lines intersected the lines of the Rock Island Railroad, and it was incorporated as a village in 1900. The community was first known as "Twist" (after a section house south of the railroad lines); then as "Twist Junction"; and then "Denrock" (from the names of the two railroads). When "Denrock" was rejected by the post office, the name of "Dalhart" (from Dallam and Hartley Counties) was submitted and accepted.

Dalhart was incorporated in 1902; a lawsuit caused it to disband and then reincorporate in 1904.

The No. 1 division headquarters of the XIT Ranch was at Buffalo Springs, 32 miles north of Dalhart. In the 1880's, the XIT Ranch, with 3 million acres, was the largest range in the world under fence. The ranch property was about 30 miles wide and reached from Lubbock northward to Oklahoma.

Dalhart is home to the XIT Museum, a collection of memorabilia of the early days of Dallam and Hartley Counties. The XIT Rodeo and Reunion is held the first full weekend in August each year.

Rita Blanca Lake & Dam are nearby. Geese, ducks, dove, quail, turkey, deer and antelope are all found in the area.

DALLAS

Dallas is located in North Texas and can be reached by Interstates 20 and 35 East, and U.S. Highways 67, 75, and 175.

Dallas County, of which the city of Dallas is the county seat, was created and organized in 1846 and was named for George Mifflin Dallas, Vice President of the United States.

The City of Dallas had its beginnings in 1841 when John Neely

Bryan, a Tennessee lawyer, arrived in the area to claim free land and to set up a trading post on a bluff above the Trinity River. He sketched out a town, designated a courthouse square with 20 streets around it, and settlers began moving in.

In 1872, a railroad line from Houston reached the new town. Dallas became the first railroad crossing town in Texas in 1873 when the East-West line of the Texas & Pacific Railroad was completed through Dallas. Because of the railroads, Dallas became a major distribution center.

Railroads currently servicing Dallas include the Atchison, Topeka & Santa Fe; Missouri-Kansas-Texas; and Southern Pacific.

By 1890, Dallas was the largest city in Texas, with a population of 38,067. It currently is the second largest city in the state and is the eighth largest in the nation, with a population of a little over one million.

Dallas has a diversified economy. It is the largest cotton trading center in the nation, and is a convention, insurance, and oil center. Manufacturing and electronics are also of importance.

Dallas is home to Southern Methodist University, University of Dallas, Dallas Baptist College, University of Texas at Dallas, and the University of Texas Health Science Center at Dallas, and Southwestern Medical School.

DECATUR

Decatur is located in North Texas and is the county seat of Wise County. It is situated at the junction of U.S. Highways 287 and 380, about 40 miles northwest of Fort Worth, and 77 miles southeast of Wichita Falls.

Col. Absolam Bishop is known as "The Father of Decatur." Bishop liked the plan of the City of McKinney in Collin County so much that he copied it for Decatur.

The City was first named Taylorsville in honor of President Zachary Taylor. However, when Col. Bishop became disillusioned with President Taylor, he petitioned to have the city's name changed to Decatur in honor of Stephen Decatur, a naval hero.

Wise County has had four courthouse buildings in its history. The present one, constructed of pink granite with an interior of Vermont marble, was completed in 1896. It is on the National Register of historic buildings.

Decatur's population is 4,700. It is a center for petroleum production, dairying, and cattle marketing. The Burlington Northern Railroad passes through the city. The average annual rainfall is a 29.7 inches. The area surrounding Decatur is a large agricultural producing area. It is one of the leading dairy producing areas in the State.

Once a year many Decatur folks gather together in a celebration and tribute to the folkways of their ancestors. This tribute is the best of Decatur's past and present . . . Decatur Chisholm Trail Days.

Red River Station, northwest of present-day Nocona, was once a busy place. It marked the jumping off point for cattle drivers from Texas to the railheads to the north and marked the official beginning of the famous Chisholm Trail. The cattle trail which led from Fort Worth past Decatur to the east was one of many which led to Red River Station.

The Chisholm Trail was a life-saving artery that restored Texas to prosperity and made millionaires out of bankrupt ranchers, speculators and traders. Trailing cattle at that time was much like a career. Trail driving became life's greatest adventure for the young men of the 1870's.

The trails were not just a narrow line, but many parallel trails. When the herds moved north, they had to spread out for miles to find grass that had not already been grazed. Generally, the drovers headed for river crossings and watering places for the cattle.

The Chisholm Trail was named after a half-Cherokee trader, Jesse Chisholm, whose main post was in Kansas where Wichita was later built. He carried his goods south into Indian Territory to the vicinity of Anadarko, Oklahoma. Unfortunately, he died in 1868 at the age of 63 of food poisoning without ever knowing of his connection with the famous trail that bears his name. He was not related to cattle baron John Chisum, who also found fame in the days of trail drives. His old home is located just east of the Wise County line near Bolivar.

The present-day "Chisholm Trail Days" is a tribute to our heritage. The Decatur Chamber of Commerce has sponsored these events since 1969.

The Chisholm Trail Days celebration has been many things to many people over the years . . . delicious barbecued brisket and all the trimmings (which was barbecued chicken in the beginning), country music, street dances, fiddler's contests, talent contests, Sheriff's Posse trail rides to Black Creek Lake with professional rodeos, gospel singing, arts and crafts, fun run, local merchants offering back-to-school western specials, rodeo banners hanging on storefronts and rodeo parades.

Chisholm Trail Days has grown and changed over the years. The Chamber now has its own large cooker that cooks briskets by the dozens and serves them during the celebration. The event currently is held during the third Saturday in June of each year. It begins with a 5K and 10K fun run and ends with the barbecue and street dance with many activities and events in between.

DEER PARK

Deer Park is a vibrant community of approximately 29,500 residents which combines the conveniences of a nearby large city with the personal charm and warmth of a hometown. The city is located in southeastern Harris County about 25 miles from downtown Houston. It is located on State Highway 225. This places residents within easy commuting distance to jobs at the numerous industrial facilities located along the Houston Ship Channel, and the nearby Bayport industrial development. Also within convenient access to the NASA Johnson Space Center, and the thriving Houston business districts.

Deer Park is well known for its generous hospitality, its state and nationally recognized public school system, its noted police and fire departments and its genuine interest in civic, social and individual development as demonstrated through its active clubs, churches, community programs and other organizations.

Deer Park got its name from the beautiful deer that roamed wild in a park area near the present townsite.

NASA, the Astrodome, Astroworld, and the Port of Houston are within a thirty-minute drive of Deer Park, while the beautiful Gulf Coast beaches of Galveston Island are less than an hour's drive away. Some of the finest fishing is available in Lake Livingston, Lake Sommerville, Lake Conroe, and Lake Houston, all not more than two hours away.

College level education is conveniently available to Deer Park residents at nearby San Jacinto College Central, a comprehensive community college of 10,000 students, or at the University of Houston at Clear Lake City, an upper-level institution. Also within commuting distance are the University of Houston Central

Campus, Rice University, Houston Baptist University, Texas Southern University and the University of St. Thomas.

A 1,840-acre industrial district north of residential Deer Park includes facilities of the major oil, chemical and other manufacturing companies. A 140-acre development for light manufacturing or supporting industry is located on the city's west side.

Deer Park is located at the heart of Texas' most historical areas. Located outside the city limits are the San Jacinto State Monument, and the Battleground State Park, a 440-acre tree-shaded park honoring the site where Texas won its independence from Mexico in 1836. A 570-foot monument within the park houses a museum which depicts the region's history from Indian civilization to Texas annexation.

The Battleship Texas, a World War I and II vintage battleship, has been berthed adjacent to the battlegrounds since 1948. The 35,000 ton ship saw action in major campaigns in Asia, Africa, and Europe. The ship has been in a Galveston dry dock being completely renovated. It is now back at the battlegrounds berth and open to the public throughout the year.

The City of Deer Park has the mayor-council-manager form of government. The city is served by the Houston Port Railroad which connects to all the five principal railroads coming into Houston: the MKT, Southern Pacific, Santa Fe, Missouri Pacific and Burlington North.

DEL RIO

Del Rio is located on the Rio Grande River in southwest Texas. It is 130 miles west of San Antonio, and it can be reached by U.S. Highways 90 and 277. It is the county seat of Val Verde County and has a population of 30,034.

Del Rio was originally named San Felipe del Rio (St. Phillip of the River) by Spanish missionaries who arrived on St. Phillip's Day in 1635. When the first post office was established in 1883, the post office suggested that the name be shortened to "Del Rio" to avoid confusion with another town called San Felipe de Austin.

Del Rio, being across the Rio Grande from Ciudad Acuna, Mexico, serves as a center for tourism and trade with Mexico. Manufacturing plants make clothing and electronic equipment.

Water from San Felipe Springs, the Rio Grande, and Lake

Amidstad (12 miles upstream from Del Rio) provide irrigation water for farming.

Laughlin Air Force Base, with a complement of 3,500 military personnel and 615 civil service employees, is located eight miles east of Del Rio.

Judge Roy Bean, known as "The Law West of the Pecos," is buried on the grounds of the Whitehead Museum in Del Rio.

DENISON

Denison is located in Grayson County and is at the Red River Border in Texas. Like many other Texas towns, the city was fathered by the railroad. Denison was born in September 1872 when the townsite of Denison had lots sold at a public auction. The U.S. Post Office designated Denison as a post office in April 1873. The railroads were in a race to see who could get a railroad into North Texas across the Red River into Oklahoma first. The first settlement in the area was Red River City; they felt like they should be designated as the Gateway to Texas, but as the railroad went through that town, the post office denied Red River City a post office and at the same time, gave it to Denison. This ensured Denison being the dominant city on the Red River.

The name Denison was given to the town by the Vice President of the MKT Railroad, George Denison. Denison's destiny was assuredly welded to the rails and Katy. However, Katy was not the sole frog in the pond. In 1873 the Houston and Texas Central Railroad arrived.

Denison had a mule-drawn street car system, which was started in 1896. Later the Denison street railway system was electrified and in 1901 was expanded to run between Denison and Sherman.

The population of Denison is 24,300. The altitude is 787 feet. The rainfall is 39.8 inches. The city has a mayor-council-manager form of city government.

Today the Missouri Kansas Texas Railroad, the Burlington Northern and the Missouri Pacific Railroads serve Denison.

The city is located on U.S. Hwy. 75 and 69 with a spur around the city (Number 303). It has Farm to Market Roads 84, 120, 690 and 1753.

Denison is the birthplace of Dwight David Eisenhower, born in a modest home along the Katy tracks in southeast Denison, October 24, 1890. His father was a mechanic who worked in the railroad shops of the Katy Railroad. He is one of a few five-star generals and admirals ever accorded the distinction of becoming President of the United States. He was the 34th President of the United States, in office from 1953 to 1961. He died March 28, 1969. This nation probably mourned no other American more than she did this World War hero. His birthplace has become a shrine and an official landmark in Texas. The shrine area has a very fine life-size sculpture of him.

Just north of the city is the Denison Dam and Lake Texoma. This is a huge reservoir and is one of the outstanding fishing lakes in the South.

At Denison is the Grayson County Junior College. Also located in Denison is the Texoma Medical Center, which is an outstanding facility. Another interesting facility at Denison is the Munson Viticulture & Enology Center. The area surrounding Denison is an excellent agriculture area. There is a large amount of beef, dairy, hogs, horses, poultry and crops raised in the area. The crops include wheat, oats, sorghums, peanuts and hay. About 4,000 acres are irrigated.

Denison is primarily a manufacturing, distribution and trade center for northern Texas and southern Oklahoma. Denison has firms that manufacture electronics, transportation equipment, process food, make clothing, furniture, plastics and many other products.

Denison advertises itself as being the Gateway to Texas and that it truly is. It has major railroads that cross the Red River from Oklahoma.

DENTON

The city of Denton is located in Denton County in North Texas. It is 37 miles north-northeast of Fort Worth and 39 miles northwest of Dallas, and can be reached by U.S. Interstate 35 and State Highways 377 and 380.

Denton County was created in 1846 by the State Legislature, and Pinneyville was named the first county seat. Later, however, the county seat was moved to Alton, then to Hickory Creek, and finally, in 1857, to Denton.

Denton was named for John B. Denton, a pioneer lawyer, preacher, and soldier.

Hiram Cisco, Bill Loving, and William Woodruff donated 100

acres of land on which to build the city of Denton. The County Commissioners had the townsite platted, reserved some land for a court house, and sold the other lots at a public sale. The city was officially established January 19, 1857. A courthouse was built with the proceeds of the lot sale. Unfortunately, that building was destroyed by fire in 1875; the second courthouse was condemned as unsafe in 1894, and the third and present courthouse was completed in 1896.

Denton's first settlers were primarily from the eastern and northeastern states. Farming, lumber, and stock raising were the mainstays of the economy. Local cattle ranches were sufficiently large to support a branch of the famous Chisholm Trail.

Denton was incorporated in 1866. Its charter provided for a mayor and five aldermen to be elected by the people.

Today, Denton has a council-manager form of municipal government, with a mayor, six council members, and a city manager. Denton has grown from 2,558 residents in 1890 to approximately 67,000 today.

Agriculture is still important to the economy of Denton County. Horses, beef cattle, and poultry are raised; and wheat, grain sorghum, hay, and nursery crops are grown. However, industry has become more important to the city's economy. Over sixty manufacturing companies, including Peterbilt, Victor Equipment, Boeing Electronics, and Sally Beauty Supplies, are located here. Such diverse products as lingerie, highway signs, precision plastic parts, coat hangers, diesel trucks, electronic antennae, paper bags, and aseptic packaging are manufactured or processed. Railroads servicing Denton include the Atchison, Topeka & Santa Fe; the Missouri Pacific (now owned by Union Pacific); and the Missouri-Kansas-Texas.

Two universities are located in Denton. North Texas State College was opened as a private institution in 1890; it became North Texas State University in 1961 and, today, its enrollment is approximately 24,000. The Girls' Industrial College was opened in 1903; it became Texas Woman's University in 1957. Its enrollment now is approximately 9,000. Housed in the Human Development Building on its campus is the unique "Collection of Gowns of the First Ladies of Texas." Included are either the actual gowns or faithful copies of the gowns worn by the wives of the Governors of Texas and Presidents of the Republic of Texas.

Of special interest are the restored homes in the Oak-Hickory Historic District near downtown Denton which feature period architecture from the 1880's to the 1950's.

One of the world's finest flying museums is located at Hartlee Field. It is the Fighting Air Command Museum; and it houses aviation artifacts and memorabilia as well as a fleet of aircraft from World Wars I and II. Some of the restored aircraft are flown in exhibitions; and other aircraft are in the process of restoration.

"County Seat Saturday," commemorating Denton's pioneering heritage, is celebrated each September.

Lakes Lewisville, Ray Roberts, and Grapevine are nearby for boating, fishing, camping, swimming, and other water sports.

DENVER CITY

Denver City is located in Yoakum County in the South Plains area of West Texas. It is fourteen miles east of the Texas-New Mexico state line, 75 miles southwest of Lubbock, and 84 miles northeast of Odessa, on State Highways 83 and 214.

The town of Wasson in northern Gaines County was founded in 1935 by representatives of the Denver Producing & Refining Co. Then a discovery well came in three miles north of Wasson that same year; and that discovery well was followed by producer wells. The Denver Producing & Refining Co. decided to move its company operations to the new site in order to be closer to the center of drilling activities; so, in 1939, surface rights to 320 acres were purchased from the Walsh brothers of Midland, Texas. The Denver Co. then moved its buildings and people from Wasson to the new townsite, named "Denver City" after the producing company.

Denver City is the last West Texas town created wholly by the discovery of oil. It was a typical oil boom town in that all activity centered along the main street which a bulldozer cleared through the mesquite and sagebrush. The first business, a Humble Service Station, was soon followed by 16 grocery stores, 16 dry goods shops, 17 lumber yards, 17 supply houses, 34 cafes, and 6 drug stores.

Living conditions were crude at first—tents, shotgun houses, public bathhouses. Better living conditions could be found outside the city limits in the fifteen company camps.

Denver City was incorporated in 1940, and a mayor and city

council elected. Within two years, the city's population grew to 5,000. Presently, its population is 6,250; and the city has a council-manager type of city government.

The petroleum industry today accounts for about 75% of the city's economy. One-fourth of the nation's oil reserves are stored beneath the South Plains. Major producers are Shell, Amoco, Arco, Texaco, Mobil, and Sun Oil. Those first wells of 1935 remain active and have been incorporated into the gigantic Wasson Pool.

During the years 1977 to 1980, Yoakum County was the top oil-producing county in the United States. In 1984, it was the fourth largest oil-producing county in Texas.

Denver City now is also the center of the world's largest complex of CO_2 recovery plants. Shell Western, Amoco, and Arco all operate CO_2 plants in the area. Cattle are also important to the economy of the city and the county, as are such crops as cotton, grain sorghum, and wheat.

Of special interest in the city is the Denver City Historical Museum.

DEVINE

Devine was created as a station on the International and Great Northern Railroad in 1881. Although scattered settlements, they date from 1840. Indian raids persisted until 1870. The town was named for Thomas Jefferson Devine, a San Antonio judge. Devine is the trade center for an irrigated district of the Medina River valley. There is a considerable amount of diversified agriculture in the region.

The population of Devine is 4,600. The city has a rather high tax rate. The breakdown of the taxes are:

City	.5374 per $100 Valuation
County	.3907
School	1.1500
	$2.0781 Total

This is on the high side of city taxes, in that, the average Texas city tax is approximately $1.75.

Devine is located 32 miles southwest of San Antonio on Interstate 35. Distances to major cities are San Antonio, 32 miles northeast; Houston, 230 miles east; Dallas, 311 miles northeast; and Corpus Christi, 114 miles southeast.

Devine is in Medina County, which is large. It has 1331 sq. miles. The average Texas county has 900 sq. miles. The county has an agricultural income of $45,000,000; 60% is from cattle, hogs and sheep. The crops are sorghum, small grain, corn, peanuts, hay, soy beans, guar, cotton and vegetables.

Medina is served by the Southern Pacific Railroad. It is on U.S. Highways 35 and 81 and on State Highway 173. It is also served by Farm-to-Market Highway 2200. One of the attractions at Devine is the Bigfoot Wallace Museum. The museum honors the famed frontiersman and Texas Ranger. It is housed in replicas of his log-cabin home and Texas Independence Hall. Artifacts of Wallace's activities in the Texas War for Independence, Mexican War and Indian fights.

DICKINSON

Dickinson is located in Galveston County Texas, seven miles west of Galveston Bay and halfway between Galveston and Houston. It is located on State Highway 3.

Its physical region is the Gulf Coastal Prairies which extend along the Gulf of Mexico from the Sabine River to the lower Rio Grande Valley. From Galveston Bay to the Sabine there is a very distinct demarcation line between the prairies and the Pine Belt forest to the north. Yet there exists in Dickinson a small, isolated, heavy stand of pines that continue to thrive.

Dickinson is an unincorporated community with a population of approximately 15,000.

Dickinson has a most interesting history. One hundred and fifty-four years ago, on August 19, 1824, John Dickinson took possession of a league of land somewhere in the general vicinity of what is known today as Dickinson, in Galveston County, Texas. The land was granted to him by the Mexican government which had finally won its independence from Spain, but which honored Moses Austin's arrangement with the Spaniards to bring worthy American settlers into Texas as new colonists. The Dickinson land grant, executed in Spanish and signed by Estevan F. Austin, Bron de Bastrop, and John Dickinson, still exists in the State Archives in Austin. The grant as originally executed makes for interesting reading. It reads as follows "We put the aforesaid John

Dickinson in possession of said tract, taking him by the hand, leading him over it, telling him in loud and audible words that by virtue of the commission and in the name of the government of the Mexican nation we put him in possession of said land . . . and the aforesaid John Dickinson in token of being in real and personal possession of said land without any contradiction whatsoever, uttered words, pulled plants, threw stones, drove stakes, and performed all other necessary ceremonies."

A league of land consisted of 4,428 acres. John Dickinson paid the sum of $135.00 for his league (or just over three cents an acre!).

John Dickinson had great plans for the development of his league of land. However, whatever the promise, John Dickinson did not live to fulfill his dreams. For in late August 1825, he was brutally murdered by Indians on the San Antonio River.

Today Dickinson is served by the G H and H Railroad. It has State Highway 3 running northwest-southeast through the town. State Highway 17 runs east and west through the city. It has farm to market highways in the area, numbers 2004, 3436, 1266. To the west of the city are the main U.S. Highways, 45 and 75, which run between Houston and Galveston. Dickinson is located twenty-eight miles southeast of Houston and about twenty miles northwest of Galveston. There is very little farming in the area. However, there is a considerable amount of beef cattle raised in the vicinity. The main economic drive of Dickinson is proximity to both Galveston and Houston. People live in Dickinson and work in one of these two cities.

DIMMITT

Dimmitt is located in the Texas Panhandle on U.S. Highway 385 and State Highways 86 and 194. It is 92 miles north of Lubbock, 69 miles southwest of Amarillo, and 45 miles east of the Texas-New Mexico state line.

The city was named for Rev. W. C. Dimmitt, and was approved as the county seat of Castro County in 1891. Lots were then surveyed and sold, and Dimmitt became a reality. Its population is now 5,019.

Dimmitt's economy is an agricultural one. It is headquarters for the Texas Corn Growers Association and is the home of American Fructose, producer of fructose corn syrup.

A spur of the Burlington Northern Railroad services Dimmitt.

More and more hunters have been discovering Dimmitt during pheasant season.

DONNA

The mid-valley city of Donna became a reality on July 10, 1904, when the St. Louis, Brownsville and Mexico Railway completed their railroad into Donna. The railroad officials recommended that the town be named after Donna Hooks Fletcher, daughter of pioneer T. J. Hooks. Mrs. Fletcher lived in Donna most of her life. She died in 1959. Donna was chartered in 1904. In 1959, a new charter was approved. A mayor and four councilmen govern the city.

Located midway between Rio Grande City and Brownsville, Donna is called "The Heart of the Valley."

Donna is in Hidalgo County and has a population of 10,200. It is in the center of the agri-business of the county. A large canning plant is located in the city. A furniture factory is located there and numerous other facilities. Hidalgo County has the largest volume of agriculture business of any county in Texas. It has $320 million of agricultural income annually. The runner-up county is Parmer, which has an agricultural income of $161 million. Hidalgo County raises cotton, citrus, grain, vegetables, sugarcane and livestock, which includes beef cattle, dairy products, hogs, poultry and horses; 350,000 acres are irrigated out of a total of 1,004,000 acres.

Donna is served by U.S. Highway 83 that runs parallel to the Rio Grande River and connects all of the valley towns, and State Highways 374 and 493 which runs north and south. The U.S. Highway 281 comes into the valley at Pharr just nine miles west of Donna. U.S. 281 runs north to San Antonio.

Donna is served by the Missouri Pacific Railroad, which is now owned by the Union Pacific Railroad.

Mexico is just eight miles to the south, with ports of entry at Reynosa and Progress.

Donna has an ideal, mild winter climate. This attracts thousands of tourists from the northern states.

DUMAS

Dumas is the county seat of Moore County, which was organized in 1892. It had a population of 12,500 in 1988. It is located in the center of Moore County at the intersection of U.S. Highway 287 running north and south and U.S. Highway 87 and F.M. 2203.

It is served by Atchison, Topeka and Santa Fe Railroad.

The average annual rainfall is only 18.3 inches, but Moore County is underlain by the huge Ogallala Aquifer and the farmers irrigate extensively with well water pumped from this water bearing strata.

The county has an average annual income of $100 million, about 75% is from cattle; crops include wheat, sorghum and corn. Approximately 200,000 acres are irrigated. The value of the agricultural and livestock produced by Moore County is $100 million.

Dumas was named for Louis Dumas, President of the Townsite Company which founded the town in 1892. The discovery of oil and gas in 1926 caused the town to grow.

All of the counties that were organized after 1875 in northwest Texas were surveyed with north-south and east-west lines. Nearly all of the counties were laid out with 36 townships, six townships on the side. A township contained 25 sections of land and was five miles square. Therefore the standard new northwest counties in Texas had dimensions, 30 miles on the side or 900 sq. miles. Moore County was laid out to have 900 sq. miles. Nearly all roads run north to south and east to west.

Dumas is 38 miles due north of Amarillo on U.S. Highway 287. It is south of the Palo Duro Canyon. The town has an elevation of 3300 ft.

DUNCANVILLE

The city was incorporated in August of 1947. The city has a home rule charter with a council/manager form of government. The city has an area of 12 square miles. The population was 39,000 in 1989.

The city is located on Interstate Highway I-20 and U.S. Highway 67.

The city is primarily a residential city. Duncanville is a remarkable city in that 85% of its residents own their homes. It is surrounded by other municipalities. It is just southwest of Dallas and is in the southeastern part of Dallas County.

The city was named after Mr. John Duncan, who assisted in the building of the Chicago, Dallas, and Mexican Railway which was under construction to Cleburne, Texas, at the time. The railroad was taken over by the Gulf, Colorado and Santa Fe Railroad in 1884. The city was first called "Duncan."

In 1882 an application for a post office was filed. The application was returned by the U.S. Post Office in Washington because there was already a city with the name of "Duncan" in Jasper County, Texas. Mr. Charles Nance, the postmaster-to-be, added "ville" to the name of "Duncan" and returned the application to the Postal Department; and it was approved as "Duncanville" in October 1882.

The altitude of Duncanville is 727 feet above sea level, 200 ft. above downtown Dallas. The annual rainfall is 34.5 inches.

The city has a favorable tax rate, broken down as follows:

City	$ .59000 per $100 assessment
School	$ .90320 per $100 assessment
County	$ .13540 per $100 assessment
County Hospital	$ .12600 per $100 assessment
County Junior College	$ .03880 per $100 assessment
State	$ .00001 per $100 assessment
	$1.79341 per $100 assessment

Duncanville offers all of the pluses of the Dallas Metroplex.

EAGLE PASS

Eagle Pass is the county seat of Maverick County and is located between Del Rio and Laredo on the Texas' border with Mexico. It can be reached by U.S. Highways 57 and 277.

Although, after the Texas Revolution, Mexicans were forbidden to trade with Texans, they continued to do so, using a route upriver from the old military trails. The new route crossed the Rio Grande at a fording place called Paso de los Adjuntos, where the Mexican Rio Escondido emptied into the Rio Grande. A few miles up the Rio Escondido was a ford known as Paso del Aguila ("Pass of the Eagle" or "Eagle Pass"), so called because of the flights of eagles to and from their nests in the pecan trees along the Rio Escondido.

In 1848, Capt. John A. Veatch of the Texas Mounted Volunteer militia, set up a camp and observation post near the Adjuntos ford. In his reports, Capt. Veatch referred to his location as "Eagle Pass."

In 1849, a trading post was established at the site by James Campbell, formerly of San Antonio. That same year, the U.S. Army established Fort Duncan two miles upriver from Campbell's store. Fort Duncan (first known as "Camp at Eagle Pass") was part of a chain of frontier posts being established across Texas.

With the discovery of gold in California, many potential miners, bound for California via the Mexican route, arrived in the area and camped just north of Fort Duncan, relying upon the Fort for protection. A San Antonio banker, John Twohig, owned much of the land along the river. He laid out a plan for a town and named it "Eagle Pass." At about the same time, a Mexican garrison was established across the river and, with settlers from nearby river towns, was known as the Village of Piedras Negras (meaning "Black Rocks" or "Coal").

During the Civil War, when there was little law or protection along the border, cattle were often run off or stolen. After the Civil War, however, the area became safer, and stock raising and ranching began to grow in importance in the area.

By 1882, the Galveston, Harrisburg & San Antonio division of the Southern Pacific Railroad reached Eagle Pass. By 1903, Eagle Pass' population was 2,729.

Although the Mexicans and Indians knew of the coal deposits in the area, it was the 1880's before coal mining was begun in the Eagle Pass area. Many tons of coal were mined and shipped; however, because of the lessened demand for coal, production was discontinued by the time of World War I.

Eagle Pass' economy is still based primarily on beef cattle and feed lots. About 16,000 acres are irrigated from the Rio Grande for growing such crops as oats, sorghum, wheat, pecans and vegetables. The tourist trade with Mexico is becoming more important.

The population of Eagle Pass is now 21,407.

EDINBURG

The history of Edinburg is a most interesting story. Early recorded history of Hidalgo County indicates that several hundred years ago the Spanish Conquistadores discovered a large salt lake which came to be known as El Sol Del Rey, or the Royal Salt Mine of King Charles IV of Spain. Salt from the mines was transported overland by oxcart to Laguna Madre, and thence, to Spain and her colonies, for more than a century. Other caravans carried the salt westward into Mexico.

Prior to 1836, the only residents of the area were those who had been given land grants by the King of Spain. Most of those favored were captains and soldiers of his army. Mexico gained her independence from Spain in 1821. After 1836, many settlers began to move into the area. By 1850 there were a sizable number of American ranchers living along the Rio Grande.

The settlers living in the area felt keenly the inconvenience of having to travel 70 to 80 miles to Brownsville, to transact land business or to pay taxes. Judge Israel Bigelow, an old stagecoach operator, introduced a bill in 1850 into the Texas Legislature to form a new county out of the then-existing Cameron County. As a result of this, a new county was formed. The county was named after Miguel Hidalgo, the famous liberator of Mexico.

John Young of Edinburgh, Scotland, secured a license to operate a ferry on the Rio Grande opposite Reynosa, Mexico. Here Young founded a town, sold lots, and ran a general store and hide yard. This new county seat town was called Edinburgh.

Raiding parties brought Colonel Robert E. Lee to Edinburgh on April 9, 1860, just five years to the day before he surrendered the armies of the Confederacy at Appomattox Courthouse. He conferred with Major John S. (Rip) Ford about the constant raiding of the Mexican bandit, Juan Cortina. The raiding was the result of the mistreatment of Latins and a lack of justice in settling their land claims. Cortina led rebels against Brownsville and burned ranch homes all along the community of Edinburgh, Relampago, and the Rosario Custom House. Lee, after riding into Edinburgh from old Fort Ringgold, sent letters to Mexican officials, the contents of which have never been disclosed. As a result, the Mexican officials sent Cortina away from the border on other missions. It is believed that the message indicated that Lee would invade Mexico with an American army if the raids were not stopped. At any rate, Robert E. Lee became the first peace-maker of Hidalgo County.

Bandit and rustler gangs began to raid the ranchers and drive off the cattle. Confederate and Union deserters, outlaws, and Cortina partisans joined the rustler bands. In 1872, ranchers estimated losses in excess of 32,000 head.

Into this troubled land rode the tall, soft-spoken Texas Ranger, Captain L. H. McNelly, and 30 other Texas Rangers. All evidence pointed to Las Cuevas Ranch as the headquarters for the biggest gang of rustlers. Las Cuevas and its counterpart ranch across the border, Las Curchas, could muster 300 men, all killers and thieves, who had run about 50,000 cattle across the border.

On November 19, 1875, McNelly and 29 Rangers rode under cover of darkness to Las Curchas and at dawn shot up the place, then stood off a determined counterattack by some 300 rancheros of the Las Cuevas. His crossing resulted in an international incident, but he refused to return across the border without the stolen cattle. In this manner, the Texas Rangers brought intermittent peace once again to Hidalgo County.

The area's real agricultural future began when, in 1902, John Closner experimented with a steam-driven irrigation pump. This proved to be successful and made irrigation a success and opened up the area to the growing of sugar cane, citrus, cotton, and corn.

In July, 1904, the first railroad was built into the area by the St. Louis, Brownsville & Mexican Railroad.

1907 was a great year in the history of the county, as Captain Fitch and Charles Volz set out the first groves of grapefruit. This was fortunate, as the bottom dropped out of the sugar market in 1910.

1907 was a year of catastrophe in the Edinburgh area. Old Edinburgh was washed away by severe floods on the Rio Grande that inundated the valley for a distance of six miles inland. The large land owner, John Closner and W. F. Sprague, offered to donate land at Chapin in the brush, sixteen miles north of the Old Edinburgh. A popular referendum passed and the courthouse was officially moved to the new town of Edinburg. It retained the name that Young had given it, honoring his hometown in Scotland, but the spelling was changed.

Since 1907, the area has grown by leaps and bounds. Today,

Hidalgo County has the largest agricultural income of any county in Texas. The 1988 income was $161 million.

Edinburg is the county seat of Hidalgo County. It has a population of 28,000. It is located 17 miles north of the Mexican border. It is on U.S. Highway 281 and is 235 miles south of San Antonio. It is served by State Highway 107 and Farm-to-Market Roads 1925, 2128, and 1426.

The Union Pacific Railroad (Missouri Pacific) serves the city.

Edinburg is the home of the Pan American University, a four-year state supported institution, with an enrollment of more than 10,000. Pan American offers programs in business education, liberal arts, health and nursing.

Edinburg has a council-manager form of city government, with a mayor and commissioners elected at large. The McAllen-Mission-Edinburg Metropolitan Statistical Area (MSA) is the fourth fastest growing area in the state and the eighth fastest growing MSA in the nation.

Edinburg has some 27 manufacturing related firms which manufacture clothing, electronic boards, corrugated boxes, ethanol, cabinetry, oilfield products, concrete products, agricultural chemicals as well as fruit and vegetable processing.

The area raises citrus, sugar cane, cotton, maize, corn and vegetables of all kinds. It is a rich agricultural area. It is, in addition, a favorite spot for winter tourists.

Edinburg is the home of the Hidalgo County Historical Museum which details the historical development of the county, as well as the entire south Texas area.

EDNA

Edna is located on U.S. Highway 59 in Jackson County, 25 miles northeast of Victoria and 100 miles southwest of Houston. State Highway 111 also passes through Edna.

Edna had its beginnings as a railroad town. In 1880, the New York, Texas and Mexican Railway Company, planned a rail line from Rosenberg to Victoria. Italian Count Joseph Telferner, on behalf of the railroad, approached the citizens of Texana (then the county seat of Jackson County) and asked them to pledge financial help in building the rail line. They refused; so when the railroad was built, it bypassed Texana by about eight miles. A new town was established on the rail line, and it was named for one of Count Telferner's daughters, Edna.

The first train reached Edna in 1882. Jackson County residents voted in 1883 to move the county seat from Texana to the new town on the railroad. Texana residents soon followed in making the move to Edna and, within two years, Texana had died.

Edna's economy is based primarily on agriculture. Rice, sorghums, corn, and cotton are grown. Jackson County is a leading rice county in Texas, with over 32,000 irrigated acres.

Oil and gas fields surround Edna, and petroleum production and operation are also important in the local economy.

Lake Texana nearby is available for recreational activities.

The Southern Pacific Railroad still serves Edna, which currently has a population of 5,650.

EL CAMPO

El Campo is the largest city in Wharton County and is located on U.S. Highway 59 and State Highway 71. It is 52 miles northeast of Victoria and 73 miles southwest of Houston.

El Campo is situated in the center of the Coastal Plains of Texas, so called because of the abundance of native grasses. The plains were used as open range for cattle from the time of the early Spanish explorers.

The early cattle drives headed northeast to New Orleans and Mobile and north to Abilene, Kansas, for rail shipment to market until the New York, Texas & Mexican Railway Company built and opened a rail line from Houston to Victoria.

"Prairie Switch" was established in 1881 as a siding, the shipping point for the railroad, and also as a station for construction workers on the railroad. Cowboys, who drove the herds to Prairie Switch, often had to camp there, holding the cattle and waiting for the next train. The cowboys began referring to the place as "El Campo," or "The Camp." In 1890, the settlement officially took the name El Campo and, in 1905, it was incorporated.

Early settlers in the area had homestead grants. Then the railroad sold some of its land to other settlers. El Campo became the largest prairie hay shipping point in the nation by the early 1900's. Rice, cotton, and corn also became important crops.

Oil was first discovered in the area in the middle 1930's, giving a boost to the area's economy.

In 1955, El Campo, adopting home rule, formed a manager-council city government.

The largest rice, maize, and soybean drying and storage facilities in Texas are in El Campo. Distribution and service facilities are maintained in El Campo by Case, Mustang, Caterpillar, John Deere, International-Harvester, Massey-Ferguson, Minneapolis-Moline, and Oliver. Ten cotton gins handle the area's cotton crop. Wharton County is the largest rice producer in the state (66,000 acres in 1988).

Master Sgt. Roy P. Benavidez (U.S. Army, retired), recipient of the Congressional Medal of Honor, is an El Campo native.

In January, 1989, the new El Campo Civic Center was officially opened, a 40,000 square foot facility with five meeting rooms. It also houses the Big Game Trophy Museum, a major tourist attraction.

El Campo, located on the Coastal Plains, is quickly becoming noted for its excellent goose hunting.

El Campo's population is now 13,500.

ELECTRA

Electra is located in the western part of Wichita County. It is 25 miles west-northwest of Wichita Falls. It is about ten miles from the Red River on the north.

The first settlement in the area followed the building of the Fort Worth and Denver Railroad through the area in 1885. The first post office was secured in 1889 and named Beaver, after Beaver Creek. It was a trading post for Chief Quanah Parker and his Comanche Indian comrades from the Comanche reservation.

Electra has a unique history that dates back to the early 1870's and is closely interwoven with the names of Dan Waggoner, the cattle baron and his son W.T. (Tom). Dan Waggoner acquired land in Wichita, Wilburger, Baylor, Knox, and Foard Counties. His ranch holdings made the largest ranch in the state with the exception of the famous King Ranch.

In 1878 the Waggoner Ranch established its headquarters near the Red River north of Beaver, which is what Electra was originally called. In 1882, the Fort Worth and Denver completed its railway to Wichita Falls. It was then extended to Beaver (Electra) in 1885. A depot was built and it was called Waggoner. In 1911 the citizens of the area decided to do away with the confusing names of Beaver and Waggoner, and they voted to change the name to Electra in honor of Tom Waggoner's daughter.

Oil was discovered in Wichita County in 1911. The famous Clayco No. 1-Magnolia Petroleum Company, now called Mobile Oil Company was the largest operator in the subsequent oil boom in the Electra area.

Electra has a population of 3,900. It is located on State Highways 29, 287, and 487, and Farm-to-Market Highway 1739.

The Burlington Northern Railroad now serves the town.

The area around Electra raises beef cattle, hogs, wheat, sorghum, cotton, and alfalfa; 13,000 acres are irrigated.

ELGIN

Elgin is the northernmost town in Bastrop County, and is located 25 miles due east of Austin on U.S. Highway 290 and State Highway 95.

Elgin had its beginnings as a railroad town and is still served by the Missouri-Kansas-Texas Railroad, the Austin and Northwestern Railroad.

By Deed of Dedication, the Houston & Texas Central Railroad named the townsite "Elgin" for Robert Morris Elgin, land commissioner for the railroad. (The correct Scots pronunciation of the family name of "Elgin" is for the second syllable to be pronounced like the "gin" in "begin".)

Elgin's current population is 6,008. It is famous for sausages. Other industry in the community includes brick plants, food processing plants, a cottonseed mill, horse breeding, training, bull breeding and a large veterinary hospital.

EL PASO

El Paso is located in the westernmost tip of Texas on Interstate 10 and U.S. Highways 20, 54, 62, 80, and 180. It is the county seat of El Paso County. Its population as of 1988 was 516,996.

Juan de Onate, a Spanish explorer, camped on the banks of the Rio Grande in 1598 and claimed the area for King Philip II of Spain. Onate crossed the river at the location of present-day El Paso and he called it "El Paso del River del Norte," meaning "the crossing of the river."

Spanish colonists and Tigua Indians, fleeing the Pueblo Indian Revolt in New Mexico in 1680, settled in the area of El Paso.

Shortly afterward, missionaries came to the area and established missions.

In 1884, Fort Bliss (a U.S. Army calvary post) was established to protect wagon trains and settlers. El Paso was incorporated as a city in 1873; and in 1881, the Southern Pacific Railroad arrived.

Ciudad Juarez is El Paso's "sister city" across the Rio Grande. El Paso is the largest port of entry on the U.S. border.

The Franklin Mountains (the southern portion of the Rocky Mountains) divide El Paso into eastside, westside, and central areas.

The city's largest industries are electronics, clothing and boot manufacture, cotton, copper, and tourism. Government and military employment are also an important component of the economy.

El Paso has a home rule city government, with a city council consisting of a mayor and six city representatives.

Fort Bliss is the largest air defense training center in the free world and is the proving ground for land-based weapons. Fort Bliss maintains museums of its history which are open to the public.

The annual Sun Bowl football game is played in the Sun Bowl stadium of the University of Texas at El Paso.

Parks of interest in or near El Paso include Chamizal National Memorial, Hueco, Tanks & State Historical Park, McKelligon Canyon Park and Amphitheater, and Tom Mays Wilderness Park and museum.

ENNIS

Ennis is located in Ellis County in North Texas. It is 34 miles south of Dallas on Interstate 45. U.S. Highway 287 and State Highway 34 also pass through Ennis. Its population is 14,000.

Ennis was established in 1871 as the northern terminus of the Houston & Texas Central Railroad, and was named for an officer of the railroad, Cornelius Ennis.

Much of the county's economy is based on farming. Many of the original settlers were from Czechoslovakia, and their descendants still operate many of the farms. Important crops are cotton, sorghums, and other grains.

Present-day Ennis also has a number of manufacturing plants, specializing in goods such as business forms, apparel and roofing.

The Southern Pacific Railroad services Ennis.

Lake Bardwell, 2½ miles from Ennis, not only furnishes the city's water supply, but is available for fishing and water sports.

The National Polka Festival is held the first weekend in May each year in Ennis.

EULESS

Indian tribes initially inhabited Euless until military expeditions opened up pioneer settlements. Bird's Fort, established in 1840, was located just south of present-day Euless. Later, land was issued for the original Peters Colony grant, located on the Grapevine Prairie. In 1841, some families did move into the fort, but because the Indians had burned off the grass and game was scarce, the settlers moved to another area along the Trinity River. Bird's Fort was used again in 1843 for the signing of a treaty with the Indians, who agreed to move farther west beyond Fort Worth. Sam Houston and officials representing the Republic of Texas agreed to establish trading posts along the treaty line. Euless is located in Tarrant County.

Settlers moved into the area in 1844 and built near the Hallford homestead, southwest of the fork of Big and Little Bear Creeks, north of present-day Euless.

A short distance south of the Bear Creek settlement, Elisha Adam Euless settled in 1881. He was a cotton farmer who built a cotton gin near the current location of the Euless municipal complex.

Other businesses followed suit, forming the nucleus of a town which was called Euless after the cotton gin. A community building was added which served as a school and as a building for three churches. The churches alternated use of the building.

The exact date of the city's incorporation is not clear. The city's master plan, said Euless was incorporated as a home rule city in 1954 and adopted a council-manager form of government.

Initially, growth in Euless progressed slowly. In 1915, the population was 25. By 1940, it had increased to only 40.

Population grew steadily in the 1960's. By 1960, the city's population reached 4,236. By 1964 it was 10,554 and two years later, it mushroomed to 15,875. By 1967, the population saw 16,500. In 1980, the city's population reached more than 21,000. It was approximately 35,000 in 1989.

Euless is served by State Highway 183. There is no railroad in Euless.

FAIRFIELD

Fairfield is the county seat of Freestone County. The town is located on Interstate-Highway 45, 83 miles south-southeast of Dallas. Fairfield was originally called Prairie Mound. In 1851 when Freestone County was formed, Prairie Mound was selected as the county seat and the new name of Fairfield was selected by an election. Fairfield was chosen because it was located in some beautiful fields.

The altitude of Fairfield is 461 feet. The rainfall is 38.5 inches per year. This rainfall is ample for agriculture and the raising of livestock. The land in the area slopes to the southeast and all of the area surrounding the city drains into the Trinity River.

Fairfield has three major highways running through it, which are Interstate-Highway 45, U.S. Highways 75 and 84. It is also served by Farm-to-Market Highways 488, 27, 1580, 2547 and 2570.

The beautiful Fairfield Lake State Recreation area is located northeast of the city, as well as the 45,000 acre Richland Creek Reservoir. The land immediately west of Fairfield has some mesquite, and there is oak with some pine in the eastern part of the county. The Freestone County Museum is located in Fairfield.

The early history of the area was the Franco-Spanish period. In the last decade of the seventeenth century, Spain occupied East Texas for a two-fold purpose; to establish her claim to that region against possible French intrusion and to carry the Catholic faith to the Asinai or Tejas Indians who had requested missions. After a brief occupation and a later abandonment of Texas for twenty-three years, the Spaniards re-established their occupancy of East Texas in 1716, this time against imminent French aggression. Two years later the site of San Antonio was occupied as a sort of halfway station between Coahiula and the locations east and west of the Sabine River.

About 1745, a notable and temporary successful attempt was made by the Spaniards to christianize the Tonkawan Indian Tribe, which then resided in and about the area. Xavier missions, after a series of adverse fortunes, were abandoned a decade later. This ill-fated project marked the nearest Spanish advance to the region of which this study treats.

In the early 1820's, Mexico opened the doors of Texas to American colonization and by the national law of August 18, 1824 and the state law of Coahuila and Texas on March 24, 1825 opened its uninhabited tracks to contractors or impresarios. One of the very first of these impresarios was Hayden Edwards, who secured a contract to colonize eight hundred families in East Texas. On April 18, 1825, his grant included practically all of Texas, east of the Navasota River. Edwards proceeded to fulfill his contract, but was prevented from doing so, on account of serious friction which arose within the boundaries of his domain and which later resulted in the Freedonian War. Hayden's grant was revoked and the territory covered by his grant plus some additional land was subsequently granted to three impresarios: Joseph Vehein, David G. Burnett and Lorenzo de Zavalla. The area which was to become Freestone County in 1850 lay within the heart of Burnett's Grant. By the time of his contract with the State of Coahuila and Texas, Burnett was to settle and colonize three hundred families within the limits of his grant in the space of six years, but this term was subsequently extended to nine years.

The Freestone County Map in the General Land Office, Austin Texas shows grants to at least four different railroad companies, the International and Great Northern being the greatest recipient. Today Fairfield does not have a railroad. The nearest railroad is the Burlington Northern and Chicago, Rock Island and Pacific at Teague, ten miles to the southwest.

Following the organization of Freestone County, came the definite location of Fairfield. On June 20, 1851, David H. Lowe deeded to the county 100 acres of land. This was the parcel of land which Freestone County had chosen for its permanent county seat. The lots were sold at auction and went at prices ranging from $6.00 to $100.01 dollars each.

About 1849, the sparsely settled western section of the county, received an increase to its population through a stimulus to the raising of cotton. In that year W. H. Parson (Smith) built a horse gin which is said to have been the first in the county. A story told in connection with the gin is that practically every piece of it was made by hand by a Negro slave. The name for the community cotton gin is believed to have arisen in commemoration of that mechanical aid to the county.

The city has a population of 4,100. It is recognized as a banking, marketing and shopping center. A rock quarry, sawmill, lignite coal mining, two electrical generation plants, and oil and gas production contribute to the town's economy. Fairfield is a major livestock country. There is no railroad in Fairfield. The county of Freestone, however, has three railroads that cross through it and they are accessible and available to Fairfield. Fairfield has a general law municipal government consisting of a mayor and five city councilmen.

FALFURRIAS

Falfurrias is the county seat of Brooks County in South Texas. It is located on U.S. Highway 281 and State Highway 285, and is 101 miles east to Laredo, 36 miles south of Alice, and 38 miles southwest of Kingsville.

Since 1904, the city has used the phrase "The Land of Heart's Delight" to describe itself. Local legend says that a Lipan Indian long ago looked upon the area and said "falfurrias," meaning "The Land of Heart's Delight." Every Spring, the countryside is covered with lavender wildflowers called "The Heart's Delight."

Ranching in the area began in the 1840's. The Beefmaster brand of cattle was established here.

Sometime after 1893, Ed Lasater moved to the area from San Antonio. He borrowed money to buy land, and then subdivided the land into small dairy farms which he offered for sale nationwide. He built the Falfurrias Creamery (still known for its "Sweet Cream Butter") to process the dairy products.

In 1930, oil wells were drilled and the petroleum potential of the area was proven. Today, there are about 20 active oil and gas fields.

Principal crops grown in the area are cotton, tomatoes, cucumbers, grain, corn, watermelons and cantaloupes.

Wild game (deer, turkey, javelina, and birds) attract hunters to the area.

The Heritage Museum houses a collection of artifacts, relics, and pictures of Texas history.

Don Pedrito, a Mexican faithhealer, came to the area in 1881 and was visited by thousands of people who came to be cured. The

Don Pedrito Shrine is still visited by many people each year. A Texas Historical Marker has been erected for Don Pedrito.

Current population of Falfurrias is 6,103.

FLORESVILLE

Floresville is the county seat of Wilson County and is located 29 miles southeast of San Antonio. It can be reached by U.S. Highway 181 and State Highway 97. Its current population is 4,381.

Sometime before 1832, Don Francisco Flores de Abryo settled in the area; he established his ranch headquarters about 6 miles northwest of present-day Floresville.

The Flores family donated land for a townsite and named it Floresville. In 1885, the county seat was moved from Lodi to Floresville. When the San Antonio & Aransas Pass Railroad reached the town in 1886, it already had two hotels, two steam gristmills and cotton gins, a newspaper, and 400 residents.

E. E. Crandel arrived in Floresville in 1886 to engage in the bee industry. By 1908, the sale of honey was an important part of Floresville's economy. Honey was shipped worldwide.

Floresville has a general law type of city government, with five elected aldermen, an elected mayor, and a salaried administrator.

Because Floresville is so close to San Antonio, a number of people work in San Antonio but live in Floresville.

Agriculture is still the primary industry. Peanuts, maize, watermelons, corn, flax, black-eyed peas, wheat, and coastal bermuda are the main crops. Dairying and livestock production are also important.

Floresville is known as the "Peanut Capitol of Texas." An annual Peanut Festival is held each year on the second Friday and Saturday of October.

The Southern Pacific Railroad serves Floresville.

FLOWER MOUND

Flower Mound is located in Denton County in North Texas. It is north of Dallas and Fort Worth on Farm-to-Market Road 1171 between Interstate 35 East and 35 West.

Flower Mound received its name from a mound (on FM 3040 near FM 2499) rising nearly 50 feet above the surrounding plains.

The mound is covered with approximately 500 varieties of wildflowers and native prairie grasses.

The main inhabitants of the area in the early 1800's were Wichita Indians, who considered the mound sacred ground.

Legend says that nothing can be built on the mound. At the time, supposedly, a church group stacked building materials on the mound but, before they could build the church, a tornado blew away the materials. The house was going to be built on the mound but, again, the materials were blown away.

Flower Mound was incorporated in 1961 to protect itself from incorporation from surrounding cities. In 1981, a town charter was adopted and Flower Mound was designated a town (because of its country atmosphere) rather than a city. The town is governed by a five-member council and a mayor.

Its current population is 15,000.

Lewisville Lake and Flower Mound boarders Lake Grapevine on the southwest.

Flower Mound's growth has resulted from its nearness to Dallas, Ft. Worth and the DFW Airport. The majority of residents in Flower Mound live in Flower Mound, but work in the surrounding area, Las Colinas, Dallas, etc.

FORT STOCKTON

Fort Stockton is located near the center of Pecos County, of which it is the county seat. It is located on Interstate 10 about halfway between San Antonio and El Paso. It can also be reached by U.S. Highways 285 and 385 and State Highway 18. Its current population is 8,688.

Comanche Springs was a well-known watering spot in the area and was an established way-stop for travelers, stagecoaches, and wagon trains. The U.S. Army established Camp Stockton in the area in 1858 to protect travelers from Comanche and Apache raiding parties. The camp was named for Commodore Robert Field Stockton, a Mexican War hero.

The Camp was abandoned by the Army in 1861 because of the Civil War, but the Army returned to the area in 1867 and rebuilt in an area north and east of the earlier post. A settlement called St. Gall grew up around the camp.

Pecos County was officially organized in 1875 with St. Gall its county seat. In 1881, the name St. Gall was officially changed to

Fort Stockton. In 1886, the Army, no longer needed for protection, vacated the fort.

Fort Stockton's economic growth was affected in 1912 by the arrival of the Kansas City & Orient Railroad, and again in 1926 when oil was discovered. Yates Field (in eastern Pecos County) is the world's fourth largest oil reserve.

Irrigation Wells and the 1950's drought combined to dry up the famed Comanche Springs.

Today's economy is based on oil and gas production, ranching, irrigated farming, tourists and sulphur mining. The newest industry is vineyards and a winery. Firestone Tire & Rubber Company has a tire test track in the area.

The Santa Fe Railroad serves the city.

Some points of interest in Fort Stockton are the old Fort buildings, the Zero Stone (a marker placed in 1859 and used as a zero reference point for subsequent surveys), Pecos County Courthouse (built in 1912), the Annie Riggs Memorial Museum, and the world's largest Roadrunner.

FORT WORTH

Fort Worth is located in north central Texas just 17 miles from the fourth busiest airport in the world and lies squarely at the commercial crossroads of business America.

The city is home to General Dynamics' F-16 program. The corporate headquarters of Tandy Corporation, American Airlines, Alcon Laboratories and of a wide variety of well-known high-tech companies are located in Fort Worth.

Fort Worth grew from a military camp established at the close of the Mexican War by General Winfield Scott. It was named for General William Jenkins Worth, who saw action in the Mexican War. Forty-two men of Company F.2nd Dragoons, established a camp on June 6, 1849. The Fort Worth to Yuma, Arizona Stageline was established in 1850. The city became the seat of Tarrant County in 1860. After the Civil War, it became a major shipping and supply depot for cattlemen.

The impressive Fort Worth Convention Center spans an area of 14 downtown blocks. Culturally, Fort Worth is known for an outstanding group of museums, plus a season for summer musicals, winter theater, symphony concerts, opera, ballet, and art galleries.

Fort Worth has become a major industrial city. It has the following major employers as manufacturers: General Dynamics, manufacturer of military aircraft, Bell Helicopter Company, who manufacture Helicopters, Tandy Corporation, makers of microcomputers and allied equipment, General Motors, who assembles automobiles, Motorola, makers of communication equipment, Alcon Laboratories, who produce pharmaceuticals, Wynn's Climate, maker of auto air conditioners, Miller Brewing Company, brewers of beverages, Justin Industries, Inc., makers of leather goods, brick, and ceramic cooling, Gerhart Industries, Inc., Oil Well logging industry, Freuhauf Corporation, manufacturers of semi trailers, American Manufacturing of Texas, manufacturers of oil field equipment, Lennon Industries, Inc., producers of heating and air conditioners, Surgikos, Inc., producers of medical supplies, ARA Manufacturing Company, maker of automotive air conditioners, Williamson-Dickie Manufacturing Company, producers of apparel products, Mrs. Baird's Bakeries, Inc., bakers of bread and cake products, Ben Hogan Company, producer of golf equipment and sportswear, Champion Parts, Rebuilders, Inc., rebuild auto parts, Menasco Aircraft, manufacturers of landing gear, R-Tec Systems, manufacturers of aircraft landing gear, and telecommunications equipment.

Carswell Air Force is located adjacent to Fort Worth. It has 6,950 military and 1,280 civilian personnel. The General Services Administration is located in Fort Worth with an employment of 1,400. The Federal Aviation Administration is located there with an employment of 1,130. The U.S. Postal Service employs 3,000 people. The U.S. Army Engineers District employs 1,700. Delta Air Lines, Inc., employs 5,000.

There are over 128 industrial parks in the Fort Worth area encompassing 22,290 acres of land and 859,000 square feet of space. Local and national developers and investors supply speculative or build-to-suit space.

The city is the home of the Southwestern Baptist Theological Seminary, the Tarrant County Junior College, Texas Christian University, Texas College of Osteopathic Medicine and Texas Wesleyan College.

There are many attractions in the city. Some of the principal ones are:

Amon G. Carter Museum of Western Art

It contains a fabulous collecton of pictures, sculptures, books and objects of western art featuring permanent collections of Remington and Russell, plus frequent traveling exhibits.

The Botanic Gardens

Which is a showcase of 150,000 living plants representing 2,500 species, displayed in both formal and natural settings.

The Casa Manana Theater

Is under a geodesic dome, and is one of the nation's most notable theaters-in-the-round, a setting for drama and musical comedies.

The Cattle Raisers Museums

Gives the history for the colorful Texas ranching industry portrayed in film, photos, and cowboy memorabilia.

The Forest Park Zoo

Contains animals, birds and reptiles from throughout the world; and includes an aquarium, a herpetarium, great apes, and a children's zoo.

The Fort Worth Museum of Science and History

Contains 100,000 artifacts and specimens for research on exhibition.

The Fort Worth Nature Center and Refuge

Grew from 35 acres on Greer Island Nature Center, currently it has 3,500 acres in a refuge that offers an interpretive center.

The Japanese Garden

Is an enchanting six-acre garden of Oriental design featuring a pagoda, moon-viewing deck, teahouse, and meditation garden and lush exotic plants.

The Kimbell Art Museum

Is based on philanthropist Kay Kimbell's Collection of 18th Century portraits and old masters.

The Sid Richardson Collection of Western Art

A downtown museum that is free to the public. It features dozens of paintings from the late Texas oil man Sid Richardson. The multimillion-dollar collection now includes works from the prehistoric to Picasso.

The LaBuena Vida Vineyards

Contains vineyards and winery which are near Springtown, some 20 miles north of Texas 199.

The Stockyards Historic Area

It gives one the feel of the old west recaptured by merchants along Exchange Avenue on the city's North Side. Renovated western-style stores and restaurants front traditional boardwalks.

There are a number of lakes in the area. These lakes are the Arlington, Benbrook, Eagle Mountain, Grapevine and Worth.

The Six Flags Amusement Park, which is nationally known, is located in Arlington. There is a Southwest Aerospace Museum which displays several military aircrafts from the huge B-36 Peacemaker to the T-33 Tweety Bird—numerous indoor and outdoor exhibits. There is the last supper, located at the Radio and Television Commission of the Southern Baptist Convention. The Will Rogers Memorial Coliseum is housed in a complex on the site of Fort Worth's major exhibitions and championship indoor rodeos. A mounted statue of Will Rogers, famous cowboy humorist, stands at the entrance grounds of the Amon Carter Square. There is the Billy Bobs Honky Tonk. This is the world's largest genuine Honky Tonk. The indoor rodeos are conducted there together with a large number of bars, dance floors, western shows, etc.

Fort Worth is the county seat of Tarrant County. It has a population of 450,000. It s located on Interstate Highways 20, 30 and 35. It has easy access to the Dallas-Fort Worth International Airport. Fort Worth is known for cowboys in "culture" and the city where the west begins. It likes to be known as "cowtown." Fort Worth has the city-manager-council form of government. The annual operating budget is approximately $350 million dollars. Besides being a cattle marketing center, there is a considerable amount of agriculture in Tarrant County.

The city has a sales tax aggregating 7.5%. The property tax in Fort Worth is high. The total tax is broken down as follows:

City of Fort Worth	$0.85600
Fort Worth ISD	0.86950
County Right-of-Way	0.15659
Hospital District	0.13300
Junior College	0.03210
Total Effective Rate	2.04719

This is considered high. 1.75% is considered the break between conservative and high taxes.

Texas Utility furnishes the electric power for Fort Worth. The average annual cost per KWH, is .0633 which is considered very reasonable. The Lone Star Gas Company furnishes the natural gas for the city. The average residential customer use 6.0 MCFF at a cost of $35.09 plus tax per month. This is a reasonable rate.

The city of Fort Worth is served by the AMTRAK passenger line, the Atchison, Topeka & Santa Fe, The Union Pacific, The St. Louis-Southwestern, and the Missouri-Kansas-Texas Railroads. There are seven main rail lines leading into and out of Fort Worth.

Fort Worth is a thriving, dynamic growing city and is a credit to the State of Texas.

FREDERICKSBURG

Fredericksburg is located in the center of Gillespie County, of which it is the county seat. It is situated at the intersection of U.S. Highways 87 and 290 and State Highway 16. It is 24 miles northeast of Kerrville, 74 miles north of San Antonio, and 80 miles west of Austin. Its current population is 7,500.

In 1845, the Society for the Protection of German Immigrants in Texas sent its first settlers to New Braunfels. Another location was needed for additional settlers being sent. Baron Otfried Hans von Meusebach selected a site in the Pedernales Valley, 80 miles northwest of New Braunfels and, in 1846, 120 settlers were led to the new site. It was named Fredericksburg for Prince Frederick of Prussia. Several other large wagon trains arrived shortly thereafter. Each settler received a town lot and 10 acres in the vicinity of the town.

In 1847, a treaty was negotiated with the Comanches. In exchange for $3,000 worth of goods, the Indians agreed not to harm or interfere with the Fredericksburg settlers. By then, fifteen stores had been opened and the town population was 966.

Until the early part of the 20th century, Fredericksburg was known for its "Sunday Houses." Farmers and ranchers spent their weekends in town—attending church, shopping and visiting—so they built small houses of one or two rooms to use for weekend stays in town. Some of the Sunday Houses are still standing, and some have been remodeled into permanent, small houses.

The Schuetzenfest, a marksmanship contest, is held each year on the Saturday and Sunday under a full moon nearest to August 1st. Oktoberfest is also celebrated annually, and Gillespie County hosts the oldest continuous county fair in Texas.

Attractions in Fredericksburg include the Admiral Nimitz State Historical Park, the birthplace of Adm. Chester W. Nimitz and the Nimitz Naval Museum, and the Pioneer Museum.

Nearby is the Lyndon B. Johnson National Historic Park, LBJ Ranch, Lyndon B. Johnson State Park, and Enchanted Rock State Park.

Gillespie County is the largest peach producing county in the state, and also has one of the largest white-tail deer populations in the state.

FREER

Freer is located in Duval County at the intersection of U.S. Highway 59 and State Highways 16 and 44. It is 35 miles west of Alice, 82 miles west of Corpus Christi, and 60 miles east of Laredo.

The first settlers came to the Freer area in 1916, lured by brochures and advertising distributed nationwide which had been designed to attract people to Texas. Many came, but only six families stayed. The area was hot, dry, and dusty; the land was covered with mesquite trees, cactus, and underbrush, and was infested with rattlesnakes, rats, spiders, and scorpions. In addition, the area was subject to raids by Indians and by Pancho Villa.

Major oil companies began leasing land in the Freer area in 1923, attracting workers and settlers to the area. In 1933, Freer was the second largest oil field in the nation. By 1935, local population was 5,000. Freer became known as the "Buckle of the Oil Belt."

In 1925, the first post office for the community was established in the home of D. J. Freer, and the town took its name from Mr. Freer.

The oil and gas industry are still important in Freer's economy, as are ranching and tourism (hunting).

Until 1965, Freer sponsored an annual Oil-Rama; emphasis then shifted to the rattlesnake hunt, and the event was renamed the Rattlesnake Round-Up. It is still held annually and attracts in excess of 20,000 people.

Freer is governed by a mayor and city council. Its population is 3,213.

FRIENDSWOOD

Friendswood is located three miles west of Interstate-45, halfway between Houston and Galveston. Friendswood holds the distinction of having citizens in two counties—Harris and Galveston.

It was founded by a group of Quakers in 1895, the heritage of this community was received from its founders based on Christ's words from the Bible: "Ye are my friends if ye do whatsoever I command you." John 15:14.

Until 1958, the Friends Church was the only church in the community which now boasts its religious influence as evidenced by more than 19 churches representing all faiths.

An historical marker designates the site of this early church. The citizens of this volunteer-oriented community have designed their own city flag, a commemorative plate, and have designated a Time Capsule and Liberty Tree in tribute to America's Freedoms. The city claims fame as having the oldest, consecutive celebration of the 4th of July in the nation. Each year since 1895, the community celebrates with a big parade, a day in the park, and an evening fireworks display.

Friendswood's population is 22,500 and growing.

FRIONA

Friona is located 66 miles southwest of Amarillo on U.S. Highway 60. It is 18 miles east of the New Mexico line. It is served by State Highway 214 and by Farm-to-Market roads 2013, 2397, 3040.

The Santa Fe Railroad runs northeast and southwest through the city.

The population of the city is 4,000. It has a mayor and council form of city government. The town is located in Parmer County.

The city is located in one of the richest agricultural areas in the United States. It is strictly an agricultural city and serves the surrounding areas. There are several grain elevators located in the city. There are fertilizer processing and packing plants. There are several very large feed lots in the vicinity. The city is a major agricultural business center.

Parmer County is the largest agricultural income county in the State of Texas. It has $163 million of income. Most of the income is from cattle, feed lot operations, hogs and sheep. The crops are sorghum, milo maize, cotton, wheat, barley, vegetables and soybeans.

The county has 260,000 irrigated acres. All of this is water pumped from the huge Ogallala Aquifer.

The town was located in Frio draw and the townspeople decided to name the town Friona.

GAINESVILLE

Gainesville is located in North Texas on Interstate 35, U.S. Highway 82, and Farm-to-Market Road 372. It is 68 miles north of Fort Worth and about five miles south of the Red River which is the boundary between Texas and Oklahoma.

Gainesville was originally called Liberty; however, that name was rejected by the post office since there was already another Texas town named Liberty. Col. Fitzhugh, who had established a Fort in the area to protect the settlers from Indians, suggested the town be named for General Edmund Pendleton Gaines, his former commander.

In 1850, Gainesville officially became the county seat of Cooke County.

Present-day Gainesville, with a population of 14,081, has factories producing pipe, garments, boots, fishing lures, metal products, and aircraft equipment. Mainstays of the county's economy are beef and dairy cattle, poultry, hogs, horses, and crops (including wheat, oats, grain sorghum, peanuts, and hay). Minerals found in the county include oil, gas, sand, and gravel.

Cooke County College is located in Gainesville.

GALENA PARK

The City of Galena Park, Texas was incorporated on September 21, 1935 and is located in Harris County on the North bank of the Houston Ship Channel (formerly Buffalo Bayou) just east of the Houston city limits. The city is located in the Ezekiel Thomas Survey, and has a population of about 11,000. The first settler in the area was Ezekiel Thomas of South Carolina, who received a grant of one league of land from the Mexican Government in 1824 as one of Stephen F. Austin's Colonists. In 1833, Isaac Batterson and his family settled in the area and named the settlement "Clinton." Batterson subsequently purchased 1000 acres from the Ezekiel Thomas estate, a tract located in the corner of present-day Galena Park. For almost 100 years, the settlement was known as Clinton, and in 1928, when the U.S. Post Office Department refused to grant the town a post office because another post office bearing the name Clinton already existed in Texas, the name of the town was changed to Galena Park, after the Galena-Signal Oil Company, the town's leading industry at the time.

Galena Park's main claim to historical fame lies in the fact, that on April 10, 1836 General Sam Houston used the floor of the Batterson house for the purpose of making rafts with which to ferry his army across the rain-swollen Buffalo Bayou. Houston also left some 260 soldiers, most of whom were ill, in the camp near the Batterson house. After crossing the bayou, Houston defeated the Mexicans under General Santa Anna in the Battle of San Jacinto and won independence for Texas.

The City of Galena Park has prospered since its incorporation in 1935, growing in population from 1500 to 11,000. It has had efficient governmental administration through the years. It has an excellent police force, and a very capable fire department. All of its major business and residential streets are paved, and the city owns and maintains its own water system and sewage disposal facilities. The city owes its progress to the many diversified industries within its borders on the Houston Ship Channel. Petroleum, petrochemicals, fertilizers, cement, gypsum products, shell products, and many other commodities are refined or manufactured in the city.

State Highway 526 runs north and south along the eastern boundary of Galena Park. I-10 Highway running east and west serves the city well. It is just one half mile north of the northern boundaries of Galena Park.

The Southern Pacific Railroad runs east and west along the northern side of Galena Park.

GALVESTON

The City of Galveston is the county seat of Galveston County and is located on Galveston Island in the Gulf of Mexico. It is 51 miles southeast of Houston and can be reached by a causeway (Interstate 45) from Houston or by a free ferry on State Highway 87 from Port Bolivar to the northeast. Its population is 61,902.

When LaSalle first visited the site of present-day Galveston, he named it San Louis (honoring his king), but in 1777, Count

Bernardo de Galvez (Spanish governor of Louisiana) renamed the island after himself, Galvez, and the settlement later became known as Galveston.

The present site of Galveston was bought in 1836 by ten men who organized the Galveston City Company; the Company was incorporated in 1841 by the Republic of Texas and lasted until 1944 when it was liquidated.

Galveston has a long history of being "first" in Texas:

1836—First post office.
1836—First Custom House, with Gail Borden as Collector of the Port (the same Gail Borden who later, in Galveston, invented condensed milk).
1841—First military company was chartered.
1845—First Chamber of Commerce.
1847—First convent (Ursuline Convent).
1854—First terminal (Galveston Wharf Co.).
1854—First telegraph.
1856—First jewelry store (N. W. Shaw & Sons).
1859—First gas lights.
1865—First Cotton Exchange and Board of Trade.
1865—First steamship line (Mallory Line).
1867—First drug store (established by J. J. Schott who was also the first druggist to import chicle from which the chewing gum industry evolved).
1868—First mule street cars.
1868—First hospital (St. Mary's Infirmary).
1871—First public library.
1876—First furniture store (Kauffman, Meyers & Co.).
1878—First telephone.
1878—First flour mill (Texas Star Flour Mills).
1880—First orphanage (Galveston Orphan's Home).
1888—First artificial lights.
1890—First building & loan association.
1891—First medical college.
1891—First electrified street cars.
1891—First black hospital.
1894—First training school for nurses (John Sealy Hospital).
1895—First brewery (Galveston Brewing Co.).
1898—First golf club and country club.

In 1901, Galveston was the first in the nation to have a commission form of government. Present-day Galveston, however, has adopted a council-manager form of government.

The area has changed a great deal from its early days when the island was a haven for pirates. Much of Galveston's economy, however, still centers around the water—its port is ranked as one of the world's largest cotton ports; related activities such as shipbuilding, ship repair, offshore oil and gas activity, fishing, and shrimping are important; tourists are attracted to the sun and sand and beach.

Galveston is home to the internationally-known Shriners Burn Institute. Institutions of higher education in Galveston include the University of Texas Medical Branch, National Maritime Research Center, Texas A & M Maritime Academy, and Galveston College.

Places of interest include Old Fort San Jacinto and Galveston Island State Park (the historical drama, "Lone Star," is performed here each summer).

GARLAND

Garland is located on the grassy plains of North Central Texas in Dallas County. It is a suburb of the city of Dallas, being situated just northeast of that city. It can be reached by Interstate 30 and Interstate Loop 635, and State Highways 66 and 78.

About 1874, a man named Moles established a store on the west bank of Duck Creek. Other settlers soon arrived and homes and businesses were built. By 1878, the little community of "Duck Creek" had a post office.

In 1886, the Santa Fe Railroad built a rail line from Dallas to Farmersville, passing a half-mile east of Duck Creek. The Missouri-Kansas-Texas Railroad then built a rail line from Dallas to Greenville and passed Duck Creek a short distance to the north. Neither railroad would build its depot at the town of Duck Creek.

Each of the railroads established its own depot, and two new towns were laid out. The one on the Santa Fe line was called "Embree" after a local doctor; and the one on the Missouri-Kansas-Texas line was called "New Duck Creek." When a fire destroyed a number of businesses in old Duck Creek early the next year, some of the residents moved to New Duck Creek and others moved to Embree.

A feud between the two towns soon developed. Both wanted the old Duck Creek settlers to move to their towns, both wanted a post office, and tempers were high. In an attempt to reconcile the two towns, a Judge Nash asked Congressman Joe Abbott to submit a bill to Congress to locate the post office halfway between the two towns. In 1888, approval was received, and the post office was established as requested. The new location was named "Garland" in honor of Attorney General, A. H. Garland, a friend of Judge Nash. The new location proved to be popular; and in 1891, Duck Creek and Embree joined to incorporate as "Garland."

A fire in 1899 destroyed about 30 of the businesses in Garland. However, the town was soon rebuilt—mostly of brick. Some of those brick stores are landmarks on the town square today.

In 1910, the population of Garland was about 965. Since then, it has grown to approximately 183,000. Garland has a manager-council form of municipal government, with the council consisting of a mayor and eight council members.

The Missouri-Kansas-Texas Railroad and the Atchison, Topeka & Santa Fe Railroad still serve the city. Present-day Garland is a center for industry and agriculture, and has more than 300 industrial plants, including E-Systems, Varo, Kraft, Continental Steel, Eckerd Drug offices, Globe Battery, Ingersoll Rand, Sherwin-Williams, and Resistol Hats.

Amber University and an East Texas State University branch are located here.

The Landmark Museum in Garland, housed in the former Santa Fe depot, features displays from early settlers' homes and businesses, and an antique rail car.

GATESVILLE

Gatesville was designated as the county seat for Coryall County in 1854 and was incorporated in 1875. It was named for Fort Gates.

It is located about 40 miles west of Waco and can be reached by U.S. Highway 84 or State Highway 36. Current population is 6,260. Mountain View and Gatesville prisons for women are located here. Fort Hood is a few miles south of Gatesville.

During the Civil War, a frontier regiment had its headquarters at Gatesville.

In 1882, a spur line of the St. Louis Southwestern Railway was run into Gatesville.

Still in use is the courthouse, built in 1898 of stone quarried in the area.

Local plants make boats, trailers, clothing, furniture and plastic medical products.

GEORGETOWN

Georgetown is the county seat of Williamson County and is located 28 miles north of Austin on Interstate 35 and State Highway 29. Its population is 16,000.

Georgetown was founded in 1848 on 174 acres of land donated for the townsite by George Washington Glasscock, Sr. and Thomas B. Huling. The new town was named for Mr. Glasscock.

The city was incorporated in 1886. From then until 1880 or so, Georgetown saw a lot of cattle. It was on a primary trail for cattle being driven up to the established trails—Western Trail, Dodge City Trail, Chisholm Trail, and Shawnee Trail—all of which originated north of Georgetown.

There are more than 50 Texas State Historical markers in Georgetown. Many of the early buildings have been fully restored; examples of early commercial buildings of Victorian architecture can be seen around Town Square. Three National Register Historic Districts showcase more than 180 historical buildings and homes.

Georgetown is an agri-business center; it has plants which make electric motors, structural products, and electronic products. Primary crops in the area are sorghum, wheat, corn, and cotton.

The Missouri-Kansas-Texas Railroad serves the area.

Georgetown is home to Southwestern University, the oldest university in Texas.

Lake Georgetown is a 1,200-acre lake with three fully developed recreational areas. Facilities include camper hook-ups, picnic shelters, boat ramps, a swimming beach and 16-mile hiking trail.

Other major attractions include Inner-Space Caverns and the Mar-Jon Candle Factory.

GIDDINGS

Giddings is the county seat of Lee County and is located at the intersection of U.S. Highways 77 and 290. It is 54 miles east of Austin and 109 miles west-northwest of Houston.

Giddings was established in 1872 and was named for Jabez Deming Giddings, pioneer citizen and stockholder in the Houston & Texas Central Railroad.

Giddings was settled primarily by Wendish Lutherans. The *Giddings Deutches Volksblatt,* the only Wendish-type newspaper in the United States, is published in Giddings.

In 1940, Giddings advertised itself as "the center of diversified farming and home of Texas' largest turkey-dressing plant," and had a population of 2,166.

Today, the Texas and New Orleans Railroad serves Giddings. Giddings' economy is based on oil field services and trucking; plants that make boats, furniture, and plastic products; livestock auctions and farming (peanuts, wheat, oats, cotton, corn, and hay). Minerals in the area include oil, gas, and lignite.

Giddings' population is now 3,950.

GILMER

Gilmer is located in northeast Texas and is the county seat of Upshur County. It is 23 miles north-northwest of Longview, 36 miles northeast of Tyler, and 120 miles east of Dallas. It can be reached by U.S. Highways 271 and State Highways 154, 155, and 300.

When Upshur County was organized by the Texas Legislature, the county seat was designted as "Gilmer" in honor of Capt. Thomas W. Gilmer who was Governor of Virginia in 1840 and Secretary of the Navy under President John Tyler in 1844.

Gilmer is located on the Old Cherokee Trace, a trail used by Indians. Gilmer was first situated, in 1846, north of Little Cypress Creek. However, because of frequent floods, the residents voted to move their community south of the creek to its present site. Gilmer has a city manager-council form of government.

Initially, the area's economy depended upon cotton. Then, in 1931, oil was discovered in southeastern Upshur County. Although the original East Texas oil field is dying, new oil and gas discoveries have been made in the county.

Gilmer now has plants making electrical conduits and fittings, ceramic bathroom accessories, and dresses. Much of Gilmer's economy still depends upon agriculture—beef, dairy cattle, hogs, poultry, timber, vegetable crops, hay, and peaches. Upshur County is one of the leading broiler and dairy-producing counties in Texas.

Gilmer is served by the St. Louis Southwestern Railroad.

At one time, Gilmer was a major yam-buying center so, in 1935, a Yamboree was held to publicize the yam. The East Texas Yamboree is still an annual event in Gilmer.

Gilmer's population is 6,400.

GLADEWATER

Gladewater is located in the northern part of East Texas at the intersection of U.S. Highways 80 and 271 and State Highway 135. It is thirteen miles west of Longview, 115 miles east of Dallas, and 26 miles northeast of Tyler. It is located mainly in Gregg County but also extends into Ushur County.

The original settlement in the area, located east of present-day Gladewater, was known as St. Clair. In 1872, St. Clair was moved to the present-day site of Gladewater and its name was changed. A spring-fed creek called the Glade ran nearby. Water from Glade Creek was used to fill a water tower for the use of the Texas & Pacific Railroad locomotives. The Union Pacific Railroad still serves Gladewater.

Gladewater, until 1930, was dependent upon farming and timber; then oil was discovered and Gladewater became another of the East Texas boom towns.

Lake Gladewater is nearby and furnishes the city's water supply. The lake is also used for fishing (bass and crappie), boating, swimming, and water skiing.

East Texas Gusher Days, celebrating Gladewater's oil field heritage, is held the first full weekend of May each year.

Another annual event is the Round-up Rodeo, held each June.

Gladewater has a city manager-council type of government. Its current population is 7,000. It is known as the "Antique Capital of East Texas."

GOLDTHWAITE

Goldthwaite is located not only near the geographic center of Mills County, of which it is the county seat, but also near the geographic center of Texas. It is about 89 miles west of Waco and

105 miles northwest of Austin on U.S. Highways 84 and 183 and State Highway 16.

Goldthwaite is another of the Texas towns founded by a railroad. In 1885, the Gulf, Colorado & Santa Fe Railroad completed its rail lines to a tent city on the site of present-day Goldthwaite. Railroad officials auctioned lots to begin a new town, and it was decided to name the town for Joe Goldthwaite, one of the railroad officials who was present at the auction.

In 1889, Goldthwaite was named the county seat of Mills County. A courthouse was built in 1890, burned in 1912, and a new courthouse built in 1913.

Goldthwaite's economy, from its beginnings, has been based on small stock farms and a few larger ranches. Sheep, beef cattle, goats, hogs, and horses are raised. Principal crops are small grains, sorghum, forage crops, pecans, and peanuts.

The Atchison, Topeka & Santa Fe Railroad serves the community today.

Goldthwaite's population is 1,783.

GONZALES

Gonzales was established in August, 1825, as the capital of Impresario Green Dewitt's Colony. This colony was located at the junction of the beautiful San Marcos and Guadalupe Rivers. It was the westernmost American settlement until after the close of the Texas Revolution. Major James Kerr drew the plans for the town and named it in honor of Don Rafael Gonzales, provisional governor of Coahuila and Texas. In July 1826, Indians attacked the settlement, killed one man, plundered and partially burned the cabins.

During 1835, unrest developed among colonists in Texas because of the over-bearing attitude of the Mexican government toward them. And as a frontier settlement, Gonzales was destined to play an important role in the resulting Texas Revolution.

The open break between Mexico and Gonzales colonists came as the result of a dispute over a small brass cannon which the Mexican authorities had given Gonzaleans in 1831 as protection against Indians. Later the Mexicans wanted it returned. First, a corporal and five Mexican soldiers were sent with an ox cart to get the cannon. When it was refused them, the Mexican officials at San Antonio sent Lieutenant Castaneda with 150 mounted soldiers to take the cannon.

When Castaneda appeared with his calvarymen on the river bank September 29, 1835, there were only eighteen men in the colony to defy their crossing. The men, now known as the "Immortal Eighteen," delayed acting on the General's demand for two days by claiming tht Alcalde Andrew Ponton was away. This tactic allowed the colonists to gather in Gonzales for the forthcoming conflict. Then on the morning of September 30th, Castaneda was met at the river by Regidor Joseph D. Clements, one of the eighteen, who read the following message: "I cannot, nor do I desire to deliver up the cannon . . . and only through force will we yield."

At 7 p.m. on Thursday, October 1st, the Texans, 50 of whom were mounted, crossed the river carrying the brass cannon. On the other side of the river they held a council of war and listened to a "patriotic address" by Rev. Smith.

When the early morning fog lifted on October 2, 1835, the Mexicans found themselves confronted by a force of Texans, commanded by Col. J. H. Moore and Lt. Col. J. W. E. Wallace, with the controversial cannon. Over the weapon proudly waved the new flag—a white background centered with a black replica of the cannon and emblazoned with the flaunting words: "Come And Take It."

Upon the first shot, the Mexican forces broke ranks and fled in terror, leaving one dead on the battlefield. The "first shot for Texas independence" had been fired and the first battle won on the second day of October 1835.

Colonel William B. Travis had been left in command of a small band of Texans in the Alamo at San Antonio. In February, 1836, Santa Anna entered Texas with an army and besieged the Alamo while a Constitution for the new Republic was being framed by the convention which had declared Texas' independence. A messenger arrived in Gonzales on the night of February 26th with Travis' dramatic appeal for help against overwhelming odds. Thirty-two men from Gonzales answered the call and succeeded in breaking through the Mexican lines on March 1st to enter the Alamo. The Alamo fell on March 6, 1836, and all 182 men were killed and their bodies burned by Santa Anna. These brave thirty-two men from Gonzales won fame and honor for all eternity. They will always be remembered as heroes in the Texas War of Independence. Four of these thirty-two have had counties in Texas named in their honor.

General Sam Houston arrived in Gonzales March 11, 1836, to take charge of gathering troops. The tragic news of the fall of the Alamo arrived with Mrs. Almaron Dickinson, her baby and two servants—the only survivors of the siege. Threatened with Santa Anna's advance, General Houston ordered a retreat. Gonzales was destroyed by fire and thus began the famous Run-Away-Scrape.

The names of those thirty-two men who volunteered to fight their way into the Alamo are George Kimball, Dr. John Sutherland, John Smith, Captain Albert M. Martin, David Cummings, Marcus Sewell, Jessie McCoy, Jonathan Lindley, Thomas Jackson, a sailor from Ireland, John Flanders, William Summers (who had been condemned to hang for murder), Lieutenant Robert White, Isaac Baker, John Cane, George Cottle, Squire Daymon, William Dearduff, Thomas Miller, Jacob Darst, John Davis, Andrew Kent, Charles Despallier, William Fishbaugh, Dolphin Floyd, George Tomlinson, George Neggan, James George, Isaac Millsaps, Johnny Kellog, John Gaston, two 16-year-olds, William King, and Galba Fuqua. The last two were the youngest men to fight in the Alamo. Note: Isaac Millsaps left a wife and seven children behind in Gonzales.

Gonzales is located centrally between Austin, San Antonio, and Victoria at the confluence of the San Marcos and Guadalupe Rivers within a nine-county trade area. The region is one of mild climate and natural beauty with many recreation activities available. The economy is largely agricultural-based with some light industry.

Gonzales is the county seat of Gonzales County which was named after the Mexican governor of Texas and Coahuila, Governor Rafael Gonzales. Gonzales is located in a rich agricultural area. The County of Gonzales is the fourth largest producer of agricultural products in the state of Texas. It produces $162 million worth of income annually. It is the top poultry and egg producing county in the state. It raises cattle and horses. The crops include grain, corn, peanuts, melons and pecans.

Highways radiate to Gonzales from all points of the compass. There are 10 highways that come into Gonzales. Gonzales is located 60 miles almost due east of San Antonio on U.S. Highway Alt. 90. The Southern Pacific Railroad serves the city.

The rainfall is 32.1 inches annually. This is an almost an ideal amount of rainfall for raising practically all crops, with the exception of rice which must be irrigated. The population of Gonzales is 7,900 as of 1989. The terrain in the area of Gonzales is rolling, with rich bottom soils along the Guadalupe and its tributaries, some sandy areas, and many oaks and pecans.

Gonzales is a most important city in Texas from a historical standpoint. Its name will always be honored and revered by Texans for the part that it played in the War for Independence with Mexico. Texans will never forget the Immortal Thirty-Two volunteers who answered Travis' call for help. They had to fight their way into the Alamo to stand by their fellow Texans and go to almost-certain death. The words 'valor' and 'bravery' can't begin to adequately describe such noble actions.

GRAHAM

Graham is located in North Central Texas and is the county seat of Young County. Graham is 61 miles south of Wichita Falls, 103 miles northeast of Abilene, and 98 miles northwest of Fort Worth. It can be reached by U.S. Highway 380 and State Highways 16, 67, and 251.

In 1871, Capt. A. B. Gant sold his Peter's Colony land on the east bank of Salt Creek, including a salt plant, to Col. Edwin Smith Graham and his brother, Gustavus Adolphus Graham, both of Kentucky. The Graham brothers planned and platted a town to be built on their land—a town that would be ideal in every way. The town square, called Commerce Park, had giant oak trees; the town square was surrounded by large blocks with wide streets; and the building lots all faced due north, south, east, and west.

All legal transactions at that time had to be recorded at Jacksboro (28 miles northeast) in Jack County, as there was no county organization in Young territory. Most travelers to Jacksboro used the Butterfield Overland Stage route which ran from Jacksboro to Fort Belknap (10 miles northwest of Graham). The stage road, however, attracted Indians and was the site of many Indian raids.

Mail came from Weatherford (35 miles southeast of Graham),

a more southern and safer route. The Graham brothers used the mails to attract settlers as well as buyers of their salt products.

Modern Graham has a population of 9,170. Its plants make computer products, apparel, fences, fiberglass products, aluminum, and floral products. Nearby recreation centers include Possum Kingdom Lake and Lake Graham, both of which offer fishing, boating, and water sports.

Fort Belknap State Park is nearby.

GRANBURY

Granbury is picturesquely situated on Lake Granbury. It is the county seat of Granbury, which is one of the smallest counties in Texas. The town area was settled in 1871, by Thomas Lambert, who united it with a settlement called Stockton to form the nucleus of Granbury. Granbury Square is on the National Register of Historic Places.

Granbury has a population of 5,001. It is located 33 miles southwest of Ft. Worth. It is located on U.S. Highway 37 and State Highway 144 and F M Highways 4, and 51. It is on the northwest side of Granbury Lake on the Brazos River.

A nuclear power plant is located between Granbury and Glen Rose in Somervell County.

The city has a mayor-council form of city government. The annual average rainfall is 31.8 inches, which is ample for the crops raised which are peanuts, pecans, and grains. 3,000 acres in the county are irrigated. Hood County is the largest producer of pecans in the state.

The Santa Fe Railroad serves the city. The nearest commercial airport is the Dallas-Ft. Worth International Airport, approximately 42 miles to the northeast.

Attractions for tourists are: Action State Historical Site; Granbury Opera House; Granbury Queen, a 73-foot replica of Mississippi River paddlewheeler that cruises on Lake Granbury; Nutt House, a historic inn; and Hood County Jail, an Old West-type jail used as offices since restoration. Tours are available.

The city gets its name from General Hiram B. Granberry.

GRAND PRAIRIE

Grand Prairie is part of the Dallas-Fort Worth metroplex. It can be reached by Interstates 20 and 30, as well as State Highway 12 and Farm-to-Market Road 1382. It is situated mainly in Dallas County, but part of it extends into Tarrant County.

A. M. Dechman was in charge of the commissary at Fort Belknap during the Civil War. While returning to Fort Belknap with supplies from Jacksonville, Texas, one of his wagons was damaged in the vicinity of present-day Grand Prairie. He traded the broken wagon, an ox team, and $200 in Confederate money for 239 ½ acres of land in the area. He later platted a townsite to be named Dechman and offered land to the Texas & Pacific Railway Co. (who were extending their line between Dallas and Fort Worth) provided that a depot be established at the site of Dechman.

In 1876, the Texas & Pacific Railway completed its lines between Dallas and Fort Worth.

Sometime after 1876, the town of Dechman evidently became known as Grand Prairie because, when it incorporated in 1909, it was in the name of Grand Prairie. The name was probably chosen because it was descriptive of the area; the Austin Map of Texas labeled this part of the state as the "grand prairie."

Grand Prairie's economy now centers around aircraft, aerospace, concrete, and chemical manufacturing. The Texas Sports Hall of Fame is located in the city.

In 1974, Grand Prairie was designated an "All American City." Its population is 71,462.

GRAND SALINE

The city of Grand Saline grew from a primitive salt works established in 1845. It is now the site of one of the largest salt plants in the United States. The salt dome under the city is about 1.5 miles across and some 16,000 feet thick. It could supply the world's need for salt for 20,000 years.

The city is located in Van Zandt County. It is 65 miles due east of Dallas. It is served by U.S. Highway 80 and State Highway 110 and FM 17. It is just south of the Sabine River. It is served by the Union Pacific Railroad. The nearest commercial airport is Love Field in North Dallas, 65 miles to the west. The Dallas-Ft. Worth International Airport is approximately 78 miles to the west.

The town got its name from the word "saline," which means consisting of salt.

The city has a population of 3,200. It has a mayor-council form of city government.

The area around Grand Saline is a rich agricultural region. The county of Van Zandt has an agricultural income of $51 million, which is almost double the agricultural income of the average Texas county; 70% of this income is from cattle, hogs, and dairy products. The crops are nursery stock, vegetables, grain, cotton and hay. The average annual rainfall is 43.1 inches. The elevation is 550 feet.

GRAPEVINE

Grapevine is located in the center of the Southwest Metroplex at the intersection of U.S. Highway 114 and U.S. Highway 26 in the northeast corner of Tarrant County, only 21 miles northwest of Dallas and 19 miles northeast of Fort Worth. Grapevine is approximately two miles from Dallas/Fort Worth International Airport.

Grapevine has a population of 28,500. The annual growth rate is projected at 11.2%. The size of the city is 32 square miles. The altitude of the city is 780 feet. The average rainfall is 32.3 inches.

Grapevine has an excellent tax rate, which is broken down as follows:

City	$ .44000
School	.85000
County	.11772
Hospital	.11125
Junior College	.03153
Right of Way	.00679
Total	$1.55891

The city is governed by a council-manager form of government. Seven council members are elected every third year. The city manager is hired by the council and he is a full time, professional executive.

The City of Grapevine is one of the oldest communities in North Texas with the first settlers arriving by wagon train as early as 1844. The city received its name from both its geographical location in the Grape Vine Prairie and near Grape Vine Springs and from the wild mustang grapes that grew abundantly in the area. The city itself was laid out in 1854 and incorporated in 1907.

On October 9, 1844, Sam Houston and commissioners representing the Republic of Texas met with members of the Comanche,

Keechi, Waco, Delaware and several other Indian tribes at Tah-Wah-Karro Creek, also known as Grape Vine Springs, and signed a treaty of "peace, friendship and commerce." This treaty was signed by the President of the Texas Republic, Anson Jones, on February 5, 1845. Among the interpreters participating in the treaty was Jesse Chisolm, for whom the Chisolm Trail was named.

The earliest wagon trains to bring settlers to the Grape Vine Prairie arrived as early as 1844. A store known as Hallford's was operating northeast of present-day Grapevine in that year.

Archibald Franklin Leonard and his father-in-law, Ambrose Foster, arrived with the Missouri Colony from Platte County, Missouri in 1845, each settling on a 640-acre section of land with adjoining boundaries. Mr. Ambrose opened a store on the land which would have been located approximately where Wall Street crosses North Main Street today. The town square was built near that area and is the site on which the restored Torian Cabin is standing at this time.

The Baylor Medical Center is located at Grapevine. This meets the health care needs of northeast Tarrant County.

GREENVILLE

Greenville is located in North Texas near the geographic center of Hunt County, of which it is the county seat. It is 52 miles northeast of Dallas and is located on Interstate 30, U.S. Highways 69 and 380, and State Highways 24 and 66. Greenville's current population is 22,161.

The First Legislature of Texas created Hunt County, and it was aproved in 1846 by Texas governor, James Pinckney Henderson. Thereupon, M. H. Wright donated land for the county seat out of his homestead tract of 640 acres. The Act creating Hunt County first called for the county seat to be named "Pinckneyville" in honor of Governor Henderson. The name of "Greenville" was later substituted, perhaps by Governor Henderson himself in honor of his close friend, General Thomas Jefferson Green. Greenville's official founding is generally listed as 1850 since it was not until then that the title to the land was perfected and the deed drawn.

Rail service was established in the area in the 1880's. Today, Greenville is served by the Kansas City Southern, St. Louis Southwestern, and Missouri-Kansas-Texas Railroads.

Greenville soon became known as the "Cotton Capitol of Texas."

In addition to a large output of cotton in the area, the largest inland cotton compress in the world was located in Greenville.

After cotton declined, the city's economy became more diversified with farming and industry (manufacturing of clothing, electronics, confections, and aerospace and communications equipment). E-Systems, Rubbermaid, Dow Consumer Products, Imperial Chemical, Wing Industries, Haggar, Tenneco, and Longmile Rubber (Goodyear) all have major manufacturing facilities in Greenville. The Mary of Puddin' Hill store is known nationwide for its fruitcakes, candy, and gourmet foods.

Lake Tawakoni, Lake Fork, Lake Lavon, and Lake Ray Hubbard are all nearby for fishing, boating, water sports, and recreational use.

Audie Murphy grew up nearby and enlisted for military service in Greenville. Of interest is the Audie Murphy Room in the Walworth Library.

GROESBECK

Groesbeck is the county seat of Limestone County. It is located 40 miles east of Waco and 95 miles south of Dallas. It is on State Highway 14 going north to Mexia, and State Highway 164 going to Waco, and Farm-to-Market Road 1245.

Groesbeck is served by the Southern Pacific Railroad, which runs north and south. The forerunner of the Southern Pacific Railroad was the Texas Central, which was built through Groesbeck in 1870. The first name of Groesbeck was Springfield. It was located just north on the Navasota River. The railroad bypassed Springfield and the settlers moved to locations along the railroad.

The town of Groesbeck was named for Abraham Groeskeeck, an early railroad builder. It was founded in 1871. It has a population of 4,200. It is located in the Navasota River Valley, which is a rich agricultural area. The Navasota River flows due south and has its confluence with the Brazos River near Navasota.

There are a number of important historical landmarks in the area. They include: Restored Fort Parker; Confederate Reunion Grounds; and a State Historical Site.

Old Fort Parker State Historic Site is a reconstructed fort which pays tribute to the Parker family. It is located about twelve miles north of Groesbeck on SH14.

The Parkers and other members of their church came to Texas

from Crawford County, Illinois in 1833. Elder Parker and three of his sons, Silas, James and Benjamin began in December of 1833 to clear the land and to construct "Parkers Fort."

The large stockade was built of split cedars buried three feet in the ground and extending up some twelve feet. Two-story block houses were erected at opposite corners, and within the fort were two rows of log cabins. The Parker families and other members of their group moved into the fort in March, 1834. Except for a short evacuation of the fort during the winter of 1836, life was reasonably secure, particularly after Texas gained its independence in the Battle of San Jacinto on April 21, 1936.

A famous story is of the Comanche Indians raiding the stockade where several farm families lived, in May of 1836, and killing five settlers and capturing Cynthia Ann Parker, then nine years old. She lived all her life with the Comanche Indians and became the wife of Chief Peta Nacona. They had three children: two sons, Quanah and Pecos, and one daughter, Topasanah. Cynthia and her daughter were captured and taken from the Comanches, leaving Quanah and Pecos, who were in their early teens. Quanah became a Comanche chief and was a wise warrior defending Comanche territory. After the Comanches were placed in a reservation, Quanah became determined to help Indians adapt to the white man's ways. Cynthia was never happy away from the Comanche life.

The City Government is a general law type of government. They have a mayor and six councilmen.

There are a number of fine universities and colleges close to Groesbeck. The distance to these institutions are:

Baylor University	40 miles
Texas A & M University	60 miles
Texas State Technical Institute	40 miles
Paul Quinn	40 miles
McLennan Community College	40 miles
Navarro Junior College	40 miles

The Groesbeck area is a rich farming country. They raise cattle, horses, hogs, sorghum, cotton, hay, oats, peaches, wheat, corn, peanuts, and pecans.

GROVES

Groves is in East Texas in Jefferson County, and is just north of Port Arthur. It can be reached by State Highways 73, 87, and 347.

The first settlers in the area arrived in 1886. The main occupation in the area in the early 1900's was rice farming. A local tale tells of a group of rice farmers who drilled a water well but, to their disgust, struck oil. They filled in the well and drilled elsewhere for water. That is why Beaumont, rather than Groves, became the Spindletop city.

The town is named for Asa B. Groves who bought a 358-acre tract of land on which 6,000 pecan trees had been planted in 1910. Mr. Groves then subdivided the land for residential homesites.

In 1952, Groves was incorporated as a township. It has a city manager-council form of government. Its current population is 17,090.

Groves is situated on the banks of Lake Sabine. Power boating, sailing, fishing, and crabbing are popular activities. The Gulf of Mexico is less than 20 miles away.

A Pecan Festival is held each year in September.

HALLSVILLE

Hallsville is in Harrison County in deep northeast Texas. It is twelve miles west of Marshal and 128 miles east of Dallas. It is located in the East Texas piney woods belt. The population is 3,800. The city is served by the Union Pacific Railroad. It is located on U.S. Highway 80 and is north of U.S. Highway 20, which runs east and west. It is also served by Farm-to-Market Road 450.

The city has a number of industries that are in the gas and oil processing business. It has lumber mills, pottery mills and a variety of manufacturing facilities. The population of the city is 3,800.

In the general area, there are two beautiful lakes that are famous for fishing. The Lake of the Pines is located north, 28 miles and Cattle Lake is located northeast, 34 miles.

Hallsville and the Marshall area east of the city, is the center of a large number of manufacturing plants. In the county, there are a total of 84 manufacturing plants employing 4,700 employes.

The county is not a large agricultural income county, because the greatest part of it is heavily timbered. The county has an agricultural income of $18 million, which is about 50% of the average county income from agriculture; 90% of this income comes from cattle, hogs, and poultry. The crops include wheat, oats, grain, corn, hay and timber.

HALTOM CITY

Haltom City is located in the geographic center of Tarrant County in North Texas. The northwest, west, and south sides of Haltom City touch Fort Worth; on the east, it adjoins Richland Hills and North Richland Hills; and on the northeast, it adjoins Watauga. Big and Little Fossil Creeks bisect the city.

Haltom City can be reached by U.S. Highway 377, State Highways 121 and 183, Northeast Loop 820 (Interstate 20), and Loop 452 (Grapevine Highway 26).

Haltom Village was founded in 1932 and was named for a Fort Worth jeweler, G. W. Haltom, whose family's ranch property comprised much of the new community.

Haltom City was incorporated in 1949 and elected a home-rule charter type of government. Current population is 29,014.

The city has a mayor-council form of city government. The population is 1600.

It is served by the Union Pacific Railroad.

HAMILTON

Hamilton is located on Pecan Creek and is the county seat of Hamilton County. It can be reached by U.S. Highway 281 and State Highways 22 and 36. It is 61 miles northwest of Temple, 105 miles southwest of Fort Worth, and 70 miles west of Waco.

The first residents to the area arrived in 1855 and settled around Pecan Creek.

The 7th Texas Legislature, in 1858, created Hamilton County, specifying that both the county and the county seat were to be named for Gen. James Hamilton, the South Carolina governor who put up $216,000 in gold to finance the Texas struggle for independence from Mexico.

Livestock raising (cattle, hogs, sheep, goats and poultry) and farming (sorghum, grains, cotton, hay, and pecans) are important components of Hamilton's economy. Local plants make garments, wood molding, steel products, and machine parts.

Deer, quail, dove, and ducks attract hunters to the area.
Hamilton's current population is 3,189.

HAMLIN

Hamlin is located in the Northwest Corner of Jones County. Part of the town is in Fisher County, which is to the west. The town is located on U.S. Highway 83, on State Highway 92 and FM Highways 57, 126, 340, 1636, 1835, 2192 and 2702.

Hamlin is 41 miles northwest of Abilene and 144 miles west of Fort Worth. The Santa Fe Railroad serves the city.

The town has an elevation of 1,700 feet and has an annual rainfall of 23.3 inches. This is barely enough rain for some crops. There is no irrigation in the county, because the county does not overlay the Ogallala Aquifer.

The surrounding area is primarily ranching country. Beef cattle, hogs, horses, sheep are raised. The crops are cotton, wheat and milo maize.

The population of Hamlin is 3,280. It has a mayor, five aldermen and a city secretary.

Hamlin was named after a Mr. Tom Hamlin, who was a prominent landowner in that area. Hamlin had its humble beginnings in the year of 1907 when it was incorporated. The site for the town was selected by the Kansas City, Mexico and Orient railroad at a point on California Creek, first, on account of the supply of water afforded, and secondly, on account of the vast expanse of fertile prairie that surrounds it. Almost a thousand sections awaited the coming of the farmer to turn its carpet of green into long rows of cotton and corn, milo maize and kaffir corn, and into broad fields of waving grain.

Within a short time the Texas Central Railroad began its westward extension to Rotan, and crossed the Kansas City, Mexico and Orient Railway at Hamlin. It did not take long for the people to see the circumstances. Here was a great section of rich country just made accessible to the farmer, who might have his choice of taking his produce to the northern markets by way of the Kansas City, Mexico and Orient Railway, or to the eastern markets and to the gulf ports by way of the Texas Central. The building of Kansas City, Mexico and Orient Railway northward and the western extension of the Texas central opened rich fields for the wholesaler and he was not slow to take advantage of the opportunity.

Lands so easy to cultivate and to be had cheaply and on long time payments, proved attractive to farmers living in communities where farm lands were high. They were rapidly taken up and put in cultivation.

Hamlin was never a village. It became a town almost overnight. Its phenomenal growth soon demanded city government, and it became incorporated in 1907.

In the spring of 1910, Col. Morgan Jones, the veteran railroad builder of the Fort Worth and Denver Railroad, the Wichita Valley Railroad, and the Abilene and Southern Railroad, visited Hamlin. Col. Jones recognized that Hamlin was destined to be a great distributing point. The Hamlin people understood Col. Jones' ability as a railroad builder, hence there was not much time wasted between the two, with the result that the Abilene and Southern Railway was extended into Hamlin in October.

Hamlin is an industrial center; it has a cotton compress, a sixty-ton cotton oil mill, twenty-ton ice plant, a cement plaster mill, an elevator, cotton gins with thirteen hundred and fifty saws, or a capacity of two hundred bales per day, electric light plant, ice cream factory and bottling works.

HARKER HEIGHTS

Harker Heights is located in Bell County in Central Texas on U.S. Highway 190. It is seventeen miles west of Temple, 69 miles north of Austin, and just east of Fort Hood.

Pinkney R. Cox and Harley Kern owned 400 acres of land about 2 miles east of Killeen, which they operated as a hog farm in the 1940's. Their dream, however, was to build a town on their property. Toward that end, in 1955, they created a water control and improvement district to secure future water resources and, in 1957, Cox began subdividing the land and selling lots (Mr. Kern became too ill to participate in the selling and died that same year.) In 1960, a modern water system was completed.

The name "Harker Heights" was chosen for the town in honor of Harley Kern ("Har" from Harley and "ker" from Kern). It was incorporated as a town in 1960 and officially changed to a city in 1963.

In 1971, Harker Heights adopted a home rule type of city government to replace the general law it previously had.

Santa Fe Railroad serves the city.

Balton Lake-Stillhouse and Hollow Lake both are nearby.
Its present population is 16,500.

HARLINGEN

Harlingen is the county seat of Cameron County in the lower Rio Grande Valley, 28 miles northwest of Brownsville and 15 miles north of the Texas-Mexico border. It can be reached by U.S. Highways 77 and 83. Harlingen's population is 43,543.

Lon C. Hill Sr. was instrumental in the development of Harlingen. He moved to the area in 1900, gave up his law practice, and worked to colonize the Valley. When the St. Louis, Brownsville & Mexico Railroad began construction of a rail line to the Valley, Hill was asked to select a name for the new townsite planned by the railroad.

The irrigation canals in the Valley reminded Hill of Holland, which was famous for its canals. When looking at a map of Holland, he noticed a town named "Van Harlingen," and he decided that "Harlingen" would be a good name for a town. When he announced his choice to Col. Uriah Lott, President of the railroad, Col. Lott was enthusiastic—his grandmother's surname was Van Harlingen and the town in Holland had been named for her family.

During the early 1900's, the railroad conductors usually referred to Harlingen as "Six-shooter Junction" because of the frequent law and order problems experienced there. It was said there were 350 people in town and 351 six-shooters.

Present-day Harlingen is an agribusiness and tourist center, as well as a wholesale and distribution center. The area is served by the Southern Pacific and Missouri Pacific Railroads.

Of particular interest is the Confederate Air Force Flying Museum, featuring World War II memorabilia and the world's largest collection of World War II combat aircraft maintained in flyable condition. The city hosts an annual Air Show every October.

Also of interest is the Rio Grande Valley Historical Museum Complex, including the home (built in 1904) of Lon C. Hill, the city's founder; "The Paso Real Stagecoach Inn;" and Harlingen's first hospital (built in 1923).

HEARNE

Hearne is steeped in Texas History. The Brazos River Valley produced many volunteers for the Revolutionary War against Mexico. Hearne is located near the Brazos River in Robertson

County. Hearne is at the crossing of the Union Pacific Railroad and the Southern Railroad. It is at the crossroads of State Highway 6 and U.S. Highway 79.

The average annual rainfall is 35.8 inches, which is ideal for any crop except rice. 15,000 acres of the land in Brazos County are irrigated. The altitude of Hearne is 300 feet. The population is 5,600. The main agricultural income in the area is from beef cattle, dairy products, hogs, horses, and poultry. Crops include cotton, sorghum, small grains, watermelons, and corn.

The history of Hearne is most interesting. On the morning of March 3, 1836, down the Brazos River at the village of Washington, a group of men from the towns and districts of the Mexican province of Texas were signing a Declaration of Independence, which had been voted unanimously the previous day. This was the beginning of the Texas Revolution against the Government of Mexico. Three days after the signing the Declaration of Independence, at Washington on the Brazos, the Alamo fell. The one hundred eighty-two brave men who fought there had lost their lives.

As the 1840's moved Texas into statehood, people were settling in the area around Hearne faster than the Comanches could kill them out. There were three towns then—Wheelock, Franklin & Stagger's Point—within a day's ride, and Sullivan's Bluff was across the river in Milam County. The land in the Brazos River bottoms was the richest in the state. The travelers from all other states who had come to Texas were not looking for a cornpatch and cabin land, but for cotton land. Texas was the cotton kingdom's last frontier.

In 1852 the Hearne's of Lowdes County, Alabama arrived in nearby Wheelock. Christopher Columbus Hearne built a large brick home and the entire numerous Hearne clan lived under this roof for a while. The Hearnes were planters—with capital, experience, and a good workforce of Negro servants. Christopher Hearne, acting for the family, acquired the lands of the former Ruiz Grant. The Hearnes were ready to move whatever needed moving aside to find their plantations. The Hearnes were spearheaders. Other planters could come. But regardless of ownership, a part of the Brazos country would always be called the Hearne Bottoms.

The Houston and Texas Central Railroad (H&TC) began building northward from Houston in 1833. The Hearnes needed a convenient shipping point for cotton. So Christopher offered the company a townsite if its route would pass his family's land. His offer was accepted.

By 1860 the tracks had reached Millican in Brazos County (near Bryan) and the right-of-way marched past Ebenezer's home in the Little Brazos Upland. In the survey maps "Hearne Station" lay 3 miles from his front door and a mile below Brown's Spring. A new town was waiting to be born. It waited eight years.

War broke out in 1861 and Texas joined the Confederacy. It was 1867 before the H&TC was revived and construction resumed on the track. The same year Christopher Hearne died, but his widow Mary Ellen deeded the townsite to the railroad company and in April of 1868 Hearne Station became the railhead.

In the next decade the International and Great Northern Railroad (I&GN), connecting Palestine with San Antonio, crossed the H&TC tracks one mile above the latter's depot—at Brown Springs.

Hearne Station was incorporated, after 3 lively years of existence on April 11, 1871.

The Golden Age of the big plantation dawned in the Brazos River Valley in 1870, even though there were no longer any slaves to work the land. At that time the clearing of the Brazos bottoms had been virtually completed. The increased cotton production was reflected by Hearne's new gins, compressors and a cotton seed oil mill.

Hearne has survived many catastrophes such as floods, fires, depressions, and wars. In spite of these troubles, she has managed to grow and prosper.

HEBBRONVILLE

Hebbronville is the county seat of Jim Hogg County. The city has a population of 4500. The average annual rainfall is 20.8 inches. This is insufficient rainfall for most crops; 2,000 acres of land are irrigated. Jim Hogg is a large county but has only about 50% of the agricultural income of the average Texas County. Hebbronville is located on State Highways 16, 285 and 359. It is 170 miles south of San Antonio and 55 miles east of Laredo on Highway 160. The city is incorporated and does not have a Chamber of Commerce.

The city was named after a rancher and land developer named Hebbron.

The Texas-Mexican Railroad goes through Hebbronville. It runs from Laredo to Corpus Christi.

The city is a market center for ranching and oil and gas operations.

The area around Hebbronville is a heavy rolling plain. The elevation is 325 feet. The terrain is covered with heavy bush. The soil is a sandy loam with acres of white blow soil; 2,000 acres are irrigated.

This is a ranching country. There is a considerable amount of oil and gas production.

The city is the center of white tail deer and quail hunting.

HENDERSON

Henderson is located in central East Texas and can be reached by U.S. Highways 79 and 259 and State Highways 43, 64, and 323.

In 1843, the 1st Legislature of Texas passed an Act creating Rusk County. Some of the land for the site of the new county seat was donated by William B. Ochiltree in 1845, provided that the town be named for his friend, J. Pinckney Henderson, the first governor of Texas.

The county's income is based on lignite coal, oil and gas, agriculture (cattle, horses, hay, and watermelon), forestry, and light industry.

Henderson's brick plant uses local clay deposits, which have been termed the best ceramic materials available in Texas.

Lakes Stroker, Martin, Murvaul, Tyler, Palestine, and Cherokee are all nearby, and are available for fishing, boating, and camping.

Henderson's current population is 11,473.

HENRIETTA

Henrietta is the county seat of Clay County. It is located on U.S. Highways 287 and 82, and State Highways 148 which leads into Oklahoma, and the farm to market Highways 1197 and 2847. The little Wichita River runs through the northern edge of the city. The population was 3250 in 1989. The elevation is 980 feet. The average annual rainfall is 31.4 inches. This is sufficient to support a good agricultural industry. The area around Henrietta raises beef cattle, dairy cattle, hogs, wheat, cotton and maize.

The Burlington Northern Railroad runs through the city.

The county borders on the Red River. It was named in honor of Henry Clay. The city was given the name of Henrietta, which is the feminine form of Henry.

Clay County was organized December 24, 1857. The county was settled by only a few ranchers prior to the Civil War because of roaming bands of Indians who preyed on the settlers.

The city is located eighteen miles east-southeast of Wichita Falls on U.S. Highway 287 and 83 miles northwest of Fort Worth on U.S. Highway 287. Lake Arrowhead on the Little Wichita River is located just ten miles southwest of Henrietta.

The area around Henrietta produces a considerable amount of oil and gas, and crushed stone for highway and street construction.

In 1860 only a few settlers dared venture into the region. With the return of troops to the region after the Civil War, settlers once again began to drift into the rich grasslands and farming region. What followed was a dark page in history—range wars. A conflict broke out between the ranchers and farmers over barbed wire fence in the open range country. The indomitable will of ranchers and farmers fueled a serious range war. The conflict was not resolved until the state legislature stepped in and passed laws making fence cutting a serious felony.

Henrietta was organized about 1875. It is the shopping center for a sizable agricultural area.

HEREFORD

Hereford is located in the Texas Panhandle at the intersection of U.S. Highways 60 and 385, and can also be reached by State Highways 1055 and 1058. It is 48 miles southwest of Amarillo and approximately 35 miles east of the Texas-New Mexico state line.

Deaf Smith County was organized in 1890, and the exact center of the county was the location chosen for a county seat. The county seat was called LaPlata. However, in 1898, the Pecos & Northern Texas Railroad from Amarillo to Roswell, New Mexico, was scheduled to cross the southeast corner of Deaf Smith County. The residents of LaPlata decided they would rather live near the railroad, and they voted to move their town. Even the courthouse and jail were loaded onto wagons and moved. Because of the deep blue color of the deep parts of nearby Tierra Blanca Creek, the new town was called "Blue Water." That same year, G. R. Jowell moved a herd of Hereford cattle to the area. A suggestion was made that the town be renamed after the cattle and, in 1906, Hereford was legally incorporated as a city.

Hereford's population is now 15,853. Its economy centers around livestock and agriculture. Principal crops in the area include sorghum, wheat, oats, barley, sugar beets, corn, cotton, and onions. The city has sugar refining and food processing plants.

HILLSBORO

Hillsboro is the county seat of Hill County. It is located on Interstate-35 and is 33 miles north of Waco and 40 miles southeast of Fort Worth. It can also be reached by U.S. Highways-77 and 81, as well as State Highways 22 and 171.

Hill County was organized in 1853. Hillsboro and Hill County were named for G. W. Hill, a Republic of Texas official. Hillsboro has a home rule type of government (mayor and council).

At the turn of the century, Hillsboro was the center of the second largest cotton-producing county in the world. Three railroads made Hillsboro a large trade-center, attracting merchants, businesses, and customers. Only one railroad remains—the Missouri-Kansas-Texas.

The Hill County Courthouse, built in 1890; the M-K-T Depot, built in 1881; and the Hill County Jail, built in 1893 are all listed on the National Register of Historic Places. The depot and jail are now museums.

In 1981, restoration work began on some of the old buildings and businesses as part of the Main Street Project. Tourism is becoming more important to Hillsboro's economy. The Bond's Alley Art Festival is always held the second weekend of June, and the Bond's Alley Holiday Bazaar is always held the weekend preceding Thanksgiving. These are chief benefactors of historical restorations and the city library.

Although Hillsboro declined in the 1950's and 1960's, its population now is 8,500.

Crops raised in the area include cotton, grains, and peanuts.

Beef and dairy cattle are also an important industry. Hillsboro is home to Hill Junior College.

Aquilla Lake is nearby. A bass tournament for fishermen is an annual event.

HITCHCOCK

Hitchcock is located in Galveston County on State Highway 6 and Farm-to-Market Road 2004. It is about 40 miles southeast of Houston and 14 miles northwest of Galveston.

Hitchcock was probably settled about 1845 and, by 1875, the Gulf, Colorado & Santa Fe Railroad was laying track in the area. Mrs. L. M. Hitchcock agreed to donate land to the railroad if they would name the town "Hitchcock" in honor of her deceased husband.

In its early days, Hitchcock was known for the finest sweet potatoes grown in the South and for the largest onions grown anywhere.

Hitchcock was a major cattle area and, at one time, the Tacquard family had 8,000 "Big Red Cows" on their ranch (now the Reitmeyer Ranch).

Hitchcock's population is 6,103. It is served by the Atchison, Topeka & Santa Fe Railroad.

HONDO

Hondo is the county seat of Medina County and is located 39 miles west of San Antonio on U.S. Highway 90. State Highway 173 passes on the eastern border of Hondo.

"Hondo," a Spanish word meaning "deep," was the name given by Alonzo de Leon (commander of a Spanish expedition) in 1689 when he crossed a deep valley with its high-banked stream. Hondo Creek runs north and east of the present-day site of Hondo.

Permanent settlers arrived at the Hondo River about 1840. In 1881, the Southern Pacific Railroad built a rail line and, in 1882, a railroad station. That same year, a post office was established and the town was officially "Hondo."

Hondo now has a city manager-council type of city government and has a population of 6,800.

Hondo is located in an area of brushy, rolling terrain which is ideal for turkey, dove, quail, and deer hunting. Hondo's economy is based on cattle ranching and feeding, farming (corn, grain sorghum, and truck crops), tourism, oil, and manufacturing (bathroom fixtures, brick and tile, metal buildings, oil field tanks, and aviation related industries. The Hondo Municipal Airport is the site of the USAF Flight Screening Program.

The Southern Pacific Railroad still serves Hondo and the surrounding area.

Of interest are the Medina County Museum and antique stores. The Medina County Fair is held the third weekend of September each year.

Hondo's famous sign, "This is God's Country, Please don't drive through it like Hell," was erected in 1930 to slow down speeding roadsters. Since then, it has been well photographed and has appeared in publications worldwide and on national television. Postcards of the sign are distributed free.

HOUSTON

Houston was named after Sam Houston, General of the Texas Army that won independence from Mexico, and the first President of the Republic of Texas. The city is the largest in Texas and fourth largest in the nation. It has experienced phenomenal growth since a small river boat landing was established on Buffalo Bayou by the Allen Brothers in August of 1836. Today, the metropolis is the industrial and financial hub for much of the State. It is the home of NASA's Lyndon B. Johnson Space Center. Houston is served by many highways including the main Interstate Highway 10, which runs east and west and Interstate 45, which runs north and south. It has U.S. Highways 59, 75, 90, 90-A, 290 and 610. It has State Highways 2, 3, 4, 5, 6, 7, 9, 11, 34, 184, 225 and 288, and numerous paved farm-to-market highways.

The city has a number of railroads which includes the Southern Pacific, the Union Pacific, Missouri-Kansas-Texas, Burlington Northern, the Galveston-Houston and Henderson and the Port Railway.

Houston has two major airports, which are the William P. Hobby Airport, southeast of the City, and the Houston Intercontinental Airport, north of the city. It is the third largest air center in the United States.

The Port of Houston is the second largest port in the United States, in terms of volume of ocean traffic moving in and out of the United States.

The Texas Medical Center was organized in 1945. It is an immense complex of hospitals, medical schools and research institutions, whose purpose is total coordination of health education, patient care and research. More than a score of buildings occupy 355 acres in the south part of Houston near midtown. Still expanding, the Texas Medical Center in a typical year will accept more than 150,000 patients and handle more than 1,500,000 outpatient visits and train some 6,000 students in all aspects of Medical Science. Major units now operating at Texas Medical Center include the Hermann Hospital, the Baylor University College of Medicine, the Methodist Hospital, the Shriners Hospital for crippled children, the Texas Children's Hospital, St. Luke Epsicopal Hospital, Ben Taub General Hospital, the University of Texas at Houston (composed of M. D. Anderson Hospital and Tumor Institute, Dental Branch including the Dental Science Institute, the School of Public Health and Graduate School of Bio-Medical Science), the City of Houston Department of Public Health, the Houston Speech and Hearing Center, the Houston Academy and Medicine Library, the Texas Institute for Rehabilitation and Research, the Texas Research Institute for Mental Sciences, the Institute of Religion, Methodist Hospital, Orthopedic, Cardiovascular Clinical Research Center, the Institute of Opthamology, the Jewish Institute for Medical Research, Texas Heart Institute and the Texas Women's College of Nursing.

The petrochemical industry production is one of the industries in Houston that is presently booming. Houston has numerous refineries, chemical plants, fertilizer plants, and many allied facilities that are strung all along the Houston Ship Channel. Houston was incorporated on August 30, 1836. It is a city with a strong mayor-city council form of government.

Harris County is a huge county, having 1,732 sq. miles, which is almost twice the size of the average Texas county. It has an agricultural income of $72,000,000 annually. This income is derived from raising livestock and crops, such as soybeans, milo maize, rice, corn, cotton, and hay. For many years Houston's economy was based to a very great extent on the petroleum industry. When the price of oil fell a few years back, the city of Houston suffered greatly. Today, Houston is coming back. There are some encouraging statistics. At least 35,000 jobs were added in Houston in 1988, helping unemployment drop to 5.4 percent in December. In June, 1986, the figure was 12.9 percent. Foreclosures in January of 1989 were down 50 percent from twelve months earlier. Sales tax revenues in 1988, were up 22.5 percent over the prior year and housing permits were up 23.4 percent.

On the other hand, some 26% of the total office space in this city was vacant as of July, 1989. A whopping 44,000,000 sq. feet, and the city sales tax increase in 1988 was largely due to state mandated expansion of the tax base.

After Houston lost the sweepstakes for both the General Motors Saturn Plant and the Navy's Home Port site selection, the city reevaluated its thinking and moved into diversification in a big way. Today, space, medicine, shipping, and petrochemicals are expanding elements of Houston's increasing business outside of the oil and gas area.

An example of the latter, was the city's response to Compaq Computer Corporation, a home-grown computer maker founded in 1982. The city gave this company a $240-million package of incentives, including new roads, expanded bus service, and tax relief.

In the electronics area, Houston now has Compaq, Texas Instruments, Toshiba International, and Kent Electronics manufacturing facilities in the area.

Shipment of electronic equipment increased from $165 million in 1980 to $770 million in 1986. Agricultural product processing is another manufacturing strength including American Rice, Coca-Cola Foods, Sysco, Nabisco, and Anheuser-Bush.

In transportation, DHL International recently added an Operations Center with 660 employees. All major air-express companies have facilities in Houston. The Port of Houston is the country's third-largest port in total tonnage, which has increased 20 percent since 1986. A $110-million cargo handling facility at the port, is under construction for an early 1990 opening.

Houston is a central location for tourism, and attractions draw 7,000,000 visitors per year, generating 3.9 billion in expenditures. With the opening of the $105-million George R. Brown Convention Center, the $20-million Menil Collection Art Galleries, and the $76-million Wortham Theater Center and expansion of the Astrodome complex, tourism is expected to increase.

Houston has a great list of outstanding attractions for the tourists and the citizens of Houston. These attractions include: Allen's

Landing, Old Market Square, the Alley Theater, the Antique Car Museum, and the Astrodomain.

The latter is a $100,000,000 entertainment complex that houses the Astrodome, Astro-Hall and the Astro-Arena.

The AstroWorld/WaterWorld—one of the nation's great amusement centers—serves as umbrella for the Battleship Texas, the Houston Armand Bayou Nature Center, Houston Garden Center, Houston Museum of Natural Science, and Lyndon B. Johnson Space Center. The Center is the headquarters of America's manned space program, the famous "Mission Control" that guided pioneering astronauts, and directs the Space Shuttle project.

Other attractions include the Miller Outdoor Theater, the Houston Museum of Fine Arts, and San Jacinto Battleground State Historic Park.

HUMBLE

Humble is located in Harris County 21 miles north of Houston on U.S. Highway 59 and Farm-to-Market Road 1960.

In 1865, Mr. P. S. Humble operated a ferry across the San Jacinto River in the area of present-day Humble, he and his family having settled there some years earlier. In 1886, Mr. Humble set up a post office in his home; he became the postmaster and Justice of the Peace, and the community was named Humble.

In 1887, the town had 50 residents. In 1904, the first gas well was brought in, and the oil rush in the Humble Field was on.

By March 1, 1905, 31 wells had been completed. Moonshine Hill, Crosby, and Humble were all oil boom towns (within five miles of each other) and had a population of 25,000.

Oil production from the Humble Field in 1905 was reportedly greater than that of Spindletop in 1902.

A railroad station was opened in 1904 to transport the oil. The Southern Pacific Railroad still serves Humble.

Perhaps the best known of the oil companies having their origins in Humble's oil boom days is Humble Oil & Refining Co., which was established in 1909 by Ross Sterling, Jesse Jones and others.

Humble's current population is 12,700. It manufactures oil field equipment and gaskets, and is the retail and commercial center for Northeast Harris County. With sales tax rebates of approximately $4,000,000 annually, Humble is the fourth largest tax center in Harris County.

HUNTSVILLE

Huntsville is the county seat of Walker County. It is 70 miles north of Houston on Interstate 45 and can also be reached by U.S. Highway 190 and State Highways 19 and 30. Its population is 31,500. Huntsville has a mayor-city manager form of city government.

Pleasant Gray, the founder of Huntsville, first visited the area in 1830-1831. He returned with his family in 1834 and established a trading post for local Indians and passing settlers. In 1835, he received a Mexican Grant for a league (7 square miles) of land, and he named the area for his hometown of Huntsville, Alabama. He sold (for a consideration of one cent) enough land for a courthouse and public square. This land was just a few hundred yards south of a spring that served as a gathering place for local Indians. Town lots were sold and residents began settling in. The town was incorporated in 1845.

Walker County was established in 1846 by the First Legislature of the State of Texas, and Huntsville became the county seat. Huntsville has had five courthouses—the first being built in 1847. The first two courthouses had defective foundations and had to be torn down; the third and fourth burned; the present one, the fifth, was built in 1970.

Early businesses in Huntsville included general merchandising, banking, blacksmithing, cigar manufacturing, leather and shoe manufacturing, and cotton raising and ginning.

In 1845, Huntsville was a stagecoach center with weekly stage trips to Houston. In 1848, a state penitentiary was established in Huntsville; prisoners were "hired out" for domestic and farm work. The Houston & Great Northern Railroad ran a spur line to Huntsville in 1872. The railroad and the prison were of prime importance in Huntsville's economy and growth.

Sam Houston moved to Huntsville in 1848 and built his Woodland home ½ mile south of the town square. He died in Huntsville in 1863 and is buried in the Oakwood Cemetery.

Austin College was established in 1850; it was later replaced by Sam Houston Normal Institute which eventually became Sam Houston State University.

Huntsville's economy is now based primarily on the university and prisons systems. However, forest and timber-related industries are also important in the local economy, as is the tourist trade. Huntsville is headquarters for the Texas Department of Corrections.

The second most decorated soldier of World War II was Col. M. B. Etherege, a Huntsville resident, educator, legislator, and banker.

Recreational opportunities are available at nearby Lake Livingston, Huntsville State Park, and Sam Houston National Forest.

Some attractions in Huntsville are The Texas Prison Museum—downtown on the Huntsville Square. It houses a great collection of the Texas Prison archives, including "Old Sparky," the electric chair. The Texas Berry Farm is located out 980 north of Huntsville. At the farm you can purchase cartons of fresh berries or pick your own, as well as fresh flowers, etc. It's a great family outing.

HURST

Tarrant County settlements began here in the northeastern section of the county when Isaac Parker, in 1850, built his log cabin in what is now Hurst. After the Civil War, more settlers moved to northeast Tarrant County, establishing schools and churches.

In 1870, William L. Hurst moved into the area with his wife and seven children. As the settlement grew, the town people decided to name the town after William Hurst. When the St. Louis Railroad came through in 1903, the local station was called Hurst's Station.

Later, growth in the small rural town was slowed when east-west rail routes were changed and routed through Arlington rather than the mid-cities.

No post office was established in Hurst until 1949 when the Souder family added a postal service to the corner of their grocery store as a service to about 1,000 residents.

Twenty-eight years ago, Bell Helicopter announced the coming installation of its $3 million plant in the small suburban Village of Hurst. Since then, the "Village" has grown into a city of some 35,000 residents.

Announcement of the construction of the Bell Helicopter plant was a catalyst which brought sudden and rapid growth to Hurst and other local cities.

Hurst was incorporated as a general law city in 1952. By 1956, the town had grown even more and was chartered as a home rule city. In five years, the population had spurted from 2,000 to 5,700. Hurst's population continued to increase at a staggering rate—from 5,700 in 1956 to 20,000 in 1966, finally reaching some 35,700 by 1981.

Hurst has an excellent ad valorem tax structure. Total taxes are 1,4335 per $100 valuation.

There are seven major colleges and universities available in the area:

Texas Christian University	18 miles
University of Texas at Arlington	10 miles
North Texas State University	30 miles
Texas Women's University	30 miles
Texas Weslayan College	12 miles
Southern Methodist University	20 miles
University of Texas at Dallas	18 miles
Tarrant County Junior College	in Hurst

The city is served by U.S. Hwy. 10, the St. Louis & Southwest, Chicago, Rock Island & Pacific, TNO & Santa Fe Railroads serves the city.

The Bell Helicopter Company is the principal employer in the area.

INGLESIDE

Ingleside is in San Patricio County, 12 miles northeast of Corpus Christi and 4 miles southwest of Aransas Pass. It is located on State Highway 361 and Farm-to-Market Road 1069. It is just a few miles from the north shore of Corpus Christi Bay and from the Gulf of Mexico.

In 1850, Marcellus and George Turner settled in the area and named their ranch "Ingleside". The name probably originated from Robert Burns' poem, "The Cotter's Saturday Night" where a fireside is referred to as "Ingleside."

Texas' first cattle drive took place in 1859 when Marcellus

Turner and Tom Coleman drove cattle from the Ingleside area to Kansas.

In 1860, the area's population was stated as "70 free individuals and 43 slaves." Its population in 1989 was 5,600.

In 1871, the Inwood post office was established at a site referred to as "Palomas." In the early 1880's, rail lines were laid to the Palomas site by the San Antonio & Aransas Pass Railway Company; the area was referred to as "Ingleside" on the railroad plats. Then, in 1892, the name of the post office was officially changed to "Ingleside."

About 1911, Gustar W. Blaschke and his family bought land in what is now the center of Ingleside. Mr. Blaschke was the postmaster, depot agent, farmer, and a public official, and is referred to as "The Father of Ingleside."

Ingleside was primarily a farming community until 1927 when a refinery and employee housing was built by Humble Oil and Humble Pipe Line Co. The refinery closed in 1945. Then, in 1950, Reynolds Metal Co. built an aluminum plant and, in the early 1970's, DuPont built a freon plant next to the Reynolds plant.

Ingleside was incorporated in 1951. It has a city council-city manager form of government.

In 1986, the U.S. Navy decided to build Naval Station Ingleside as home port for the Battleship USS Wisconsin; the Aircraft Carrier USS Lexington; an unnamed guided missile cruiser (possibly the USS San Jacinto); a destroyer and a "Craft of Opportunity." In 1989 based on the recommendations of the base re-alignment and closure commission, five additional ships were to be re-located from Lake Charles, Louisiana, and Galveston, Texas. An oiler, 2 frigates, and 2 mine-warfare ships as yet to be named will homeport in Ingleside. A total of 4735 civilian and navy personnel will support Naval Station Ingleside and the ten ships. Naval Station Ingleside is to be constructed with anticipated completion in October, 1991.

In 1987 (Oxychem) Occidental Chemical Corporation purchased a large portion of DuPont's production capacity of chlorine at the Ingleside plant. Oxychem then expanded the plant considerably and is now in the process of building a 250 million dollar chemical plant on the acreage purchased from DuPont.

IOWA PARK

Iowa Park is in Wichita County. It is 11 miles west of Wichita Falls and is located on U.S. Highway 287 and State Highway 370 and FM Highways 368 and 1814.

The city has a population of 6,500. The annual rainfall is 27.2 inches, and the elevation is 980 feet. It is approximately 13 miles south of the Red River and the Oklahoma Border.

One hundred years ago when the Fort Worth and Denver City Railroad inched its way over the prairie lands of North Texas, a switch in the center of Wichita County was called "Daggett" after a pioneer Fort Worth family.

General Grenville M. Dodge, hero of the Civil War, was the engineering genius behind this line as well as the Union Pacific and the Texas Pacific railroads. He purchased an 80-acre site at Daggett Switch with the railroad running diagonally through it. D. C. Kolp and his wife, Jennie, purchased 550 adjacent acres. In October of 1888 the three of them filed the town plat of Iowa Park. General Dodge's home was at Council Bluffs, Iowa and the Kolps also came from that state. Included in the plat were many parks as well as named park areas in the spacious boulevards, hence the name "Iowa Park." Many other families from Iowa also settled in the area.

The town government incorporated July 3, 1891. The next growth spurt came in the middle 1920's when the damming of Lake Kemp provided irrigation water to thousands of acres of fertile land south of town.

The City of Iowa Park is a general law city. The city is governed by a council composed of a mayor and five councilmembers. The city established an ordinance to appoint a city administrator.

The terrain is gentle rolling prairie with a sandy loam; 20,000 acres of cotton farm land are irrigated.

Wichita is one of the smaller counties, having only 606 sq. miles. The average county has 900 sq. miles. It has an average agricultural income of $23 million.

The area around Iowa Park raises beef cattle, hogs, horses and dairy products. The crops are cotton, sorghum, wheat, other grains and hay.

The city's economy is based on retail trade for a large area. There is also a considerable amount of manufacturing. Cryovac

Manufacturing Company is one of the cities largest plants. The production of oil and gas is sizable. Iowa Park has plants that manufacture fertilizer and oil field equipment.

The Buffalo Creek Reservoir is twenty miles west of Iowa Park, just north of U.S. Highway 287.

The Burlington Northern Railroad serves Iowa Park. Commercial air transportation is available at Wichita Falls.

IRVING

Irving is located in Dallas County just west of the city of Dallas and is part of the Dallas-Fort Worth metroplex. Irving is on U.S. Highway 356 and State Highways Loop 12, 183 and 114.

In 1902, J. O. Schulze and Otis Brown were surveyors for the Rock Island Railroad for a branch line from Fort Worth to Dallas. They set up their headquarters in a tent near what is now Irving and decided it would be a good location for a town. They thereupon purchased 80.21 acres of the heavily wooded (post oak) land from the owner (H. W. Britain). About two acres of the land had been cleared and planted in watermelons, and it was this land they donated to the railroad for a depot and switching yard. The townsite was then platted and, in 1903, a public sale of town lots was held; 40 lots at $50 each were sold. During the lot sale, the first issue of the *Irving Index* (forerunner of the *Irving Daily News*) was distributed.

After much discussion, Schulze and Brown had agreed on the name of "Irving" for the new town—the reason for the name, however, is unknown. Shortly after the lot sale, Schulze opened a lumber yard, and the new property owners began to build homes and businesses.

The Irving Independent School District was created in 1905. The Merchants and Planters Bank (now the Irving Bank & Trust Co.) was organized in 1907. A branch of the Frisco Railroad north to Carrollton was built in 1907. And, in 1910, Lone Star Gas Co. built its lines in Irving, and a water meter system was installed.

The city was incorporated in 1914 and it grew slowly until the mid-1950's. In 1950, Irving's population was 2,621; now it is 156,800.

Irving is home for dozens of Fortune 500 companies and is also regional, national and world headquarters for many others.

Throughout this growth into an urban mecca, Irving has retained its community spirit.

Texas Stadium (where the Dallas Cowboys play) and the Dallas/Fort Worth International Airport also call Irving home.

JACKSBORO

Jacksboro is located in North Texas in Jack County, of which it is the county seat. It is 62 miles northwest of Fort Worth and 59 miles southeast of Wichita Falls. It can be reached by U.S. Highways 281 and 380 and State Highways 59 and 148.

Jack County was created by the Texas Legislature in 1856; settlers in the area asked that their community be designated "Mesquiteville" because of the many large mesquite trees there. However, in 1858, the name of "Mesquiteville" was changed to "Jacksboro."

Jacksboro, as well as Jack County, is named for William H. Jack and his brother, Patrick C. Jack. The brothers were born in Georgia; both became attorneys and were patriots of the Texas Revolution.

Fort Richardson was built at Jacksboro in 1868; and the famous Sixth Cavalry was stationed there for protection of residents and travelers. The building of Fort Richardson spurred a building boom in the town. For the next ten years, Jacksboro was the outfitting point for ranchers to the west and for buffalo hunters. Grand balls for officers and citizens were held in the newly-built Wichita Hotel.

In 1898, the Rock Island Railroad arrived in Jacksboro.

The present economy of the town is based on oil field services, livestock, farming, manufacturing, tourism, and recreation.

Some of the old fort buildings at Fort Richardson State Park have been restored and others are in the process of restoration. Campsites, picnic areas, nature trails, fishing, and swimming are available to the public in the park.

Nearby Lake Jacksboro offers picnic areas, a boat ramp, and fishing dock.

Of interest in Jacksboro are the many historic homes built in the late 1800's and early 1900's.

Jacksboro is also home to the most famous wedding cakes in the country—Ida Mae Stark Wedding Cakes. There is a shop downtown.

A "Weekend in Old Mesquiteville" festival is held the second weekend of June each year.

JACKSONVILLE

Jacksonville is located in Cherokee County in the central part of East Texas on U.S. Highways 69, 79, and 175 and State Highways 204 and 347. It is 27 miles south of Tyler and 115 miles southeast of Dallas. Jacksonville's population is now 15,000.

The present city of Jacksonville came into being because of the railroad. The International & Great Western Railroad constructed a rail line in 1872 through Cherokee County. Since the rail line was a mile or so north of the old town of Jacksonville, the townspeople quickly realized their town was doomed. They met with railroad officials to decide on a site for a new town on the railroad line and agreed on a site at Fry's Summit. Sarah Fry sold 75 acres to the railroad company with the provision that a depot would be located on the land. The railroad company sold townsite lots and the people of old Jacksonville moved to the new site. Buildings were dismantled or moved by ox cart and, within a few days, only three buildings remained in old Jacksonville. What had formerly been corn and cotton fields soon became a thriving community.

In 1873, the new town was incorporated as Jacksonville and the railroad depot was designated as the center of the city.

The old town of Jacksonville had been laid out by Jackson Smith in 1847. Some people thought Smith named the community "Jacksonville" because he previously had lived in Jacksonville, Illinois; others thought it was named for a Dr. Jackson whose office was the first building on the townsite.

Although cotton remained the county's main crop until 1929, peaches and tomatoes were also important. In 1912, Jacksonville was recognized as the "Peach Center of the State;" and in the 1930's, Jacksonville became known as the "Tomato Capital of the World." Both crops, however, have since declined.

Today, ranching and the raising of beef cattle are of more importance. Jacksonville is the nation's largest manufacturer of wooden baskets and boxes for fruit containers. More than 75 industries have located in or near Jacksonville in recent years, making such diverse products as particle board, charcoal, furniture, plastics, air conditioner coils and vents, fiberglass boats, and wooden pallets, baby accessories, health care products for the medical industry.

Lake Jacksonville is just south of town and is available for water activities.

Lon Morris College, the oldest junior college in Texas, and the B M A Theological Seminary are located in Jacksonville.

Jacksonville has one of the most beautiful views at Love's Lookout Park, overlooking miles of hills and valleys. The Tomato Fest celebrates Jacksonville's heritage of being the "Tomato Shipping Capital," each year in September, with many fun activities.

JASPER

Jasper is in East Texas and is the county seat of Jasper County. It is located on U.S. Highway 96 just north of State Highway 63, and is 33 miles west of the Texas-Louisiana state line. It is 73 miles north of Beaumont and 138 miles northeast of Houston.

The City of Jasper, as well as Jasper County, is named for Sgt. William Jasper who was born in South Carolina about 1750 and who became a hero in the Civil War.

Eight states in the nation (Georgia, Illinois, Indiana, Iowa, Mississippi, Missouri, South Carolina, and Texas) have a Jasper County—all named for Sgt. William Jasper—but only Texas has a city of Jasper as the county seat of a Jasper County.

Jasper's current population is 7,824. Since most of Jasper County is forested, the economy is based primarily on the timber industry—sawmills, plywood mill, and various industries. Crops raised in the area include vegetables, fruit, and pecans.

As a result of Jasper's close proximity to Lake Sam Rayburn, Toledo Bend Reservoir, and Lake B. A. Stienhagen; the tourism industry comes closer and closer to taking over as the "number one" industry.

JUNCTION

Junction is located in the center of Kimble County, of which it is the county seat. It is located 116 miles northwest of San Antonio on Interstate 10 and State Highway 377 and is 93 miles southeast of San Angelo.

Although the area had already been settled for some time, it was not until 1876 that Kimble County was organized and Denman was named as the county seat. Soon thereafter, the residents voted on a town name and "Junction City" (because of the town's location at the junction of the North and South Llano Rivers) was chosen over "Denman."

In 1882, the town had about 300 residents, a courthouse and jail, a general merchandise store, a furniture store, and a newspaper, *The Western Texas*. Two churches and a school were being built.

In 1927, the city was formally incorporated as "Junction."

Today, Junction has thirteen churches, three public schools, an eighteen-bed hospital staffed by three physicians, a public swimming pool and library, a weekly newspaper, *The Junction Eagle*, a radio station and three banking institutions.

The primary income in the area is from livestock (sheep, goats, and cattle) and crops (pecans and fruit). Junction has a cedar oil plant, cedar log plant, sheet metal plant, pecan processing, and is a tourism center, with canoeing, fishing and hunting being the most popular recreations. Lake Junction is nearby.

Junction's population is 3,050.

KARNES CITY

Karnes City is in Central County and is the county seat. It is located on the Southern Pacific Railroad. It is located 57 miles southeast of San Antonio. The city had a population of 3,600 in 1989. The average annual rainfall is 31.9 inches which is enough rainfall for most crops.

The city is at the crossroads of five highways. U.S. Highway 181 runs through the city. The other highways are farm-to-market roads. The city was incorporated in 1914.

The San Antonio and Aransas Pass Railroad was constructed through the area in 1891 and a shipping point was established at the present location of Karnes City. A settlement grew up there. Karnes City was named after Henry Wax Karnes, a famous Texas Ranger and scout for General Sam Houston.

The flourishing town of Karnes City won the county seat election from Runge, Kenedy, and Helena in 1893. The election was contested. The county records were carted away to Karnes City in the night in January, 1894; and the county seat has been there ever since.

Karnes City and the surrounding area were settled by a varied ethnic mix of Mexican, German, Bohemian, Polish, Czech, Irish,

Scottish, French, Negro, and Anglo-Americans. The Old Helena Panna Maria is Texas' oldest Polish settlement.

The terrain around Karnes City was originally heavily covered with mesquite brush with large oak trees along the streams. The hardworking farmers cleared and grubbed the land and put it into cultivation. The area raised cotton, corn, maize, truck, and livestock. Karnes County is only about 75% the size of the average Texas county; however, its agricultural income is $35 million which is slightly higher than the average county income.

There was a considerable amount of oil and gas production in the area. There is only one producing oil field located in Karnes County. It is the Chevron field located five miles north of Karnes City.

The San Antonio River runs southeast across Karnes County about 9 miles north of Karnes City.

Karnes City has a commission-mayor form of city government.

Karnes City has a number of manufacturing plants which process agricultural products and manufacture fiberglass products.

KATY

Katy was laid out as a townsite by Mr. James Oliver Thomas, in 1895. He donated 320 acres of land for the townsite. The first post office was authorized in 1896, and Mr. J. O. Thomas was the postmaster. The post office was part of his general store.

Another person who is very special to Katy's history was Mr. Eule from Germany. In 1897, he grew rice, using surface water for irrigation. The second year he dug wells to irrigate the fields. Since that time the raising of rice has grown to be a major source of agricultural income.

The Missouri-Kansas-Texas Railroad was completed through the settlement that is now Katy in 1895. The railroad was referred to as the Katy railroad and it was natural that the town be named Katy.

Today the town of Katy has a population of 8,000. The Katy Independent School District surrounds the town. It is one of the largest school districts in Texas. The population served by this School District is 80,000. Katy claims this to be its metropolitan population. The school district has a student population of approximately 17,500.

Katy is in the extreme western part of Harris County. A large part of its trade area is in Waller and Fort Bend Counties. The town is 26 miles west of downtown Houston, but only seven miles from Houston's western city limits.

Katy is served by I-10 Freeway, and several farm-to-market highways.

The agricultural income in the area is from beef cattle, horses, hogs, poultry, and dairy products. The crops include rice, nursery crops, soybeans, grains, hay, corn and vegetables.

Katy was chartered in 1945. The charter provides for a mayor and five aldermen. In 1983 the city adopted a zoning ordinance dividing the city into residential areas and four commercial areas.

One of Katy's major assets is its proximity to Houston, and to its higher education facilities, to the two airports, library facilities and medical centers.

Katy is located on the edge of a huge salt dome with a series of satellite domes. This geological structure has created one of the largest gas and oil fields in Texas.

Attractions to the area include Alkek Veladrome and the Great Southwest Equestrian Center.

KAUFMAN

Kaufman is the county seat of Kaufman County and is located 33 miles southeast of Dallas on U.S. Highway 175 and State Highways 34 and 243. Its population is 4,658.

Dr. William P. King led 40 pioneer families from Holly Springs, Mississippi, to this area in 1840 in search of the "Three Forks of the Trinity." Upon arrival, they built a fort and called it "King's Fort." The community was called "Kingsboro."

Kaufman County was created by an Act of the Texas Legislature in 1848. When Kingsboro was designated the county seat in 1851, it was renamed "Kaufman" in honor of David Spangler Kaufman, a member of the Texas and United States Congresses. In the early 1870's, Kaufman was incorporated.

Kaufman had stage coach service for mail and passengers once a week. Then, in 1881, a rail line of the Texas Grand Trunk Railway was completed to Kaufman; and, in 1883, the Texas Central Railroad reached Kaufman. The railroads spurred growth in the town.

A Civilian Conservation Corps (CCC) camp was established in

Kaufman in the 1930's, and was used as a German prisoner-of-war camp in the 1940's.

Cedar Creek Lake is nearby, as are a number of large ranches. Many Kaufman residents work in Dallas but prefer to live in the more rural atmosphere of Kaufman.

KELLER

Keller is located in Tarrant County. It is 24 miles due north of downtown Fort Worth.

This is another Texas town that was born as a result of a railroad being built through the settlement. In 1881, the Texas and Pacific Railroad was built between Fort Worth and Texarkana. The first train ran on the track May 9, 1881. The day the first train came through Athol (Keller) was a big event.

As the railroad was being built, the residents of Athol wanted the railroad to come through their community. They knew that the town that would dominate the area depended on where the railroad located the depot. John C. Keller, the railroad construction boss, told the citizens of Athol that if they would name the town after him, he would see that the depot would be located in their community. That is how Keller got its name.

Keller is on U.S. Highway 377 and is located between Fort Worth and Denton. Keller was incorporated in February, 1958. It has a mayor/council form of city government. The town, of course, had existed for 77 years prior to that. The first post office was established in 1886.

The original railroad is now the Missouri Pacific Railroad, which is owned by the Union Pacific.

Keller benefits by its proximity to Fort Worth. It is just west of the Dallas-Fort Worth International Airport. The city has increased in size to encompass nineteen square miles. The current population is 10,265.

One of the Air Force's largest installations is Carswell Air Force Base. Keller is close to major educational institutions such as Texas Christian University, University of Texas at Arlington, Arlington Baptist College, and Bauder Fashion College.

Located in the area is Six Flags Over Texas and the Texas Ranger's Baseball Club.

Keller is primarily a residential city; however, it has a considerable amount of industry.

KENEDY

The early history of Kenedy is very interesting. In the days of its youth, the town of Kenedy, Texas, was known as "Six-shooter Junction." It deserved the name—conceived in a quarrel, born in a gun fight, and nurtured in adversity. Kenedy was a son-of-a-gun . . . a real tough town.

Even Kenedy's leading citizens admit there never was much reason for Kenedy in the first place. It was willed into being by strong men who decided there ought to be a town there. Today, there still isn't much reason for Kenedy to exist. But that doesn't discourage the ever-growing number of people who live there and are proud to call it home.

Kenedy's story is that of the Old West; it has all the elements of cowboy lore that have so captured the imagination of America: Indians, cowboys, cattle barons, range wars, bad men, fearless lawmen and six-gun justice. A writer of westerns could locate in Kenedy and occupy himself for a lifetime writing nothing but the truth about the place.

In 1758, bold Spanish ranchers began settling in the area. One of these was Don Carlos Martinez, son of one of the founders of San Antonio. In 1773, Don Carlos petitioned his Imperial Majesty, the King of Spain, for eight leagues of land, specifying that the tract should border three leagues along the San Antonio River and running five leagues west. Don Carlos' petition was answered in 1788 when he was granted a tract of land measuring three by five leagues. The King's arithmetic was correct in addition: three and five do make eight, but he multiplied instead. Thanks to the error of the royal mathematician, Don Carlos found himself the owner of 15 leagues, or 65,000 acres of land. On this tract, where modern Kenedy is located, Don Carlos operated a horse ranch until the year 1815 when he died at the hands of Comanche warriors.

The settlement of Karnes County was given a major impetus when 800 immigrants from Poland came to Texas in 1854. The arrival of the colony was one of the most picturesque scenes that had ever occurred in that area. The highway between Port Lavaca and San Antonio passed directly in front of the house of an early pioneer who gave this account. He said, "Up until that time, the people of Texas were entirely English-speaking but for a few colonies from Germany. The consequence of this was, that simple frontier people like ourselves have never seen anything like the crowd which passed along the road that day. There was some eight or nine hundred of them. They wore the costumes of the old country. Many of the women had what, at that time, were regarded as very short skirts, showing their limbs, two or three inches above the ankle. Some had on wooden shoes and, almost without exception, all wore broad-brimmed, low-crowned black felt hats, nothing like the hats that were worn in Texas. They also wore blue jackets of heavy woolen cloth, falling just below the waist and gathered into folds at the back with a band of the same material." These Polish immigrants founded the town of Panna Maria and it exists today as one of the concentrated ethnic groups. This Polish settlement is located 19 miles north of Kenedy.

Helena which was one of the early towns in Karnes County, has a population of over 3,000. It had also acquired the reputation of being the "toughest town on earth." The town was on the Chisholm Trail over which great herds of Longhorn steers were trailed to market in Kansas. It was an important stagecoach stop, as well. As there was little organized law enforcement, the region became infested with bandits and rustlers who came to prey on stagecoach passengers and freighters and to steal cattle and horses. It was in this vicinity that John Wesley Hardin began building the infamous reputation that earned him national notoriety as a gunman and a killer. These outlaws originated a bloody form of personal encounter known as the Helena Duel. It consisted of tying the left hands of the duelists together with rawhide, giving each a knife with a three-inch blade, whirling them around rapidly a few times and turning them loose. The shortness of the knife blades prevented a single fatal stroke and the fight became a gory slashing match with the contestants hacking away furiously. No quarter was given or expected.

Not until the Karnes County vigilance committee and the Texas Rangers began to apply their six-gun justice was the area cleared of the "gentry of the brush."

In the year 1884, exciting news swept through Karnes County. A Corpus Christi man named Uriah Lott had secured a charter to build a railroad from San Antonio to Aransas Pass on the Gulf. The line was to pass through Karnes County and would bring new prosperity and progress. By 1886, the S. A. & A. P. (SAP as it would always be called) had arrived at the northern edge of the county. Agents of the railroad came in advance of the track-laying crews to dicker for right-of-way and establish the route.

Citizens of Helena naturally expected that the SAP would come through their town which was the largest community on the proposed route and an important center. However, it was the policy in those days to demand favors of communities desirous of rail service. Officials of the SAP informed the city fathers that if they wanted a railroad, they would have to provide free right-of-way through the town plus $60,000 in cash. Convinced that the SAP had to come through Helena whether it wanted to or not, the townspeople concluded the railroad men were bluffing and rejected the demands. This proved an unfortunate decision. The railroad bypassed Helena to the west and made plans to lay out a new townsite.

As a site for their new town, the railroad men began negotiating with a rancher named Fate Elder to buy a section of land some five miles northwest of Kenedy's present location. Before the deal could be closed, however, fate in the form of a blood feud altered the decision.

Fate Elder was sheriff of Karnes County and head of the clan of Elders who were pioneer settlers and ranchers with extensive holdings in the county. Their neighbors to the south were the Butlers. William Green Butler, the family patriarch, was a Mississippian who had arrived on the banks of the San Antonio River in 1852. He began buying land and soon became one of the largest landowners and ranchers in the county.

For reasons which Karnes Countians will not discuss even today, Elder and Butler quarreled. Other members of the families got into the act and finally, on September 6, 1886, the feud came to a head. It was election day; Sheriff Elder was running for reelection. The polling place was a little general store at the tiny settlement of Daileyville.

Bill Butler and his men went there to vote. They met Sheriff Elder. His brother, Bud, and four deputies were there. In the dusty street outside the little store, the Butlers and the Elders had a showdown.

Sheriff Elder was fast on the draw; his 45 colt roared first. But the bullet only clipped Butler's ear. Butler didn't miss, nor did the other Butler men. When the shooting was over, Fate and Bud Elder and the four deputies lay dead.

That ended the Butler-Elder feud, but it created new problems for the railroad officials. When they learned that Fate Elder was dead, and that his heirs consisted of a widow and four minor children, they grew concerned over their ability to acquire a sound title to the Elder property. To play it safe, they decided to select some other tract instead.

Bill Butler, J. M. Nichols, and other ranchers whose properties were located farther south urged the railroad to acquire a tract five miles south of the original location on the banks of the Escondido Creek. Accordingly, the railroad purchased 677 acres of land there from George A. Little and proceeded to plat the present township of Kenedy.

It was called Kenedy Junction at first, but this was later shortened to Kenedy. For years, the original townsite five miles to the north was known as Old Kenedy.

The new town immediately began to grow . . . and proud Helena, to whither.

The Texas Historical Commission established a bronze historical plaque at the Highway in Kenedy, this plaque reads as follows:

The town of Kenedy occupies a site that once was part of a royal spanish land grant to Don Carlos Marinez. American settlement in the area began after the Texas war for independence (1836). Land for a townsite was purchased in 1886 by railroad promoter Mifflin Kenedy, for whom the community was named, and a post office was established the following year.

Kenedy's early growth was attributed to its position as a major stop on the San Antonio and Aransas Pass Railroad. Early buildings in Kenedy included a church, store, and cotton gin. By 1906, businesses in the town included newspaper offices, a bank, livery and feed stables, and one of the largest cotton compresses in the state. Incorporated in 1910, Kenedy gained a reputation for gunfighting that earned it the name "Six Shooter Junction."

In 1915, hot mineral water was discovered near the depot. And the Hot Wells Hotel and Bath House was a thriving business for nearly 25 years. An alien detention camp was located on the outskirts of town during World War II.

Although passenger train service no longer runs through Kenedy, this historic town remains an economic center for the surrounding agricultural area.

Kenedy is in Karnes County. It is located on U.S. Highway 181 and State Highways 72 and 239. The Southern Pacific Railroad serves the city. The San Antonio River is twelve miles to the east. Kenedy is 95 miles north-northwest of Corpus Christi and 62 miles southeast of San Antonio. Kenedy is in a rich agricultural area. Karnes County has an agricultural income of $35 million and is smaller than the average county with 753 sq. miles. The average size of Texas counties is 900 sq. miles. The average agricultural income of a Texas county is $29 million. 80% of the agricultural income is from beef, dairy cattle and hogs. The crops include maize, wheat, corn, oats, and flax.

The rolling terrain in the area around Kenedy is covered with mesquite and oak trees. The soil is principally sandy loam. The average rainfall is 32.9 inches per year. This is adequate for most crops.

The population of Kenedy is 4,800. The city was incorporated in 1886, with a mayor-council form of city government. The town celebrated its 100th anniversary in 1986.

The city was named in honor of Mifflin Kenedy who was the President of the San Antonio and Aransas Pass Railroad.

The nearest commercial airport is the San Antonio International Airport, 69 miles to the northwest.

KERMIT

Kermit is located on the West Texas plains and is the county seat of Winkler County. It is 47 miles west of Odessa, 51 miles northeast of Pecos, and ten miles south of the Texas-New Mexico state line. It can be reached by State Highways 18, 115, and 302. Its population is 8,015.

In 1880, Col. McKenzie put an end to the Comanche threat in the area and the first settlers began arriving. The population in 1890 was 19; in 1900, it was 66; and by 1910, enough homesteaders had filed on land that a petition for county organization was granted. The new town (consisting of three houses, a four-room hotel, and a court house) was named "Kermit" in honor of Theordore Roosevelt's son and was designated the county seat. Although the town was established in 1910, it was not incorporated until 1938.

Ranching was the primary activity around Kermit until 1926 when a major oil strike led to the development of the Hendrick Field (10,000 acres). Today, Kermit is an oil activity center; Winkler County is among the leading petroleum-producing counties in the state. Primary agricultural activities center around beef cattle. The Missouri-Pacific Railroad provides rail service to Kermit.

Monahans Sand Hills State Park is nearby.

KERRVILLE

Kerrville is located in Central Texas and is the county seat of Kerr County. It is approximately 67 miles northwest of San Antonio on State Highways 16 and 27. Its population is 19,500.

In 1849, Joshua D. Brown established a camp on the Guadalupe River to make cypress shingles. He was forced to leave the area because of Indian problems, but, a few years later, returned and reestablished the camp.

In 1856, Kerr County was created by an Act of the Texas Legislature. The residents of the county picked Brown's campground as the site for a county seat. Thereupon, Joshua Brown donated four acres for a public square and courthouse and, as soon as the town was platted, he began to sell lots.

Brown insisted the town be named for a close friend of his from Gonzales—Major James Kerr, a soldier, statesman, surveyor, and the first American settler on the Guadalupe River. The town was first named "Kerrsville," but was renamed "Kerrville" in 1866.

Present-day Kerrville is an area of hills covered with cedar and live oak trees, green valleys, and streams edged with cypress. It has become a health and recreation center and has many camps (for boys, girls, and adults) and dude ranches.

Kerrville is also a center of wool and mohair production. Local manufacturing includes aircraft, recreational equipment, jewelry, and glass. Schreiner College, Kerrville State Hospital, and the Veterans Hospital are all located here.

Of interest in the area are the Hill Country Museum (formerly the home of Capt. Charles Schreiner, an early resident), Cowboy Artists Museum, Classic Car Showcase, Wax Museum, and James Avery Craftsman, Inc.

Kerrville State Park on the Guadalupe River is very popular.

The Kerrville Music Festival and the Texas State Arts and

Crafts Fair are held every year on the last weekend in May and first weekend in June. The Point Summer Threatre Productions run from June through August.

KILLEEN

Killeen is located in central Texas in Bell County on U.S. Highway 190. It is about 25 miles west of Temple and 78 miles north of Austin located at the main entrance to Fort Hood.

The township of Killeen was platted by the Gulf, Colorado and Santa Fe Railroad and was named for Frank P. Killeen, assistant general manager of the railroad.

The first train reached Killeen in 1882 and, because of the railroad, Killeen quickly became a marketing and distribution center for the area. Business property was in great demand; lots that sold for $75 in the 1880's sold for $1,000 in the 1890's.

A depot was built by the railroad in 1913; the building is now used by the Greater Killeen Chamber of Commerce for its offices.

Killeen has 11 sites designated with markers by the Texas Historical Commission. One of those sites is the birthplace of Oveta Culp Hobby.

Killeen is home to Central Texas College and American Technological University. Killeen has varied manufacturing facilities, but much of its economy depends on Fort Hood. Its present population is 46,296.

KINGSLAND

Kingsland is an unincorporated area in Llano and Burnet Counties. It is located on the Llano River on Farm-to-Market Roads 1431 and 2342, just at the north end of LBJ Lake. The lake is on the Colorado River, just below the confluence of the Llano and the Colorado. The population is 3,500; elevation is 830 ft., Kingsland rainfall is 29.8 inches per year.

Kingsland was originally known as Kingsville, having been given that name by Martin D. King who had purchased land in the area in the late 1870's. In 1892 the Western and Northwestern Railroads came to Kingsville. The name was changed to Kingsland, since another town claimed the name of Kingsville.

In 1900, Kingsland had two general stores, three churches, a blacksmith shop, meat market, barbershop, a drugstore, two saloons, a newspaper, and a post office.

In 1901, the Austin and Northwestern Railroads built the Antlers Hotel for traveling salesmen. It soon became known as a resort hotel, and promotional excursions came from Austin on weekends.

Until 1914, the only way across the rivers was by boat, by fording the Llano at Harvey Crossing, or by walking across the railroad bridge. In 1914, a wagon bridge was built near the place where the Colorado River bridge is today.

In the 1930's, Buchanan Dam was built across the Colorado River, bringing an influx of people who worked on the project. They gradually moved on after it was completed in 1936. After Granite Shoals (now Wirtz) Dam was completed in 1951, forming Granite Shoals Lake (now known as Lake LBJ) Kingsland began to come alive as a resort community once again. Fishing camps became common and lodges began to spring up along both rivers and down the lake. Until the 1960's a ferry carried people across the Llano River when a bridge was built near the ferry crossing. Subdivisions were built as the demand for lake and river properties grew. The area became a haven for retirees wanting to leave the city for peace and quiet in a small town atmosphere.

In the 1970's and 1980's Kingsland grew from a retiree/resort community into a thriving town that is also home to many young families. There are doctors, pharmacies, banks, grocery stores, beauty salons and barber shops, service stations, garages, boat dealers, auto sales, repair shops, welders, contractors, equipment sales, shops for all types of merchandise, churches, restaurants, library, and volunteer fire department. The town is now truly a city.

Area attractions are Longhorn Caverns, Enchanted Rock, LBJ State Park, Inks Lake State Park, a fish hatchery, and Chain of Seven Lakes and Dams.

Yearly events are the Bluebonnet Festival, bass tournament, softball tournament, Aqua-Boom, and arts and crafts festival.

The town is located 60 miles northwest of Austin in Burnet County.

KINGSVILLE

Kingsville is located on the Gulf Coastal Plain of South Texas in Kleberg County, of which it is the county seat. It is 39 miles southwest of Corpus Christi and 110 miles north of Brownsville on U.S. Highway 77 and State Highways 141 and 428.

The area at one time was known as the Wild Horse Desert and was visited only by Indians and miners headed for the California gold rush. In 1853, Richard King, a riverboat captain, bought an old Spanish land grant on Santa Gertrudis Creek and there founded the Santa Gertrudis Ranch.

After King's death in 1885, the ranch was managed by his widow and his son-in-law, Robert J. Kleberg, Sr. Kleberg was instrumental in getting the St. Louis, Brownsville & Mexican Railroad to build a line from Corpus Christi to Brownsville. The rail line, of course, passed through the ranch property. A community along the tracks was first referred to as the "Townsite on Santa Gertrudis Ranch" but later was named Kingsville in honor of Capt. King. Mrs. King changed the name of the Santa Gertrudis Ranch to the King Ranch in honor of her husband. The King Ranch is world famous, not only for its size but for the Santa Gertrudis breed of cattle developed there.

The first passenger train arrived in Kingsville on July 4, 1904. At that time the population of Kingsville was about 400; four years later, it was 2,000; today it is 28,808.

Kingsville was incorporated in 1911. The town's early economy was based on railroad, ranching, and farming (cotton, corn, hay, vegetables, citrus fruits, grapes, and figs).

The Texas College of Arts & Industries (now known as Texas A & I University) opened in 1925.

During World War II a naval air station was built just east of the city. Today that base is one of the largest jet training facilities in the world.

After oil and gas were discovered in the area, Celanese built a petrochemical plant north of Kingsville, Exxon built the world's largest gas plant on the King Ranch.

Currently Kingsville's economy is based primarily on petrochemicals, agriculture, and ranching. To a lesser extent, light manufacturing, trade, the military installation, and higher education are important. Kingsville is on the main line of the Missouri-Pacific Railroad.

Baffin Bay is southeast of the city and offers public piers, free boat launches, and saltwater fishing.

Points of interest in the area include the King Ranch Loop Road and the John E. Conner Museum on the Texas A & I University campus.

KIRBY

Kirby is located on U.S. Highways 35 and 81, six miles northeast of the center of San Antonio. It is located in Bexar County and has a population of 6,500. It is just outside Loop 410 and is inside Loop 1604.

The city is served by the MKT Railroad.

The town is a bedroom community near San Antonio. It has no reason for existence except that as a separate city, it may possibly enjoy some tax benefits by virtue of a lower municipal tax.

The city was named in honor of a prominent citizen of San Antonio, who was a large property owner.

LA GRANGE

La Grange is the county seat of Fayette County. It is on the Colorado River. The city is located where the old Indian trail, later known as La Bahia Road, crossed the Colorado River. It is located in Southeast Central Texas. It is 65 miles southwest of Austin, 120 miles southeast of San Antonio and 100 miles northeast of Houston. It is located on U.S. Highway 71 and 77 and State Highway 159.

The terrain around La Grange consists of beautiful rolling hills covered with graceful oaks and pines, and in the spring, with bluebonnets. The early immigrants were of German and Czech heritage.

The population of La Grange is 4500. The elevation is approximately 300 feet. The average annual rainfall is 35.6 inches, which is sufficient for the raising of nearly all crops. The land around La Grange is very productive. Fayette County is an average sized county and yet produces 80% more agricultural income than the average county; 75% of the income comes from beef, dairy cattle, hogs and poultry. The crops raised are corn, sorghum, hay, peanuts, and pecans.

The minerals in the area are oil, gas, clays, sand, gravel, lignite and Fullers earth.

The City of La Grange is served by the MKT Railroad.

The County of Fayette was named in honor of General Lafayette. It is the general opinion that the early settlers named La Grange for their home town in Tennessee.

There are a number of historical and interesting points in the area of La Grange. Some of these are:

1. Fayette Heritage Museum and Archives.
2. Kreische Brewery State Historic Site—Ruins of the stone brewery and home built by Stonemason Heinreich L. Kreische, who came to La Grange in the early 1840s.
3. Lake Fayette.
4. Monument Hill State Historic Site.
5. Scenic Drives—FM 153 west from U.S. 77 to community of Winchester traverses the Colorado River Valley amid tall pines.
6. Winedale Historical Center—A restored farm home and buildings of the 1830 period.
7. Fashion Home Museum.

The City enjoys an excellent tax rate. A breakdown is:

City	.2280
County	.2115
School	.9300
	$1.3695 per $100 valuation

The city has a council/city-manager form of government.

The nearest commercial air service is in Austin, 65 miles away.

LAMARQUE

LaMarque is a separate city, but its growth has merged with Texas City, to the extent that they have almost become one industrial complex. The map below shows this clearly.

LaMarque is located on S.H.-146 and S.H.-3. It is in Galveston County. It is sixteen miles northwest of Galveston. It is on the west side of Texas City and contiguous to it. It is 40 miles southeast of Houston.

LaMarque's future was assured when the first railroad was laid to LaMarque in 1859. This forever changed its destiny. The first town that grew around the railroad was known as Buttermilk Junction, because confederate soldiers traveling from Houston to Galveston would stop there to buy buttermilk.

The area grew slowly after the Civil War, with cattle and farming being the main ways of earning a livelihood.

Buttermilk Junction was later changed to Highland, but this

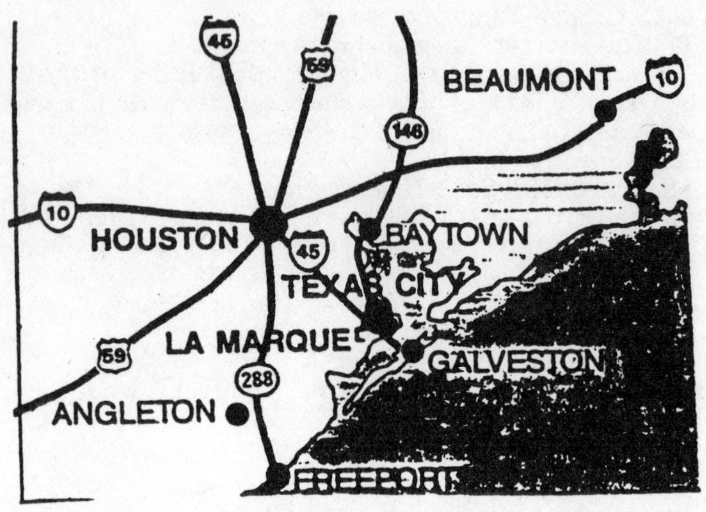

was change to LaMarque to avoid confusing the town with High Island. The choice of naming the town LaMarque is credited to Madame St. Ambrose, a French nun and school teacher who lived there. LaMarque is French for "the mark" or "the place."

Five railroads now serve the LaMarque/Texas City area. They are the Missouri-Kansas-Texas Railroad, Southern Pacific, Santa Fe, Union Pacific, and the Burlington Northern railroads. Goods may be shipped by water through the ports of Galveston or Texas City.

A number of nationally known manufacturers are located in the LaMarque-Texas City area. They are:

Amoco Oil Company
Amoco Chemical Company
Amoco Gas Company
Amoco Production Company
Amoco Pipeline Company
Amoco Transport Company

Sterling Chemicals
Marathon Petroleum Company
Tri-Sen Systems, Inc.
Sikes Fabricating Co.
Monsanto Chemical Co.
GAF Chemicals
Texas City Refining Company
Union Carbide Corporation

The LaMarque/Texas City area suffered serious damage from Hurricane Carla in 1961. This prompted the beginning of a major flood control project. A seventeen-mile levee sea wall was constructed with accompanying large pumps. Thus, when Hurricane Alicia hit the Texas Coast in 1983, the flooding was on a very small scale. The final completion of the Texas City/LaMarque Hurricane-Flood Control Protection Levee was dedicated in July, 1987. This $54.6 million project encompasses 36 square miles and includes 16 miles of earthen levee 23 feet high and 1.3 miles of concrete floodwall.

LaMarque has access to a number of outstanding colleges and universities. They are:

University of Houston at Clear Lake
University of Houston at Houston
Rice University at Houston
Houston Baptist University at Houston
University of St. Thomas at Houston
University of Texas A & M at Galveston
University of Texas Medical Branch at Galveston
Texas Southern University at Houston
College of the Mainland—Texas City
Lee College at Baytown

LaMarque has a mayor/council/city manager form of city government. It has a population of 16,000. The city was incorporated in 1953.

LaMarque's future is tied to the industrial development in the Texas City-Houston Ship Channel complexes. It benefits from its proximity to Houston.

The city has air transportation available at the Intercontinental Airport, north of Houston and the Hobby Airport at Houston, only 35 miles away.

LAMESA

Lamesa is the county seat of Dawson County in the plains area of West Texas. It is 45 miles northwest of Big Spring, 58 miles north of Midland, 60 miles south of Lubbock, and 68 miles east of the Texas-New Mexico State line. It is located on U.S. Highways 87 and 180 and State Highway 137. Its population is 11,790.

In the early days, the area around Lamesa was the domain of Indians and buffalo; later, it became open cattle range. The first Dawson County census in 1900 counted 36 people.

When Dawson County was organized in 1905, there were four large ranches in the area—one of them being the Slaughter Ranch (with the Lazy S brand).

In 1903, 160 acres from the home section of Frank Conner (a former employee of the Slaughter Ranch) was surveyed and platted into town lots. A. L. Wasson suggested the name "La Mesa" (Spanish for "table land") for the new town. The name was approved, but the spelling of it changed to "Lamesa".

An election was held to determine the county seat of Dawson County and Lamesa won. After the election, the residents of Chicago, a small town two miles away, moved their residences, stores, and other buildings to Lamesa—and Chicago ceased to exist.

The Santa Fe Railroad arrived in Dawson County in 1910. From the early 1900's, farming and ranching were the main sources of income in the area. Livestock is still important, but field crops—especially cotton and grain sorghum—are of greater importance. Dawson County is one of Texas' major cotton-producing counties. The area's economy is also based on oil.

Lamesa has a council-city manager form of Government.

Dal Paso Museum (renovated & restored this past year) is an attraction in the City.

The Lamesa Campus of Howard County Junior College is located in Lamesa.

LAMPASAS

Lampasas is located in Central Texas, 79 miles northwest of Austin, 124 miles north of San Antonio, and 28 miles west of Killeen and Fort Hood. It can be reached by U.S. Highways 183, 190, and 183.

The springs of Lampasas were valued by the Indians for their curative powers; and the springs served as watering places for buffalo, wild horses, bears, and panthers. Lipan, Apaches and Comanches roamed the area; and it wasn't until after 1875 when the Indians were forced onto reservations, that the Indian threat to the settlers was over.

John Burleson was the first permanent settler in the area, arriving about 1850. He had received 1,280 acres of land in 1838 for his services in the Texas Revolution. In 1854, he deeded the property to his two daughters; and the town of "Burleson" was laid out in 1855 by his daughter, Elizabeth, and her husband, George Scott.

Lampasas County was created by an Act of the Texas Legislature in 1856 and that Act specified that the county seat would be located at Burleson, but that Burleson's name would be changed to "Lampasas", the same as the county. In 1873, therefore, the City of Lampasas was chartered and, in 1883, the city was incorporated and the courthouse was completed.

There is some disagreement as to the origin of the name "Lampasas." The nearby river was known as the Lampasas over a hundred years before the county was created. Some contend the name is of Indian origin and refers to the sulpher springs which supply water to the river. Others contend the name was borrowed from the Mexican town of Lampazos (spelled slightly differently). More likely, however, is that the river was named Lampasos (a Spanish word meaning "cockleburs") by the Spanish Aguayo expedition in 1721 because of the many cockleburs in the region. Then, over time, the spelling of "Lampasos" became "Lampasas." The *Texas Almanac,* however, states that "Lampasas" is Spanish for "lilies" which are found in area streams.

In the 1870's, Lampasas was a typical wild west frontier town—cattle drives, trail drivers, shoot-outs, rustling, and the Texas Rangers stationed there to maintain law and order.

In 1882, the Santa Fe Railroad arrived in Lampasas and the town grew rapidly; 653 residents in 1880 grew to 2,408 by 1890. Lampasas became a supply stop for travelers heading west; and cotton and wool in large quantities were shipped east. A spa resort was developed around the nearby sulpher springs; the railroad promoted excursion trips to the spa, and Lampasas became known as the "Saratoga of the South."

The population of present-day Lampasas is 6,165. It is a ranching and hunting center. Agriculture is important to its economy; the primary crops grown in the area are oats, wheat, fruit, and pecans. There is some manufacturing in town, such as feed, plastics, western boots, apparel, nut harvesters, rubber products, brooms, and mops. The city is served by the Atchison, Topeka & Santa Fe Railroad.

Lampasas has many State Historical Site markers and medallions. Some of the buildings date back to 1860.

Lampasas participated in the Texas Main Street project and many of the older buildings have been restored.

LANCASTER

Lancaster is located in the southern part of Dallas County. It is 12 miles south of the Dallas City Hall. It is located on S.H. 342 and FM 1382. It is served by the MKT Railroad.

Lancaster operates under a home rule charter with a council/city manager form of government. The city was founded in 1852 as a trading post. The first name of the town was Hardscrabble, started in 1845. Then, in 1848, the settlement was named Pleasant Run and had a post office. The town then became known as Lancaster in 1852, at which time, it had a mayor and city council. The town was first incorporated in 1856, but it developed that the title to all the city property was flawed, so in 1876 all property owners gave a "Quit Claim" to their property and new titles were issued, and properly recorded. The city was formally incorporated in 1876.

Lancaster has a population of 21,500. The city was founded by A. Bledsoe in 1852. He named the town Lancaster after his hometown Lancaster, Kentucky, which had been named after Lancaster, England.

Lancaster is probably the only town in Texas with a city square with the streets entering the square in the middle of the square. It is called Independence Square, after the one in Philadelphia, Pennsylvania.

The taxes of Lancaster are slightly on the high side, at $1.862 per $100 of assessment.

The city is served by the MKT Railroad, and the Southern Pacific Railroad. The nearness to the Dallas/Ft. Worth International Airport and Love Field Airport is a real asset.

The City has access to these institutions of higher learning:

SMU	Dallas, 20 miles
University of Texas-Arlington	Arlington, 35 miles
Cedar Valley Jr. College	Lancaster
Mountain View Community College	Dallas, 15 miles

A large number of manufacturers are located at Lancaster. A few of the larger ones are:

	Employees
Amrep Inc.—Industrial Chemicals	56
Bilco Corp.—Cement Brick	44
Bramton Co.—Janitorial Supplies	40
Brass Craft Western—Plumbing	229
Cupp Illustrated—Plastic cups	65
Dana Corp.—Hydraulic Cylinders	144
Lancaster Mfg.—Packaging	55
Lasco, Bath Fixture Div.—Fiberglass/Acrylic Tubs	96
Longhorn Gasket—Custom Die Cutting/Fab	52
Magna Homes—Manufactured Housing	100
Southwestern Bell—Distribution Center	250
Tidwell Industries—Cabinets	172
TU Electric—Repair/Service Center	83

The main asset that Lancaster has, is its close proximity to the Dallas Metroplex.

LAREDO

Laredo is situated on the Rio Grande in South Texas and is the county seat of Webb County. It is 154 miles south-southwest of San Antonio and 145 miles west of Corpus Christi. It can be reached by Interstate 35, U.S. Highways 59 and 83, and State Highway 359.

In 1747, Jose de Escandon, a Spanish colonel, organized a colonization expedition to the area around the Rio Grande. One of his men, Captain Don Tomas Sanchez de Barrera y Gallardo located a ford on the Rio Grande which he called "El Paso de Jacinto"—it was later called "Indian Ford"—just west of what is now downtown Laredo. The Captain requested, and was granted, permission to found a town at the site. In 1755, he moved three families to the site and called the settlement "Villa de San Agustin de Laredo." The name was chosen to honor Colonel Escandon who was from the city of Laredo in the Spanish province of Santander.

Within two years, the population of the new town numbered 85, and sheep, goats, and cattle numbered 9,000. The residents, for the next fifty years or so, faced all the hardships of a frontier town, including flood and drought, gangs of roving bandits, and raids by the Apache and Comanche Indians.

The Laredo residents remained loyal to Spanish rule but, when Spain was defeated, they accepted the new flag of Mexico; and life continued much as usual.

In 1836, when Texas won its independence, Laredo had 2,000 residents and was in a "no-man's land". Mexico claimed the Texas-Mexico boundary was the Nueces River north of Laredo; and Texas claimed the Rio Grande as the boundary.

In 1840, the Republic of the Rio Grande was founded with Laredo as its capitol; it was an independent country for 283 days.

Laredo became the center of military activity in 1846 during the war between Mexico and the United States. After the signing of the Treaty of Guadalupe Hidalgo, making the Rio Grande the boundary line, Laredo became a part of Texas. Families loyal to Mexico simply crossed the Rio Grande and formed their city—Nuevo Laredo, Mexico. And, again, life for the residents of Laredo continued much as usual. Indian raids and outlaw gangs were still a problem.

By 1878, large ranches had been established in the area. Webb County had 239,000 sheep and goats and 9,000 cattle. In 1881, the Texas Mexican Railway was completed from Corpus Christi to Laredo and, for the first time, Laredo had direct access to a deep-water port. The following year, the Missouri Pacific Railroad joined with the National Lines for Mexico City at Laredo; and Laredo became the "Gateway to Mexico" for international freight.

By 1900, most of the local ranchers concentrated on cattle rather than sheep. Irrigation had been developed, and fruits and vegetables were being grown. Laredo was noted for its Bermuda onions, cantaloupes, and tomatoes.

After World War I, natural gas and oil were both discovered in quantity in the area, and Laredo became the center of one of the most important producing areas in the state.

With the completion of the Pan American Highway in 1935,

Laredo's tourist trade began to develop. Then, in World War II, the Laredo Army Air Field was set up (closed in 1974).

Laredo has a population of 120,000; its sister city has a population of more than 350,000. Laredo is still a major rail and highway gateway to Mexico; the Missouri Pacific and Texas Mexican Railroads serve the area. Laredo is also a center for tourism and for oil and gas operations. Brick, clothing, shoes, and electronics, among other products, are manufactured in the city.

Laredo has many historical buildings and sites. Two of the most popular are the Museum of the Republic of the Rio Grande (which is housed in the building constructed in 1834 that served as the Capitol for the Republic of the Rio Grande) and the Nuevo Santander Museum (which is housed in four restored buildings from old Fort McIntosh and is located on the campus of Laredo Junior College and Laredo State University).

Annual events of special interest are Washington's Birthday Celebration, (an annual event since 1898 and held during the week of February 22nd), the recently added "Jalapeno Festival" celebrated at the same time, the Border Olympics, (the first major outdoor track and field event in Texas in which university, college, and high school students from the southwestern states and Mexico compete, and which is held the first week in March), and BorderFest, a July 4th celebration of folklife in South Texas.

Bullfights and traditional Mexican events are scheduled periodically in Laredo's sister city—Nuevo Laredo, Mexico—five minutes away.

LEVELLAND

Levelland is the county seat of Hockley County in North Texas. It is 31 miles west of Lubbock on U.S. Highway 385 and State Highway 114. Its population is 13,809.

C. W. Post bought the Oxsheer Ranch in 1906 and designated a site for a new town on his ranch. In 1912, he placed a marker, "Hockley City," at the spot he gave for a building site for the courthouse of Hockley County. Hockley County, however, was not organized until 1921. When, in 1922, a petition for a post office for Hockley City was sent to the postal authorities, the petition was turned down—a town named "Hockley" already existed in Texas. At a town meeting, Mrs. T. W. Bowers suggested a name descriptive of the area—level land, which was then spelled as one word and thus became "Levelland."

Levelland today is a farming and petroleum center. The county is one of the leading oil-producing counties in the state. Principal crops grown include cotton, sorghum, wheat, soybeans, corn, hay, and sunflowers.

Levelland is home to South Plains College, a fully-accredited two-year public school.

LEWISVILLE

Lewisville is located in North Texas in the southeastern corner of Denton County. It is at the north-northwestern edge of Dallas on Interstate 35 East and is part of the Dallas-Fort Worth metroplex.

Early settlers were attracted to the area by the rich soil as well as by the offer of free land. John and James Holford from Missouri were two of the early settlers. In 1855, they sold their land to Baseal W. Lewis, and Mr. Lewis laid out what would become the town of Lewisville. Almost immediately, a grist mill, trading post, and dry goods store were built.

With the arrival of the Dallas & Wichita Railway in 1881, the town became an important trading center. Its population in 1900 was 500; in 1925, it was 825; and today, it is 45,600.

In early times, Lewisville's economy was primarily based on farming (cotton, fruits, and vegetables).

The routing of Interstate 35 through Lewisville in the 1950's greatly enhanced its growth and expansion. Present-day Lewisville has varied industries. The city is served by the Missouri-Kansas-Texas Railroad. Many Lewisville residents work in the Dallas-Fort Worth area.

Lake Lewisville is nearby for all water sports.

LIBERTY

Liberty is located in the southern part of East Texas and is the county seat of Liberty County. It is 39 miles northeast of Houston and 44 miles west of Beaumont on U.S. Highway 90 and Farm-to-Market Road 1960. Its current population is 7,945.

The area around present-day Liberty had been claimed by both the Spanish and the French in by-gone years. In 1756, the Spanish built two missions and presidios on the Trinity River. The northern post was known as Atascosito, and the trail connecting the two settlements to other Spanish settlements deeper in Texas was known as the Atascosito Road. The road became a popular and well-used route into Texas when the United States bought Louisiana in 1803.

The Mexican government encouraged people to colonize the area and, by 1826, 407 people lived in Atascosito. In 1831, the Mexican government issued titles to the land and laid out a town and named it "Villa de la Santissima Trinidad de la Libertad"—which was then shortened to "Liberty" by the residents.

Liberty became a major port on the Trinity River when steamboats began making regular runs up the river; then the railroads came to the area in 1860. Cattle and cotton were transported to Galveston, both by boat and by rail. During the Civil War, much of the beef for the Confederate army in Louisiana came from Liberty. One of the companies of men from Liberty who fought as part of Hood's Brigade in the Confederate Army was known as the "Liberty Invincibles."

Liberty remained a farming and ranching center until 1925 when oil was discovered (the South Liberty Oil Field). Today, Liberty is a center for oil pipe manufacturing and oil field services.

Transportation access has always been a big factor in Liberty's economy, and it continues to be a key to Liberty's future. Liberty's port is located on the Trinity River, the longest navigable river in the State. Liberty is 60 barge-miles from the Houston Ship Channel and 73 barge-miles from the Intracoastal Waterway. It is on a main line of the Southern Pacific Railroad. Oil, sulphur, chemicals, timber, steel, and farm products are processed and shipped. Principal crops grown in the area are rice, soybeans, grain sorghum, and wheat.

Liberty has a mayor/council/city manager form of government. The city is rich in history. William Barrett Travis, Sam Houston, and David G. Burnet all practiced law in Liberty.

The Sam Houston Regional Library and Research Center, the official regional historical resources depository for the ten counties of Southeast Texas, is located in Liberty. The Center is available to both professional researchers and amateur geneologists.

Deer, dove, pheasant, and quail are bountiful. Ducks and geese winter here.

LITTLEFIELD

Littlefield is the county seat of Lamb County. This county is one of the largest agricultural producing counties in Texas. Together with its beef stock income and its agriculture, it has an income of $113,000,000 worth of agricultural products a year. This is almost four times the average income of Texas counties.

Littlefield is located on U.S. Highway 385 and on State Highway 54. The Atchison, Topeka and Santa Fe railroads serve the City. The nearest commercial airport is the Lubbock International Airport, 34 miles away. This airport has several major airlines serving it.

In 1830, Major Long, of the United States Army, and his companions explored the area that the present town of Littlefield occupies. In his written report, he and his party pronounced this land unfit for cultivation, that no one would ever live here and that the land would forever remain the unmolested haunt of the Indian hunters, the bison and the jackal.

Thirty-five years later (1876) the people of Texas voted to trade this worthless land to anyone who would build a magnificent State Capitol building in Austin, Texas. The decision to do this trading at $.50 an acre was based on Major Long's report about the harshness of the area. This trade of three million acres of Texas land for a building was so unique that it was published in newspapers throughout England, Europe, and the United States.

The trade was made, the huge new State Capitol Building was built, and the three million acres in West Texas became the largest ranch in the world. Named the XIT, it covered the better part of nine Texas Panhandle counties. The magnificent State Capitol Building remains in use today, but the XIT Ranch is gone, a victim of sixteen unprofitable years of operation (1885 to 1901). The owners of the XIT began selling off the ranch to pay accumulated debts. The first tract of some 312,000 acres was sold to Major George W. Littlefield, Austin banker and cattleman, in 1901, at $2.00 per acre.

In 1912, the Major hired Authur P. Duggan, who laid out the townsite and held the grand opening on July 4, 1913. The town was therefore named after Major George Littlefield. The people take great pride in the good farmland and its abundant production, and in the city itself.

Lamb County is situated in the middle of the huge Ogallala Water Aquifer. This supplies the water to irrigate 300,000 acres of farmland in Lamb County.

In 1974, the citizens organized and began construction on a new 30,000 head capacity cattle feedyard. On February 22, 1975, the intended construction of a $30 million denim textile mill to be built in Littlefield was announced by American Cotton Growers. Construction began early in May of 1975. The ACG Textile Mill is one of the most modern denim operations in the world. It now employs about 600 people with an annual payroll of about $3.3 million. It consumes about 65,000 bales of raw cotton, producing 20 million yards of denim annually. This is enough denim to make about nineteen million pairs of blue jeans. The ACG Mill has made Littlefield the denim capital of the West.

Littlefield now has a population of 8,000 people.

The City of Littlefield has a council-manager form of government. The city council consists of four councilmen and a mayor and these officials are elected for two-year terms. They set policies and hire a city manager, who serves as a chief administrative officer. The city of Littlefield has no zoning ordinances. The city of Littlefield has a very good tax rate. The breakdown of the taxes are as follows:

City	.3969
County	.1576
School	.7850
State	-0-
Other	.0450
	1.3845 per $100 Assessment

Littlefield has access to four major educational colleges and universities. They are as follows:

Texas Tech University, Lubbock	34 miles
Wayland Baptist University, Plainview	52 miles
South Plains College, Levelland	22 miles
Lubbock Christian College	34 miles

The agricultural industry is "Big Business" in the Littlefield area. It is listed among the biggest of Lamb County's industries.

Over $113,000,000 is brought into the county each year as a direct result of agricultural production. Cotton is the leader in agriculture income in Lamb County, accounting for 33% of the total agriculture income. This amounts to approximately $40,000,000 derived from 918 farms producing 265,000 acres, averaging 350 pounds per acre.

Following close behind cotton is the second largest agriculture product in the county . . . corn, which produces $20,000,000 or 17% of the total agriculture income. Corn in Lamb County is grown on more than 60,000 acres, averaging 129 bushels per acre. Wheat with 50,000 acres in production, averages 40 bushels per acre for an income of $6,000,000 or 5% of the total agricultural income. Other agricultural income is derived from grain, sorghum, alfalfa, soybeans, vegetables and forage hay.

Beef cattle production is the major livestock enterprise with numbers exceeding 108,000 head grazing 250,000 acres in the county.

LIVINGSTON

Livingston is located in the East Texas Piney Woods and is the county seat of Polk County. It is 75 miles north of Houston on U.S. Highways 59 and 190 and State Highway 146.

In 1836, Moses L. Choate came to the area and established the town of Springfield, so named because of the numerous springs in the area.

In 1846, a committee was asked to choose a county seat for Polk County. Three towns were under consideration—one of which was Springfield. The matter was decided when Mr. Choate offered to donate 100 acres of land if Springfield were chosen and if its name would be changed to Livingston.

There are conflicting stories as to the reason for Mr. Choate's selection of the name "Livingston." Some people say Mr. Choate was from Livingston, Tennessee, and others claim he was from Livingston, Alabama; some claim the town was named for either Robert or Edward Livingston.

Livingston today has a population of 6,100. It is a center for lumbering, tourism, and oil. The Southern Pacific Railroad lines run through Livingston.

Livingston is on the eastern shoreline of Lake Livingston (approximately 90,000 surface acres) which was built and is owned and operated by the Trinity River Authority. Lake Livingston is the largest lake constructed for water supply purposes located entirely within the state. Full-service marinas, boat ramps, camping, and motel accommodations are available at the lake.

The Livingston area is a popular seasonal hunting spot—duck, dove, quail, and deer.

Nearby places of interest include the Big Thicket National Preserve (located southeast of Livingston) and the Alabama-Coushatta Indian Reservation (one of only two Indian reservations in Texas, and located east of Livingston).

The "Pine Cone Festival" is held the first Friday, Saturday, and Sunday of October each year.

LLANO

Llano is located in the central mineral region of Texas on the Llano River. It is the county seat of Llano County and is 72 miles northwest of Austin and 113 miles north of San Antonio. The community can be reached by State Highways 16, 29, and 71. Its current population is 3,323.

In 1535, Alvar Nunez Cabeza de Vaca led an expedition of exploration in the area. However, it was over 300 years later before settlers began to arrive. After a peace treaty was made with the Comanches in 1845, settlers were brought to the area by the Adelsverein, a German group which aided emigration to Texas. The town of Llano was founded in 1855 and became the county seat in 1856.

The name "Llano" (meaning "plain" in Spanish) seems to be a misnomer, as the town is in the Texas Hill Country and is located on a spring-fed river. It is said the river was originally called "Rio de Los Chanas"—the Chanos being a band of Tonkawa Indians. Over time, the words "Chanos" and "Llano," having similar sounds, were confused and "Llano" gradually replaced "Chanos" when referring to the river, for which the town was named.

The threat of Indian raids on the area settlements was finally resolved in 1873. Packsaddle Mountain (now used by hand gliders), east of Llano, was the site of the last battle between the settlers and the Comanches. With the Indian threat removed, the settlements began to grow.

Llano experienced a boom in 1886 when large deposits of magnetic iron ore were found. 10,000 people crowded into Llano but, in 1893, when no coal was found in the area (to make steel), the boom was over.

Minerals found in Llano County (but not necessarily in commercial quantities) include gold, silver, iron ore, serpentine, manganese, and graphite. A rare type of brown granite with sky blue crystals and rusty-pink feldspar is called "llanite" and is found nowhere in the world but in Llano County. And, surprisingly, pearls have been found in the area. Northeast of Llano is Lake Buchanan, fed by the Colorado River; the freshwater mussels in the Colorado yield pearls.

Many houses and buildings in Llano date back to the late 1800's. Of particular interest are: the Llano County Museum (featuring a large collection of Indian and early Texas artifacts and a large display of area gems and minerals); the Confederate Monument; the Llano County Courthouse (built in 1893); the Llano County Jail (built in 1895); and the World War I Monument (on the Courthouse Square).

Present-day Llano has an aldermanic form of city government, with a mayor and five aldermen. Its economy is based on livestock production (cattle, horses, goats, and hogs); manufacturing of such diverse products as livestock feed, handmade boots and saddles, and cabinets; granite finishing; and some peanut farming and grape growing. The Southern Pacific Railroad serves the area.

Llano County has been termed the "Deer Capital of Texas." The density of deer in the Llano Basin is greater than that of any other area in the nation.

Enchanted Rock State Natural Area is 22 miles south of Llano and is a popular spot for climbing, backpacking, camping, and picnicking.

The "Old Boom Days in Llano" celebration is held the first weekend in June each year.

LOCKHART

Lockhart is the county seat of Caldwell County and is located 30 miles south of Austin and 70 miles northeast of San Antonio. It can be reached by U.S. Highway 183 and State Highway 142.

Byrd Lockhart was a sureyor with Green DeWitt's Colony. As payment for his survey work in the area, he requested and received the land around the springs (site of present-day Lockhart).

When Caldwell County was newly-created in 1848, Lockhart was designated the county seat.

Lockhart's early economy was based on cattle. Many trail drivers lived in the town, which was the gathering point for trail drives heading north.

The coming of the railroad resulted in greater growth for the town. Lockhart had a number of hotels and saloons and was a regular stop for drummers (traveling salesmen). An opera house provided plays and musical programs; the Lyceum featured speakers such as President Grover Cleveland.

Present-day Lockhart has a mayor/council type of government. The Union Pacific Railroad serves the community. Lockhart has various manufacturing plants, although agriculture is still important to its economy. Primary crops are cotton, sorghum, wheat, corn, and watermelons. Its population is 9,944.

Lockhart has a number of buildings and sites listed in the National Register of Historic Places. Of particular interest are the Courthouse, the old County Jail, the Emmanuel Episcopal Church (completed in 1856), the Dr. Eugene Clark Library (built in 1899, the oldest continuously used library in Texas); the Brock Log Cabin (built in 1850 and believed to be the oldest building in the county still standing).

The "Chisholm Trail Roundup" festival is held in Lockhart each June, during which event the Battle of Plum Creek is reenacted.

LONGVIEW

Longview is located in East Texas in the eastern part of Gregg County and, partly, in the western part of Harrison County. Longview is 128 miles east of Dallas and 41 miles west of the Texas-Louisiana state line. It can be reached by Interstate 20; U.S. Highways 80 and 259; and State Highways 42, 149, 300, and 31.

O. H. Methvin deeded 100 acres of land to the Southern Pacific Railroad in 1870. It is said that railroad surveyors, when laying out the railroad right-of-way and townsites, were so impressed by the long view, or the distance they could see from a nearby hillside (called Rock Hill) that they named this townsite "Longview."

Longview was chartered in 1871 and, in 1873, designated the county seat of Gregg County.

By 1887, Longview was a prosperous trade center. Area farmers brought in cotton to be ginned, baled, and sold, and, in turn, bought needed farm supplies.

Currently, Longview is the center of the East Texas oil industry. Local plants manufacture such diverse products as: plastics, chemicals, heavy equipment, recreational vehicles, metal cans, hats, steel products, railway equipment, yard trailer jockeys, equipment for the lumber industry, signs, truck parts, and boats.

LeTourneau University and Kilgore College (Longview Center) are located in Longview.

LUBBOCK

The history of Lubbock is as varied and fascinating as that of any western community in the United States. The one unique factor that has made Lubbock the "Diamond of the West" is that of plenty of underground water. Tracing back, some 150 million years ago, this whole area (now known as the Plains) was one vast lake area. The passing of time combined with the force of the wind and other of nature's happenings created the level surface of the plains as it appears today.

It was across these plains in 1540 that the Spanish explorer, Captain Francisco Vasques de Coronado, came to explore the Southwest. Coronado was in search of the golden city of Quivira. In fact, historians and archaeologists have evidence that these expeditions camped in the famous "Lubbock Lake Site and Yellow House Canyon." Lubbock Lake Site, located north of the city, is one of the archaeological wonders of the United States. There experts can trace chronologically year by year, all cultural groups of people who lived in the Southwest. They can trace from elephant hunters 20,000 years ago to the Comanches of a hundred years ago.

These Spanish explorers named many of the natural geographical features, and these names are still being used today. The Lubbock Lake Site was known as *La Punta de Agua* or the Place of Water, *Llano Estacado* was called Southern High Plains, *Canon Casas Amarillos* was Yellow House Canyon, and *Canon de Rescate* was Canyon of Ransom. In this Canyon of Ransom, trading was done between the Indians and the Spanish traders for captives and goods. Many relics of the Coronado Period are on display in the West Texas Museum of the Texas Tech University Campus.

Later, Indians of the Comanche Tribe roamed this whole area

because it was a haven for the buffalo, antelope, lobo, prairie dog and coyote. This lasted until the 1870's when the hunters began to kill the Indian's livelihood. These hunters were responsible for many of the Indian uprisings and later caused General N. S. MacKenzie to come into the area to clear the Plains. MacKenzie Park, located within Lubbock, bears this man's name. After the slaughter of the buffalo, very few people stayed on these level plains where the grass grew to saddle-stirrup height, and the cottonwood trees and other vegetation grew abundantly in the canyons and lake areas.

Lubbock is the seat of Lubbock County. It is the major city of the south plains. The city is 118 miles due south of Amarillo. The early settlers complained of prairie fires, sand storms, tumbleweeds and occasional droughts. The average annual rainfall is 18.4 inches, which is less than required to consistently grow most crops.

Lubbock is located in the center of a rich agricultural area. Thanks to irrigation, the county produces over three times the average Texas counties agricultural income. It has an annual income of $100 million. 225,000 acres of land are irrigated. The water comes from the huge high plains Ogallala Aquifer.

Lubbock has a population of 185,000. It has an altitude of 3240 ft. The city is on U.S. Highways 27, 62, 82, 84 and 87, State Highways 289 and 331, and FM 40, 835, 1729, 1730, 2341 and 2641.

The first train pulled into Lubbock from Plainview with steam hissing, smoke billowing, to be met by the entire town at the depot with the old "Brass Band" on September 25, 1909. Lubbock had arrived as the "Hub of the Plains"—transportation-wise at least. The arrival of old "John Santa Fe" was the ending of many years of work on the part of many people. Many "paper railroads" were proposed and many false starts were made before the Santa Fe built their line. The chief credit goes to Monroe G. Abernathy, a Lubbock realtor, who served as the town's representative with the Santa Fe officials.

The city is served by the Burlington Northern Railroad and the Santa Fe Railroad. The city of Lubbock has an airport with several commercial airlines offering service.

Lubbock, as were almost all towns in West Texas, was named after a signer of the Texas Declaration of Independence and a

Texas Hero, Tom S. Lubbock. He was a former Texas Ranger, Confederate officer (he organized the Terry Rangers), and brother of Francis R. Lubbock, the Civil War governor of the State.

Reese Air Force Base is located in Lubbock.

Many cattle ranches surrounded the community of Lubbock. There were ranches with such names as XIT with its three million acres to the north of Lubbock, Colonel C. C. Slaughter with his lazy S of 50,000 acres, the Matador Ranch, the T Bar, the Spade, the Spur, the Pitchfork and many others. The main problems that these ranches had were: the level plains with little protection for cattle, the undependable surface water and the grass fires. Then came the discovery of plentiful water at shallow depth and ranching flourished. On many ranches the windmill crew did nothing but go from windmill to windmill repairing them. This was not only a full-time job, but one of the most important, since each cattle herd was dependent on the water supply, and each mother cow drank about twenty gallons a day. As more wells were drilled, water flowed abundantly using the new pumps run by gasoline, and the plows cut open the grass prairie for the farming of cotton, grain and other crops. Land became too valuable for grazing of cattle. The ranchers on the high plains started to cut them into farms and sell the land at $25.00 per acre. This, considering the original cost of $1.00 to $2.00 an acre, made an unbelievable profit. (Today some of the same land sells for approximately $2,500 an acre.)

Lubbock is in the center of a huge agricultural area; 75% of the income is from crops, including cotton, wine grapes, sorghum, wheat, corn, sunflowers and soybeans. The other agricultural income is from feedlot cattle, hogs and poultry. The largest cotton seed processing plant in the world is located at Lubbock.

Located at Lubbock are: many manufacturing plants, including major electronic company's consumer products headquarters, manufacturers of earth manning equipment, mobile homes, food containers, fire protection equipment, clothing, and many other products.

There are many things of interest in the Lubbock area, some of these are:

Lubbock County Museum
Lubbock Fine Arts Center
Lubbock Lake Landmark

MacKenzie State Park
Museum of Texas Tech
Ranching Heritage Center

LUFKIN

Lufkin is the county seat of Angelina County in East Texas. It is 124 miles north-northwest of Houston, 86 miles south of Longview, and 46 miles west of the Texas-Louisiana state line. It can be reached by U.S. Highways 59 and 679 and State Highways 103 and 287.

Angelina County, founded in 1846, has had four county seats—Marion, Jonesville, Homer, and then, in 1892, the courthouse was moved to Lufkin.

From the early days, the East Texas forest (and related lumber and timber industries) have been important to the economy of Lufkin. Even today, 70% of Angelina County is in commercial forest and the county is the leading timber-producing county in Texas.

Present-day Lufkin is a leading manufacturing center. Its population is 28,562. Angelina College is located in Lufkin, as is the Lufkin State School (for the mentally retarded). There are many historical markers and points of interest in the city. Among them are the birthplace of Allen Shivers (Texas governor, 1949-1957); Mantooth Street (turn-of-the-century homes); the Texas Forestry Museum; and the Ellen Trout Park Zoo.

Lake Sam Rayburn, the largest freshwater lake located entirely within Texas, is southeast of the city.

LULING

Luling is located in southern Caldwell County, 56 miles east of San Antonio, 45 miles south of Austin, and 145 miles west of Houston. It is 1 mile north of Interstate 10 on U.S. Highways 90 and 183 and State Highway 80. Its population is 5,039.

In 1870, the western terminus of the Galveston, Harrisburg & San Antonio Railroad was in Columbus (64 miles east of present-day Luling). Col. Thomas W. Pierce of Boston had purchased the railroad franchise and had the option of continuing the line to San Antonio or to Austin. He chose San Antonio and, when surveying a proposed route, he indicated the site for a new town to be called "Luling"—which was his wife's maiden name. The rail line to Luling was completed in 1874 and Luling soon became a cattle shipping center.

(Incorrect versions of the origin of the name "Luling" attribute the name to Pierce's Chinese cook, Loo Ling, or to a railroad official's daughter, Lula.)

The discovery of oil in 1922 brought a new spurt of growth to Luling. Today, ranching, agriculture and oil are the basis of Luling's economy. The Southern Pacific Railroad still serves Luling.

A three-day "Watermelon Thump Festival" is held the last weekend in June each year on Thursday, Friday, and Saturday.

Nearby is Palmetto State Park with campsite, nature trails, fishing (crappie), swimming, birding, and picnicking.

LUMBERTON

Lumberton is located in Hardin County, whose eastern boundary is the Neches River. It is ten miles north of Beaumont. The first name of the settlement was Chance-Loeb. When the first railroad came through the town, it was a major lumber shipping point. The railroad named it Lumberton.

The city is located on U.S. Highway 69 and State Highway 96. The city is served by the Santa Fe Railway Company and the Southern Pacific Railway Company. The nearest deep water port is Beaumont. The nearest Commercial Airport is Jefferson County Airport, and the Houston Intercontinental Airport, 110 miles to the west.

The city has an average annual rainfall of 54 inches. This is one of the highest in the state.

Hardin County has an annual agricultural income of only $5,000,000; 85% of the agricultural income is from forestry products. The area around Lumberton is heavily forested. This is the piney woods of Texas. Much of the area to the west of Lumberton is covered by the "Big Thicket."

There is considerable industry in the city and the surrounding territory. Paper making, wood processing and food processing are the principal industries.

The city has a mayor-council form of city government. The population of the city is 7,700. The city enjoys an excellent tax structure. The breakdown is:

County	0.46 per $100 Assessment
City	0.00 " " "
School	1.26 " " "
	$1.72

Lamar University is an excellent four-year university and is located 10 miles south at Beaumont.

Two of the recreational attractions in the area are the Big Thicket National Preserve, and the Big Thicket Museum at Saratoga, 18 miles to the west. The Village Creek State Park will open in 1991.

MADISONVILLE

Madisonville is a handsome East Texas Community, with a population of 4,000. It has been an incorporated township for 77 years. Madisonville today boasts some of Texas' finest cattle and horse country, highlighted by a half dozen showplace working spreads, including the famed McDermott Ranch, the Great Western, the Santa Elena and La Mejor. There are many other smaller ones, as well as much more land waiting to be covered with horses and cattle. Now that pari-mutuel betting and race tracks are coming to Texas, it's only a matter of time until more breeders and trainers establish operations around Madisonville.

The city of Madisonville has a general law form of government, which calls for a mayor-city manager and six councilmen. The Burlington and Northern Pacific Railroad serves Madisonville. The Huntsville Municipal Airport offers air transportation.

The taxation for the City of Madisonville is as follows:

City	$0.6739 Rate Per $100 Assessed Value
County	$0.64271
School	$1.0800
	$2.39661 Per $100 Assessed Value

This is extra high, in that the optimum Texas City ad valorem tax rate is $1.75 per $100 of Assessed Value.

Two higher educational facilities are available within 45 miles of Madisonville: Texas A&M University at College Station, and the Sam Houston State University at Huntsville.

In the Madisonville area, there are several important historical sites, which include the Fort Trinidad and Robbins Ferry Crossing on the Trinity River. The El Camino Real or Old San Antonio Road, which ran from Laredo, Texas to San Augustine passed nearby.

Madisonville is located 96 miles north of Houston on I-45 and 36 miles east of Bryan on State Highway 21. Madisonville is located on a league of land granted by the Mexican Government on May 28, 1835, to Job Starks Collard, a member of Austin's Colony. In 1854, Mr. Collard donated 200 acres of land to the county for the purpose of establishing a county seat. Mr. Collard operated the town's first business establishment, a hotel, and a general store. Today Madisonville is the only incorporated town in Madison County. The county was named Madison after the U.S. President James Madison. When Madison County was created in 1853 and organized in 1854, Madisonville was named as the county seat and took the name, Madisonville.

MALAKOFF

Malakoff is located in Henderson County, 75 miles southeast of Dallas, 93 miles northeast of Waco, and 43 miles southwest of Tyler. It can be reached by State Highways 31 and 198 and Farm-to-Market Road 3441.

An early settler in the area was Dr. John Collins. In 1850, he applied to the postal authorities for a post office for his settlement, and he proposed the name of Malakoff—naming it for a Russian town that became prominent during the Crimean War.

A little silver was being mined in the Wild Creek area, but the town primarily depended upon farming for a livelihood. By 1860, there were two cotton gins in town.

The St. Louis and Southwestern Railroad arrived in Malakoff in 1880, making it easier and faster to get the cotton to market.

Then, in the early 1900's, lignite was found and mining began. To serve the mines, the Malakoff Fuel Company Railroad was built.

Brick clay deposits were also found in the area and, in 1904, a brick plant was built.

Malakoff has never been a big town. Its population in 1900 was 376; in 1950, it was 1,283; and today, it is 2,082. Malakoff still has the brick factory. Crops grown in the area include grain, hay, fruits, vegetables, melons, and nursery crops.

MANSFIELD

Although Mansfield is located at the southern boundary of Tarrant County, part of it extends into Johnson County. It is five miles south of Arlington and eighteen miles southeast of Fort Worth, and can be reached by U.S. Highway 287 and Farm-to-Market Roads 917 and 157.

Before 1850, nomadic tribes of Tonkawa, Comanche, Kiowa, Wichita, and Hasini Caddo Indians inhabited the area of present-day Mansfield. In 1856, Julian Feild bought 540 acres from the William Price Survey; and by 1860, he had built and was operating a steam-powered grist mill with his partner, Ralph S. Man. The community that grew up around the mill was called "Mansfeild"—"Man" for Ralph S. Man and "feild" for Julian Feild. Misspellings of the name over time resulted in the present spelling of "Mansfield."

After the Civil War, many families moved to Texas, and Mansfield became a major trade and educational center. The Mansfield Male and Female College was established in 1869; and the Mansfield Academy in 1901.

Mansfield has a couple of "firsts" in its history: (1) The Mansfield Cardinal Road was the first paved road in Tarrant County; and (2) The Mansfield Independent School District was the first school district in Texas to be desegregated by court order (in 1955).

At the time of its incorporation in 1890, Mansfield had 418 residents. It has grown to its present population of 16,261. Various products are produced in Mansfield's industrial parks. The Southern Pacific Railroad services the city.

The southern end of the newly opened Joe Pool Lake meets Mansfield's city limits.

MARBLE FALLS

Marble Falls is located in the middle of the Texas Highlands and the Highland Lakes area. It is located in Burnet County on U.S. Highway 281, FM 1431, and FM 2147. It is on the Colorado River.

The city was named for the Colorado River waterfalls flowing over marble out-croppings. The city has a population of 4,600. It has an elevation of 770 feet. The city has a mayor-council form of government.

Granite Mountain is a huge 866 foot high dome of high-quality pink and red granite, prized worldwide. It is located just west of Marble Falls. Quarrying began in 1880 for construction of the Texas Capitol building. Texas traded 3.5 million acres of panhandle land for $0.50 an acre to pay for building the Texas Capitol. The owners formed the famous XIT ranch. The marble for the Texas Capitol was quarried with the aid of Texas convicts. The Stone Cutters Union raised a strong protest, and boycotted the project. The contractor went to Scotland and brought in 62 stone cutters. The convicts also built the narrow gauge railroad from Burnet to Granite Mountain.

An un-ending flow of the superb material has continued to come from Granite Mountain ever since, yet the bulk of the dome has hardly been diminished. The granite dome is located just off FM 1431.

The Marble Falls area is served by the Southern Pacific Railroad which starts at the Granite Mountain, west of Marble Falls, and goes north to Burnet, at which point it turns east toward Austin.

Marble Falls has an average annual rainfall of 29.8 inches. This is sufficient for most crops. The county has a very low agricultural income of $15.8 million; 85% of this income is from cattle, sheep, and goats. Other income is from pecans, hay, grain and cedarposts.

There are a number of manufacturing plants in the area producing precision instruments, sporting goods, stone quarrying and graphite products.

The nearest commercial air transportation is at Austin, 45 miles to the east.

Marble Falls was the home of Oscar J. Fox, the composer. He studied and lived in Europe and New York, and became the favorite composer of Franklin D. Roosevelt. Fox gained world fame with his collection of western tunes like "Home On The Range," "Git Along Little Doggie," and "Old Paint;" his musical inspiration still came from this countryside. His most famous tune "The Hills of Home" was written with this view in mind.

The Highland Lakes Bluebonnet Trail takes place each year around the first of April. This trail tour is a beautiful sight.

Marble Falls is located south of Lake Marble Falls. Lake LBJ is further north up the river. Still further up the river is Lake

Buchanan. A new dam is under construction on the Colorado River in Coleman County. This will be the Stacy Lake down the river from Marble Falls, and Lake Travis.

MARLIN

Marlin is the county seat of Falls County. It is located in central East Texas. It is almost equal distance from Dallas, San Antonio and Houston. It is almost 115 miles due south of Dallas. It is 170 miles north-northeast of San Antonio, 140 miles northwest of Houston and 27 miles southeast of Waco. State Highways 6 and 7 intersect at Marlin. Farm-to-Market 147 runs northeast to Groesbeck.

The population of Marlin is 7,100. The city has a mayor/council/city manager form of Government. The annual rainfall is 32.5 inches, which is sufficient for all types of crops. The city is east of the Brazos River. The fertile Brazos Prairie lands are very productive from an agricultural standpoint. The area around Marlin is heavily farmed. The altitude of the city is 400 feet.

The Union Pacific railroad serves the city. The nearest commercial airport is Waco, 27 miles to the northwest.

On January 21, 1851, citizens of Falls County met at Dr. Allensworth Adams' home to select a new location for a county seat to replace Fort Milam. Twenty votes were cast favoring the selection of Adams, located on a spring near Dr. Adams' home. Three months later, the name was changed to Marlin, in honor of John Marlin, the dead alcalde of Robertson's colony.

Marlin's location near the Brazos River prospered in the rich prairie land abundant in timber and game.

In 1892 efforts to obtain an adequate water supply for drinking and domestic water were thwarted when drillers, employed by the township to sink a well, struck a stream of hot mineral water. Because of the bad taste and the hardness, the water was allowed to drain into the nearby creek.

In 1895 the benefits of the healing waters were discovered and the first bath house spa was built. It was followed by other spas, clinics and doctors. Word of the medicinal properties of the water spread quickly, and Marlin soon became a mecca for those suffering from a long list of illnesses and disease. Daily trains brought passengers to the spas for treatment. With the advent of modern drugs, Marlin's spas and clinics faded in popularity.

Marlin's main industry today is stocker cattle, with over 80,000 steers raised annually in the county, along with forage crops, and retail business as its economic base.

The city has a good tax rate, the breakdown is as follows:

City	.4106
County	.5750
School	.7000
Fire District #1	.0300
Total Tax Rate per $100 Assessed Value	$1.7156

This rate is considered good, in that anything under $1.75 per hundred valuation is considered good in Texas.

There is a considerable amount of industry around Marlin. The major manufacturers are:

Wallace Computer	
Marling Mfg. Co., Inc./Prestige Business Fashions	*Business forms*
Tex Style Carpet Mill	*Uniforms/Career apparel*
Wolf Manufacturing Co.	*Carpet*
U.S. Silica Co. of Texas	*Garments*
(Kosse)	*Mine—sand & clay*

The largest employers in the area are the Marlin Veterans Administration Medical Center and the Texas Department of Corrections, which has a prison farm in the area.

One of the main sites for tourists is the famous Highlands Mansion which has been restored and is a very interesting and attractive old mansion.

The area around Marlin is a rich agricultural area. The county has a $34,000,000 average annual income; 75% of this income is derived from beef cattle, hogs, turkey, eggs and crops.

The crops raised are sorghum, hay, cotton, wheat and oats.

MARSHALL

Marshall is located in East Texas and is the county seat of Harrison County. It is eighteen miles west of the Texas-Louisiana state line, 72 miles south-southwest of Texarkana, and 151 miles east of Dallas. It can be reached by Interstate 20, U.S. Highways 80 and 59, and State Highways 43, 154, and 390.

The first settlers reached the area of present-day Marshall in the early 1830's. After Harrison County was created by the Texas Legislature in 1839 and organized in 1842, Greensborough was first designated the county seat; later the county seat was moved to another community, Pulaski. However, in 1842, because both Greensborough and Pulaski were found to be "unsanitary," commissioners were appointed by the Republic of Texas to select a seat of justice. Peter Whetstone, one of the commissioners, owned 4,444 acres in the area and invited the other commissioners for a meeting on his property. After spending some time drinking spring water and whiskey, the commissioners agreed that Whetstone's land was a good site for the seat of justice. Whetstone thereupon donated some land, and the town of Marshall (in honor of Chief Justice John Marshall) was laid out.

The site of present-day Marshall has been under seven flags—that of Spain, France, Mexico, the Republic of Texas, the United States, the Southern Confederacy, and the State of Missouri.

Under the Republic of Texas flag, Marshall was a cultural and educational center and became known as "The Athens of Texas." James Pinckney Henderson, the first governor of Texas, and Senator Wigfall both lived in Marshall.

After the fall of Vicksburg, Marshall became the Western Capitol of the Confederacy. Several generals were stationed in Marshall and lived on Burleson Street on what is now known as "Generals' Row."

From 1863 to 1865, Marshall served as the Capitol of the State of Missouri. Governor Thomas Reynolds of Missouri conducted state business, in absentia, from Marshall. He had chosen Marshall because of its good stagecoach connections with St. Louis.

Present-day Marshall has a population of 24,921. Its economy is dependent on petroleum and lumber processing, chemicals, steel products, tile, pottery, aluminum products, bus frames, apparel, and other products. Cattle, hogs, and poultry are raised in the surrounding area; the principal crops include wheat, oats, grains, corn, and hay. The Missouri Pacific Railroad services the area.

Wiley College and East Texas Baptist College are located in Marshall, as are many historic buildings and sites.

MATHIS

Mathis was founded in 1889; it is located in the northwest part of San Patricio County. A large settlement of Irish farmers and ranchers lived there during the earliest days of Texas history.

Mathis is 110 miles south-southeast of San Antonio, 50 miles north of Kingsville, 160 miles north of the Mexican border at Reynosa and 33 miles northwest of Corpus Christi.

Mathis is located on State Highway 359, just west of U.S. Highway 37 which goes from San Antonio to Corpus Christi.

Mathis is on the southeastern shore of the large Corpus Christi Lake, located on the Nueces River. This is one of the principal sources of water supply for the City of Corpus Christi. It is a favorite fishing spot for sportsmen.

The City of Mathis was founded by Mr. Thomas H. Mathis, a prominent South Texas Rancher. He gave the town his name when it was organized.

The population of Mathis was approximately 6100 in 1989. The County of San Patricio produces $65 million dollars worth of livestock and agricultural products annually. This is double the average county agricultural income in Texas. The town is the principal commercial center for the agricultural area, featuring livestock and cotton, also producing large quantities of grain, sorghum, flax and varied truck crops.

The area around Mathis has extensive oil and gas production, and many petrochemical plants are located in the general area.

The rainfall of the area is 30.6 inches per year. This is on the borderline of needing irrigation. Although many of the crops can be raised very successfully with this amount of rainfall, it is quite often necessary to do some irrigation. The county of San Patritio has five thousand acres under irrigation.

During the early days, Mathis was an important center for truck farming. The area produced large volumes of onions, cabbage, carrots and spinach. However, the market for this produce no longer exists. Other areas in the state took over this truck farming, and the farmers in the Mathis area turned to the production of maize, corn and cotton which they produce now in large quantities. The land around Mathis is in the Blackland Coastal belt and is very fertile and productive.

There is a considerable amount of manufacturing in the city. There are a number of manufacturing plants located there.

The city is served by the Missouri Pacific Railroad.

McALLEN

McAllen is located in Hidalgo County in the Rio Grande Valley in South Texas. It is located 60 miles west of Brownsville, 150 miles southwest of Laredo, 144 miles south-southwest of Corpus Christi, and 7 miles north of the Texas-Mexico border. It can be reached by U.S. Highways 83 and 281 and State Highway 336.

There are at least four accounts, all different, of the founding of McAllen. There is even dispute as to what constitutes "founding." The general belief is that McAllen was founded in 1909 and incorporated in 1911.

The Missouri Pacific Railroad reached the McAllen area in 1905. Ordinarily the arrival of the railroad led to the founding of a town; in McAllen's case, however, that was apparently not true, even though a depot was built. Some people think the depot was called "West McAllen"—but no one is sure.

There seems to be agreement, however, that James McAllen, a Scottish immigrant, operated a 65,000 acre ranch in the area and, about 1909, deeded 1,200 acres to the McAllen Townsite Company. A community was established on that land, which was some distance east of the railroad depot. There is dispute, however, as to who established the first business in the town. By 1910, the town's population was 150.

Irrigation of the land began early in the town's life, and grapefruit and other citrus fruits and vegetables were grown; 6,000 acres were under irrigation by 1914.

Banditry and outlaw gangs were a continuing problem, not only for McAllen but the entire border area. On July 4, 1916, 12,000 soldiers from northern and eastern states were sent to McAllen to stop the banditry. At the time the soldiers arrived, McAllen was a small town; existing facilities were stretched to their limits to provide housing, food, drink, and other necessities and entertainment for the soldiers. Restaurants were set up under tents, boarding houses were constructed, and new businesses begun—the town boomed and there was work for everyone. By the time the soldiers left in March, 1917, McAllen had grown into a city.

Two years later, broom corn became a big money crop; 35 broom corn buyers headquartered in McAllen, and McAllen became a broom corn center. The successful sales of the product with its high prices helped the other business in town to grow also.

McAllen today has a population of 92,000. It is a popular tourist center because of its weather and its proximity to Mexico; McAllen is host to many northern residents each winter. McAllen is also a center for petroleum processing, food processing, and packing and shipping. Rubber products, medical equipment, hospital furniture, electronics, food equipment, and apparel are made here. The Missouri Pacific Railroad serves the McAllen area.

McGREGOR

McGregor is located in McLennon County nineteen miles southwest of Waco and 92 miles north of Austin on U.S. Highway 84, State Highway 317, and Farm-to-Market Road 2416.

When the Gulf, Colorado and Santa Fe Railroad was considering its route westward, Dr. Gregor Carmichael McGregor (who lived in Waco but owned property west of the city) offered them a right-of-way through his property. The railroad accepted the offer and, in 1882, after the railroad was built, lots were sold and a new community came into being. It was named "McGregor Springs." Later the "Springs" was dropped and the town became known as just "McGregor."

Present-day McGregor has a population of 4,513. Products manufactured include rocket motors and fuel devices and office supplies. Farm crops grown in the area include cotton, sorghum, wheat, oats, and hay.

McGregor is served by the Santa Fe and AMTRAK Railroads.

McKINNEY

McKinney is located in North Texas 33 miles north of Dallas on U.S. Highways 75 and 380. It is the county seat of Collin County. Its estimated population in 1986 was 20,500.

When Collin County was created in 1846, it was named for Collin McKinney, a signer of the Texas Declaration of Independence and a member of the committee drafting it. Initially, Buckner was designed the county seat of the new county. In 1848, however, the county seat was moved to a point near the geographical center of the county, and the new county seat was named "McKinney" as a further honor to Collin McKinney.

Champion International, Fisher Controls, Leightner Electronics, Montgomery Elevator, and Texas Instruments all have manufacturing facilities in McKinney. Other manufacturers make such diverse products as saddles and leathergoods, packaged chile mix, ultra light aircraft, epoxy adhesives, and microphones.

Crops (sorghum, wheat, hay, and cotton) and livestock (beef cattle and horses) are also important to McKinney's economy. The city has a council-manager type of government. The Southern Pacific Railroad serves the city.

McKinney has numerous sites listed in the National Register of Historic Places. The Old Collin County Jail was built about 1880 and the County Courthouse in 1875. There are numerous antique shops and art galleries. Of special interest are the Heard Natural Science Museum and Wildlife Sanctuary, Bolin Wildlife Exhibit, Bolin Antique Museum, Collin County Farm Museum, the Old Post Office Museum, and the Chestnut Square Historical District.

MEMPHIS

Memphis is the county seat of Hall County and it is located in the extreme northeast corner of the county. It is located on U.S. Highway-287, State Highway-256 and Farm-to-Market-257. Memphis is located 87 miles southeast of Amarillo. The city has a population of 4,500. In 1990, it will celebrate its one hundredth birthdate. The area has an annual rainfall of 19.5 inches which is insufficient to raise most crops. There are 20,000 acres of irrigated farmland in Hall County.

Memphis is burdened with a high tax rate. The breakdown on the taxes are as follows:

County	.4500	
City	.4500	
School	.9500	
Special Dist.	.1500	
	2.0000	per effective rate on current values.

The city has a mayor-alderman form of city government.

The county has an agriculture income of $24 million annually, which is just under the average of the Texas counties. The farm crops are cotton, sorghum and wheat. The city also raises a considerable amount of beef cattle, and hogs. The minerals in the area around Memphis are gas, oil and gravel.

The city is served by the Burlington Northern Railroad. The nearest commercial airline service is at Amarillo.

College level schools in the area are:

Clarendon Jr. College	22 miles
Vernon Jr. College	80 miles
West Texas State University	100 miles
Amarillo College	87 miles

The altitude is 2,067 feet.

It is not definitely known how Memphis got its name. The name was selected by J. C. Montgomery, "the father of Memphis." He bought land and started the town of Memphis. It is thought he named the town after Memphis, the early-day capitol of Egypt.

The city was incorporated in 1906, and today calls itself the Cotton Capitol of the Panhandle.

MESQUITE

Mesquite is located in Dallas County. It is on the east side of Dallas and in fact, is almost encircled by the Dallas incorporated limits.

Mesquite is one of the most rapidly growing cities in Texas. In 1988 it had a population of 102,000. It is a residential city with varied industrial and distribution businesses.

Mesquite was incorporated in December of 1887. The railroad had named the town "Mesquite." This name was obviously selected because of the Mesquite trees which grow in profusion throughout the area. The incorporated area of Mesquite is now 20.7 square miles.

The Texas & Pacific Railway Company built its line through Mesquite in 1873. This resulted in Mesquite's rapid growth. The railroad ran from Dallas to Shreveport, Louisiana. Mesquite is served by I-635 and I-30 and I-20 Highways.

Mesquite has a large number of business firms. Today there are more than 3000 business firms that hold sales tax identification numbers. Big Town Shopping Center, the first enclosed mall in the Metroplex area, is here; Town East Mall opened its doors in 1971 with 1.2 million square feet of retail space.

A major industrial breakthrough occurred in 1969. Western Electric Co. (now AT&T), started the construction of its major manufacturing facility in Mesquite. They call it the Mesquite Works, which is the largest manufacturer of power equipment for the telephone industry in the world. It is Mesquite's largest single employer. The Mesquite works employ approximately 3,400.

The Dallas County Community College District in 1968 constructed the Eastfield Community College on I-30. It opened its doors to the public in 1970. It now has an enrollment of 8,500 students.

Mesquite has a council-city manager form of city government. The city is one of Texas' showplace growing cities.

MEXIA

Mexia is located 40 miles east-northeast of Waco and 83 miles south of Dallas. It can be reached by U.S. Highway 84 and State Highways 14 and 171.

General Jose Antonio Mexia (a friend of Sam Houston, Stephen F. Austin, and William B. Travis) and his wife owned a large land grant in Limestone County which they passed on to their children, Matilda and Enrique. Enrique spent part of each year in Limestone County on the family property and part of each year in Mexico on the family holdings there.

When the Texas & Central Railroad reached Limestone County in 1871, Enrique donated land to the railroad for a right-of-way and a townsite. And the townsite, of course, was named "Mexia" for the Mexia family.

Mexia experienced an oil boom in the 1920's, and oil and gas are still produced in the area. Mexia is now an agribusiness center and its economy centers on wholesale grocery distribution as well as furniture, sportswear, and other products. Crops grown in the area include sorghum, cotton, hay, peaches, oats, wheat, corn, peanuts, and pecans. Cattle, hogs, and horses are also raised. Mexia State School is located here. Mexia's population is now 7,094.

Lake Mexia is nearby for recreational purposes.

MIDLAND

Midland is located in West Texas on Interstate 20. It is 306 miles east of El Paso, 118 miles south of Lubbock, and 148 miles west of Abilene. It can also be reached by U.S. Highway 80 and State Highways 158, 191, 250, and 349.

Starting in the mid-1860's and continuing for thirty years, approximately 10 million cattle crossed this area on trail drives. Indians roamed the area but there were few, if any, settlers.

In the 1880's, the Texas and Pacific Railway built a rail line from Fort Worth to El Paso. A water stop on the line was called "Midway" because it was about half-way between the two cities. However, when application was made to the postal authorities for a post office, it was found there was already a town called "Midway" in Texas. The name, therefore, was changed to "Midland," and a post office was opened in 1884.

The first settlers were mainly cowboys and sheepherders. Land was available at 50 cents an acre. There was no surface water, however, so wells had to be dug and windmills built to pump the water to the surface. Midland soon became known as "Windmill Town" because of the numerous windmill structures.

John S. Scharbauer was one of the early ranchers in the area. He developed his cattle herd until he had the largest and most famous Hereford cattle in the world.

By 1895, Midland was an important rail shipment center for cattle; Midland cattle had the reputation of being the best on the market. Midland is still a livestock sale center; beef cattle, sheep, and horses are still raised in the area and form an important part of Midland's economy. The principal farm crops are cotton, sorghum, and small grains.

Midland did not change much until 1923 when oil was discovered. Midland is situated near the geographic center of the oil-rich Permian Basin. Oil fueled Midland's growth, and oil and associated industries continue to be an important component of Midland's economy.

Midland today has a population of 70,525 and is the county seat of Midland County. It is a center for petroleum and petrochemical operations. Local manufacturers make clothing, oil field and petroleum-related equipment, plastics, electronic calculators, and other products. The Missouri-Pacific Railroad services Midland's needs.

Midland College is located here.

MINEOLA

Mineola is located in northeast Texas in Wood County and is 81 miles east of Dallas, 47 miles west-northwest of Longview, and 88 miles west of the Texas-Louisiana state line. It can be reached by U.S. Highways 69 and 80 and State Highway 37.

L. R. Graham, a storekeeper, was apparently the first settler in the Mineola area (then known as Sodom). Other settlers arrived in the 1840's, and by 1859 there was even a sawmill in the area.

In 1873, both the Texas & Pacific Railroad and the International & Great Northern Railroad were building rail lines—one from the East and one from the West—and the lines were scheduled to meet at Sodom. Railroad officials had agreed that the railroad which reached Sodom first would win crossing rights and would own the terminal property, and the winner was the International & Great Northern.

The railroad was instrumental in attracting settlers and businessmen to the town which centered around the railroad station. The *Wood County News,* published in Mineola, stated: "In 1900 there were four drug stores, three restaurants, four saloons, an ice and beer house, three or four blacksmith shops, two photograph galleries, one tin shop, three cotton yards, two wagon yards, one lumber yard, two newspapers, two barber shops, three railroad repair shops, two fresh meat markets, five physicians, two dentists, two hardware stores, five dry goods, a steam gin and mill, a compress and furniture factory."

There have been several versions as to how Mineola got its name. The most widely accepted story is that the town was named for Minnie Patten (daughter of A. L. Patten) and Ola Evans (daughter of Major Ira H. Evans, an official with the International & Great Northern Railroad); and the name was approved by I. E. Ward, a Construction Engineer from Mineola, New York.

Today, Mineola has 4,346 residents. It is a farm trade center as well as a tourism and railroad center. Its manufacturers make clothing, camping and boating equipment, livestock feeds and other farm products, precision machinery, and electronics. Crops grown in the area include watermelons, sweet potatoes and other vegetables, hay, corn, and small grains. The Missouri-Pacific Railroad serves the area.

MINERAL WELLS

Mineral Wells is located in North Texas at the eastern edge of Palo Pinto County, extending partly into Parker County. It is 48 miles west of Fort Worth, 90 miles south-southwest of Wichita Falls, and 109 miles east-northeast of Abilene. It is located at the intersection of U.S. Highways 180 and 281.

The story of the founding of the city of Mineral Wells is as follows: James A. Lynch of Virginia suffered from acute arthritis and, in the late 1800's, he and his family headed west to settle in a warmer climate. They camped in the area of present-day Mineral Wells and decided to stay. After digging a well and drinking and bathing in the sulfurous water, Lynch gradually became stronger and healthier. He was convinced the water was medicinal; he shared it with his neighbors and they began reporting miraculous cures. More wells were dug, and more and more people came to see if the water could cure their afflictions.

By 1882, there were more than 140 wells. Drinking pavillions, rooming houses, hotels, and bathhouses sprang up to accommodate the people who came to "take the waters." Not only was the water being drunk and bathed in, but it was being bottled and sold, and even the salt residue (after boiling off the water) was packaged into boxes and marketed.

The greatest popularity for the health spas was in the 1920's and 1930's. The Baker Hotel, built in 1929, was known as the South's greatest health resort. Its customers included such well-known persons as Marlene Dietrich, Mary Pickford, Helen Keller, Will Rogers, and General John Pershing.

Mineral Wells today has a population of 14,468, and it is still a tourist center. Manufacturing of such varied products as clay pipe, aircraft systems, plastics, electronic products, brick, feeds, and clothing are also important to its economy. Beef cattle, hogs, goats, sheep, and horses are raised; and pecans, peaches, vegetables, grains, and hay are grown in the area. The Weatherford, Mineral Wells & Northwestern Railroad services Mineral Wells.

Possum Kingdom Lake and Palo Pinto Creek Reservoir are nearby for water recreational activities.

MISSION

Mission is located in the Rio Grande Valley just a few miles north of the Rio Grande. It is situated at the intersection of U.S. Highway 83 and State Highway 107 in Hidalgo County. It is 40 miles west of Harlingen, 154 miles southwest of Corpus Christi, and 134 miles southeast of Laredo.

The Oblates of Mary Immaculate established La Lomita Mission (about 3 miles south of the present-day city of Mission) in 1845, and most of the activities in the area centered around the mission. Later, the La Lomita Land Company was organized and purchased land from the Oblate Fathers. When the Missouri Pacific Railroad ran a rail line through the Land Company property in 1908, a railway station was built near the center of the new development. The town that grew up around the railway station was named "Mission" in honor of the chapel.

Citrus was first planted in the Rio Grande Valley in the Mission area. Citrus is now a multimillion dollar business, and Mission is still the center of the Valley citrus industry. The "Citrus Fiesta" is an annual event.

Mission's population is now 22,653. The Missouri Pacific Railroad still serves the area.

Of interest in the area are Lomita Plaza (in the center of downtown Mission); La Lomita Mission and the surrounding historical park (3 miles south of Mission); and Los Ebanos Ferry (the only hand-operated ferry still operating across the Rio Grande, and located about 10 miles west of Mission).

MONAHANS

Monahans is located in West Texas in pioneer Ward County. It is 240 miles east-southeast of El Paso and 36 miles southwest of Odessa. It is situated at the intersection of U.S. Highway 80 and State Highway 18, 1 mile north of Interstate 20, and is 32 miles south-southeast of the southeast corner of New Mexico. Monahans is the county seat of Ward County, and its population is 8,397.

Historically, Monahans was born with the coming of the Texas and Pacific railroad. It was a water stop between two section points (Sandhills and Aroya) where the T&P surveyor John Thomas Monahan had dug a well and found plenty of good water in the summer of 1881. On September 12, 1881, Texas and Pacific sent the first railroad line, known as "Monahan's Well." Years later the name was shortened to "Monahans."

In 1882, Monahans abounded in game and livestock, with grass knee high as far as one could see. Game of all kinds was plentiful. After the Civil War the country was overrun with unbranded cattle. Cowhunting was a community project, and it was not unethical to catch unmarked cattle, brand them and establish ownership, and ranching became a primary occupation of the area. In 107 years, there have been great changes in Monahans and Ward County in the cattle industry. From "cows" to fine, pure bred Herefords, a cross-breeding with some of the exotic breeds and Angus Cattle—from the cowboy on a horse, to the mustang, to a fine quarter horse, to the pickup, the jeep and now the helicopter.

On November 2, 1928 oil was discovered in Ward County, and Monahans experienced an oil boom. Another significant development was the construction of the Million Barrel Tank by Shell Oil. It was built to take care of an oversupply of oil being produced in the Permian Basin, but could not be used due to leakage. A museum has been established on this site, and is a tribute to early-day Monahans, the 1928 oil discovery, 1909 Holman House, antique farming equipment, windmill, jail, railroad section houses and caboose.

Today, oil, gas and other minerals dominate the economy of Ward County, with Monahans a center for oil activities and oil field equipment. There is also a gasoline plant. Beef cattle are still raised; primary crops are alfalfa and hay. The Missouri Pacific Railroad provides rail service to Monahans.

On the governmental side, in April, 1955, Monahans adopted a home rule charter and a city manager form of government.

Other attractions besides the Million Barrel Museum include the Sandhills State Park, 15-square miles of "snow-mountain sand," with museum, picnic grounds, and sand sledding. The Rattlesnakes Bomber Base Museum, located in Pyote, fifteen miles west of Monahans, is a must for all World War II buffs.

MOUNT PLEASANT

Mount Pleasant is in the northeast corner of Texas. It is the county seat of Titus County and can be reached by Interstate 30, U.S. Highways 67 and 271, and State Highway 49. It is 63 miles southwest of Texarkana, 119 miles north-northeast of Dallas, about 53 miles west of the Texas-Louisiana state line, and about 50 miles south of the Texas-Oklahoma state line.

Titus County was created by an Act of the Texas Legislature in 1846. John Binion Sr., Richard Moore, and L. Gilbert laid out a 48-block townsite to serve as the county seat for Titus County. The townsite was founded in 1848 and named "Mount Pleasant."

The name of the town originated with the Caddo Indians. Red mineral springs had attracted Indians to the area for many years. The vicinity of the springs was dominated by mounds constructed by some prehistoric race. One large mound, in particular, was well-known to the Caddoes and was called, in their language, "Pleasant Mound." To early settlers, then, it became "Pleasant Mount," and later, "Mount Pleasant."

The economy of early Mount Pleasant centered around farming and timber. There was an abudance of hardwood trees in the area. The town population was 227 in 1850 and had grown to over 3,000 by 1900.

In 1861, Titus County voted in favor of secession, and over 2,000 men went east to fight on the Confederate side in the Civil War. A Confederate transportation depot was based in Mount Pleasant. Blacksmiths, carpenters, harness makers, and wheelwrights were employed to fashion harnesses and wagons to transport men, army supplies, and cotton (one of the major crops in the area).

Mount Pleasant sent many men to the Confederate Army. Some of them fought and died on battlefields whose names still haunt the American past: Shiloh, Gettysburg and Chicamauga.

The "Tyler Tap," a 3-foot-gauge line, was Mount Pleasant's first railroad. The following year (1879), the Texas and St. Louis Railroad bought the Tyler Tap and connected it with a through line from St. Louis to Waco. In 1887, a branch line was built from Mount Pleasant to Sherman, Texas. Later, the Paris and Mount Pleasant Railway also built a line to serve Mount Pleasant. The result of all these rail lines was to make Mount Pleasant the "Hub of Northeast Texas."

From 1900-1910, Dellwood was a popular resort and health spa in the area; it centered around Mount Pleasant's mineral spring—but then the development company went broke and the hotel burned. After years of neglect, Dellwood has once again been developed into a recreational area.

In 1934, during the depression, a Civilian Conservation Camp was established in Mount Pleasant. The Works Progress Administration and the Public Works Administration also provided many jobs in the area.

Today, Mount Pleasant has a population of 14,800. Its economy is based on oil, agribusiness, tourism, and lignite mining. Titus County is one of the leading counties in Texas in broiler production, and Mount Pleasant has beef and poultry processing plants. Crops grown in the area include corn, watermelons, sorghum, hay, and peanuts. Rail service is provided by the St. Louis Southwestern Railroad.

Northeast Texas Community College is located at Mount Pleasant.

Fishing and other water recreations are available. Four lakes within twenty minutes of Mount Pleasant offer 17,000 acres of water fun known as the "Bass Capital of Texas." Mount Pleasant is home to some of the best fishing and water recreation anywhere.

MOUNT VERNON

Mount Vernon is the county seat of Franklin County. This county is the smallest one in Texas. Mount Vernon is located on U.S. Highways 30 and 67 and on State Highways 37 and 423. It is served by Farm-to-Market Roads 21 and 115. The city is located 110 miles east of Dallas. The city was named after George Washington's home.

It is served by the St. Louis and Southwestern Railroad.

The terrain is rolling country, heavily wooded with pine, gum and hardwoods. There are many small streams in the area.

There are several lakes in the vicinity, including Lake Bob Sandlin, which has a large paddlewheeler, the Queen Maria, which offers dinner and cruises. Other Lakes are Cypress Springs and Montecello. The population of the town is 3,000. The altitude is 476 feet above sea level. The annual rainfall is 44.8 inches which is sufficient for raising all crops.

There is some industry in Vernon including clothing factories, beef packing plants. The town is a major livestock, marketing and supply center.

Even though the county is just about ⅓ of the size of the average Texas county, it has an average agricultural income of $30 million per year. Approximately 90% of the income is from dairy products, beef cattle and poultry. The principal crops are timber and hay.

MULESHOE

Muleshoe is located in the High Plains of the Texas Panhandle 18 miles east of the Texas-New Mexico state line, 66 miles northwest of Lubbock, and 100 miles southwest of Amarillo. It can be reached by U.S. Highways 70 and 84 and State Highway 214, and is the county seat of Bailey County.

In 1885, the XIT Ranch, with its 3 million acres, was spread over ten West Texas counties. In 1913, E. K. Warren bought some of the XIT land and named it the Muleshoe Ranch. Many stories have been told as to why Warren chose the name Muleshoe for his ranch; perhaps the one told most often is that one day while walking over the property, one of the men with Warren picked up an old rusty muleshoe, and the ranch became known as the Muleshoe Ranch.

Muleshoe is located in the famous High Plains Ogallala Aquifer. The farmers have wells to irrigate their farmlands which are very productive. The average annual rainfall is 17.4 inches.

The county produces $61.0 million of agricultural income. This is double the average county agriculture income.

The city of Muleshoe is located on most of Sections 39, 40, and 54 of Block Y of the Muleshoe Ranch.

Bailey County was created by an Act of the Texas Legislature in 1876 and was organized in 1917, and Muleshoe was designated its county seat.

Muleshoe's population today is 4,842. It has a council-manager type of city government. The Atchison, Topeka & Santa Fe Railroad services the city.

Farming and ranching are the primary activities in the area. Beef and dairy cattle and hogs are raised. Principal crops are milo, wheat, cotton, corn, alfalfa, soybeans, and sunflowers. Food processors in the area include Galante (picante sauce, salsa, and jalapeno strips) and Valley Grain (masa and tortilla chips).

Muleshoe Wildlife Refuge was established in 1935 and is the oldest national refuge in Texas. It is located 20 miles south of the city of Muleshoe. Waterfowl, including the Sandhill Crane, winter here.

Of special interest is the National Mule Memorial located on Highway 84 Downtown and the Muleshoe Heritage Center (featuring the old Muleshoe Depot, the Jane's Ranch house, and the old Muleshoe Ranch cookhouse), on Highway 84 West.

NACOGDOCHES

Nacogdoches is referred to by some Texas historians as "The Indian Town." The Tejas Indians lived in East Texas, and the name of Texas is derived from their name.

It is recounted that in the days of long ago, an old Caddo chief lived on the banks of the Sabine, the river of the cypress trees.

To him, twin sons were born: Natchitoches, swarthy of features, with straight black hair and flashing black eyes; and Nacogdoches, fair of complexion, with blue eyes and yellow hair. As the old man neared the end of his days, before being ushered into the happy hunting grounds, he called his twin sons into his presence to receive his final blessing and instructions. He commanded that immediately following his death, Natchitoches should gather his wife and children together and turn his face toward the rising sun, and after a three days' march should build his home there and rear his tribe; while Nacogdoches was instructed to travel a like distance toward the setting sun where he should rear his children and his children's children. Thus the twin tribes of Nacogdoches and Natchitoches were founded 100 miles apart, and thus Nacogdoches was the father of the Tejas, the white Indians of eastern Texas, and the name given to the city of Nacogdoches.

Less than 50 years after Columbus sighted America, Hernando De Soto, in the winter of 1541-1542, penetrated as far west as Nacogdoches where he spent the winter, sending out scouting parties further west to search for the Seven Cities of Cibolo.

The first definite description of Nacogdoches and its aboriginal population is in the accounts of La Salle's visit in 1685 to Nacogdoches.

De Leon and his followers, in 1691-1692, made the first serious attempts to educate the Tejas Indians in European ways by taking several of the young members of the tribe back to the College of Zacatecas in Mexico.

The first permanent European settlement in the town of Nacogdoches was made in June 1716, when Fray Antonio Margil de Jesus founded the Mission Nuestra Senora de Guadalupe de Nacogdoches.

During the struggle between the French and Spanish for mastery of eastern Texas, the Mission Guadalupe had an eventful history.

With the French cession of Louisiana to Spain in 1764, the Spanish took an increased interest in Texas. Mexico rebelled against Spain in 1810 and won its independence in 1821. Under Mexican rule, Nacogdoches regained its former prestige as the largest town in East Texas.

The Americans began to emigrate into Texas in the early 1800's, and many of them entered by way of Nacogdoches. Stephen

F. Austin and his 300 families began to settle in Texas between the Colorado and Brazos Rivers beginning in 1822.

During the Texas war against Mexico in 1835, Nacogdoches played an important support role.

Nacogdoches has been under nine flags: The Lilies of France with La Salle in 1686; the flag of Castile and Aragon of Spain in 1716; the green flag Magee-Guitierrez Expedition in 1813; Long's flag of the First Republic of Texas in 1819; the white and red flag of the Republic of Fredonia in 1826; the flag of the Mexican Republic, 1821-1836; the Lone Star Flag of the Republic of Texas; the Stars and Bars of the Southern Confederacy, 1861-1865; and finally the Stars and Stripes.

Today Nacogdoches is a modern city of 29,500. It is the county seat of Nacogdoches County. It is located in deep East Texas, just east of the Angelina River. It is 138 miles north-northeast of Houston on U.S. Highway 59. It is also served by State Highways 21, 7, 224, and 343 and Farm-to-Market Roads 1279, 2863, and 1879.

Nacogdoches is a rich agricultural area. It has a rainfall of 58 inches annually. The county has a large agricultural income of $190 million, which ranks it in the ten largest agricultural counties. The area produces a large quantity of lumber, plywood, cotton, cattle, poultry, dairy products; it is the leading broiler-producing county in the state.

Nacogdoches is a large industrial city. It produces valves, aluminum furniture, feed, fertilizer, business forms, transformer, candy, dresses, and motor homes.

The city is served by the Southern Pacific Railroad.

It is located eighteen miles north of the north end of Sam Rayburn Lake.

NAVASOTA

Navasota is located in Grimes County. It is two miles east of the Brazos River on Highway 6. It is 70 miles northwest of Houston, 189 miles south-southeast of Dallas-Ft. Worth and 114 miles east of Austin. The highways serving Navasota are State Highways 6, 90 and 105 and Farm-to-Market Highways 362, 1227, and 3090.

The Navasota River runs east of Navasota and joins the Brazos River ten miles south of Navasota. The land between these two rivers in the area of Navasota and for some fifteen miles north of that, are possibly the richest and most productive farmlands in Texas. Washington-on-the-Brazos is about seven miles southwest of Navasota across the Brazos River. Before the railroads came to this area, they wanted to go down the westside of the Brazos, through the settlement of Washington-on-the-Brazos, but the leaders of that town denied granting any railroad right-of-way. The railroads moved their line location across the river to the east and went through Navasota. This was the making of Navasota.

Today, there are three railroads serving Navasota, the Union Pacific, the Southern Pacific and the Santa Fe.

There is some uncertainty as to exactly how the town of Navasota got its name, but originally the Indians had given the river the name Navasota; and it is presumed that when the town of Navasota was formed, it took the name of this river.

Navasota has the council-city manager form of government. The city has an elected council composed of five members.

The city has a rather high tax rate, which totals $2.115 per $100 of Assessment. The tax for the Navasota Industrial District is $.33 per $100. This is what runs the tax rate up.

Navasota's principal identifying landmark is a statue of the famous French explorer, Rene Robert Cavelier Sieur de LaSalle who was murdered by his own men on March 19, 1687 near Navasota, approximately at the confluence of the Navasota and Brazos Rivers. Facts are sketchy, but it is believed that LaSalle was attempting to reach Canada overland after losing his ships in Louisiana when his crew turned on him and murdered him.

In 1930, citizens of Navasota joined hands with the Texas Society of the Daughters of American Revolution to erect a 14½ foot statue of LaSalle on the Washington Avenue esplanade near downtown. This statue has had historical importance and interest through the years. The French government officially recognized Navasota as the place of LaSalle's death and has presented a bust of the famous explorer to the Historical Commission for display in the P. A. Smith Hotel, which is being restored.

The mining of lignite and the generation of electricity from it will play a major role in expanding the economy of Navasota and Grimes County during the next 100 years.

The Texas Municipal Power Agency has built its Gibbons Creek plant on 23,000 acres near Carlos, in Grimes County. The plant went into operation in August, 1983. The plant was built at a cost of approximately $600,000,000 and generates 400 megawatts of electricity for four cities. 1,200 persons were employed during the construction phase, and upon completion the plant retains 500 permanent workers with a payroll estimated at $12.5 million, an average of $25,000 per employee annually. Of vital interest to Navasota is the 2500-acre reservoir and dam, which is already stocked with Florida bass. The lake in reservoir is to be used as a cooling lake for the plant.

In the planning stage is a similar, but much larger, mining and generating operation called Brazos Coal Ltd., to be located just across the Grimes County line in Brazos County. Planners say it will be two and a half times larger than the TMPA and will be built at a cost of almost $2 billion, generating 1,080 megawatts of power.

Two of Grimes County's most popular tourist attractions are the Navasota Nostalgia Days and the Texas Trek at historic Anderson, the county seat, during which the public is invited to make tours of some of the most beautiful Victorian, East Lake Victorian and Classic Greek Revival homes in the Southwest. Some of these homes are more than 100 years old. One of the most beautiful homes is that of Mr. and Mrs. W. J. Terrell, one of Navasota's most historic residences. "Nostalgia Days" are held on the first weekend of May each year. A wide variety of activities are planned for the two-day festival, including antique shows and sales, arts and crafts shows and sale, quilt exhibit, juried art show and juried doll show.

Lifeblood of Grimes County's economy is the centralization of industries in the Navasota Industrial Park where nineteen different companies employ in excess of 1400 persons and will greatly exceed that number in the immediate future.

Navasota was organized on June 24, 1854, when it received postal service. The population of Navasota today is 7,500.

Texas A & M University is located only 26 miles north at College Station.

NEDERLAND

In December of 1897, Nederland was officially put on a map prepared by civil engineer Robert Gilham. He placed that name on the map of approximately 42,000 acres belonging to the Port

Arthur Townsite Company. They named the acreage "Nederland" to pay tribute to the Dutch who financed the Kansas City Railroad. It was also said that the area resembled the low, flat land of Holland.

The Port Arthur Rice and Irrigation Company was established in 1897 to irrigate 5,000 acres of land, using a steam-powered pump to irrigate the land. This was the start of an extensive rice growing industry in the area.

After the Franco-Prussian War of 1870, which caused severe economic conditions in Holland, many of the Dutch emigrated to the Nederland area. The Orange Hotel was built in late 1897 by the Port Arthur Land Company for the Dutch who needed a place to stay while raising money to buy land and to build their homes. The hotel was built on the west bank of the Neches River in Port Arthur.

Nederland is located 12 miles north of Port Arthur on U.S. Highways 69, 96, and 297, and 12 miles south of Beaumont. It is in Jefferson County, which is in the extreme southeast corner of Texas.

It is served by the Southern Pacific Railroad.

Nederland is an industrialized city with a population of 18,000. It has a number of oil and chemical plants.

The principal agricultural products of the area are beef cattle, rice, soybeans and timber.

NEW BOSTON

New Boston is located in Bowie County, Texas. This county is in the northeast corner of Texas. The county is bordered on the north by Oklahoma and Arkansas and on the east by Arkansas.

Intrastate Highway 30 runs generally from east to west and goes through New Boston and thence into Texarkana to the east. U.S. Highway 82 also runs east and west through New Boston. It comes from Paris. New Boston is well served by farm-to-market highways.

There is a confusing name situation in Bowie County. Boston is the county seat, but only has a population of 250. Old Boston is located south of Boston, and was destroyed by fire a few years ago; New Boston, located north of Boston, has a population of 6,000.

New Boston is located 150 miles east-northeast of Dallas and

23 miles west of Texarkana. The average rainfall is 49 inches which supports lush vegetation. The city is located in the pine belt of Texas.

The city was named for an early storekeeper in the settlement, W. J. Boston. The coming of the railroads led to the location of two more Bostons.

The city has a mayor-council form of government. The city has low taxes:

City	0.1345
County	.3350
School	.7800
	$1.2495 per $100 assessment

The city is served by the Union Pacific Railroad.

The Red River Army Depot is located just east of New Boston. It employs 5,340 people. The Lone Star Ammunition Plant is located nearby. Also the International Paper Co. has a lumber mill located in the area, and is the most modern plant of the company. The plant produces 60 million board feet of lumber per year and sixty thousand cords of chips.

Lake Wright Patman, formed by a dam on the Sulphur River, makes the area one of the leading recreational areas in the state.

NEW BRAUNFELS

This city has had a most interesting history. In the June 22, 1844 issue of the *Orleans Republican*, was the following news item concerning a mass German immigration project in Texas: "His Serene Highness, the Prince-Zu-Solms-Braunfels, near relative of the King of Prussia, with four individuals is on his way to Texas. He is going there for the purpose of inspecting lands which have been sold or granted by the Government of the Country, to an emigration's agent or specialist, who has been negotiating in Europe, for the transport of German Emigrants."

Prince Carl of Solms Braunfels landed at Galveston July 1844 and traveled on horseback through the territory of Texas to acquire exact knowledge of where best to locate the German emigrants, who were to follow in a few months. On July 24 the Prince found Captain John Coffee Hays, who was Commander of a Texas Ranger Company, and employed by the Republic of Texas to make surveys of the frontier. Captain Hays gave the Prince valuable information about the frontier.

In December, 1845 Prince Carl arranged for a landing port for the emigrants at Indian Point, which he named "Carlshafen," which was on the Texas coast near to where Indianola was established in 1849.

In March 15, 1845 Prince Carl crossed the Guadalupe River at the ford of the military road from Nacogdoches to San Antonio, with 25 men to inspect the land he had purchased for the first settlement in Texas that was being made by the German Emigration Company. That night they camped on the Comal River. He established the German Colony there and gave it the name New Braunfels.

New Braunfels was founded on March 21, 1845, Good Friday. The first wagons of emigrants crossed the Guadalupe and were placed in an encampment erected on a bluff overlooking the Comal River.

The founding of New Braunfels, often referred to as the "City of a Prince," had a major impact upon the immediate area, as well as opening west Texas to a civilized economy. The many artisans and craftsmen among the 6,000 settlers generated industry and commerce for the entire central Texas area.

New Braunfels now has a population of 28,000. It is the county seat of Comal County. Comal County is one of the smaller of the 254 Texas counties. It has 555 sq. miles of area which is less than half of the average size of the counties. The city is located on both banks of the Guadalupe River at the point where it crosses the Balcones fault zone. The Comal River rises in the city limits of New Braunfels and flows into the Guadalupe River all within the city limits. The Comal is one of the shortest rivers in Texas. Its origin is a series of large perennial springs that flow from the base of the Balcones Fault.

This major fault begins in Mexico and runs all across Texas, from Del Rio by way of Uvalde, San Antonio, New Braunfels, San Marcos, Austin, west of Fort Worth and crosses the Red River in Cooke County, just west of Gainesville. The fault is the geological feature that separates the Edwards plateau from the blackland belt.

The elevation of New Braunfels is approximately 700 ft. above sea level. The elevation of the heights 2 miles north of New Braunfels is 1700 feet. This 1000 differential in elevation varies along the fault line; it becomes less as the fault progresses north.

New Braunfels is located on U.S. Highway 81 and Interstate Highway 35, and on State Highways 46, 482 and 483, and it is served by several farm to market highways.

The city has a considerable amount of industry. It has firms that manufacture textiles, boots, ice chests, apparel, furniture, metal, electrical, and concrete products, lime, sand, gravel, and crushed limestone.

The city attracts a large number of tourists. It has many attractions, including the Comal Springs, Landa Park, Natural Bridge Caverns, the Comal and Guadalupe Rivers, the hill country and Canyon Dam and reservoir, located 20 miles northeast of the city.

New Braunfels is attractive, neat, clean, and modern as well as picturesque. The population is still largely of Germanic origin, and the town is proud of its German people. They are proud, hard working, thrifty, clean, and believe strongly in education.

New Braunfels is located 32 miles northeast of San Antonio. This distance is measured from Comal to Bexar County courthouses. This proximity to San Antonio gives access to the International Airport and the many facilities offered by San Antonio.

ODESSA

Odessa was established in 1881 as a stop on the Texas and Pacific Railroad. It is said that the name originated from the area's resemblance to the region around the Soviet city of Odessa in the Ukraine. The city is in the heart of a vast area that was once an ancient sea. This area is known geologically as the Permian Basin. It was created over 250 million years ago, and contains tremendous quantities of anhydrite, potassium salt, natural gas, and oil. It is called a "basin" because the rocks slope inward from all sides toward the middle; it encompasses an area 250 miles wide and 300 miles long in West Texas and eastern New Mexico.

The population of Odessa is approximately 104,800. It is the county seat of Ector County. The elevation is approximately 2,890 ft. The annual rainfall is 13.8 inches. The Colorado River Municipal Water District furnishes the area's water.

The Texas & Pacific Railroad came to Odessa in July 1881. The city started from a railroad camp and stock pens, and emerged into a thriving city.

Oil was discovered in Crane County, just south of Odessa, in 1926. The discovery of the Penn well was the beginning of a long series of successful discoveries that made Odessa what it is today—the oil capitol of West Texas.

Odessa is served by the Missouri Pacific Railroad (owned by the Union Pacific Railroad). U.S. Highways 20, 80, and 385 run through the town. The city is also served by State Highways 191, 302, and 338 and Farm-to-Market Roads 1882, 1936, 2020, and 2227.

Even though the oil industry supplies the economic drive for the city, the ranching industry continues at its normal healthy pace. The county produces beef cattle, sheep and wool, poultry, pecans and hay. Odessa has begun to diversify from a totally oil-based economy to one that is attracting a wide variety of manufacturing entities to the area.

Odessa was organized and chartered for incorporation in the spring of 1927.

ORANGE

Orange is located in Orange County in East Texas. It is located on the Sabine River, which forms the boundary between Texas and Louisiana. It is 28 miles east of Beaumont, 115 miles east-northeast of Houston, and about 30 miles north of the Gulf of Mexico. It can be reached by Interstate 10, U.S. Highway 90, and State Highways 62 and 87.

There are at least three versions of how Orange acquired its name. One tradition holds that the name came from a citrus grove, owned by George A. Patillo, on the east side of the Neches River. Another maintains that it was named for "a large grove of native orange trees that once grew in that vicinity." The most likely version is that it was named after Orange, New Jersey, the hometown of A. H. Reading, county surveyor and one of three commissioners authorized to organize the county in 1852.

The first widely-accepted name for the site of present-day Orange was "Green's Bluff." It is generally agreed that Reason Green is the man who named it, or for whom it was named, but there is dispute as to just when Green was in the area. Dates range from 1822 to 1836. In any event, by 1840, Green and his family had moved from the area, as they are listed in the Liberty County census for that year.

In 1840, the site was also referred to as "Pine Bluff" and a town called "Huntley" (for General Memucan Hunt) was being laid out. The site was also referred to as the "Town of Jefferson" and also "Lower Town of Jefferson" and "East Jefferson."

In 1842, the Congress of the Republic of Texas changed the name to "Madison" (most likely to honor U.S. President, James Madison). The town of Madison was incorporated by the Texas Legislature in 1856. However, shortly thereafter, the residents requested a name change—"Madison" was often confused with another commmunity called "Madisonville." In 1858, the Texas Legislature adopted the name "Orange" for the community, naming it after the county of which it was the county seat.

A big step for the city came in 1914, when the harbor was dredged to accommodate large ships. The deepening of the waterways was a great improvement to water transportation and enabled the construction of ships here during World War I. Wartime production resulted in a decided increase in the city's population. Then came the Depression, with World War II marking the end of those trying times.

Almost overnight, the small town of Orange, with its 7,000 residents, became a bustling, "boom town" of approximately 60,000 residents. Its shipyards again built ships, and other industries were expanded to meet the tremendous wartime demands. A United States Naval Station was installed, and additional housing was provided for thousands of defense workers, servicemen and their families.

After the adjustment was made from wartime production to peacetime operations, the population in the Orange area stabilized to approximately 35,000. The shipyards, lumbermills, port, and naval station continued to operate in the city, and, by this time, additional industries, such as the petrochemical plants and other businesses were started.

Orange has a beautiful civic plaza consisting of the W. H. Stark House, built in 1894. This example of Victorian Architecture is recognized by the National Register of Historical Places as one of the best preserved examples in this area. The Stark Museum of Western Art is a masterpiece museum that houses a valuable and extensive collection of Western American Art. The First Presbyterian Church was the first air-conditioned building in the U.S., built in 1912 of Texas granite and imported Italian white marble.

The spectacular Frances Ann Lutcher Theater, a 1,500-seat performing arts center, offers Broadway-caliber stars and has professional touring attractions and shows throughout the year.

Orange has an educational and cultural center for the benefit of Lamar University. The Brown Center was built in 1956 and is a copy of an antebellum plantation in Natchez, Mississippi. This is a true tour through the old south located on 62 acres of landscaped grounds. Orange also offers beautiful historic homes and extensive recreational areas and camp-grounds.

Orange is famous for its great seafood cuisine, caught fresh daily from the nearby Gulf of Mexico. You can shop where the real cowboys shop and leave with handmade boots, hats, belts and a saddle for ole Trigger.

Orange today has a population of 23,620. Its economy is based on its seaport, shipping, timber processing, farming, and industry. Local plants make petrochemicals, container board, ships, cement, carbon black, steel, plastics, and marble products. Rice and soybeans are the principal area crops.

OZONA

Ozona is the county seat of Crockett County and is located at the intersection of Interstate 10 and State Highway 163. It is 131 miles southeast of Midland, 81 miles southwest of San Angelo, and 210 miles northwest of San Antonio. Its population is approximately 3,500.

Crockett County was formed by an Act of the Texas Legislature in 1875. Legend says that in 1891 a group of men got together on a hot July afternoon under a spreading live oak tree to organize the county and to set dates to elect county officers. At the same time, it was decided to organize a town to be built at the meeting site. Someone suggested the name of "Ozona" for the town because the air had the freshness of ozone. That may or may not be the true story of the founding and naming of Ozona—no one knows for sure.

Ozona is the state's largest unincorporated town and the only town in the entire county. It is one of the nation's top areas in wool production. More than two million pounds of wool is marketed annually.

Oil production in the county led to a large number of local millionaires. Ozona is known for its mansions built by oil. Today, oil is still important to Ozona's economy, as is ranching. Crockett County is a major sheep producing county.

Of special interest in downtown Ozona is the Davy Crockett sculpture. It was accepted by Ozona after being turned down by the city of Crockett in East Texas.

Ozona has a number of historically-recognized and significant buildings. Among them are the Crockett County Courthouse and the old Ozona National Bank building.

Fort Lancaster State Park is west of Ozona.

PALACIOS

Palacios is located in Matagorda County about halfway between Houston and Corpus Christi. It is on Tres Palacios Bay, just off Matagorda Bay and the Gulf of Mexico. State Highway 35 is the only road into the city.

The land on which present-day Palacios is situated was once part of the ranch of cattle baron, A. H. "Shanghai" Pierce. Pierce sold approximately 20,000 acres to a group of investors who platted the land for a townsite and began selling lots in 1902. The city was incorporated in 1909 as "Palacios."

The name "Palacios" comes from a legend of long-ago Spanish sailors who became lost during a storm on Matagorda Bay. They were blown by a southern wind into another bay (now called Tres Palacios Bay) and, to the north, saw three magnificent palaces surrounded by beautiful grounds. The palaces, of course, were a mirage. The sailors, however, were so inspired by the vision and so grateful to reach land safely, they christened the spot "Tres Palacios," meaning "Three Palaces."

Palacios today has a population of 4,667. It is governed by a mayor and city council. There is an airport with three, 5,000 foot lighted runways. There are three turning basins and access to Intracoastal Waterways, Matagorda Ship Channel and Gulf of Mexico. Its economy centers around tourism, seafood processing, agriculture and petrochemicals. It has seven miles of shoreline, two free lighted fishing piers, public boat ramps, golf course, city parks and a public library.

The Marine Fisheries Research Station is located 7.5 miles west of Palacios on Texas 35 and then south 5.5 miles on Well Point Road. The Research Center studies, among other things, adaptability of salt water species to fresh water.

Historical sites include the Luther Hotel (built in 1902 and still in service), Palacios Pavilion (1902-1961, then partially rebuilt in 1988), Texas Baptist Encampment (built in 1906 and still in service).

PALESTINE

Palestine is the county seat of Anderson County in central East Texas. It is 153 miles north of Houston, 180 miles northeast of Austin, and 109 miles southeast of Dallas. It can be reached by U.S. Highways 79, 84, and 287, and State Highways 19 and 155.

The first settlers in Anderson County were Daniel Parker and his colony of 25 families from Illinois. They arrived in the area in 1833.

In 1835, Old Fort Houston (about two miles west of present-day Palestine) was built for the settler's protection; soon thereafter, a store and several cabins were built next to the fort, and a community was established.

When Anderson County was created in 1846 by an Act of the Texas Legislature, the community around Old Fort Houston was suggested as the county seat for the new county. However, it was then decided that the fort was not centrally-enough located, and the following year, a site two miles northeast was chosen as the site for the county seat. The new townsite was called "Palestine" for the former home of some of the Parker colonists—Palestine, Illinois.

Palestine has a mayor-council form of government.

From its beginnings, Palestine was the marketing and distribution center for the agricultural lands around it. Salt was an important component of the town's early economy—the Palestine Salt Dome was one of the largest in the United States and had been known and used for many years by Indians in the area.

In 1872, railroad lines were run to the foot of the hill on which the town of Palestine was located. At first the city had streetcars running up and down the hill, but that proved to be an unprofitable venture. Old businesses then moved down the hill, and new businesses were built below the hill near the railroad station.

The Civil War slowed settlement in Anderson County, but after the war, settlement increased rapidly. New residents were drawn by the good land and the abundance of game and timber.

Palestine today is a transportation and shipping center as well as an agribusiness center. Dairying, agriculture, and timber are the mainstays of Palestine's economy. The city has local plants manufacturing automotive parts, clothing, metal, and wood products. The National Scientific Balloon Facility is located here, the only one in the nation.

Primary crops grown in the area are cotton, vegetables, fruit, and cane syrup. Hickory, pine, oak, and sweet gum trees are all found in commercial quantities.

Palestine's population has grown to 22,736. The city is served by the Union Pacific Railroad for freight service; the Texas State Railroad carries passengers between Palestine and Rusk, (a tourist attraction—not for actual transportation).

Trinity Valley Community College has a campus in Palestine.

Palestine became a Texas Main Street Project city in 1986. Many historic buildings have been renovated.

The Dogwood Trails Festival is held each year the last two weekends in March and the first weekend in April. The Museum for East Texas Culture is in Palestine.

PAMPA

Pampa is the county seat of Gray County and is located in the Texas Panhandle. It is 56 miles northeast of Amarillo and 59 miles east and 71 miles south of the Texas-Oklahoma state line. It can be reached by U.S. Highway 60 and State Highways 70 and 152.

Pampa is located on land that was once part of the White Deer Lands owned by an English syndicate. The city owes its beginnings to the Santa Fe Railway. When a rail line was completed to the area in 1888, George Tyng, manager of the White Deer Lands, laid out a townsite and called it "Ontario." That name was changed to "Sutton" and, later, to "Glasgow." Then Mr. Tyng thought of the name "Pampas"—the grass in the area reminded him of the grass of the Argentine Pampas. He submitted the name "Pampa" (meaning "plain") to the postal authorities when requesting a post office for the community, and both the name and the post office were approved.

T. D. Hobart has been referred to as "the father of Pampa." He sold land only to settlers, not speculators, and most of his land sales were parcels of 160 to 640 acres. According to the sales contract, the new owner was required to make improvements on the land.

In the beginning, the area around Pampa was cattle country. Then, beginning in 1903, eastern speculators sold western land to eastern farmers. Many of the farmers went west by rail to reach the land they had bought sight unseen.

To encourage settlement in the Pampa area, an exhibit house was prepared and booklets were printed, telling of the area, the kinds of crops grown, the price of the land, and future plans for the area. When trains carrying the farmers stopped in Pampa for water, the farmers saw the exhibit house and were given the booklets. Some settled there, and others recommended the area to their friends back home.

The first gas well in the Panhandle was completed in 1918, and three years later, oil was discovered. Pampa is in the heart of a six-county, 150-mile long oil field containing more than 6,000 producing oil wells, over 2,000 natural gas wells, and 25 carbon black plants.

Pampa's population has shown a steady increase. The population in 1910 was 500; by 1930, it had increased to 10,470; and today, Pampa has 21,396 residents.

Oil ranching, and farming still form the basis of Pampa's economy. Pampa has chemical plants, petroleum processing plants, feedlots, and meat packers; laminated windshields and tempered window glass are manufactured. Chief agricultural crops are wheat, grain, sorghum, barley, corn, hay, oats, and rye. Cattle and hogs are raised.

The Atchison, Topeka & Santa Fe Railroad still serves the area.

PARIS

Paris is located in northeast Texas in Lamar County, and it is the county seat. It is eighteen miles south of the Red River (part of the boundary between Texas and Oklahoma) and 114 miles northeast of Dallas. It can be reached by U.S. Highways 82 and 271, as well as State Highways 19 and 24.

In 1839, George Wright purchased 1,000 acres of land; he donated 50 acres of it for a townsite which was first called "Pin Hook" (after a general store with that name).

Lamar County was created in 1840 and organized in 1841. The community of Lafayette was first designated as the county seat;

then Mount Vernon; and then, in 1844, Pin Hook. However, the residents believed a more elegant name than "Pin Hook" was needed for the county seat. At the suggestion of T. H. R. Poteet, an employee of George Wright and a man of French descent, the town was renamed "Paris" after the city in France.

At the time of the Civil War, Paris' population was 700. The residents opposed secession; however, once Texas voted on secession, the residents joined the side of the Confederacy.

The Texas & Pacific Railroad entered Lamar County in 1876. Other railroads soon followed—the Gulf, Colorado & Santa Fe in 1887; the Paris & Great Northern in 1888; the Texas Midland in 1895; and the Paris & Mount Pleasant in 1910.

Paris has been destroyed twice by fire—first in 1877 and then again in 1916. Each time, however, the residents have rebuilt.

Today, Paris' population is 25,498 and the city is thriving. Local plants make canned soups, steam generating equipment, apparel, food products, and farm supplies. Principal crops grown in the area are wheat, peanuts, sorghum, soybeans, cotton, and hay. The city is still served by two railroads—the Missouri-Pacific and the Atchison, Topeka & Santa Fe. Paris Junior College is located there.

In 1984, Paris was officially designated a Texas Main Street Project City.

PASADENA

Pasadena, known as the "Birthplace of Free Texas," has a population of 117,000 and a market area of 350,000. It is in Harris County and is east and contiguous to the city of Houston. It is one mile north and three miles east of Ellington Field. It is five miles from Hobby Airport.

The Southern Pacific Railroad runs through the northern part of the city. With connection by way of the Port Terminal Railroad, the city also has connections to the Santa Fe, Burlington Northern, Missouri-Kansas-Texas, and the Union Pacific Railways. State Highway 225 runs east and west through the northern part of the city.

The city has a strong mayor and council type of government.

Pasadena is highly industrialized. It has facilities belonging to 19 nationally-known industrial companies employing 12,430 people.

Pasadena is close to a number of colleges. These are: San Jacinto Junior College (3 campuses, 1 extension center, 17,000 students), Texas Chiropractic College (500 students), University of Houston Main Campus, University of Houston Clear Lake, Texas Southern University, Houston Baptist, South Texas School of Law, University of Houston School of Law, Baylor College of Medicine, University of Texas Medical and Dental, Texas Women's College, Houston Community College, and Rice University—all within 20 miles.

Pasadena was founded in 1895 by Colonel J. H. Burnet, a native of Georgia. He named his new city-to-be "Pasadena" after the famed California city which he had never visited, although he had heard of its beauty and lush vegetation. Colonel Burnet was a man of vision and planned his city with great detail. Pasadena would be the hub of a vast, rich agricultural area. For many years it was just that, as fruit and vegetables were produced in abundance. Thousands of refrigerated freight cars were loaded with delicious strawberries. Pasadena was the "Strawberry Capitol of the Gulf Coast."

The industrial revolution struck the Gulf Coast with such force that strawberries were forgotten. Its invasion point was the Pasadena area with the development of the Houston Ship Channel, the petrochemical industry, and the space industry.

The average rainfall is 48 inches. The elevation is 33-34 feet above sea level. The geographical location is longitude 95 degrees 10 minutes west, and latitude 29 degrees and 45 minutes north.

PEARLAND

Pearland is located on State Highway 35 and Farm-to-Market Road 518 in Brazoria County. The northern city limit boundary of Pearland touches the southern city limit boundary of Houston.

Pearland is another of the Texas towns that owes its beginnings to the railroad. In 1883, the Gulf, Colorado & Santa Fe Railroad completed its line from Alvin to Houston. The town established about halfway between the two points was originally called "Mark Belt" after one of the early residents. However, because of the numerous pear orchards in the area, the name was changed to "Pearland" and was recorded as such in 1894.

In its early days, the economy of Pearland was based primarily on prairie hay and livestock shipping. Later it became more diversified with rice and truck farming, dairying, and cattle raising. Then, in 1935, oil was discovered five miles south (the Hastings Oil Field) and, in 1946, Stanolind Oil & Gas Company constructed a refinery there.

Pearland's population is now 13,248. Rail service is still provided by the Atchison, Topeka & Santa Fe Railroad. Many of Pearland's residents work in Houston or other surrounding towns.

PEARSALL

Pearsall is located in South Texas in the geographic center of Frio County, of which it is the county seat. It is 54 miles southwest of San Antonio and 100 miles north of Laredo. It can be reached by U.S. Highways 35 and 81, and Farm-to-Market Roads 140, 1582, and 2779. Its population is now 7,400.

Frio County was officially organized in 1870 and "Frio Town," the first settlement in the county, was designated as the county seat.

A popular spot on a sheep ranch southeast of Frio Town was called "Waggoner's Well" because wagons stopped there for water. When the International & Great Northern Railroad extended its rail line through Frio County in 1880, Waggoner's Well became a regular water stop for the train. As was usual, a community grew up around the train stop; it was named "Pearsall" in honor of John W. Pearsall, a vice president of the railroad. The first passenger train reached the new town of Pearsall on July 4, 1881. In 1883, the county seat was moved from Frio Town to Pearsall.

Pearsall's form of government consists of elected officials-mayor and city council persons.

Frio County is a leading county in Texas for peanut production. Pearsall is an oil and ranching center. Food processing, livestock shipping, and crop raising (such as melons and vegetables) are all components of Pearsall's economy. Cotton, grain, sorghum and vegetables grow on 54,000 acres of the land.

A giant peanut monument in downtown Pearsall salutes the area's primary crop. Over 55 million pounds are marketed annually.

Pearsall also grows potatoes; a Potato Festival, celebrating the end of the harvest, is held the first weekend in June.

This is great hunting area for white tailed deer, javelina, dove and quail.

The city is served by the Union Pacific Railroad.

PECOS

Pecos is the county seat of Reeves County in West Texas. It is 209 miles east-southeast of El Paso, 77 miles southwest of Odessa, 376 miles northwest of San Antonio, and 52 miles south of the Texas-New Mexico state line. It can be reached by Interstate 20 and U.S. Highways 80 and 285.

Pecos had its beginnings as a station of the Texas & Pacific Railway when the railroad built its line across Texas in 1881. The town grew up on the banks of the Pecos River, but because of repeated flooding, the town was moved to the higher ground of its present location.

When Reeves County was created in 1883 and organized in 1884, "Pecos City" was designated the county seat. "Pecos" is an Indian word meaning "crooked"—and apparently referred to the meandering course of the river.

Shortly thereafter, two other railroads also came through town—the Santa Fe in 1890 and the Pecos Valley Southern in 1909.

Pecos was the site of the world's first rodeo on July 4, 1883. The rodeo is still an annul event—the "West of the Pecos" Rodeo is held each year during the week of July 4th.

Another annual event is the "Cantaloupe Festival" which is held the first weekend in August.

Special places of interest include the West of the Pecos Museum, one of the most complete historical museums in West Texas (it reflects life in the late 1880's); the grave of Clay Allison, the famous Pecos "Gentleman Gunfighter;" a replica of Judge Roy Bean's Jersey Lilly Saloon; the hanging tree; the jail; and the oldest house in Pecos.

The economy of present-day Pecos is based on ranching, farming, oil, gas, and sulphur. The area is still served by three railroads—the Union & Pacific, the Santa Fe, and the Pecos Valley Southern. Primary crops include cotton, cantaloupe, bell peppers, alfalfa, and onions. Pecans, watermelons, and pistachios are also grown.

The city has a mayor/council/manager type of government. Its current population is 12,855.

Major employers in the area are Pennzoil Sulphur, Smithers

Test Center (tire testing), Intratex (Enron) Gas Co. (natural gas distribution), and Foster Frozen Foods (vegetable processing).

PHARR

Pharr is the "Hub City" of the Rio Grande Valley where Expressway 83 and U.S. 281 intersect, and lies in the center of the Hidalgo County business district. Pharr is 65 miles from South Padre Island, seven miles from Reynosa: 151 miles from Monterrey, Mexico, and 235 miles south of San Antonio.

Henry Newton Pharr and John C. Kelly were co-founders of the town of Pharr in the early 1900's. The Pharr Townsite Company, operated by John C. Kelly, built a city hall in 1911. And, that same year, a post office was applied for and approved. The city was incorporated in February 1946.

To entice settlers to the area and to promote the sale of townsite lots, the Pharr Townsite Company published a brochure about the advantages of the area, mentioning their new school building. By 1914, the school had 73 students.

Today, Pharr's population is 35,000, and it is an agribusiness and trading center. Citrus fruits, vegetables, cotton, livestock and tourism are major compounds of the local economy.

The area is served by the Union Pacific and Southern Pacific Railroads.

The City of Pharr has a commission-city manager form of government. Their tax rate is based on 100% of assessed value. The tax rate is high: $2.10 per hundred dollars of evaluation.

Pharr has a very pleasant climate. The annual average temperature is 73.7 degrees. The average humidity is 65%. The average annual rainfall is 20.48 inches. The altitude is 40 ft.

Three transcontinental natural gas transmission lines have their point of origin in the county. There are approximately 1600 wells in Hidalgo County, with an estimated appraisal value of $740,000,000 as of 1988.

Pharr is at the heart of the wildlife country where deer, javelina, quail and whitewing dove hunting is available. The hunting in northern Mexico is one of the main attractions to the area. There are fresh water lakes in the area and the Rio Grande offers excellent fishing. Saltwater sportsmen have access to the Gulf of Mexico where both edible and game fish abound. Falcon Lake, one of the largest man-made lakes in the U.S., offers excellent fishing for bass, catfish, and crappie.

An estimated 70,000 Winter Texans reside in the Valley during the peak period of February of each year. Reports indicate that 65,200 Winter Texans live in recreational vehicles and motor homes, while 5,700 reside in apartments, condominiums, hotels and motels.

Pharr has the industrial development foundation and the city has the Las Milpas Industrial Park, which contains 1495 acres of planned unit development.

The city airport is located south of the city. The Continental Airline serves McAllen. The Southwest Airline serves Harlingen, which is just a few miles to the southeast.

Pharr and the surrounding area offers a number of attractions. The All Valley Winter Vegetable Show is held in Pharr. It is a Valley-wide event with elementary and high school students entering over 55 varieties of vegetables grown locally. There is an annual parade, German Night Dance, Valley Arts & Crafts Show. Pharr has a very active Winter Senior Citizens Club that meets regularly at the Civic Center for potluck dinners, cards, bingo, arts & crafts, etc.

PITTSBURG

Pittsburg is the county seat of Camp County in northeast Texas. It is 129 miles east-northeast of Dallas, 42 miles north-northwest of Longview, and 65 miles southwest of Texarkana. It can be reached by U.S. Highway 271 and State Highway 11.

W. H. Pitts came to Texas in 1854 and, the following year, settled in the area of present-day Pittsburg. He bought 200 acres, built a lot cabin, and began clearing his land. A community grew in the area and took the name of its oldest and most prominent settler, "Major" W. H. Pitts.

Pittsburg's main claim to fame may be as the home of the Ezekial Airship. The Reverend Burrell Cannon was an inventor and machinist as well as a minister. He was intrigued by a biblical reference in the Book of Ezekiel of strange flying creatures propelled by wheels; and he spent 20 years drawing plans and making models of a flying machine. In 1901, he formed the Ezekiel Airship Manufacturing Company and built his first airship at P. W. Thorsell's Machine Shop (which exists to this day). The aircraft was first flown in 1902. (The Wright Brothers did not make their Kitty Hawk flight until 1903.) However, while being shipped by rail to be exhibited at the St. Louis World's Fair, the aircraft was completely destroyed when it was blown off the flatbed car by a high wind. A replica of that Ezekiel Airship is on display in downtown Pittsburg.

Pittsburg's population today is 4,561. The area is heavily timbered, and is a commercial center for farming, poultry, and livestock. Peaches, blueberries, vegetables, and hay are the main crops. The city's industries include manufacturing of furniture, clothing, oil field products, air filters, steel castings, and process feed. Both the St. Louis Southwestern and the Kansas City Southern Railroads provide service to Pittsburg.

Annual events in Pittsburg include the Spring Chick Fest (held the first Saturday in April), the Pittsburg and Camp County Rodeo (held the second weekend in May), and Pioneer Days Festival (held the third Saturday in September).

Six nearby lakes furnish water sports and fishing.

Pittsburg is a main street city.

PLAINVIEW

Plainview is the county seat of Hale County and is located on the South Plains in North Texas—one of the richest agricultural areas in the United States. It is 47 miles north of Lubbock and 76 miles south of Amarillo. It can be reached by Interstate 27, U.S. Highway 70, and State Highways 194 and 445.

Z. T Maxwell and E. L. Lowe settled in the area in 1886, and the following year founded a town called "Plainview." The name was chosen because of the terrain—the view of the plains was unobstructed in all directions.

Agriculture, of course, was and is the main component of Plainview's economy. Principal crops are grain, sorghum, cotton, soybeans, corn, and vegetables. Much of the grain sorghum is used for cattle feed in Plainview, which is the center of the cattle feeding industry in the county.

Plainview has approximately 4,300 wells, each 250 ft. to 250 ft. deep, which are used for irrigation. In fact, Plainview is known as the shallow water irrigation capital of the world.

Presently, Plainview's population is 25,000. Wayland Baptist University is located here.

The Burlington Northern Railroad and the Santa Fe Railroad serve the city. Several major industries are located in Plainview, including a Wal-Mart Regional District Center, AZTECA Milling Company, Rand and Excel.

PLANO

Plano is located in the southern part of Collin County in North Texas. It is 19 miles north of downtown Dallas and part of the Dallas-Fort Worth metroplex. It can be reached by U.S. Highway 75, State Highway 5, and Farm-to-Market Road 2514.

Collin County, in 1845, was basically open prairie. A few settlers had moved into northern Collin County and settled near some of the small creeks, so water was readily available and trees offered some protection. In 1846, the first settlers arrived in the area of present-day Plano. As the community grew, the residents requested a post office. The names of "Fillmore" and "Foreman" were submitted to the postal authorities as the name for the community, but neither name was approved. The residents were informed the post office could not take a man's name. Dr. Henry Dye then suggested "Plano" which he thought was the Spanish word for "plains." That name was submitted to the postal authorities and approved as the name of the new community.

For the first 75 years of its existence, Plano was a trading center for the surrounding agricultural area. Today, Plano is one of the country's fastest growing cities. Its population grew from 17,867 in 1970 to 71,956 in 1980. Many residents work elsewhere in the metroplex area but choose to live in Plano. Local industry includes boats, metals, newspaper printing, computer forms, satellite communications, and bakery equipment. The Southern Pacific Railroad serves the city.

PLEASANTON

Pleasanton is located in Atascosa County 33 miles south of San Antonio and 112 miles northwest of Corpus Christi. It is located about 5 miles west of Interstate 37, at the intersection of U.S. Highway 281 and State Highway 97.

Atascosa County was established by an Act of the Texas Legislature in 1856. Col. Jose Antonio Navarro, a signer of the Texas Declaration of Independence, was one of the first settlers in this area, and he donated land for the building of the first county courthouse. The community which grew up around the Courthouse was called "Navatasco." Because of the frequent Indian attacks there and at nearby Amphion, the residents voted on a new location for the county seat. A site around the mouth of Bonita Creek on the Atascosa River (which belonged to John Bowen) was chosen. Bowen donated land for the townsite and he named it "Pleasanton" after his best friend, John Pleasant.

Pleasanton remained the county seat of Atascosa County until 1910. Then, one Saturday night during a dance, some men from Jourdanton (five miles southwest) raided the courthouse, took all the papers and records to Jourdanton, and established the new county seat there. Today, Jourdanton remains the county seat.

Pleasanton is recognized as being the home of the American cowboy. It was in this area that "El Rancho de Atascoso" (also called the "San Jose Mission Ranch") was established. 177 Indians were sent to work on the ranch by the San Jose Mission in San Antonio; those men developed the techniques and methods of working cattle that have come to be known as the essence of the American cowboy. They have an Annual Cowboy Homecoming Celebration held the third week of August to honor their outstanding local cowboys.

Pleasanton's population was 206 in 1870; it had grown to 4,000 in 1956; today it is approximately 7,200. The economy of the town is based on agriculture, cattle, hogs, peanuts, grain and hay.

The Longhorn Museum on the east side of Pleasanton features the early life of the American cowboy and genuine covered wagons and stage coaches.

PORT ARTHUR

Port Arthur is part of the Beaumont, Port Arthur, Orange Golden Triangle in Southeast Texas. Port Arthur is located on the west bank of Sabine Lake which is part of the Texas-Louisiana boundary. It is in Jefferson County, 93 miles east of Houston, and can be reached by U.S. Highways 69, 96, and 287, and State Highways 73, 87, 214, 215, and 347.

John Sparks, an early settler, built a home on the banks of Lake Sabine. His family soon joined him, other settlers arrived, and a community came into being. The community was called "Aurora," after a nearby railroad junction called "Aurora Junction," and was established in 1840.

The town prospered until it experienced a double blow—an epidemic swept through the town in the winter of 1885 and then, the following year, a hurricane struck. The discouraged families packed their belongings, and Aurora soon became a ghost town.

A few years later, Arthur E. Stilwell wanted to extend his Kansas City Gulf Coast Railroad from Kansas City to the Gulf of Mexico. He traveled to Texas to visit Sabine and Galveston, two towns he was considering as the southern terminus of the railroad. He was not satisfied with either location and, on his way home, passed Sabine Lake and the old site of Aurora. He was so impressed with the site and its possibilities—he could build a canal to the Gulf and the site would be safe from storms. He decided this was where he would build his railroad terminus. He gave the location his first name and called it "Port Arthur."

In 1901, the first oil well was brought in at the nearby Spindletop Field and the entire area changed forever. Port Arthur, with its port location and transportation facilities, soon became greatly involved in oilfield activities with refineries, petrochemical plants, shipbuilding, and oil field equipment manufacturing.

Today, Port Arthur has a population of 61,251 and is a center for oil, chemical activities, shipping, drydocking, food processing, rice milling, and tourism. The Southern Pacific Railroad still serves the area.

A branch of Lamar University is located here.

PORT LAVACA

Port Lavaca is located on Lavaca Bay about halfway down the Texas Gulf Coast. It is the county seat of Calhoun County and is 138 miles southwest of Houston, 116 miles southeast of San Antonio, and 72 miles northeast of Corpus Christi. It can be reached by U.S. Highway 87 and State Highway 35.

In 1519, Alonso Alvarez de Pineda visited the area while on an expedition of exploration. Then, in 1528, the area was visited by Cabeza de Vaca, and in 1685 by LaSalle. LaSalle landed at the site of the old town of Indianola (fifteen miles southeast of present-day Port Lavaca) and established Fort St. Louis nearby. The last of LaSalle's four ships was wrecked during a storm in the bay. (There is a wreck in North Lavaca Bay which is thought to be LaSalle's ship.) LaSalle set out on foot from the fort to try to locate the mouth of the Mississippi River. Because of illness and a shortage of food, he was forced to return to the fort shortly thereafter. He set out a second time but was killed by his own men near present-day Navasota. LaSalle's men who had been left at the fort became prisoners of the Spanish.

In 1830, John Linn, a German immigrant, built a warehouse and wharf about 3 miles north of present-day Port Lavaca. A small settlement called "Linnwood" grew in the area. Boats arrived from New York and New Orleans with goods to be transported by wagon to San Antonio and points west. In 1840, Linnwood was ransacked and burned by the Comanches; most of the residents managed to escape safely.

Although the town of Port Lavaca was laid out in 1843, the site was already a prosperous port. Seven large wharves accommodated steamships and schooners; cotton, hides, tallow, and cattle were shipped. Nearby rendering plants made tallow and preserved hides. The port took the name "Lavaca" meaning "the cow" in Spanish; "Port Lavaca," therefore, means "port of the cow."

Transportation has always been a key to Port Lavaca's growth. For many years, Port Lavaca was headquarters for wagon trains traveling west. Texas' second railroad was chartered in 1852 and projected to run between Port Lavaca and Victoria; and the Morgan Steamship Company established regular service between New York and Port Lavaca.

In 1846, Calhoun County was organized and, in 1856, Indianola became the county seat. Indianola had built a wharf to deep water and had captured much of the business formerly handled by Port Lavaca. The U.S. government landed camels at Indianola in 1856. The Army planned to use them to transport goods to frontier forts. The experiment, however, was unsuccessful.

During the Civil War, Port Lavaca was shelled by cannons from gunboats anchored offshore. Using slave labor, the Confederate Army built Fort Esperanza on Matagorda Island. On Christmas Eve, 1863, Union forces defeated the Confederates; some of the Union soldiers were then quartered at Port Lavaca.

Indianola suffered considerable damage in 1875 from a gulf storm; then in 1886 a tidal wave swept over Indianola and the town never really recovered. Port Lavaca became the county seat of Calhoun County. Severe gulf storms in 1914 and 1919 led to the building of a seawall to protect Port Lavaca.

During World War I, Indianola became a training base for the armed forces, during World War II a permanent Air Base was built on Matagorda Island.

Today, Port Lavaca has a population of 10,911. Its port facility makes it an important center for commercial and pleasure fishing; ranching and agriculture and diversified industries all contribute to Port Lavaca's economy.

Of special interest in the area are the Calhoun County Museum, Halfmoon Reef Lighthouse, Indianola County Historic Park, LaSalle Monument, and Port Lavaca Causeway State Recreation Park.

PORT NECHES

The history of the city goes back more than 150 years to 1834, when Joseph Grigsby, Port Neches' first settler, came there with his family and established a community which he named after himself. Other families came to Grigsby's Bluff in the 1840s and 1850s, and by 1860, census records reveal that 80 persons were residents of the growing community. During the Civil War the Confederacy founded Fort Grigsby to guard the Neches River.

With the erection of refining and petrochemical plants in the area after the turn of the century, Grigsby Bluff became Port Neches in 1901, according to state historical archive records in Austin. The city took its name from the Neches river.

World War II and the government project that furnished synthetic rubber to the rubber-starved war needs, really put Port Neches on the map. The Neches River provides deep water transportation. Port Neches is surrounded by large industry and has a population that has grown to more than 15,000. Modern up-to-date schools, churches, and business firms round out the modern community.

The area of the city is fourteen square miles. The city has a city manager, mayor and council form of government.

Texas Highway, U.S. 287 runs just to the west of Port Neches. State Highways 87, 136 and 347 serve the city as well as Farm-to-Market Highways 365 and 366.

The city has a fairly high tax structure. A breakdown of this tax is:

City of Port Neches	$ .690
Port Neches ISD	1.135
Jefferson County	.225
	2.05

The backbone of Port Neches' economy is the industrial installations that border the city. On the city's southern edge are two synthetic rubber plants, a butadiene plant, an oil and asphalt refinery, and a petroleum chemicals plant. Just north of the city is an oil refinery. Within quick driving distance are seven other plants where many hundreds of Port Neches people work. Through their payrolls and purchases of goods and services, these industries exert a steadying influence on Port Neches' economy.

Lamar University is located in the Beaumont-Port Neches area. It is a four-year university and offers degrees in the arts, sciences, engineering and pre-med.

Port Neches was incorporated in 1927. The city is served by the Santa Fe Railroad.

Port Neches is in Jefferson County, which has an agricultural income of $23,000,000 per year. This income is 80% from crops, chiefly rice and soybeans. The other 20% comes from the raising of beef cattle; 38,000 acres of Jefferson County is irrigated.

PORTLAND

The original townsite of Portland came into existence as the result of 640 acres being purchased by John C. Willacy in November of 1890. The land was located on both sides of the San Antonio and Aransas Pass Railroad and overlooked both Corpus Christi and Nueces Bay. On February 6, 1891, Willacy sold ths land to the Portland Harbor & Improvement Company and on June 19, 1891, Officers of the Portland Harbor & Improvement Company filed a map of the city at the county courthouse.

Portland was called the "Gem City of the Gulf" and was described as being the most attractive and pleasant spot in Texas. It was situated on a beautiful 30-40 foot bluff overlooking 150 square miles of dancing waves and fronting the deepest water in Corpus Christi Bay. As a summer and winter resort, Portland is fortunate in her mild climate and prevailing bay breezes.

As a place for sportsmen, Portland offered great attractions. Ducks and other game are abundant, while the bay abounds with red fish, tarpon, and other varieties of fish. More fish and oysters have been taken from these waters than at any other point on the Gulf Coast.

The New England Land and New England Real Estate Company purchased 1280 acres of land east and northeast of the original 640 acres. Most of the stockholders of these companies resided in Portland, Maine, and that town's name was selected to be the name of their new town.

Portland is a city of 9.12 sq. miles, located in San Patricio County on the South Texas Coastal Plain, fronting on the Corpus Christi Bay and Nueces Bay. The Portland city limit is contiguous with that of Corpus Christi, Texas. The city is joined with other major cities in the state by two major highways, U.S. 181 and State Highway 35. It is the gateway city into Corpus Christi and other points south.

The Corpus Christi International Airport is within 20 miles of Portland and offers daily flights by Continental Southwest, and American airlines.

The 1989 population of Portland was 13,500. The city's tax rate is slightly high. The breakdown of the tax is as follows:

Portland	$.5155	100% Assessment
San Patricio & State County	.4456	
ISD District	.9000	
	$1.8611	Total

The average of Texas towns and city taxes is approximately $1.75.

San Patricio County is a relatively small county, having only 693 sq. miles, whereas the average Texas County has 900 sq. miles. However, in spite of its smaller size, it has a large agricultural income of $65,000,000, whereas the average Texas county has approximately $30,000,000. The income is from sorghum, cotton, vegetables, corn, hay, beef cattle, hogs, goats, horses, poultry, and cattle feed lots; 5,000 acres are irrigated.

Rail services are provided by the Missouri-Pacific Railroad (now the Union Pacific), Southern Pacific Railroad and Texas Mexican Railroad. The Port of Corpus Christi is available for shipping to all major shipping centers in the world.

Portland has a home rule charter with the council-manager system of city government. There is a mayor and six city councilmembers elected at large for two years, on staggered terms. The city also has a Planning & Zoning Commission and an Economic Development Commission.

POST

Post is the county seat of Garza County and is located 42 miles southeast of Lubbock, 117 miles northwest of Abilene, and 115 miles northeast of Midland. It can be reached by U.S. Highways 84 and 380, State Highway 207, and Farm-to-Market Roads 651 and 669.

Post is just three miles from the Cap Rock escarpment and is known as the "Gateway to the Plains of West Texas."

In 1907, the town of "Post City" was founded by Charles William Post of the Post cereal family. It was his "dream city"—a planned community located on his ranch. Post divided his ranch into 160-acre lots and built five- and six-room houses to sell to settlers. He wanted every settler to be a homeowner.

After the death of its founder, C. W. Post, the city became known as just "Post."

The Burlington textile mill was established in Post in 1912. When the mill closed in 1983, the community formed a nonprofit organization to take over the operation. Today, the textile mill, along with oil and farming, forms the basis of Post's economy. Primary crops in the area are cotton and grains. Cattle and hogs are raised.

Post's population is now 3,961. The city is served by the Atchison, Topeka & Santa Fe Railroad.

Post was named a Texas Main Street City in 1987. A number of historic buildings (including the Algerita Hotel, the Garza Theatre, and the Santa Fe Railroad Depot) have been restored and renovated.

The Post "Stampede Rodeo" is held in early August of each year.

POTEET

Poteet, known as the Strawberry Capital of Texas, is located in Atascosa County which is 30 miles south of San Antonio and off State Highway 16. Poteet is also served by FM 1470 and 476.

Originally, the town was part of Mexico until 1834, when the Mexican government gave Joaguin de la Garza Poteet and several thousand acres of land. At this time, Poteet was almost desert-like, with nothing but sand, cactus and jackrabbits. This, however, did not last long. Once Texas gained her independence, the town began to grow in both development and population.

In 1902, there was a dreadful drought. This drought ruined the cotton crop but proved to be the beginning of Poteet. Since the drought, Poteet's annual average rainfall is 26.5 inches.

The drought led Henry T. Mumme to search for a new source for water. And, in 1904, Mumme's crew drilled the first artesian water well in Atascosa County as well as the first in South Texas. The well was located in a field near the store Mumme owned. The well proved to be the one thing that opened the area to irrigation farming and a larger population. Known as "The Artesian Belt," Poteet is one of the lushest farming areas within the state.

In 1909, a railroad was built, which gave Poteet a connection to the outer world. Today, the Union Pacific Railroad runs north and south through Pleasanton, which is eight miles east of Poteet.

It wasn't until June of 1910 that Poteet officially became Poteet. This occurred when Henry T. and Ida Fischer Mumme generously donated three hundred acres of pasture land as a townsite for the expanding community. Until 1910 "Poteet" was actually a general store located approximately one and a half miles north of the present townsite.

The name of the town came from Francis Marion Poteet, a blacksmith, who established the general store prior to the turn of the century. Mr. Poteet used a wooden box for the area residents' mail box, and when the Mummes bought the store, the Poteet name continued to be used.

By 1910 the once small community was booming. A new Mumme store was opened and a train depot completed.

It was not until 1926 that Poteet was incorporated and its first mayor, Tom Dean was elected. Since Dean, there have been fourteen succeeding mayors, one being a woman, Mrs. Elva Copeland, who served one term in 1978.

Located off Highway 16, Poteet has a population of approximately 3,084. The community is mainly made up of Caucasians and Mexican-Americans.

Atascosa is a large county, having 1218 square miles, while the average Texas county has 900 square miles. The area around Poteet is a rich agricultural area. The county has an annual agricultural income of $50 million. Cattle, dairy products and hogs make up about 60% of the income. The crops are peanuts, grains, hay, pecans, and strawberries. The county has 60,000 irrigated acres.

Poteet is one of five towns within Atascosa County. Each town has some kind of special celebration. Poteet's celebration is probably the largest of all five in the county and draws anywhere between 50,000 and 100,000 people. This celebration is held the second weekend in April when Poteet celebrates the "Poteet Strawberry Festival."

PRAIRIE VIEW

Prairie View is located in Waller County. It is on U.S. Highway 290 and is approximately 45 miles northwest of Houston. The 1989 population of Prairie View was 4,000.

The city of Prairie View received its name from the plantation home of Col. Jack Kirby, who had named his plantation Prairie View. A girl's school was originally established at the present location of Prairie View University. Later the property was deeded to the State of Texas. In 1876 the Texas Legislature established a college for black youths on the present site. It is now known as Prairie View A and M University.

The city is served by the Southern Pacific Railroad. In addition to U.S. Highway 290, Farm-to-Market Road 1098 serves the city. The Houston Intercontinental Airport is approximately 48 miles east of Prairie View.

The city was incorporated April 12, 1969. The form of city government is known as general law.

The main purpose of Prairie View city is to support the Prairie View A and M University. Most of the professors, instructors and employees live in the environment of Prairie View.

The area surrounding Prairie View is a rich agricultural region. The income from beef cattle, hogs, poultry and horses is substantial. The crops are rice, cotton, corn, and milo maize. The agricultural income of Waller County is about 50% higher than the average Texas county income. The annual rainfall is 41.6 inches.

QUANAH

Quanah is the county seat of Hardeman County. The county borders on the Red River and Oklahoma, and is at the eastern base of the Panhandle.

Quanah is 70 miles west of Wichita Falls and 127 miles north of Abilene. The city is located on U.S. Highway 787 and State Highways 6, 285, and 133, FM 104, 2568, and 2640.

The population of the city is 4100. The altitude is 1450 ft. The average annual rainfall is 24.3 inches.

The Burlington Northern Railroad serves the city.

Quanah is an agricultural business center. It has a plant that manufactures gypsum wall board, a cotton seed oil mill, a cotton compress, and a large meat packing plant.

The crops raised in the area are wheat, cotton, and milo maize. There are 6800 acres of irrigated land. There is no good aquifer underlaying the area.

The city was named for Quanah Parker. His mother was a kidnapped white girl named Cynthia Ann Parker. Quanah was the last great war chief of the Comanche Indians.

•

RANGER

Ranger derived its name from a Texas Ranger Camp established three miles east of the present city to protect citizens from the Indians. The Ranger Camp became a tent city when workers building the railroad spent some time working on the "high bridge" in Wiles Canyon near the camp. After the bridge was completed and the trains came, houses and businesses of a more permanent nature were built at the present site. This was in the early 1880's.

Ranger was incorporated in 1919. It has a city council-city manager type of government and a mayor. Ranger's current population is 3,200.

Industries include oil and gas production, farming, ranching, railcar repair facilities, and cinder block manufacturing.

Ranger is served by the Missouri-Pacific Railroad. It is on Interstate 20 and U.S. Highway 80. Ranching and peanut farming are the major agricultural activities.

In 1917, the spectacular McKlesky Well No. 1 roared in and started the wildest drilling campaign ever witnessed. Ranger grew from a sleepy village of 600 to a population of over 30,000 almost overnight. The majority of the Ranger oil went to the aid of the Allied forces in Europe during World War I. The Ranger field gained the reputation as the "Boom That Won The War."

Roaring Ranger Museum contains pictures, tools, and artifacts from the "Boom Town Days." It is open from 10 AM to 2 PM weekdays.

Lake Leon is a 28,000-acre lake with 35 miles of shoreline offering fishing, boating, swimming, and other water sports. Lone Cedar Country Club on Lake Leon features a very competitive nine-hole golf course and other club facilities.

RAYMONDVILLE

Raymondville is the county seat of Willacy County in South Texas. It is about 55 miles northwest of Brownsville and the Texas-Mexico border, 103 miles south of Corpus Christi, and 27 miles west of the Gulf of Mexico. It can be reached by U.S. Highway 77 and State Highway 186.

Raymondville was founded as a railroad town. The Texas-Mexican Railroad had a rail line at Robstown; then, in 1904, the St. Louis & Mexico Railroad built a line from Robstown to Brownsville. A townsite at Mile 95 was set up and named "Raymondville" in honor of Edward Burleson Raymond (who was a Cameron County Commissioner and foreman of the El Suaz Ranch).

In 1908, E. B. Raymond purchased 24,000 acres. His land on the north adjoined the southern boundary of the famed King Ranch.

Merchants and settlers soon formed a community. By 1909, the town had a post office, general store, inn, two doctors, seamstress and milliner, an 18-room hotel, hospital, drug store, bakery, two churches, and a bank. The Raymondville State Bank, established in 1907, is the oldest bank in the Rio Grande Valley. Dry land farming was an important part of the local economy. Principal crops were potatoes, onions, cabbage, peas, corn, maize, and cotton. There are 377,000 acres of land in the county. Ten percent of the land is irrigated. The remainder is dry-land farms. The area has 25.0 inches of rainfall annually.

Raymondville was incorporated in 1912 and reincorporated in 1921. When Willacy County was created by an Act of the Texas Legislature in 1921, Raymondville was named the county seat. Raymondville has the commission-manager form of government.

Today, Raymondville's population is 9,493. It is an agribusiness and oil center. Clothing and fiberglass products are manufactured. Vegetables and seafood are processed and shipped. Raymondville is the winter home of many northern visitors, and is a popular tourist center.

A bilingual museum is housed at the Raymondville Historical and Community Center. It features prehistoric and pre-Columbian artifacts, items from a 1554 shipwreck, King and Kenedy Ranch memorabilia, and a picture history of Willacy County.

Port Mansfield on the Gulf of Mexico is just 18 miles to the east on Farm-to-Market road 497. This is a fishing port and a well known sportsman's fishing place.

REFUGIO

The Spanish built their last mission in Texas in 1795 at Refugio, in an attempt to Christianize the Karankawa, a feared Indian tribe they believed to be cannibalistic. The mission was called "La Mission de Nuestra Senora del Refuge" (the Mission of Our Lady of Refuge). The town took its name from the name of this mission.

During the Texas Independence movement of 1836, the mission church at Refugio was destroyed in the "Battle of Refugio," where Captain King and Colonel Ward took refuge. There were a total of five battle actions fought within the county lines, as well as the massacre of King's forces. The Mission of Our Lady of Refugio is no longer in existence.

Refugio has many large and stately old homes that are well preserved and very beautiful. Many of them are well over 125 years old. The collection of these beautiful homes is a great tourist attraction.

Refugo is governed by a mayor-aldermen home rule form of government. The city is the county seat of Refugio County.

The population of the city was estimated to be 3,900 in 1989. The average annual rainfall is 33.7 inches. This is ample to raise nearly any crop except rice, which must be irrigated.

The city is served by the Union Pacific Railway Co.

The taxes on real property are:

City	.8244	per $100 assessment
County	.1550	per $100 assessment
School	.5402	per $100 assessment
	1.5196	Total

Refugio historically has been classified as an oil and gas producing, farming and ranching area. The county has an average agricultural income of $23.5 million yearly. This is about 60% of the average Texas county income. There is no manufacturing performed in the city. The income from oil and gas production, while still substantial, is becoming less each year.

Refugio is on U.S. Highway 77 and 183, and on State Highway 202, and FM 2678 and 774. The city is 55 miles north-northeast of Corpus Christi and 116 miles south-southeast of San Antonio.

RICHARDSON

Richardson is located 22 miles north of the center of Dallas at the extreme northern edge of Dallas County. Part of the city overflows into Collin County. U.S. Highway 75 goes through the center of Richardson and the Santa Fe Railroad crosses Highway 75 at the center of the city.

In 1989, the population was 76,500. The city has an excellent ad valorem tax base. The total of the various taxes is 1.63218 per $100 of assessed value. This is below the Texas average for cities over 50,000 population. It is, in fact, the lowest tax rate of any Texas city with a population over 50,000.

The city has a home rule form of city government, which consists of a mayor, council, and city manager.

The average rainfall of Richardson is 25 inches. The city has an excellent transportation service, in that it is 22 miles east of the Dallas-Ft. Worth International Airport and is twelve miles from Love Field in Dallas, which is southwest of Richardson. It is served by two railroads, the Southern Pacific and the Santa Fe.

Richardson is a very industrialized city. There are a number of large manufacturing and service-type companies based in Richardson. The companies who employ over 250 people are as follows:

Name	Product	Employment
E.D.S. Technical Products	Computer Software	250
Electrospace Systems, Inc.	Airborne Communications	2167
Ericsson Network Systems	Telecommunications	700
Honeywell Optoelectronics	Components & subassemblies	291

MCI Telecommunication Corp. System	Microwave communication	1000
Northern Telecom	PABX & Switching Equipment	1800
Rockwell Int's Corp.	Radio Div.-Microwave	6600

The history of the city of Richardson is inseparable from that of the blackland belt reaching from Dallas to Denison. From the original stage coach route, through the eras of the Houston and Texas Central Railroad, the Interurban, the old brick road which is Greenville Avenue, to the latest addition—Central Expressway, the Richardson area has been the gateway through which the products and culture of this great belt flowed into Dallas.

The Civil War saw many of the townsmen take up arms for the Confederacy, including Col. Coit (grandfather of Henry C.), Wm. A. Loveless, Frank Armstrong and A. D. and W. L. Campbell. Some saw duty with Morgan's Men in the Battle of Mansfield in Louisiana.

The forefathers of Richardson settled in a small township they called Breckenridge around 1853. This was located just east of what is now Restland on Spring Valley Road and Abrams Road at the site of the giant old tree which still stands today.

During the years that followed, the township's wealth was often judged by the number of chickens that were owned. No one thought much about it, but poverty was always just around the corner for many folks.

In the years that followed, the quiet little community of Breckenridge heard more and more talk about a railroad. Finally in 1872 Ryley and Jack Wheeler gave land for a townsite (Richardson's present location), and a right-of-way to the Houston and Texas Central Railway. The new town now needed a new name.

If the townspeople had had their way, they would be living in Wheeler Texas, today, but Mr. Wheeler did not like the idea, so they chose Richardson for Mr. George Richardson, (then president of the H&TC Railroad).

Richardson has had a record of being struck by tornados. One hit at 3:00 in the morning of May 27, 1867. A black funnel of destruction ripped through, south of the tiny community leaving death and destruction in its path. After a few minutes of horror, all seven members of the Caldwell family, one of the Prigmore girls and an entire Negro family were dead. The Mt. Calvary Baptist Church lay in ruins. It was a devastating blow to the town.

In 1924, a second tornado struck Richardson. A black finger of destruction dropped from the sky ending the life of L. W. Jacobs.

There are a number of colleges and universities within a reasonable distance from Richardson. The University of Texas at Dallas is located in Richardson with 7,000 students. Richland College is two miles away. Southern Methodist University is eight miles away, Texas Christian University is located in Ft. Worth.

ROBSTOWN

Robstown is located in Nueces County in the Coastal Bend area of South Texas. It is 10 miles west of Corpus Christi on U.S. Highway 77 and State Highway 44.

The railroad tracks of the Texas-Mexican Railroad (running from Laredo to Corpus Christi) crossed the tracks of the Missouri Pacific Railroad (running from St. Louis to Brownsville) on land owned by the Driscoll family. About 1905, Robert Driscoll established a store, called Rob's Store, at the intersection. Settlers, storekeepers, and businesses soon moved to the area, and the settlement was referred to as "Rob's Town," which later became "Robstown."

To encourage settlement of the area, the prairie land around Robstown was promoted as a prime area for farmers. Excursion trains called "Blackland Specials" brought prospective farmers to see the area. Many of the visitors bought property and farmed it, helping Robstown become one of the country's largest cotton and vegetable farming areas.

The community began to grow even more when, in 1907, George H. Paul bought all the Driscoll land north of the Texas-Mexican Railroad tracks—some 12,000 acres—and began construction. A city charter was received in 1912.

Since that time, Robstown has evolved into an agribusiness center with 12,100 residents. Beef cattle, dairy cattle, and horses are raised; grain sorghum, corn, and cotton are grown. Local industry includes a cold storage locker plant, cotton gins, delinting plant, grain elevators, clothing manufacture, and oil production and servicing. The Missouri Pacific and the Texas-Mexican Railroads still serve the city.

ROCKDALE

Rockdale is located in the southern part of Milam County, 61 miles northeast of Austin, 133 miles northwest of Houston, and 69 miles south-southeast of Waco. It can be reached by U.S. Highway 79 and Farm-to-Market Road 487, and is just a short distance west of the intersection of U.S. Highway 79 with U.S. Highway 77.

By 1873, the International and Great Northern Railroad had reached Hearne (30 miles northeast of present-day Rockdale). When plans were announced for extending the rail line west, land was sold to the railroad by B. F. Ackerman, George Green, and Frank Smith. The first buildings erected were tents, which were replaced by wooden buildings, and later by brick.

In 1874, when the first official passenger train reached the new townsite, the town was officially founded and was named "Rockdale."

The name "Rockdale" is generally attributed to Mrs. B. F. Ackerman. She had been asked to suggest a name for the new town, and, so the story goes, she remembered a large rock she had seen two miles north of the townsite. She thought of the rolling hills in the area. Combining the two features, she thought of the name "Rockdale."

Rockdale was the railroad terminus for two years; then the rail line was extended farther west.

Vast deposits of lignite underlie Milam County. A large open pit mine extracts lignite for the nearby power plant.

Rockdale today has a population of 5,611. It is a lignite mining center; Alcoa Aluminum is located here. Crops grown in the area include sorghum, cotton, wheat, hay, and corn. The Missouri Pacific Railroad services the city.

Lake Alcoa is nearby. The Rockdale area is popular for hunting and fishing.

ROCKPORT

Rockport is located on Aransas Bay of the Gulf of Mexico, just west of San Jose Island. It is in Aransas County and is 35 miles north-northeast of Corpus Christi, 161 miles southeast of San Antonio, and 173 miles southwest of Houston. It can be reached by State Highway 35 and Farm-to-Market Road 881.

The Rockport area has been known for hundreds of years. The Spanish explored and charted the area in 1519. The French attempted to colonize the area, but were resisted fiercely by the Karankawa Indians. Spanish colonization finally began in 1746 when two forts were built nearby. Spanish ranchers have lived in the area since about 1766.

The site of present day Rockport has been known by different names at different times—Rocky Point, Rockport, Aransas Pass, and then Rockport again. The name of "Rockport" was apparently derived from a rocky ledge in the area; the possibility of a port at the site was recognized by at least the mid-1800's.

In 1865, the northern portion of the townsite of Rockport was laid out on 640 acres by Joseph F. Smith and Colonel John H. Wood, while the southern half was platted by J. M. Doughty, T. H. Mathis, and J. M. Mathis. Col. Wood has been referred to as the "Father of Rockport." In addition to the Rockport land, the Wood family acquired ownership of St. Joseph's Island (now known as San Jose Island) and operated a cattle ranch there.

The first cattle pens, warehouse, and wharf were built at Rockport in 1866 by Richard M. Wood (son of Col. J. W. Wood) and J. M. Doughty. Two years later, a larger wharf was built in the bay and, the following year, an even larger one.

From 1867 to 1875, Rockport was a center for the hide, tallow, packing and canning industry.

Today, Rockport is known for its seafood packers, oil and gas industry, fishing, and tourism. Its population is 6,500.

Three annual events in the area are the Fulton Oysterfest (the first weekend of March), the Rockport Art Festival (the weekend of July 4th), and the Rockport Seafair (Columbus Day in October).

The Fulton Mansion, built in 1876, is open to the public. It was refurbished by the Texas Parks and Wildlife Department and is a leading example of authentic restoration with its original period pieces and interior design.

The Aransas National Wildlife Refuge, the winter home of the whooping crane, is located 38 miles north of Rockport.

ROCKWALL

Rockwall is the county seat of Rockwall County in North Texas. The city is located on the east side of Lake Ray Hubbard, about 20 miles northeast of downtown Dallas. It is one mile north of U.S. Highway 67, at the intersection of State Highways 66 and 78.

Although settlers were in the area by 1841, the town of Rockwall was not founded until 1854. The original townsite was platted by Elijah Elgin and was named for unusual rock formations in the county. The naturally-occurring rock walls resemble man-made walls.

When Rockwall County was organized in 1873, the town of Rockwall was named as the county seat. The city was incorporated in 1874.

The railroad reached Rockwall in 1886, helping to make it a trading, distribution, and shipping center for the surrounding area.

Rockwall today has 5,939 residents. Local plants make aluminum, leather goods, windows, apparel, and steel products. Beef cattle and horses are raised in the area; local crops include wheat, cotton, sorghum.

A local newspaper, *The Rockwall Success,* begun in 1883, is still published today.

Texas' first woman dentist, Dr. Jessie Castle La Moreau, practiced here, beginning in 1901 or 1902.

ROUND ROCK

Round Rock is located in Williamson County. It is 18 miles north of Austin and can be reached by Interstate 35 and U.S. Highways 79 and 81. It is located in the heart of the hill country, on the Edwards Plateau.

Round Rock is named for an actual round rock in Brushy Creek and marks a safe fording place in the stream. The Tonkawa and Comanche Indians used the rock as a crossing guide, as did the settlers and cattlemen who came later. The Old Chisholm Trail ended near here.

In 1835, Tumlinson Fort was built at the headwaters of Brushy Creek (west of present-day Round Rock) and, in 1839, Kinney's Fort (also called Fort Cazeneau) was built for the protection of settlers and friendly Indians in the area. Kinney's Fort was the site of Texas' Archives War, the historic battle in which no shots were fired. Also, from this fort, President Lamar of the Texas Republic dispatched the Santa Fe Pioneers on exciting, disastrous expeditions.

A settlement called "Brushy" grew up around the creek crossing. However, when a post office was established in 1854, the town officially became "Round Rock." Actually, there were two Round Rocks. Old Round Rock and New Round Rock—and Brushy Creek was the boundary line between the two settlements.

Growth of the community was spurred in 1876 when the Texas Land Company helped develop the townsite and invested in the town that was to become the terminus of the International & Great Northern Railroad. With the coming of the railroad, the town became a prosperous trade and marketing center.

In 1878, Round Rock had a population of 1,500. Its businesses included fourteen general merchandise stores, four drug stores, four lumber yards, a bakery, and six hotels. Today the city has a population of 32,000. Round Rock has a city council and city manager form of city government.

Round Rock has had its share of famous, or infamous, characters. John Wesley Hardin, son of a preacher, and known as "the fastest gun in the West," graduated from the Round Rock High School in 1870.

Sam Bass, a notorious outlaw, was casing a bank to rob in Round Rock when he was shot to death (on his 27th birthday) by a Texas lawman. Bass' grave is in Round Rock. A reenactment of his last gunfight is staged each year.

"Soapy" Smith grew up in Round Rock. He met trains at the depot and solicited business for his mother's hotel; then later went north and became the most notorious "conman" in Alaska.

Round Rock's economy is quite diversified—from high tech industries to the production of lime and limestone products, stone quarries, and burned dolomite processing plants. Some of the leading employers in Round Rock are DuPont Photomask, Advanced Custom Molders, Westinghouse Motor Company, Abbot Laboratories, Weed Instrument, and Carroll Touch. Rail service is provided by the Missouri Pacific and Greater Georgetown Railroads.

Boutiques, antique shops, and craft centers are located in the historical buildings downtown.

Nearby Lake Travis is a popular spot for water recreational activities.

ROWLETT

Rowlett is located on the west bank of Lake Ray Hubbard, primarily in Dallas County but also extending into Rockwall County. It is about 20 miles northeast of downtown Dallas and is part of the Dallas-Fort Worth Metroplex area. It can be reached by Interstate 30, U.S. Highway 67, and State Highway 66.

Prior to 1836, the community of settlers at the site of present-day Rowlett was referred to simply as the "German Settlement." Then, in 1836 or 1837, for his services in the Army of the Republic of Texas, Daniel Owen Rowlett of Kentucky was given a large land grant in the area. A creek on the tract was described in early tax records as "Rowlett's Creek" (it is a tributary to the East Fork of the Trinity River). Over time, the community assumed the name of the creek.

However, the area was also referred to as "Pleasant Valley" because of the surrounding rich farm lands. And when the first post office was established in the area in 1880, it was called the "Morris" Post Office—named for Austin Morris, the first postmaster.

Rowlett was officially named as the post office was officially established on February 19, 1889. Rowlett's Centennial was celebrated in 1989. The railroad came to Rowlett in 1886. The railroad, of course, brought growth and by 1912, Rowlett had a bank, barber shop, telephone exchange, four stores, depot, corn mill, blacksmith shop, doctor, school, three churches, cotton market, and two gins.

The town was incorporated in 1952, and a home rule charter was adopted in 1980. The city has a council-manager form of government. The Missouri-Kansas-Texas Railroad provides service to the area.

Rowlett's population grew from 1,015 in 1960 to 7,522 in 1980. Its 1988 estimated population is 19,522. Because of its location, Rowlett's growth and economy are tied very closely to that of the Dallas-Fort Worth Metroplex. Local industries manufacture such diverse products as appliance controls, store fixtures, labels, cabinets, truck body hardware, gymnastic equipment, furniture and inspection equipment.

Picnicking, boating, fishing, and other water activities are available at Lake Ray Hubbard and Lake Lavon.

RUSK

Rusk is the county seat of Cherokee County in the central part of East Texas. It is 129 miles southeast of Dallas, 201 miles northeast of Austin, and 167 miles north of Houston. It is situated at the intersection of U.S. Highways 84 and 69.

Thomas Jefferson Rusk, for whom the town is named, is said to have held more high official positions than anyone else during the days of the Texas Republic. He was a soldier, attorney, judge, and statesman; he was one of the signers of the Texas Declaration of Independence and served as Secretary of War, Chief Justice of the Supreme Court, and a Major General of the Army of the Texas Republic.

When Cherokee County was created by an Act of the Texas Legislature in 1846, the county seat was given the name "Rusk" to honor T. J. Rusk. At that time, however, there was no town; John Kilgore was the only white man living within the townsite boundaries. All the other residents were Indians. Settlers began moving to the area and, in 1847, a post office was established. By 1850 the town's population had increased to 355.

The first train reached Rusk in 1852 and helped the city develop as a trade and marketing center.

Later, iron ore was discovered, and in 1884 a foundry was built to develop the iron ore industry. During the Civil War, Rusk was an industrial site and supply depot for the Confederacy, especially as an iron products manufacturing center. Wagons, saddles, harnesses, guns, plows, and skillets were made here. A Union prisoner-of-war camp was established in Rusk, as well as a C. S. A. training camp and conscript district office. Cherokee County sent 2,000 men to the Confederate armed forces between 1861 and 1865.

Oil development occurred in 1914-1945. By 1932 there were 42 producing wells in the county. Active oil fields are located southeast and northwest of Rusk.

Today, Rusk's population is 4,681. Its economy is based on agriculture and timber. Cattle and poultry are raised; greenhouse plants, hay, vegetables, and fruits are grown. Timber production includes the growing of Christmas trees. Rusk is a pulpwood shipping center and milk processor, and has woodworking plants and other factories. The city's largest employer is the Rusk State Hospital which cares for more than 2,000 mentally ill patients.

The St. Louis Southwestern Railroad provides freight service to the city: passenger service is provided between Rusk and Palestine by a line of the Texas State Railroad.

Rusk is the birthplace of two famous Texas governors—James Stephen Hogg and Thomas Mitchell Campbell. There are numerous historical sites in and near Rusk. In addition, the nation's longest footbridge (546 ft.) is located here at the Footbridge Garden Park. It was originally built in 1861 for crossing the valley during the rainy season and was rebuilt in 1889 and 1960.

Nearby are I. D. Fairchild State Forest, Jim Hogg State Historical Park, Love's Lookout Park, and Caddo Mounds State Park.

SAN ANGELO

San Angelo was established in December, 1867, to protect the surrounding area from Indian attacks across the North Concho River from Fort Concho by Bart J. DeWitt, merchant and businessman. It was called "Over the River" by Fort Concho soldiers. The town was only a cluster of gambling houses, saloons, and trading posts in those early days. DeWitt named the village Saint Angela in honor of his deceased wife, Carolina Angela de la Garza. Residents unfamiliar with proper Spanish grammar corrupted the name to San Angela. In 1883, the federal post office officials changed the name of the post office to San Angelo in order to make the name masculine.

San Angelo is the county seat of Tom Green County. It was incorporated in 1903. The 1989 population is estimated to be 90,000. The elevation of the city is 1900 feet. The average annual rainfall is 17.6 inches which is insufficient to successfully grow certain crops without irrigation. There are 15,000 acres currently being irrigated in Tom Green County.

San Angelo is on U.S. Highways 67, 87, and 277 and State Highways 208, 378 and FM 765, 380, 2288, 2104. It is 95 miles south-southwest of Abilene, and 188 miles northwest of San Antonio.

San Angelo is served by the Atchison, Topeka and Santa Fe Railroad. San Angelo is known as the "Sheep and Wool Capital" of Texas.

There are 101 manufacturing plants in San Angelo, employing 5,100 people. The annual payroll is $70,200,000. The product value is $363,100,000. Items manufactured are sportswear, footwear, surgical supplies, millwork, aircraft parts, oilfield equipment, and many other products.

The city is located at the confluence of the north and middle Concho Rivers. The Concho flows into the Colorado River 42 miles east of San Angelo. There are three lakes near the city. Twin Buttes Lake, on the middle Concho River, is five miles south of town and Lake Nasworth, also on the middle Concho, is just two miles south of town. Lake O. C. Fisher on the North Concho is in the city limits to the northwest. These are beautiful lakes and afford excellent fishing.

The famous Concho River pearls range in color from pink to rich purple. These are the only pearls of such color from fresh water. The average size is three millimeters.

The Old Fort Concho is among the best preserved of Texas Frontier military forts in the United States. It has 16 buildings; 15 have been reconstructed and are still standing and in use. It was established in 1867. It is a living monument to the western heritage. Marvelous exhibits depicting life on the frontier are displayed year-round at both the fort's museums.

San Angelo has the second largest livestock auction in the state. A large volume of cattle, sheep, horses and hogs are marketed at this auction.

Tom Green County has an annual agricultural income of $52 million. This is almost double the average agricultural income of the average Texas county. The region produces beef cattle, dairy cattle, sheep, goats, and is the leading producer of wool. Mohair, cotton, wheat, oats, and sorghum are also grown.

The Angelo State University and Texas A & M Research and Extension Service are located at San Angelo. San Angelo is a modern, growing, vibrant city and is a credit to the state.

San Angelo has a favorable property tax:

San Angelo—City	0.69500
School District	0.69000
State & County	0.28323
	$1.66823 per $100 assessment

SAN ANTONIO

The City of San Antonio owes its origin to a nation of Payaya Indians who lived at their rancheria along the upper headwaters of the San Antonio River, a stream they called the Yanaguana. Although two expeditions to establish missions in the country occupied by the Tejas Indians had been made by the Spaniards under the leadership of Alonzo de Leon, the first in 1689, the second in 1690, it was not until 1691, during the third expedition led by Domingo Teran de los Rios that the Payaya Indians were encountered.

It was the good fortune of Padre Damian Massanet and Captain Joseph de Urrutia, who accompanied Teran, to meet them. The party arrived on June 13, the feast day of St. Anthony. Massanet was impressed with the beauty of the country. It so happened that the following day was the feast of Corpus Christi. It was decided that the expedition should not continue its journey, but rather spend the day in religious celebration and physical rest.

Accordingly, a large cross was set up, an altar erected and Mass was said. The Indians were present during these ceremonies. Massanet explained their meaning through the chief of the Pacpul nation, who accompanied the expedition as interpreter. After rosaries and other gifts had been distributed among the Indians, Massanet christened the stream San Antonio de Padua River. The expedition then moved to the country of the Tejas Indians. With the return of the party to Mexico the following year, and with the departure of the missionaries and the total abandonment of the missions in 1693, the Indians were left in undisturbed possession of the country for many years.

In 1718, at an Indian village in a pleasant wooded area of spring-fed streams at the southern edge of the Edwards plateau, Spain established Mission San Antonio de Valero (later called the Alamo). A customary accompanying presidio (Fort) San Antonio de Bexar protected the mission and its work.

Today's city and county names derive from those 18th century

Spanish beginnings that predate the founding of the United States by more than half a century.

Several other Spanish missions soon followed, but the city's real growth dates from the establishment of a Villa or Civil settlement in 1731. This was Spain's first step to colonize Texas. The original colonists were Spanish Canary Islanders, to whom many Texas families proudly trace their roots. San Antonio remained the chief Mexican stronghold in Texas until the Texas Revolution.

The Mission San Antonio de Valero, later to become famous as the Alamo, was established in 1718. It was founded in San Antonio to Christianize and educate the Indians living in the upper San Antonio River Valley. As the four missions that were to follow became active, the Alamo was abandoned.

Rebelling against the repressions of Mexico's self proclaimed dictator, Santa Anna, a band of 187 Texas Volunteers defied the Mexican Army of several thousands for thirteen days of siege in the Alamo. On March 6, 1935, the Alamo fell and the Alamo defenders died to the last man. Among the defenders were such storied names as William Travis, Davy Crockett and Jim Bowie.

Unsheathing his sword during a lull in the virtually incessant bombardment, Colonel William Barrett Travis drew a line on the ground before his battle-weary men. In voice trembling with emotion, he described the hopelessness of their plight and said, "Those prepared to give their lives in freedom's cause, come over to me."

Without hesitation, every man, save one, crossed the line. Colonel James Bowie, stricken with pneumonia, asked that his cot be carried over.

For twelve days after February 23, when Travis answered Mexican General Antonio Lopez de Santa Anna's surrender ultimatum with a cannon shot, the defenders had withstood the onslaught of an army which ultimately numbered 4,000 men.

Committed to death inside the Alamo were 189 known patriots who valued freedom more than life itself. Many, such as the 32 men and boys from Gonzales who made their way through the Mexican lines in answer to Travis' plea for reinforcements, were colonists. Theirs was a fight against Santa Anna's intolerable decrees. Others were volunteers such as David Crockett and his "Tennessee Boys" who owned nothing in Texas, and owed nothing to it. Theirs was a fight against tyranny wherever it might be.

A handful were native Texans of Spanish and Mexican descent who suffered under the same injustices as the other colonists.

Now, with ammunition and supplies all but exhausted, yet determined to make a Mexican victory more costly than a defeat, those who rallied to the Texas cause awaited the inevitable. It came suddenly in the chilly, pre-dawn hours of March 6.

With bugles sounding the dreaded "Deguello" (no quarter to the defenders) columns of Mexican soldiers attacked from the north, the east, the south and the west. Twice repulsed by withering musket fire and cannon shot, they concentrated their third attack at the battered north wall.

Travis, with a single shot through his forehead, fell across his cannon. The Mexicans swarmed through the breach and into the plaza. At frightful cost they fought their way to the Long Barrack and blasted its massive doors with cannon shot. Its defenders, asking no quarter and receiving none, were put to death with grapeshot, musket fire and bayonets.

Crockett, using his rifle as a club, fell as the attackers, now joined by reinforcements who stormed the south wall, turned to the chapel. The Texans inside soon suffered the fate of their comrades. Bowie, his pistols emptied, his famous knife bloodied, and his body riddled, died on his cot.

Present in the Alamo were Captain Almeron Dickinson's wife, Susanna, and their 15-month-old daughter, Angelina. After the battle, Santa Anna ordered that Mrs. Dickinson, her child, and other noncombatants be spared. Other known survivors were Joe, Travis' servant; Gertrudis Navarro, 15, sister by adoption to James Bowie's wife, Ursula; Juana Navarro Alsbury, sister of Gertrudis, and her 18-month-old son, Alijo; Georgio Esparza's wife, Ana, and her four children (Enrique, Francisco, Manuel and Maria de Jesus); Trinidad Saucedo and Petra Gonzales. Another survivor was Louis "Moses" Rose, who by his own choice, left the Alamo on the fifth day of March.

Santa Anna, minimizing his losses (which numbered nearly 600), said, "It was but a small affair," and ordered the bodies of the heroes burned. Colonel Juan Almonte, noting the great number of casualties, declared, "Another such victory and we are ruined."

The Texans' smoldering desire for freedom, kindled by the funeral pyre of the Alamo, roared into flames three weeks later at

Goliad when Santa Anna coldly ordered the massacre of more than 300 prisoners taken at the Battle of Coleto Creek.

On April 21, forty-six days after the fall of the Alamo, less than 800 angered Texans and American volunteers led by General Sam Houston launched a furious attack on the Mexican army of 1,500 at San Jacinto. Shouting, "Remember the Alamo! Remember Goliad!," they completely routed the Mexican army in a matter of minutes, killing 630 while losing nine. Santa Anna, "the Napoleon of the West," was captured and treated humanely by General Houston. The independence of Texas was won by this one battle. Texas was free; a new republic was born.

An independent nation for nearly 10 years, Texas was officially annexed to the United States on December 29, 1845. With the change in government, and the lowering of the Texas flag on February 19, 1846, outgoing president Anson Jones declared, "The final act in the great drama is now performed; the Republic of Texas is no more."

HEROES OF THE BATTLE OF THE ALAMO

Juan Abamillo, San Antonio
R. Allen
Mills DeForrest Andross, Vermont
Micajah Autry, N.C.
Juan A. Badillo, San Antonio
Peter James Bailey, Ky.
Isaac G. Baker, Ark.
William Charles M. Baker, Mo.
John J. Ballentine
Richard W. Ballantine, Scotland
John J. Baugh, Va.
Joseph Bayliss, Tenn.
John Blair, Tenn.
Samuel C. Blair, Tenn.
William Blazeby, England
James Butler Bonham, S.C.
Daniel Bourne, England
James Bowie, Tenn.
Jesse B. Bowman
George Brown, England
James Brown, Pa.
Robert Brown
James Buchanan, Ala.
Samuel E. Burns, Ireland
George D. Butler, Mo.
Robert Campbell, Tenn.
John Cane, Pa.
William R. Carey, Va.
Charles Henry Clark, Mo.
M. B. Clark
Daniel William Cloud, Ky.
Robert E. Cochran, N.J.
George Washington Cottle, Tenn.
Henry Courtman, Germany
Lemuel Crawford, S.C.
David Crockett, Tenn
Robert Crossman, Mass.
David P. Cummings, Pa.
Robert Cunningham, N.Y.
Jacob C. Darst, Ky.
John Davis, Ky.
Freeman H. K. Day
Jerry C. Day, Mo.
Squire Daymon, Tenn.
William Dearduff, Tenn.
Stephen Dennison, England

Charles Despallier, La.
Almaron Dickinson, Tenn.
John H. Dillard, Tenn.
James R. Dimpkins, England
Lewis Duel, N.Y.
Andrew Duvalt, Ireland
Carlos Espalier, San Antonio
Gregoria Esparza, San Antonio
Robert Evans, Ireland
Samuel B. Evans, N.Y.
James L. Ewing, Tenn.
William Fishbaugh, Ala.
John Flanders, Mass.
Dolphin Ward Floyd, N.C.
John Hubbard Forsyth, N.Y.
Antonio Fuentes, San Antonio
Galba Fuqua, Ala.
William H. Furtleroy, Ky.
William Garnett, Tenn.
James W. Garrand, La.
James Girand Garrett, Tenn.
John E. Garvin
John E. Gaston, Ky.
James George
John Camp Goodrich, Tenn.
Albert Calvin Grimes, Ga.
Jose Maria Guerrero, Laredo, Tex.
James G. Gwynne, England
James Hannum
John Harris, Ky.
Andrew Jackson Harrison
William B. Harrison, Ohio
Charles M. Haskell, (Heiskell), Tenn.
Joseph M. Hawkins, Ireland
John M. Hays, Tenn.
Patrick Henry Herndon, Va.
William D. Hersee, England
Tapley Holland, Ohio
Samuel Holloway, Pa.
William D. Howell, Mass.
Thomas Jackson, Ireland
William Daniel Jackson, Ireland
Green B. Jameson, Ky.
Gordon C. Jennings, Conn.
Damacio Jimenes, Tex.
Lewis Johnson, Wales
William Johnson, Pa.
John Jones, N.Y.
Johnnie Kellog
James Kenney, Va.
Andrew Kent, Ky.
Joseph Kerr, La.
George C. Kimball, (Kimble), N.Y.
William P. King
William Irvine Lewis, Va.
William J. Lightfoot, Va.
Jonathan L. Lindley, Ill.
William Linn, Mass.
Toribio Losoya, San Antonio
George Washington Main, Va.
William T. Malone, Va.
William Marshall, Tenn.
Albert Martin, Rhode Island
Edward McCafferty
Jesse McCoy, Tenn.
Wiliam McDowell, Pa.
James McGee, Ireland
John McGregor, Scotland
Robert McKinney, Ireland
Eliel Melton, Ga.
Thomas R. Miller, Tenn.
William Mills, Tenn.
Isaac Millsaps, Miss.
Edward F. Mitchusson, Va.
Edwin T. Mitchell
Napoleon B. Mitchell
Robert B. Moore, Va.
Willis Moore, Miss.
Robert Musselman, Ohio
Andres Nava, San Antonio
George Neggan, S.C.
Andrew M. Nelson, Tenn.
Edward Nelson, S.C.
George Nelson, S.C.
James Northcross, Va.
James Nowlan, Ireland

George Pagan, Miss.
Christopher Parker, Miss.
William Parks, N.C.
Richardson Perry
Amos Pollard, Mass.
John Prudy Reynolds, Pa.
Thomas H. Roberts
James Robertson, Tenn.
Isaac Robinson, Scotland
James M. Rose, Va.
Jackson J. Rusk, Ireland
Joseph Rutherford, Ky.
Isaac Ryan, La.
Mial Scutlock, N.C.
Marcus L. Sewell, England
Manson Shied, Ga.
Cleveland Kinlock Simmons, S.C.
Andrew H. Smith, Tenn.
Charles S. Smith, Md.
Joshua G. Smith, N.C.
William H. Smith
Richard L. Stockton, Va.
A. Spain Summerlin, Tenn.
William E. Summers, Tenn.
William D. Sutherland, Ala.
Edward Taylor, Tenn.
George Taylor, Tenn.
James Taylor, Tenn.
William Taylor, Tenn.
B. Archer M. Thomas, Ky.
Henry Thomas, Germany
Jesse G. Thompson, Ark.
John W. Thomson, N.C.
John M. Thurston, Pa.
Burke Trammel, Ireland
William Barret Travis, S.C.
George W. Tumlinson, Mo.
James Tylee, N.Y.
Asa Walker, Tenn.
Jacob Walker, Tenn.
William B. Ward, Ireland
Henry Warnell, Ark.
Joseph G. Washington, Tenn.
Thomas Waters, England
William Wells, Ga.
Isaac White, Ky.
Robert White
Hiram J. Williamson, Pa.
William Wills
David L. Wilson, Scotland
John Wilson, Pa.
Anthony Wolfe, England
Claiborne Wright, N.C.
Charles Zanco, Denmark
John (Negro)

In addition to the Alamo, four other San Antonio missions were established by Franciscan friars in the early 18th Century. The Mission Nuestra Senora de la Purisma Concepcion, was established in 1731. The church was more than 20 years under construction. It is a massive church with twin towers and cupola. It is the oldest unrestored church in the United States. Its acoustics are comparable to the Mormon Temple in Salt Lake City.

The Mission San Francisco de la Espada was also started in 1731. It is the favorite of many students of the Spanish period in Texas. The little church has been restored several times and is in use today.

The Mission San Jose y Miguel de Aguayo is known as the "Queen of Missions." It is both a State and National Historical Site. This mission housed a sizable Indian population, who irrigated the adjacent land with water from the San Antonio River. All of the missions developed extensive irrigation systems, involving the construction of retention dams on the San Antonio River, canals, aqueducts and laterals to supply the land between the canals, paralleling the river and constructed at a flatter gradient than the river and the river bed.

Mission San Juan Capistrano, like both Espada and Concepcion, was established in 1731. This church still serves the community of Berg's Mill. This mission is approximately ten miles downriver from the Alamo.

There is an extensive military base complex at San Antonio. Fort Sam Houston is headquarters for both the U.S. Fifth Army and Brooks Army Medical Center.

Kelly Air Force Base is headquarters for the Air Logistics Center and the Air Force Electronics Security Command. It is the nation's oldest military airfield.

Randolph Air Force Base is the official Air Force Records Center, and also provides pilot training.

A young aviator named Charles Lindbergh trained here, as did Billy Mitchell, and "Hap" Arnold. Lackland Air Force Base was founded in 1943 and is the only training base in the United States through which all Air Force trainees must come. Many of today's airmen receive their first training here. Wilford Hall USAF Medical Center is on Lackland and is the Air Force's largest (1,000-bed) medical facility."

Brooks Air Force Base was founded in 1918. It is now headquarters for the USAF School of Aerospace Medicine and the Human Systems Division.

Such higher education facilities as Trinity University, sometimes referred to as the Harvard of the South), the University of Texas at San Antonio, St. Mary's University, Incarnate Word College, San Antonio College, St. Phillip's College and Our Lady of the Lake University are all found in San Antonio.

The city's most famous attraction is the Alamo. There the Alamo Centaph is located, and the Alamo museum, maintained by the Daughters of the Texas Revolution.

Another famous structure is the arsenal constructed in 1860 by the U.S. Army. The arsenal was the munitions storehouse required to supply all the military operations located in Texas at that time.

San Antonio has an endless list of famous attractions. To name a few: the Botanical Gardens with its 33 acres of formal gardens, Brackenridge Park, and the General Cos House, an outstanding example of an early San Antonio home. This is where the capitulation of General Perfesto de Cos was signed. HemisFair Plaza was the site of the 1968 World's Fair. The River Walk (Paseo del Rio), one level below the busy streets of downtown, is San Antonio's premier attraction. The river meanders for several miles through downtown. Sea World is a new attraction in San Antonio. It is becoming world-renowned and is drawing huge crowds.

San Antonio has an annual rainfall of 27.5 inches. It has an average elevation of 550 feet below the Balcones Fault. That part of the city above the fault has an elevation of approximately 1200 feet. San Antonio is located at the foot of the Balcones Fault. It is the source of numerous springs which are fed by the Edwards Aquifer. The Edwards Plateau, known as the "Hill Country," has an elevation varying from 400 to 900 feet higher than the foot of the Balcones Fault.

San Antonio today is the third largest city in Texas with a population of 914,350. It is the state's largest military center. It is one of the most popular tourist cities in the United States. It has the council-manager form of city government.

San Antonio is a wholesale, retail, financial, and distribution center for a wide area. Local manufacturing includes aircraft, construction equipment, concrete production, dairy products, soft drinks, clothing, aircraft components, fabricated steel, penitentiary cell-block equipment, and various high-tech items.

San Antonio is the county seat of Bexar County. It is 221 miles west-southwest of Houston, 81 miles southwest of Austin, and 154 miles northwest of Corpus Christi. It can be reached by Interstates 10, 35 and 27; U.S. Highways 87, 181, and 281; and State Highway 16.

San Antonio has an extensive agricultural industry. Bexar County is a large county. It is 25% larger than the average county. The agricultural income is $63 million, which is about 200% of the average county agricultural income.

The city has three railroads: the Southern Pacific, the Union Pacific and Amtrak.

SAN JUAN

San Juan Plantation is where the city gets its name. John Closner of New Glarus, Wisconsin, founded a sugar cane plantation on the Rio Grande River, and sold the land on the north end of his property to establish the city. His Mexican employees revered him and called him "San Juan," so the city inherited a most appropriate Spanish name, even though its beginning was a sugar plantation owned by a man from the north.

San Juan is in Hidalgo County, which has the second largest agricultural income of any county in Texas. San Juan is a progressive town in the beautiful and rich lower Rio Grande Valley. It is located 236 miles south of San Antonio and is only seven miles from Mexico. It is on the main expressway between McAllen and Brownsville and the Gulf of Mexico.

This fertile garden spot, in the center of the Lower Rio Grande Valley, in which San Juan is located, was a wilderness of cactus and mesquite only 80 years ago. Now it is a huge vegetable garden and citrus orchard. San Juan's residents and winter visitors have easy access to all parts of this fabulous empire, as well as to points of interest in romantic old Mexico.

San Juan's population is approximately 9,400. The city owns its own water treatment plant and distribution system, sewage treatment plant and sewage collection system. It is proud of its newly paved streets. It is surrounded by groves of citrus fruits and fields of vegetables, irrigated through a multi-million dollar system supplied with water from the nationally famous Falcon Reservoir on the Rio Grande River.

Colorful banks of scarlet bougainvillea line the edges of the highways and are found everywhere.

The Shrine of La Virgen de San Juan del Valle is located in San Juan. This is an elaborate Catholic Church completed in 1954. It includes many imported objects of art. It was destroyed by fire after an airplane crash (apparently deliberate) in 1970. A wooden statue of Our Lady of San Juan was, however, undamaged. Ten years later the small statue was placed in a new $5 million dollar shrine built mostly from small contributions. The new Virgin de San Juan del Valle Shrine can now seat over 1,800 people. As many as 20,000 visitors now come to the imposing edifice on the weekend.

The Santa Anna Refuge is located near San Juan. The Refuge was established in 1943 to preserve 1,980 acres of the largest single tract of native subtropical vegetation remaining in South Texas, and is habitat for a large number of birds and animals found nowhere else in the United States.

Points of interest available to residents of San Juan and to visitors of San Juan include South Padre Island, Falcon Lake, quaint Old Mexico, the Confederate Air Force Museum, the Gladys Porter Zoo, the restored San Juan Hotel, the San Juan Shrine, Los Ebanos Ferry and the Santa Anna National Wildlife Refuge.

San Juan is served by the Missouri Pacific Railroad. It is located on U.S. Highway 83, and State highway 374, and Farm to Market road 2557.

One of the largest concrete pipe manufacturing plants in the United States is located in San Juan.

SAN MARCOS

The city of San Marcos is located in the southeastern part of Hays County and serves as the county seat of 670 square miles of territory. It is situated at the head of the San Marcos River, which has played a great part in the development of the city. San Marcos is 52 miles northeast of San Antonio on U.S. Highway 35.

According to legend, a group of Franciscan monks discovered the San Marcos while paddling up the Guadalupe River in 1790. A most unusual river, the San Marcos is fed by several large springs. It gushes from the foot of the Balcones Fault; the springs are fed by the Edwards Aquifer. Since the discovery was on St. Mark's Day, the river was named San Marcos in honor of that saint.

In 1845 two rangers, William W. Moon and Mike Sessom, brought their families and settled near the present site of San Marcos, the first of a long line of pioneers to settle in that area. In 1851, William Lindsey, Edward Burleson, and Eli T. Merriman bought the Juan Martin de Veramendi land and laid out the town of San Marcos. The new county of Hays was created by an act of the State Legislature on March 1, 1848. It was named in honor of Captain Jack Hays, a noted Indian fighter and Texas Ranger. When the county was organized, it had a population of 387 people.

Shortly after the first settlers arrived, the little town of San

Marcos became a stopping point in the three-day stagecoach trip from Austin to San Antonio. In 1849, a courthouse was built which also served as a school and church until other buildings could be completed. The stagecoach route was on the famous Spanish Road, El Camino Real.

The population of San Marcos increased slowly but consistently after the county was offically formed. From a population of 5,134 in 1930, it had grown to 34,650 by 1989. The average rainfall for Hays County is 34.4 inches, which is sufficient to raise all types of crops. The temperature averages 53 degrees in January and 96 in July. North of San Marcos is the Edwards Plateau and three miles north of San Marcos the elevation is 1500 feet, whereas three miles south of San Marcos, in the blackland farming district, the elevation is 600 feet. This gives the difference in elevation of the land lying above and below the Balcones Fault. To the east and south of San Marcos is blackland prairie. With its rich fertile soil, it offers the state's finest agricultural opportunities. Crops include cotton, hybrid corn seed, small grains and hay. To the west and north, the hill country is largely devoted to ranching.

Industry in San Marcos is diverse and includes high-tech electronics, injection plastics, oilfield valves, couplings, industrial lighting fixtures, specialized photographic equipment, and metal building fabrication. The newest facility will produce composite components for jet engines.

San Marcos is served by U.S. Highway 35 and by State Highways 12, 21 and 123 and by Farm to Market roads 621, 3107 and 3409. It has two railroads going through the town, the Union Pacific and Amtrak Railroads.

SANTA FE

Santa Fe was organized on January 20, 1977. On that date the towns of Arcadia and Alta Loma combined to form one municipal corporation, Santa Fe, Texas. The town took its name from the Santa Fe Railroad, which runs through both towns. Alta Loma was originally given that name because it was on fairly high ground. Alta Loma in Spanish means "high land."

Originally the settlers that were attracted to the Alta Loma area were brought in to raise pears, oranges, figs, and strawberries, but due to freezes, the boom ended. They turned to truck and dairy farming.

The first artesian water well in the area was dug at Alta Loma. The town of Arcadia, which is right next to Alta Loma, received its name from settlers who had come from Arcadia, Louisiana. They were lured into the area by the landsharks who promoted the land to be ideal for raising oranges, figs, strawberries, pears and peaches. There again, due to frequent freezes, the boom ended and the promise for an agricultural area to raise these products vanished.

The people of these two towns combined to form the flourishing new town of Santa Fe, Texas. It is located on State Highway 6. It is 23 miles northwest of Galveston and 40 miles south-southeast of Houston. The Santa Fe Railroad goes through the town and runs parallel to State Highway 6. The region surrounding Santa Fe is used for raising rice, soybeans, grain, sorghum, hay, corn and honey, and grazes beef cattle and horses. The town is in Galveston County.

The population of Santa Fe is 6,500 and growing. The town is supported by the agricultural activity in the surrounding region. The rainfall of the area is 42.2 inches per year. This is sufficient for any agricultural product that the farmers wish to raise, with the exception of rice, which must be irrigated.

The town of Santa Fe is close enough to Houston and Galveston for people to reside there and work in either of these two cities. The proximity of Houston is of particular importance to Santa Fe, because the citizens have access to seven universities located in the Houston area. They are close enough to the gulf for all types of water recreation and fishing.

SEAGOVILLE

The town of "Seago" was founded in 1876 by a gentleman named T. K. Seago. Mr. Seago cleared his land of dense timber and built the first store in town. His stock consisted of $200.00 in dry goods and groceries. In 1881 he was postmaster of Seago.

The first school in Seago was built around 1867. It was a one room log building with split log seats. It is known that some forty children attended this school, known as the Brinegar School.

The T&NO Railroad came through Seago, and upon its completion in 1880, helped the area become a busy and thriving rail terminal center. This was a great help because the farmers and other citizens no longer had to go to Lawson for their mail. Also, the farmers could market their cotton, alfalfa and other crops by shipment on the railroad instead of carrying them to Dallas by wagon. Before the railroad, there were locks on the Trinity River, several miles south of the city, and freight for the area could also be transported via the river on barges.

The first official plat of the city was recorded in the Dallas County deed records in 1883, and a second plat was filed in 1926, at which time the city was incorporated.

In the meantime, in 1910, the Post Office Department added the "ville" to the name "Seago," and the town became "Seagoville."

Seagoville is located in the extreme southeastern corner of Dallas County. It is located on U.S. Highway 175 and is 25 miles southeast of Dallas. The population is 8,500.

Seagoville was founded in a perfect agricultural region. The town proper was built on sandy soil and was surrounded by the richest blackland in the state at that time. The land during the early years of the 1900's sold for $100 per acre. In 1912 Seagoville had one of the largest farms in the state. The farm was owned by Mr C. C. Cobb and covered several thousand acres.

In the 1930's the Federal Prison System built the Detention Station on Highway 175 west of the city proper, and it is the present Federal Correctional Institute. Since its inception, the institution, under whatever name, has contributed enormously to the economy of the city with its payroll fund and great influx of employees from almost every state in the union.

In 1979 Seagoville celebrated its 100th birthday with the biggest celebration that has ever been held in the city. Letters of greetings were received from then President Jimmy Carter, Governor Bill Clements, and many others from all over the country.

Today, Seagoville has a population of 8,850 with an area population of 33,000.

The economy of Seagoville is primarily dependent upon the agricultural income of the area. It serves as the marketing and trade center serving the agricultural industry.

SEALY

Sealy is located in the first county to be settled in the state of Texas. Austin County's history dates back to 1821, when Stephen F. Austin came to San Antonio in August to carry on the Texas colonization enterprise which his father Moses Austin had been working on until his death the previous June. Austin was authorized to continue his father's work, and the governor of Mexico, whose flag flew over Texas at the time, permitted Austin to explore the coastal plain area between the Brazos and the San Antonio Rivers to select a site for colonization.

Austin chose an area west of the Brazos River which today includes Austin County, and the present-day Sealy and San Felipe. He chose this area partly because it was located on the Atascocito crossing of the Brazos River, providing a good link with San Antonio, San Augustine, and Liberty. The first colonists began arriving in the area in December 1826.

During the years that Austin was carrying on negotiations for his colonization plans, he managed to succeed in fulfilling the terms of his official April, 1823 contract with the Mexican government. By 1826, he had brought 297 people to colonize Texas under a legal contract with the government of Mexico; they have come to be known as the "Old Three Hundred."

In 1836, Texas won its independence from Mexico; it was in the same year that Stephen F. Austin died. By 1837, Austin County was officially organized and named for the man who originally settled the area. The county occupies 662 square miles, partially bounded on the west by the San Bernard River, and on the east by the Brazos. Today the area's historic importance is paid tribute in San Felipe where the 664-acre Stephen F. Austin State Park is maintained in honor of the first impresario of Texas.

Like many Texas towns of the late nineteenth century, Sealy owes its existence to the railroads born of America's Golden Age of Capitalism. The construction and expansion of countless railroad lines characterized the decade following the Civil War in this country, and it was during this period, and largely because of this activity, that the town of Sealy was created.

In 1877, a Galveston businessman named George Sealy created an organization to work for the extension of the Gulf, Colorado, and Santa Fe Railroad line further into Texas. The line had been chartered in 1873, and, at the time this extension was planned, it consisted of 50 miles of track reaching to Fort Bend County.

George Sealy was a successful Galveston businessman whose association with the railroad stemmed from his brother John's business interests. John Sealy was a prominent Galveston banker and capitalist who had an interest in several railroad lines, including the Gulf, Colorado, and Santa Fe Railway Company, of which he eventually became president.

Some accounts have it that George Sealy's organization originally hoped to extend the railroad through San Felipe but did not because that town's government and citizenry rejected the idea. Instead, George Sealy, acting on behalf of the Gulf, Colorado, and Santa Fe line, reached an agreement in 1878 with the San Felipe de Austin Town Corporation whereby the town corporation would sell him a parcel of land on which to establish a new town through which the railroad line could pass.

George Sealy bought 11,635 acres of land at a price of $0.10 per acre and the sale was made under the condition that Sealy would do his best to secure the establishment of a railroad depot on the land. George's brother John became president of the Gulf, Colorado, and Santa Fe Company that same year, and through the brothers' combined efforts, the railroad did reach the area in December 1879. By then, the final steps were being taken to create an official town on the recently acquired land.

The railroad quickly made Sealy quite a lively trading post in Austin County. Sealy was a particularly important stop on the Gulf, Colorado, and Santa Fe line because the roundhouse, where railroad engines were worked on and crews changed, was located there.

Sealy's first cotton gin was built in 1898 and in short order, there were three gins operating in or around the town.

Sealy is located on State Highway 36 and Interstate Highway 10 and U.S. 90. It is also served by farm to market roads 3019, 1094 and 1458. It is 47 miles west of Houston. It has a population of 4100. It is served by the Missouri-Kansas Texas Railroad and Atchinson, Topeka and Santa Fe Railroad.

The city has a considerable amount of industry. The famous Sealy Mattress Company is located there.

The city is supported primarily by the agricultural trade. The area raises livestock, poultry, sorghum, grains, rice, corn, cotton, peanuts, and hay. Incidentally, it is in the center of the Bluebonnet Trail in the spring.

In 1949, Sealy finally voted to incorporate and to adopt a commission form of government for the town. In 1968 the citizens voted to implement an aldermanic system of government with a mayor and five aldermen. This is the system that continues to serve Sealy today.

Sealy is a unique city. Its architecture attest to the fact that it is a blend of Anglo-Saxon, German and Czech cultures in the community.

SEGUIN

Seguin is located on the Guadalupe River on U.S. Interstate 10, 34 miles east of San Antonio. It is served by U.S. Highways 90 and 90A, State Highways 46 and 123, five Farm-to-Market Roads, and the Southern Pacific Railroad. The Old Spanish Trail (Highway 90A) is Seguin's main east-west artery.

The average annual rainfall is 30.6 inches. The altitude is 550 feet; the population is 22,500.

Seguin was built on land granted by the Mexican government to Sir Humphrey Branch under the Emprasario Grant of Green Dewitt. This land grant, recorded in the State Land Office at Austin, bears the date of May, 1830. Branch perfected his grant by actually settling on the present townsite in November, 1831. The terrors of untamed wilderness, the savage Indians, and growing difficulties with the Mexican government, Branch accounted for selling his league in 1834 and leaving the area.

Founded by Texas Rangers in 1838, Seguin was named "Walnut Springs." When it was discovered in 1839 that another locality in Texas had previously recorded the name "Walnut Springs," the shareholders voted to adopt a new name—"Seguin"—in honor of native son, Juan N. Seguin, who had been a colonel in the Texas Cavalry and had led the only company of the Texas Army totally comprised of men of Spanish or Mexican descent all the way to San Jacinto.

On March 24, 1846, an Act by the First Legislature read as follows: ". . . be it enacted by the Legislature of the State of Texas that the town of Seguin be declared the Seat of Justice in the County of Guadalupe." Then, on March 30, 1846, Guadalupe County was created from parts of Bexar and Gonzales counties. By this Act, Guadalupe County became one of the first ten counties created by the Legislature of Texas, and Seguin actually became a county seat before there was a county.

The city of Seguin was incorporated in 1853. The city adopted a home rule charter in 1971. A charter change in 1986 changed the form of government from mayor-council to city manager-council.

The first U.S. post office opened in 1846. The first newspaper, *The Texas Mercury,* appeared in 1853; and the Galveston and Harrisburg Railroad arrived in 1875. With the city's main street formerly a part of the Old Chisholm Trail, many local pioneers gained fame on the cattle drives from 1866 to 1877.

Seguin has been historically noted for its interest in quality education. The first school was taught by Rev. D. T. Thompson in 1842. Today St. James Church operates a modern parochial school which is housed partially in the old Male Academy built in 1849. In point of continuous usage as a school facility, it is the oldest school in Texas. The first public school was built in 1889. Seguin is the home of Texas Lutheran College.

Guadalupe County has always been famous for its stock raising. One of the most famous race horses of post-Civil War Seguin was named after the city; he carried the city's colors to win in the State Races in Austin. Texas, the horse ridden by Theodore Roosevelt in the charge of San Juan Hill in the Spanish-American War, was given to Roosevelt by his wife's Seguin cousin.

Today Seguin boosts its downtown oak trees, some over 500 years old; Max Starcke Park with outstanding public recreational facilities and an 18-hole golf course; a modern coliseum; a beautiful Central Park; mgnificent Victorian homes; restored historic sites and homes; and the soon-to-be-completed renovation by Texas Parks and Wildlife of Sebastapol, an 1850's plantation home called "the most beautifully constructed home in antebellum Texas" by the U.S. Advisory Committee in 1934.

Geography dictated that the early economy should be based on the soil. Today, a wide diversity of businesses provide income for the area. Along with traditional crops of pecans, cotton, grains, livestock, and poultry, there are agribusinesses, along with considerable production of oil, gas, sand, gravel, and clay.

There are nineteen industrial plants in the area which employ 3,800 employees, manufacturing microwaves, digital panels, electrical instrument controls, structural steel, dressed poultry, roadside maintenance equipment, composite fabrics, dry wallboard, architectural millwork, cotton goods, metal stamping, and plastic bags.

SEMINOLE

Seminole, the county seat of Gaines County, is located in the Texas Panhandle. It is 79 miles southwest of Lubbock, 187 miles west of Abilene, and 25 miles east of the Texas-New Mexico state line. It is situated at the intersection of U.S. Highways 180 and 385.

In 1905, Mr. and Mrs. W. B. Austin of Decatur, Texas, established a general store and post office about two miles south of the center of Gaines County. They called their community "Caput" (Latin for "head").

When an election was held that same year for the purpose of creating Gaines County, the Austin store was one of four voting places for the 175 qualified voters in the area. The location of the county seat was selected, land was donated by a New York syndicate whose estate was handled by Judge Caldwell of Midland, and a list of possible names for the new county seat was prepared for submission to the United States postal authorities. With the list of names, the post office could select one not already used by some other community; and, from that list, the post office approved the name "Seminole" for the county seat.

The Commissioner's Court thereupon accepted the name of "Seminole," and accepted the township plat as it was surveyed and presented in 1906. Mr. and Mrs. Guy Stark opened a store in the new community; Mr. and Mrs. Austin moved their store from Caput; a temporary court house was erected; and a small hamlet began to grow. Seminole was not incorporated until 1936.

Today, Seminole is a market for farmers and oil field workers. Gaines County is one of Texas' leading oil-producing counties. Seminole has petrochemical plants and a cotton delinting plant. In addition to cotton, leading crops in the area are sorghum, wheat, vegetables, peanuts, sunflowers, peaches, and pecans. Over 400,000 acres are irrigated. Cattle, sheep, and hogs are also raised.

SEYMOUR

Seymour is the county seat of Baylor County. It is located squarely in the center of the county. Seymour is 85 miles north-northeast of Abilene and 50 miles southwest of Wichita Falls. The town has a population of 3,800. The entire population of the county is 5,900.

Baylor County is like most of the counties in northwest Texas and the Panhandle. It is laid out approximately square, with 30 miles on the side. This is six townships square or 36 townships, each having 25 sections. Most of the counties have approximately 900 square miles.

The town of Seymour was laid out in 1878. The settlers named it Seymour, presumably after a Texas Cowman, Seymour Munday, who lived near Seymour Creek.

During the early days of Seymour when the country was largely free range, the Millet Brothers Ranch had headquarters ten miles south of Seymour. The Millet outfit kept up a running battle with the farmers who bought small parcels of land and put up fences. The cowhands cut their fences and harassed them in every way.

In 1884, the Texas Legislature passed a law, making it a serious felony offense to cut a fence. The Millets realized law and order had come to the free range. They sold their ranch. The sale included 25,000 cattle and 1,000 horses. The Simpsons were the buyers. This was the largest transaction of that time.

The Concord StageOcoach came through Seymour, making its run from Wichita Falls to Abilene. The Butterfield Trail, a branch of the Chisholm Trail, and the Old Cheyenne Trail passed through Baylor County, driving great herds of cattle from South Texas to Kansas markets. Some of the herds contained as many as 6,000 cattle.

The now famous Cowboy Reunion was started in 1896 by Jeff Scott, a retired cowboy. This has become a nationally known event. In 1897, Chief Quanah Parker, the half-breed Comanche chief and 300 Indians attended. They staged an Indian war dance, dressed in full battle regalia, dancing around a huge bonfire. It was a spectacular event and thousands watched.

Chief Quanah Parker was the son of the Parker girl who was kidnapped when she was nine years old and grew up with the Comanches and learned to love them. She had three children, one was Quanah, the famous Chief Warrior and Indian diplomat and reformer.

The Burlington Northern Railroad serves Seymour.

Seymour is located on U.S. Highway 277, 283 and 183, and

State Highways 422, 82 and 114 and by farm to market Highways 1286, 1919 and 2582.

Seymour is on the north bank of the Brazos River. The annual rainfall is 26.3 inches. The altitude is 1250 feet above sea level. The main agricultural products are cattle, wheat, cotton and grain sorghum.

Lake Kemp on the Wichita River is located ten miles north.

SHERMAN

Sherman is the county seat of Grayson County, which has its northern boundary as the Red River. The county was organized in 1846. Today the population of Sherman is 33,000. Sherman is located on U.S. Highway 69, 75 and 82 and on State Highways 11, 59, and 93. The city is also served by Farm-to-Market Roads 697, 1417 and 2729. The city is located 61 miles north of Dallas on U.S Highway 75.

The Burlington Northern Railroad, the Southern Pacific Railroad and the MKT Railroad serve the city.

The city has a well equipped municipal airport. Today Sherman is an educational, medical, commercial and industrial center with a wide variety of industrial products. With the establishment of several colleges in the area as well as a dramatic club, Sherman has earned the title of Athens of Texas.

On March 17, 1846, the birth certificate for Sherman was signed when the First Texas Legislature cut off a part of Fannin County, and named the area Grayson County for Peter Grayson, Texas statesman, and called the county seat Sherman for General Sidney Sherman, a calvary officer. At that time of course, they did not know that he would be the scourge of the Confederacy some eighteen years later.

Two years after Sherman was organized, the town had a log courthouse and a public well. It grew, sprawling over the 80-acre townsite on which Indian campfires were hardly cold. Log piled on log chinked with mud, windows without panes, walnut lumber export and courage, avarice and buffalo hides, ambition, cotton, wheat, cows, oil, a tinge of the Old South, much of the New West, elbow grease, family pride and love all went into the making of Sherman.

In 1852 when the town was just starting to grow up, it had 400 people. In 1858 it was incorporated. The Butterfield Trail Overland Mail with its galloping teams tied the town to the outside world.

Then came the strife-ridden and bloody 60's of the Civil War. At the end of this fratricidal struggle, farms were run-down. There was little money and no industry, but cattle were plentiful. The big drives north began. Hunters from plains to the west scented the Sherman square with their profitable, but fetid buffalo hides. As farming recovered, wheat and cotton buyers flooded the town. Crafts multiplied and trade flourished. There were new mills, a brickyard, candy factory, tannery and iron foundry.

Just north of Sherman is the huge lake at Texoma on the Red River. This is a favorite camping and fishing spot in North Texas.

Today Sherman is a thriving, growing city and serves as the trading and marketing center for a large agricultural area that raises beef cattle, dairy cattle, horses, hogs, poultry and grows cotton, wheat, oats, and sorghum grain.

Sherman has the Austin College located there. This is a Presbyterian affiliated school.

SILSBEE

Silsbee is the largest city and the principal commercial center of Hardin County in the Big Thicket National Preserve in Southeast Texas. It is 15 miles north of Beaumont, 97 miles northeast of Houston, and 90 miles southeast of Lufkin. It can be reached by U.S. Highway 96, State Highway 327, and Farm-to-Market Road 92.

Nathaniel D. Silsbee, a Boston lawyer, was one of the original incorporators of the Gulf, Beaumont & Kansas City Railway. Silsbee and his partner, John Henry Kirby, worked together to develop the virgin pine forests of southeast Texas. When a line of the G. B. & K. C. railroad was run north from Beaumont, Kirby named the first terminal "Silsbee" in honor of his partner and the second (30 miles northeast) "Kirbyville" after himself. The rail line reached Silsbee in 1894 and Kirbyville in 1895. Both towns were established as sawmill towns; Kirby's first sawmill was built in Silsbee the same year the railroad arrived.

When the Santa Fe Railroad selected Silsbee for its junction point with the Gulf, Beaumont & Kansas City line in 1901, the town that was to become Silsbee was formally laid out. A few years later, the Santa Fe Railroad established shops at Silsbee and made the city its division point. Today, Silsbee is a division point on the Southern Division of the Atchison, Topeka & Santa Fe Railway, headquartered in Chicago.

John Henry Kirby formed the Kirby Lumber Company, now known as Kirby Forest Industries. Kirby Forest Industries was sold to Louisiana-Pacific Corporation in January 1987. The sawmill is no longer in operation and plans for the complex have not been announced by the new owners.

Over 85% of Hardin County is forested. Much of the county's economy is based on forestry products. Silsbee, with a population of 7,684, is a trade and manufacturing center. Manufactured products include lumber, paper, and particle board. Sawmills, and oil and gas processing plants are also located here. Many of the city's residents are employed at Temple-Inland Forest Products Corporation, a paper mill which is located six miles from Silsbee in Evadale.

SINTON

The history of Sinton dates back to the year 1826 when Jim McGloin secured a contract from the Mexican government to form the townsite of San Patricio. The agreement provided for a town one mile wide and five miles long.

San Patricio, the first county seat, is located on the Nueces River about 35 miles west of Corpus Christi.

After receiving the grant, McGloin went to Ireland and recruited colonists. There were 42 families who settled on a site selected on the Nueces River. They named their settlement San Patricio, after the patron saint of Ireland, Saint Patrick. It was named by McGloin and McMullen, empresarios of the Irish colony.

The settlers, all of Irish descent, included lawyers, doctors, priests and engineers. The lack of farmers proved to be a real hardship to the little community. Also, the town did not grow as the founders had envisioned because the leaders of the community refused initially to permit a railroad to go through. To this day, San Patricio has no railroad and is now a small community with few residents.

Empresario Col. James Power, born in Ireland, signer of the Texas Declaration of Independence, received a contract from the Governor of Coahuila and Texas in 1828, for a settlement of 200 Catholic families, half Irish and half to be Mexican. Included in his settlement were Captain Felipe Roque de la Portilla and family. Power married successively two of Portilla's daughters. He married Tomasita after the death of Dolores. In 1830, Francis Welder came to America from Bavaria, and he and two sons landed at El Copano Bay in 1883. One of the sons, John, married Dolores Power (daughter of John and Dolores Portilla Power).

In the year 1886, the San Antonio and Aransas Pass railroad was begun through the county. This gave a great thrust to the growth of Sinton.

In 1887, a group consisting of J. V. Schofield and his son, L. D. Schudder of San Antonio, and a rich stockholder and landowner, David Sinton, an Irish millionaire who lived in Cincinnati, Ohio, formed a company which bought part of the Coleman-Fulton Pasture Company from Francis Welder and his son, John Welder. Incidentally, David Sinton was the father-in-law of Charles Taft, for whom Taft, Texas, a nearby town, was named.

In 1893 a company was formed called Sinton Town and procured a charter to form a town. They purchased 1,000 acres from the Coleman-Fulton Pasture Company and laid out the present townsite of Sinton. Two hundred acres of land were initially surveyed into town lots and these lots were sold.

The town was named for David Sinton, the rich landowner in the area.

An interesting story concerns the two mansions built by partners of the Coleman-Fulton Pasture Co. Fulton Mansion built in 1873 and Coleman Mansion shortly thereafter. Coleman's wife, after seeing the Fulton Mansion, desired one larger and better, and her husband built it for her.

After the turn of the century, the farmers found that the rich blackland in the Sinton area was ideal for cotton farming. J. J. McWhorter, his brother, A. E. McWhorter and the latter's son, Jack, invented and built the first steam-engine cotton picker in the United States. It took a long time for this technique to be developed to the point where the cotton-picker was really a successful machine. Today however, you no longer see cotton pickers toiling in the field picking cotton; it is all done by mechanical cotton-pickers.

About 1935, the area around Sinton became a major onion and truck-farming area. One hundred and eighteen carloads of vegetables were shipped from Sinton in 1940. The loads consisted of

26 cars of mixed vegetables; spinach, 12 cars; carrots, 13 cars; beets, 3 cars; cabbage, 25 cars; beans, 3 cars; and onions, 36 cars. Vegetable buyers were predicting even bigger yields of onions in the future. The prediction would prove correct, since San Patricio County led the nation in onion acreage planted, 26,000 acres, in 1944.

Paralleling the agricultural boom was the oil boom. Oil fields were developed by Plymouth Oil Company on the Welder leases north of Sinton. The first well was drilled in 1934. In 1935, the Welder "C-1" came in at 5508 feet with the production of 336 barrels daily. The discovery prompted Plymouth Oil Company to move its district offices to Sinton on May 7, 1936.

Sinton is the home of the nationally-known foundation, the Rob and Bessie Welder Wildlife Foundation. The Foundation's refuge and research area is located on an uniquely situated 7,800 acre tract and was established in Mr. Welder's will. It was founded in 1954, yet the design and furnishing of the facilities give it the appearance of having been there since the Spanish settlers came to this area when it was conveyed to the ancestors of the Welder family, the de la Portilla family, in 1807.

After the town of Sinton was settled, the company petitioned the commissioner's court for the relocation of the county seat from San Patricio, which was located in the extreme southwest area of the county, to Sinton, a more suitable and central location. The commissioner's court complied with the request and ordered an election to be held for this decision. The election carried and Sinton became the county seat of San Patricio County.

Even though the area around Sinton remains as a major agricultural area, oil still plays a most important part in its income. Since 1920, more than 350 million barrels of oil have been produced, and there is presently a renewed interest in oil exploration and production.

Sinton, originally incorporated with a commission form of city government, has changed to a council-manager form of government. There is a mayor and four councilmen.

Sinton is located 31 miles north of Corpus Christi, 126 miles south of San Antonio, 146 miles north of Laredo and 205 miles south of Houston.

The annual rainfall at Sinton is 31 inches. The elevation of the town is approximately 45 feet.

The real property ad valorem tax in the area is high. The total of the city, county and school tax is $2.1445 per $100 of assessment.

The nearest commercial airport is at Corpus Christi, a distance of 25 miles. The airlines serving the area are the American Airlines, Continental Airlines, Southwest Airlines and Conquest.

Sinton is served by major highways, U.S. 181, U.S. 77, Farm-to-Market 881 and the newest interstate, Highway 37.

Sinton is served by the Southern Pacific Railroad and the Union Pacific Railroad. There are a number of colleges a short distance from Sinton. The Corpus Christi State University is 50 miles away, Delmar College is 30 miles, the Bee County College is only 30 miles, and the Victoria-Houston College is 75 miles. Texas A and I University at Kingsville is 44 miles from Sinton.

SMITHVILLE

Smithville is located on the Colorado River in Bastrop County in Central Texas. It is 43 miles southeast of Austin, 100 miles northeast of San Antonio, and 118 miles west-northwest of Houston. It can be reached by State Highways 71 and 95 and Farm-to-Market Road 535.

The first recorded European visitors to the area were the members of the expedition of Don Domingo Teran de Los Rios in 1691; however, it was much later before any settlers arrived in the area.

The village of "Old Smithville" was laid out on 640 acres of land granted to Thomas J. Gazley and Lewis Lomas. The date of the founding of the village is apparently unknown; however, it is known that Frederick W. Grasmeyer was in the area and operating a ferry on the Colorado River in 1836. A post office was established in 1876; and the name of "Smithville" was apparently in honor of William Smith, a pioneer settler.

When, in 1887, the Taylor, Bastrop and Houston Railroad arrived in the area, the town relocated along the railroad tracks. Legend says that a coin was tossed to decide if the town's name would remain "Smithville" or if it would be changed to "Burlesonville" in honor of Murray Burleson who donated the land for the railroad depot. "Smithville" apparently won, and the town was incorporated in 1895.

Today, Smithville's population is 4,587. The city is located in a rich farming area; from its beginnings, agriculture has been an important component of its economy. Principal crops are grain sorghum, pecans, corn, wheat, oats, and fruit. The city is served by the Union Pacific Railroad (formerly MKT).

The Smithville Jamboree is an annual celebration held the first weekend after Easter.

Bastrop County is in the center of the "Lost Pines" region, and is a popular fishing and hunting area. Bastrop and Buescher State Parks are nearby, as are Lake Bastrop and Shipp Lake.

SNYDER

Snyder is the county seat of Scurry County, located on the rolling plains of West Texas with its sandy, red soil. It is 87 miles southeast of Lubbock, 80 miles northwest of Abilene, and 88 miles northeast of Midland. It is located at the intersection of U.S. Highway 180 and State Highway 350, just west of U.S. Highway 84.

The town was founded by W. H. "Pete" Snyder, a Dutch buffalo hide trader, who established a trading post on the banks of Deep Creek in 1878. Other businesses and settlers arrived, and a townsite was laid out in 1882. The site of the present Scurry County Courthouse was once the site of a buffalo hide house. The city was incorporated in 1907.

In 1948, Magnolia Petroleum opened the Kell-Snyder Oil Field of 52.52 acres. Within a year of the discovery of oil, Snyder's population increased from 4,000 to 12,000 and peaked above 15,000 in the early 1950's. At one time, over 4,000 trailer houses were in the city.

Scurry is one of the leading oil producing counties in the nation; and Snyder is now the center of the largest unitized oil field in the world. Other minerals produced in the area are natural gas, sand and gravel, and bentonite. Deposits of magnesium, copper, salt, gypsum, volcanic ash, limestone, coal, and clay loam are also found here.

In 1969, Snyder was designated an All-American City. Snyder's population today is 12,705. Its economy is based on oil production, ranching, farming, and manufacturing. Livestock and poultry are raised; and cotton, grain sorghum, wheat, fruits, and vegetables are the principal crops grown. Local industries process oil, gas, and magnesium, and manufacture apparel, wax, brick, and other products.

Scurry County has more than 50 registered Texas Historical Markers; Snyder has seven around the downtown square area.

Of special interest in Snyder is the Scurry County Museum which features Indian relics and pioneer ranch and home artifacts, and the Diamond M Museum of Fine Art which includes thirteen original paintings by N. C. Wyath.

Also of interest in the downtown area is a white buffalo statue at the courthouse square. It commemorates the shooting of a rare albino buffalo in the county. Reportedly, only eight white buffalo were ever killed in the United States. A "White Buffalo Days" celebration is held each October.

Western Texas College, a two-year community college, was opened in Snyder in 1971.

Deer, wild turkey, quail, and dove attract hunters to the area. Lake J. B. Thomas is nearby for fishing and other water activities.

SONORA

Sonora is located on the western slope of the Edwards Plateau, and is the county seat (and only town) in Sutton County. It is located at the intersection of Interstate 10 and U.S. Highway 277, 173 miles northwest of San Antonio, 64 miles south of San Angelo, and 91 miles north of Del Rio.

Sam Merck, while trailing Indians for the cavalry at Fort Clark, discovered a spring in the desert which had been used for years by the Indians passing through the area. Later, Ed Wall and Tom Birtrong camped at the spring while on a hunting trip. With their discovery of water in the area, they returned with their sheep herds and established a camp (later a ranch) at what they called "Wall's Well."

A well, drilled in early 1889, promised free water at the wellsite to all settlers who moved into the area. The well was the beginning of a town, drawing settlers to the desert-like area. Later, steam power was used to draw the water into a 20,000-gallon wooden tank.

When Sutton County was organized in 1890, Sonora became the county seat. The settlement was located on the Old San Antonio-El Paso Road. Typical of the old wild west days, shootings, drinking, gambling, and lawlessness marked the town's beginnings.

By 1891, the town had two hotels, several saloons, a restaurant, meat market, saddlery shop, barber shop, stage stop and post office, general store, drug store, newspaper, feed and wagon yard, blacksmith shop, jail, lawyer and land agent, and two physicians and surgeons.

A fire in 1902 destroyed all but the First National Bank building on the east side of Main Street, but the town was soon rebuilt.

The Fort Worth & Rio Grande Railroad purchased a 250-foot-wide right-of-way between its railhead at Brady and Sonora, and fenced the entire 100-mile distance—making it the longest fenced cattle trail in the world. This was a profitable venture until 1930 when another rail line ran directly into Sonora.

Today, Sonora's population is 4,387. Its economy is based on agriculture, tourism, hunting leases, and oil field services. Cattle, sheep, and goats are raised; and Sonora has become a cattle, wool, and mohair marketing center. Oil, gas, and stone are produced in the area. Sutton County is one of the leading hunting counties in Texas.

A Texas A and M Agricultural Research Substation is located here.

Of special interest are the Miers Home Museum (a furnished pioneer home built in 1888) and the Caverns of Sonora (about eight miles west of Sonora).

SOUTH HOUSTON

South Houston is in Harris County and it is southeast of Houston on U.S. Highway 75 and State Highway 3. It is about nine miles from downtown Houston.

The city had a population of 14,500 in 1989. It has an area of 3.0 sq. miles and is wedged between Pasadena and Hobby Airport.

The city took its name from Houston, its big sister. It is primarily a residential city, even though it has a number of small business establishments. The city was incorporated in February 1927. The city has a mayor-alderman type of government.

The city draws its economy from Houston.

South Houston is in the Pasadena Independent School District.

A very influential and colorful part of South Houston's history, was the Christy Brothers Circus. This circus traveled throughout the U.S., Canada and Hawaii. South Houston was the winter quarters for the circus. Christi pastured fourteen elephants in a prairie south of Spencer Rd. In 1944, George Christy disbanded the circus.

George Christy became a resident of South Houston in 1925. He became mayor for the first time in 1949, and was elected seven times thereafter. Mayor Christy would not accept any pay for his services.

South Houston has a high tax rate. The breakdown rate is as follows:

City	0.55 per $100 evaluation
County	.65 per $100 evaluation
School	1.06 per $100 evaluation
	2.20 per $100 evaluation

The average tax rate for Texas cities is approximately $1.75 per $100 evaluation.

The city is served by the Galveston, Houston and Henderson Railroad.

SPEARMAN

Spearman is the county seat of Hansford County, at the top of the Texas Panhandle. It is 91 miles northeast of Amarillo and about 20 miles south of the Texas-Oklahoma state line. It can be reached by State Highways 15 and 207 and Farm-to-Market Roads 759 and 760.

Spearman had its beginnings as a town on the Santa Fe Railroad in 1917. It was named for Thomas E. Spearman, Vice President of the railroad.

In the area where water can never be taken for granted, the Palo Duro River Authority was formed to provide water for the cities of Dumas, Cactus, Sunray, Gruver, and Spearman. With the completion of Palo Duro Reservoir in 1991, the residents of these cities will have a reliable water supply.

These several cities currently draw their water from the Ogallala Aquifer. Studies have indicated, however, that these wells may be depleted between the years 2000 and 2037.

Community leaders in the area recognized the problem of impending water shortage nearly two decades ago and began looking for a solution. As a result of their efforts, the State Legislative authorized the formation of the Palo Duro River Authority.

The dam is located twelve miles north of Spearman at the confluence of Palo Duro Creek and Horse Creek.

The oil and gas boom in Spearman began in 1954; oil, gas, and associated oil field businesses continue to be important components of Spearman's economy. Hansford County has five gas compressor stations, a gas-cracking plant, and a helium plant.

The area around Spearman has an annual rainfall of 22.1 inches.

Farming and cattle ranching are also important to the area. There are eight feedlots in the county. Hansford County has an agricultural income of $104,000,000 annually. This is approximately 300% of the average agricultural income of Texas Counties.

Spearman's local government consists of a mayor, city manager, and five councilmen. Spearman, with a population of 3,590, is a center for grain marketing and storage and gas processing. Crops grown in the area include sorghum, wheat, and corn. Over 200,000 acres of land are irrigated. The Santa Fe Railroad serves Spearman.

Hansford County has a considerable population of ring-neck pheasants, and in season, Spearman is a popular spot for pheasant hunters.

The Stationmaster's House Museum in Spearman features a restored depot agent's home, farm machinery, and a general history of the local area.

STAMFORD

Stamford is located in Jones County in North Texas; part of the city, however, extends north into Haskell County. It is 126 miles southwest of Wichita Falls, 160 miles west of Fort Worth, and 23 miles northwest of Abilene, at the intersection of U.S. Highway 277 and State Highway 6.

Land grants were purchased from the Texas Central Railroad by settlers associated with the Swenson Land and Cattle Company in 1900. The townsite on the railroad line was named "Stamford" after Stamford, Connecticut, but there seems to be some disagreement as to whether it was because most of the settlers were from Stamford, Connecticut or because the hometown of the railroad's president was Stamford, Connecticut. Most of the older streets in today's Stamford are named for the town founders.

Today, Stamford has a population of 4,542; and it is a retail, banking, and commercial center for a three-county area. Its industries include grain elevators, cotton gins, delinting plant, cotton compress, cottonseed oil mill, feed mill, oil well machinery, clothing factory, and wholesale outlets. Beef cattle, hogs, horses, and sheep are raised in the area; and cotton, wheat, and milo are grown.

Stamford is known for its Texas Cowboy Reunion held each year around July 4th and generally acknowledged as the greatest amateur rodeo in the world.

Also of interest in the area are the MacKenzie Trail Monument (which tells of the famous MacKenzie Trail and what it meant to the area in the late 1800's) and the Texas Cowboy Museum (which features paintings by cowboy artists and early farm and ranch artifacts).

STEPHENVILLE

Stephenville is located on the upper Bosque River Valley in Central Texas. The city is in the geographic center of Erath County, of which it is the county seat. It is 71 miles southwest of Fort Worth, 93 miles northwest of Waco, and 110 miles east-southeast of Abilene. Stephenville is well served by major highways with three U.S. highways, one state highway and three major farm to market highways coming into the city. The nearest interstate highway is only 23 miles north of Stephenville. The Santa Fe Railway provides rail service, including switching service, to the city. Stephenville is accessible by air with a 4,200-foot lighted, hard surface airport.

The first land patent in the area was obtained in 1853 by John M. Stephen, who donated the original townsite. When the county of Erath was organized in 1856, "Stephenville" (named for the Stephen family) was designted the county seat.

Stephenville's historic courthouse was built in 1893.

The early settlers raised oats, corn, sorghum, and garden produce. Most of the county was open range. By 1880, Indians were no longer in the area, having been driven east and north. Cotton was the principal crop in the county from 1890 to 1915.

Stephenville today has a population of 15,000. Stephenville has a very diversified economic base. Agriculture is the leading industry in the area having contributed $118 million, $80 million of which was from the dairy industry, to the county economy in 1987. Tarleton State University, a part of the Texas A&M University system, is an integral part of the community and has a major impact on the local economy. Stephenville has a good manufacturing base, boasting five major manufacturing plants with a total employment of 1,028 people. It is also the center of a retail trade area of approximately 72,000. Farming and ranching are still important to its economy. Dairy and beef cattle are raised. Erath County is the state's second leading county in milk production, and is also a leading producer of Coastal Bermuda range grass. Peanuts are the major cash crop; and small grains, fruit, and sorghum are also grown. One of the largest tree nurseries in the southwest is located in Stephenville.

The existing manufacturing industries in Stephenville are all strong and growing. Presently under construction is a $19 million AMPI cheese processing plant which created 90 new jobs for Stephenville when it opened in April 1989.

Stephenville is well equipped to provide all human services needs. Medical services are provided by the Harris Hospital, a modern, 98-bed hospital; a modern medical and surgical clinic; 28 doctors and nine dentists. Also available for special needs is Pecan Valley Mental Health and Mental Retardation, The Foster Home for Children and five nursing homes.

Housing is readily available in all price ranges, either rental or purchase. A total of 1,384 apartment units from 1 to 3 bedroom are also available.

Stephenville has 45 restaurants available which provide for quick lunches for a work force as well as after hours dining pleasure.

Recreational opportunities are abundant in Stephenville. Two parks and an active city parks and recreation department provides continuous programs for all ages. Also available are: a museum, a modern library, two golf courses, six baseball fields, a six screen cinema, a new 20-lane bowling center, two miniature golf courses (one indoor), a rodeo arena, and a fine arts center for the visual and performing arts.

The Atchison, Topeka & Santa Fe Railroad services Stephenville and the surrounding area.

Tarleton State University (begun as John Tarleton Agricultural College in 1899) offers a four-year program with a wide selection of degree programs. The university works closely with local industry to provide student labor, both graduate and undergraduate, in fields closely associated with the individual student's field of study. Tarleton provides a ready supply of dependable, highly motivated part-time labor. Tarleton State University is one of the fastest growing universities in Texas. Enrollment for the fall semester of 1988 was just under 5,800, an increase of 8% over 1987.

SULPHUR SPRINGS

Sulphur Springs is the county seat of Hopkins County in Northeast Texas. It is 80 miles east of Dallas, 38 miles south of Paris, and 100 miles west of Texarkana. It can be reached by Interstate 30 and State Highways 1,119, and 154.

For many years, only the Indians enjoyed the flowing springs. Their trails became the track for the wagons heading west. A few days rest under the shade of stately oak trees with abundant fresh water, was a blessing for the weary traveler. About 1845, a trading post was established by Eli Bibb. The town was founded by Dr. O. S. Davis, selling the first lot in 1851. Named for the springs and the sulphur content found in many of them, the town has always been called Sulphur Springs. The post office was named Bright Star, because there was already a post office in Texas called Sulphur Springs. In 1871, the post office name was changed to Sulphur Springs.

After the Civil War, in the fall of 1868, a federal garrison was established in Sulphur Springs. The federal commander moved the county court from Tarrant (formerly the county seat) to Sulphur Springs due to their inability to reach the county seat because of rain swollen creeks. When the last troops left, the citizens of Tarrant moved their records back to the old wooden courthouse in Tarrant. July 1, 1870, the Government officially made Sulphur Springs the county seat. The first courthouse in Sulphur Springs was built in 1881, and destroyed by fire in 1894. The present courthouse of Texas red granite and limestone was built in 1895.

After its beginning as a camping ground, Sulphur Springs became a market center for agricultural crops such as cotton, peaches, watermelons, potatoes, tomatoes, peanuts and hay. From 1929 to 1936, Hopkins County was primarily a cotton and fruit county. A slogan was adopted, "Where the Fruit Belt Begins."

Fruit was shipped out by the train carloads. A cotton compress was built in Sulphur Springs to meet the needs of some 30 gins in the county.

Then, in 1936, with the building of the Carnation Milk Company plant in Sulphur Springs, dairy farming became more important. Today Hopkins County produces more milk and dairy products than any other county in Texas. More than 500 dairies are located there. The county is also a leader in beef cattle production.

Today Sulphur Springs has a population of 17,646. Besides trade and agriculture, lignite mining and manufacturing are important to the city's economy. Doors and shutters, fired brick and clay, flow control valves, office furniture, plastic film and research balloons are manufactured. Hay, grains, and soybeans are the principal agricultural crops. The St. Louis Southwestern and Kansas City Southern Railroads serve the city.

Of special interest in Sulphur Springs are the Loe St. Clair Music Box collection (on the second floor of the Public Library); Hopkins County Museum and Heritage Park (an eleven-acre complex featuring a number of historic buildings and artifacts, including the oldest brick house (Atkins House) built in 1873); and The New Heritage Square (a restoration project for the downtown area).

Annual events include the Folk Festival in May (which features old-time crafts), Dairy Festival in June, Art of Woodcarving in June, Fall Festival in September (which features the World Champion Hopkins County Stew Contest, arts and crafts, and livestock and dairy shows), and Civil War Encampments and Drills in October.

Sulphur Springs Lake is nearby for recreational activities, as well as Lake Fork which holds several state records for bass fishing.

SWEENY

Sweeny is located in western Brazoria County on Farm-to-Market Roads 524 and 1459, 5 miles south of State Highway 35. It is about half-way between Bay City and Angleton and less than 20 miles from the Gulf of Mexico.

In the mid-1820's, "Move to Texas" excitement swept through Tennessee. When two of the sons of a Tennessee farmer, John

Sweeny, were sent to town to sell mules, they used the proceeds to buy a land grant. In 1831, John Sweeny's brother and son, William Sweeny and William Burrell Sweeny, traveled to Texas to look at the newly-purchased land; and two years later, John Sweeny himself, with his wife, 9 children, and 250 slaves, moved to Texas. The original homesite of the John Sweeny family was located just across from the present Sweeny cemetery.

The St. Louis, Brownsville & Mexico Railroad laid a construction sidetrack in the area in 1905, and gave the name "Adamstown" to the site (although no one apparently remembers or knows why or for whom it was named). Also that year, a sample of Sweeny soil won first place for fertility and germination at the Paris Exposition. With the combination of a railroad line and excellent soil, it was only a matter of time before more settlers arrived. By 1908, a store and cotton gin were built near the railroad tracks.

Application was made for a post office. The application was approved; William Sweeny was named the first postmaster, and the community was designated "Sweeny." There is some question, however, as to whether the town was named for William Sweeny (the postmaster) or for his father.

Sweeny's present city layout was designed in 1911 by Burton D. Hurd, a land development county agent.

Today, Sweeny's population is 3,538. Primary crops grown in the county are rice, cotton, commercial turf, and soybeans. Sweeny is served by the Missouri Pacific Railroad.

What is currently the Phillips 66 plant in Sweeny was originally an aviation gasoline plant built by Plancor for the federal government during World War II.

SWEETWATER

Sweetwater is the county seat of Nolan County in central West Texas. It is 42 miles west of Abilene, 106 miles northeast of Midland, and 125 miles southwest of Lubbock. It can be reached by Interstate 20, U.S. Highway 70, and State Highway 432.

During the 1870's, the site of present-day Sweetwater was a favorite camping place for buffalo hunters in the area. Kiowa Indians called the nearby creek "Mobettie" (meaning "sweet water") and the buffalo hunters called it "Sweet Water" because its clean, sweet-tasting water did not have the bitter gypsum taste of other streams in the area.

In 1877, a combination trading post and post office was established in a dugout on the banks of the creek (2½ miles southeast of present-day Sweetwater). Settlers and their families lived in tents. When the settlement applied for a post office, it was learned there was another "Sweetwater" in Texas. The settlement therefore became "Mobettie," although the residents continued to call it "Sweet-water". The name of the town was not formally changed to "Sweetwater" until 1918.

In 1881, the Texas & Pacific Railroad extended its rail line to the area. Nolan County was then officially organized and Sweetwater declared the county seat. Shortly thereafter, the town relocated itself next to the railroad track and the first permanent structure was erected.

Sweetwater was incorporated as a town in 1884. However, many people left the area because of a severe blizzard and drought in 1885-86, and the town charter lapsed. Sweetwater did not become fully incorporated until 1902. The city has a mayor-council form of government.

Oil development, begun in the 1950's, remains important to Sweetwater's economy, along with oilfield servicing and supply businesses. There are over 3,500 producing oil and gas wells within 30 miles of the city.

Today, Sweetwater's population is 12,738. The city is a banking and commercial center as well as a manufacturing and agricultural center. Cattle, hogs, and sheep are raised; and cotton, grains, and sorghum grown. Major employers are Genstar, Lone Star Industries, Ludlum Measurements, U.S. Gypsum, and Walls Industries.

The Sweetwater Commercial Historic District is listed on the National Register of Historic Places and includes more than 90 sites. Also of interest is the Pioneer City-County Museum.

The Rolling Plains Campus of Texas State Technical Institute is located in Sweetwater.

The Atchison, Topeka & Santa Fe Railroad and the Missouri Pacific Railroad both serve Sweetwater.

An annual event (held in March) is the Rattlesnake Roundup.

Lake Sweetwater and Oak Creek Lake are nearby for camping, fishing, and other water activities.

TAFT

Taft is near the center of San Patricio County on Highway 181 and Southern Pacific Railroad (established as San Antonio and Aransas Pass). It came into being shortly after the railroad came through the Coleman-Fulton Pasture Co. land in 1886. First, it was a flag stop installed at the request of Tom Coleman. A ranch windmill nearby was known as the Mesquital Mill, and when the railroad company built cattle pens on the railroad to ship out the ranch cattle, the small company settlement which grew up was known as Mesquital. In 1900, when Joseph F. Green took over management of the Coleman-Fulton Pasture company, he decided to build a town at the location, naming it Taft, after Charles P. Taft of Cincinnati. The change in name took place in 1904. For the next seventeen years it existed completely as a company town.

At the time that Green took charge of the ranch all of the land in and around Taft was ranchland. Starting in 1903, the company began planting cotton near Taft, the first plot containing 200 acres. By 1909, 2,300 acres were devoted to cotton and Taft was fast becoming the agricultural center for the company.

A surplus of buildings were available in Portland, Aransas Pass and Rockport due to fizzled land booms and Green moved several buildings across the open pasture land to Taft and started the nucleus of a town. A bunk house was moved from the ranching headquarters on the Rincon. Later it was turned into a hotel. A school was established in the back of a warehouse and several businesses were built on the south side of the railroad. Imogene Warburton was named the first postmaster on May 5, 1904.

The Coleman-Fulton Pasture company had made a decision to improve the land and sell it to farmers. In 1909 the first dependable water supply on the coast was discovered at Taft. Within a few weeks the company started construction of an agricultural-industrial complex to process farm products. Funds were authorized to build a slaughter and packing house, cold storage and ice factory, light plant, cotton seed oil mill and cotton gins. Later a feed mill, cotton compress and a creamery were added to the list of agriculture-related industries. These industries played big roles in the selling off of company land in the next two decades. These industries enabled the company to assure anyone who bought land that a market would be readily available to buy their products. It also afforded an opportunity for the company to make more money from their farm and ranch land.

During the next decade the company town grew with the addition of a hospital, bank, and a new school which doubled as a meeting hall. In 1909 President Howard Taft spoke in the school. In 1918 the directors decided to sell their entire ranch, including the city of Taft—utilities, industries and businesses, as well as city lots and farm land. In June of 1921 a huge auction sale was attended by well over 5,000 people and the city of Taft was launched as a privately owned community rather than being a company town. The company sold its last holdings in 1928. Green, who died in 1926, had purchased a considerable amount of choice land and businesses in the sellout. His heirs still own part of the land. The company's last office, which also housed the two company-owned banks, now belongs to the Taft Blackland Museum, displaying pioneer items from the ranch area.

The city was incorporated in 1929, with Ben Ivey named as its mayor. Aldermanic government was voted in 1960. Business continued to prosper as the community grew. The depression hit the city hard in the early 1930s, but in 1935 oil was discovered north of the city and the boom which followed helped Taft survive the depression. During the 1930s farmers in the area began planting vegetables, and packing sheds were built in Taft along the railroad. Vegetables continued to be packed in Taft until the 1950s when the last shed was torn down. Two large grain elevators now serve the area farmers, who largely plant sorghum grain, cotton and a limited amount of corn.

Immediately after WWII Taft enjoyed a residential boom and a growth in its school system. Retail business has declined; however the population has remained stable, due to jobs being opened in industries on the ship channel and in Corpus Christi. Major industrial employers in Taft are Reynolds Metals, DuPont, and Occidental Chemical. The Southern Pacific Railroad serves the area. Oil and petrochemicals are important to the area's economy.

The population in the city and Southwest Taft (not in city limits) is estimated at 6,000 (1985 figures put Taft at 3,686 and Southwest at 2,050).

Blackland Museum, located in the Taft Building, contains memorabilia of the early days of the area. A mural on the side of a packing and shipping shed beside the railroad attracts a lot of attention. It features the town's slogan, "The Best Cottonpickin' Town in Texas," and has everything from palm trees, cacti, a cotton field, oil well derrick, cattle, Pilgrims, the Mayflower, to astronauts.

TAYLOR

Taylor is located in Williams County in Central Texas. It is 35 miles northeast of Austin, 77 miles south of Waco, and 154 miles northwest of Houston. It is situated at the intersection of U.S. Highway 79 with State Highway 95.

When the International & Great Northern Railroad announced its plan to run a rail line from Chicago to Laredo through the area of present-day Taylor, the Texas Land Company bought acreage in the area. An auction of city lots was held in 1876 for the new town of "Taylorsville," named for Edward Moses Taylor, part-owner of the railroad.

Within two years, the town had a population of 1,000 and 32 businesses, including a gin and a grain elevator. Cotton and grain were the primary crops grown; and cattle and sheep were raised.

Most of the business district of Taylorsville was destroyed by fire in 1879. The residents quickly rebuilt, however, replacing wooden structures with more substantial ones. In 1882, the rebuilt town was incorporated as "Taylor." That same year, another railroad line—the Taylor, Bastrop & Houston Railroad—reached Taylor. Work on the rail line and in the railroad machine shops and roundhouse provided much employment.

By 1890, Taylor had Texas' first savings and loan association, as well as two banks. By 1900, the population of the town had reached 4,212; and had increased to 7,875 by 1940. Williamson County became the leading cotton producer in the state.

Today, Taylor's population is 12,500; it is an industrial, agribusiness, and publishing center. The city still operates under a commission form of government (which was designated in 1914 by city charter). The city is served by the Union Pacific Railroad.

Sorghum, wheat, corn, and cotton are grown in the county; and cattle, hogs, poultry, sheep and goats are raised.

Taylor is a Main Street City. The downtown area has been renovated and restored. A number of the buildings date from 1877 to 1894.

Of special interest is the Governor Dan Moody House, built in 1900. (Moody was governor of Texas from 1927-1931.)

TEAGUE

Teague is located in Freestone County, 63 miles east of Waco, 96 miles south-southeast of Dallas, and 157 miles north-northwest of Houston. It can be reached by U.S. Highway 84, State Highway 179, and Farm-to-Market Road 80, about 10 miles west of Interstate 45.

Settlers from Alabama, Florida, and Georgia came to the area of present-day Teague about 1849. They were farmers and grew cotton and corn. The community of "Brewer" (sometimes referred to as "Brewer Prairie") soon came into being, with the first post office being established in 1880. Brewer was named for Green Berry Brewer, who had a land grant in the area.

In 1906, Brewer was selected by the Trinity & Brazos Valley Railway as the site for its railroad shops and as the main division point between Houston and Fort Worth. The Trinity & Brazos Valley Railway was part of the Burlington-Rock Island Complex. The railroad was popularly known as the "Boll Weevil" Railway, so-called for the many special trains which were run to conferences about combating the insect devastation of cotton fields. Cotton was a staple of the local economy, and any threat to cotton was a serious matter.

That same year the town was renamed "Teague" for B. F. Yoakum's family. Yoakum was a railroad magnate and was largely responsible for the local rail line; his mother's maiden name was Teague.

With the railroad, prosperity came to the community. A town lot sale was held, brick buildings were erected, and the population grew. The town's population was close to 5,000 by 1910. Then, with the decline of passenger train service, Teague's growth also began to decline.

Today, Teague's population is 4,029. Cattle, hogs, and poultry are raised in the county; the primary crops are peaches, berries, pecans, and oats for grazing. Work in the area consists mainly of employment at the railroad, Big Brown Steam Plant in Fairfield, Nucor Steel, Jewett and the H L & P Plant in Jewett.

Of special interest in Teague is the Burlington-Rock Island Railroad Museum, located in the 1906 depot of the Trinity &

Brazos Valley Railroad. It features memorabilia of early-day life in the Teague area, as well as historical railroad material. Teague has the honor of hosting the second largest amateur rodeo in the State of Texas. This is always held during the July 4th weekend. The week preceding the rodeo is aptly called Western Week—a street dance on Main Street kicks off the entire week's events; there is a pageant to select Miss Western Week, several performances of a variety show featuring all local talent, a Main Street Jail used as a fund raiser, and then three nights of Rodeo, with a parade on opening night.

Teague also has city parks, a city pool, tennis courts, two baseball fields, picnic facilities and a large open pavilion available for family reunions, parties, etc.

Teague has an aldermanic form of city government consisting of five aldermen and a mayor.

There are also several large ranches in the area which need recognition as suppliers of fine cattle for show and breeding stock.

TEMPLE

Temple is located in Bell County in Central Texas, 36 miles south of Waco, 61 miles north-northeast of Austin, 169 miles northwest of Houston, and just a few miles east of the Fort Hood army installation. It can be reached by Interstate 35, U.S. Highways 81 and 190, and State Highways 36 and 95.

The Gulf, Colorado & Santa Fe Railroad selected a site as a division point for the railroad—branch lines would go to Fort Worth and Killeen—and named it "Temple" in honor of Bernard Moore Temple, their chief construction engineer. Although Mr. Temple lived in Galveston, he traveled throughout Texas working on various rail projects.

The railroad paid $27 an acre for 181 acres for a townsite in 1881, and sold the first town lots that same year for $45 to $300 each. Railroad shops were established at the site, and that was the beginning of Temple. The town was incorporated the next year and, two years after that, already had two banks, two newspapers, three churches, a flour mill, and 3,000 residents. The railroad played a key part in Temple becoming a trading and agricultural center.

Today, Temple's population is 45,044. Its industry is diversified (railroad shops, computer equipment, furniture, plastics, and oil field machinery); and it is a rail, marketing, and distribution center.

Temple, with four major hospitals and clinics employing approximately 20,000, is internationally known as a medical center. The Scott and White Memorial Hospital and Clinic, established in 1897, is often referred to as the "Mayo Clinic of the Southwest."

Temple Junior College is located here. The Missouri, Kansas & Texas Railroad and the Atchison, Topeka & Santa Fe Railroads serve Temple. Nearby are Lake Belton and Stillwater House Reservoir, which offer sailing, water skiing, fishing, camping, and picnic sites.

Of special interest are the Czech Heritage Museum in the SPJST (Czech) Insurance Company Building; and the Railroad and Pioneer Museum housed in a restored 1907 Santa Fe depot from Moody, Texas, which features a collection of local history and culture. An actual Santa Fe locomotive can be boarded and inspected.

The Texas Train Festival, an annual event, is held the third weekend of September.

TERRELL

Terrell is the principal commercial center of Kaufman County in North Texas. It is 30 miles east of Dallas and is located at the intersection of U.S. Highway 80 and State Highway 34. Interstate 20 and State Highway 205 also go to the city. Terrell's slogan is "The City of Tomorrow With the Charm of Yesterday."

Although the first settlers in the area arrived about 1848, Terrell was not founded until 1873 by John G. Moore and C. C. Nash when a railroad line was built into the area. The city was incorporated in 1875. It is assumed by all Terrell citizens that the city was named in honor of R. A. Terrell, a prominent land owner in the area.

Terrell today has a population of 13,953. It operates under a home rule charter and has a council/city manager form of government. Terrell is a banking and marketing center for the surrounding agricultural area. Its economy is based on general commerce, retail and wholesale trade activity, commuters, construction, industry, mental health care (Terrell State Hospital), and agriculture. Principal agricultural products are cotton, beef cattle, and dairying. Local plants make clothing, plastic goods, school supplies, machine parts, and wood fabrication.

Terrell has a high tax rate. The breakdown is as follows:

County	$0.2722 per $100. assessment
City	0.8500 per $100. assessment
School	0.8000 per $100. assessment
Spec. Road Dist.	0.0633 per $100. assessment
Highway 175	0.0064 per $100. assessment
Jail	0.0337 per $100. assessment
Trinity Valley Community College	0.0615 per $100. assessment
	$2.0871

The main line of the Texas and Pacific Railway serves Terrell. The nearest air transportation is Love Field in Dallas and the Dallas/Ft. Worth International Airport.

Southwestern Christian College and Trinity Valley Community College are located here.

Places of special interest in Terrell include the following:

The R. A. Terrell Homeplace is located on the campus of Southwestern Christian College. It was one of the first homes constructed in the area and is unusual in that it was built in an octagonal shape to give better protection from Indian attacks; it also contained the first glass windows in Kaufman County.

The Dr. L. E. Griffith Homeplace is the historic house of Dr. Griffith who was a personal friend and physician of Sam Houston. He administered medicine during the Battle of San Antonio, later becoming U.S. Surgeon-General.

The Porter Farm is recognized as being the birthplace of the Agricultural Extension Service in the United States.

The Terrell Carnegie Library Museum features historical items of local history. The Museum is housed in the Carnegie Building, built in 1904.

The Silent Wings Museum is located at Terrell Municipal Airport and is dedicated to the memory of all World War II Airborne Personnel. It features a completely restored WWII Waco CG-44 Glider and other wartime memorabilia.

The Spring Festival held annually in April features a Tour of Historic Homes, Livestock Show and Agricultural Exposition,

Arts and Crafts Exhibition, Antique Car Contest, Stew Cook-off, and Fiddler's Contest.

Lee's Silver Fox, the third largest country-western nightclub in the United States, is located in Terrell.

Three nearby lakes—Ray Hubbard, Tawakoni, and Cedar Creek—offer fishing, boating, skiing, picnicking, and camping.

TEXARKANA

Texarkana is located in Bowie County in the northeast corner of Texas, on the Texas-Arkansas border. It is located in two states and is named for three. It is 180 miles northeast of Dallas, and is situated on Interstate 30 and U.S. Highways 59, 67, 71, and 82.

The area around present-day Texarkana was occupied and settled many years before the first white settlers arrived. The Grand Caddoes lived in villages on the banks of the Red River and raised crops of maize, beans, pumpkins, and melons. The Great Southwest Trail, used by Indians traveling between the Mississippi Valley and the West and Southwest, crossed the area.

Hernando DeSoto was in the area in 1542; the French had set up a fort and trading post by 1719; and the survivors of the LaSalle expedition of 1867 passed through the area. About 1840, the community of "Lost Prairie" was established about fifteen miles east of present-day Texarkana.

The city of Texarkana itself, however, owes its founding to two railroads. The Texas & Pacific Railroad's lines crossed Texas to Arkansas; and the Cairo & Fulton Railroad crossed Arkansas to Texas. Texarkana was founded at the point where the two railroads met; the first town lots were sold in 1873 by the Texas & Pacific Railroad.

Although there is agreement that the city's name is derived from TEXas, ARKansas, and LouisiANA, there is no agreement as to who proposed the name.

Today, Texarkana is served by three railroads—the Missouri Pacific, the Kansas City Southern, and the St. Louis Southwestern. The population of Texarkana is estimated at 56,600, of which 33,900 live in Texas.

The post office and the Justice Center (with courts and jail) of Texarkana are located on the Arkansas-Texas line so they can serve two states, two counties, and two cities. Each side of the city has its own mayor/city manager government. A popular photo spot is in front of the post office where one can stand with one foot in Texas and one foot in Arkansas. Also downtown is the Scott Joplin ("King of Ragtime") mural; Perot Theatre (neo-renaissance); Draughn-Moore House (built in the shape of a playing card—the ace of clubs); and the Texarkana Historical Society and Museum (housed in the city's first brick structure, built in 1879).

The Red River Army Depot and Lone Star Army Ammunition Plant are located here, as are Texarkana Community College and East Texas State University at Texarkana.

Thirty manufacturing plants, both large and small, provide 12,500 primary jobs and 18,700 support jobs. Payrolls from these companies fuel an economy that is growing 6.75% per year (average since 1979). In the county, timber is harvested; beef, dairy cattle, poultry, and swine are raised; and wheat, soybeans, and hay are grown. Lake Wright Patman, southwest of Texarkana, offers fishing, boating, and other water activities.

Annual events in Texarkana include the Strange Family Bluegrass Festival, Memorial Day and Labor Day weekends; Quadrangle Festival in September; and the Four States Fair in October.

TEXAS CITY

The city of Texas City springs from a cluster of small settlements along Galveston Bay. Its roots go back before the Civil War, the Texas Revolution and even before the arrival of Stephen F. Austin and his first settlers. Texas City was originally called "Shoal Point," where the U.S. Government built a lighthouse to mark an oyster reef which was a menace to navigation in Galveston Bay.

In 1892, financiers from Minnesota purchased a large tract of land, developing a port, which grew and created a need for shipping terminals and refineries. As the city grew, the founders changed the name of the town to "Texas City", a name better suited, they felt, for greatness.

Texas City is located 35 miles southeast of Houston on Interstate U.S. 45. It is ten miles northeast of Galveston. Other major roads that run through the city are State Highway 146 and State Highway 3.

The city is a pleasant residential area and also a major industrial port. The port which is located in the Houston Ship Channel is the third largest in Texas.

Major industries include several oil and chemicals refineries, a tin smelter, metal fabricating plants, and is the future site of a copper smelting facility.

College of the Mainland, a two-year junior college, is located in Texas City, and offers vocational and technical instruction.

The Texas City Dike, the world's longest fishing pier, extends five miles into Galveston Bay and provides excellent fishing, boating, and swimming.

Today the city has a population of around 45,000.

TOMBALL

Tomball is located in the northern part of Harris County about 30 miles northwest of downtown Houston. It can be reached by Farm-to-Market Roads 149 and 2920.

The area around present-day Tomball was settled in 1849 by German immigrant farmers; as more settlers arrived, a community called "Peck" was established.

After the Rock Island Railroad constructed a rail line through the area in 1906, the town became an agricultural trade center and was renamed "Tomball" in honor of Thomas H. Ball who was instrumental in bringing the railroad to town. Mr. Ball was a prominent Houston attorney and U.S. Congressman from Texas.

In 1933, the discovery of oil in the area (The Tomball Oil Field) made Tomball an overnight boom town.

Today, Tomball's population is 6,228. It is a petrochemical and retail center. David Wayne Hooks Airport, located in Tomball, is the state's largest privately-owned airport. Tomball is still served by the Burlington Northern Railroad.

Of special interest in Tomball is the Community Museum Center which features a collection of antique farm machinery as well as several historical buildings—the Griffin House, a country church, a cotton gin, and a rural doctor's office.

TULIA

Tulia is the county seat of Swisher County. It has a population of 5,100 people. It is 47 miles south of Amarillo on U.S. Highway 87. State Highway 86 runs east and west through the city and Farm to Market 2301 runs east from Tulia.

The elevation is 3500 feet which makes for a good climate. The rainfall is 18.9 inches which is insufficient for the raising of most crops without irrigation. However, Tulia is located in the huge Ogallala Aquifer. One hundred eighty nine thousand acres of land in Swisher County are irrigated with water drawn from this huge Aquifer. The agricultural income in Swisher County is $125 million, which is roughly five times the agricultural income of an average Texas county. Sixty percent of this income is from the cattle feed lots. Some of the largest cattle feed lots in the world are located in the vicinity of Tulia. The crops which comprised the 40 percent of the income includes milo maize, wheat, cotton, corn and soybeans.

The Santa Fe Railroad runs north and south through Tulia. Swisher County came into existence in 1890. It was named after James Gibson Swisher, who was a man of distinction and a hero in the history of Texas. Tulia was named the county seat. Where did Tulia get its name? It has been accepted knowledge that Tulia was to be named "Tule," but when the application was sent to Austin in the year of 1890 (written in longhand) the letter "e" was misread to be "ia"—and so the word Tulia was given to the city. It has never been known exactly what it means. However, the word "Tule" is a Spanish word meaning "marsh-grass," a grass grown in Tule Canyon and along branches of Tule Creek.

The cattle feedlots which contribute to the prosperity of Tulia are located in three directions. Four lots within a 16 mile radius of Tulia contain 169,000 head of cattle on any given day and employ 173 people. The Tulia livestock auction sale is held every Monday. The magnet that draws the cattle feedlots to Tulia is the ability to raise grain on this rich irrigated agricultural land cheaply.

The Missouri Beef Packers plant is located 19 miles south of Tulia on I-27 (Highway 87). This plant has the largest beef-kill capacity under one roof in the world. Many Tulia families work at this plant.

A 35-minute drive north of Tulia is the Panhandle-Plains Historical Museum. This is the finest collection in the southwest. C. Boone McClure, a retired museum director, has been proclaimed the greatest living historian of the area.

One of America's most famous living "western" artists, Kenneth Wyatt, lives in Tulia. Wyatt's paintings are hanging in homes of movie stars, governors, museums, and private collectors plus individuals in every state and most countries.

Tulia has had an interesting prehistoric record. The Apaches, the Kiowas, and the Comanches fought to make the Tule area their homeland. In the year of 1541, Captain Fransisco Vasquez de Coronado's expedition, consisting of 1,500 men, with horses, stock, and supplies, set up camp in Tule Canyon (13 miles east of Tulia). From the Tule camp, Coronado took thirty mounted men and six foot soldiers on his trip north into Kansas looking for "The Seven Cities of Cibola" gold. He ordered the balance of his expedition back to Mexico. Coronado did not find the cities of gold, but the trip was not in vain as it opened the route for the founding of Santa Fe in 1565, twenty-four years later.

After the Coronado expedition, the Spaniards took notice of the area and sent several expeditions which crossed the now present site of Tulia, Swisher County, and all camped in the Tule Canyon. Two such were the Mares-Santos-Martin expedition of 1787 and the Texan-Santa Fe expedition from Austin, in 1841.

Some one hundred years ago, on September 25, 1874, Colonel Ronald S. MacKenzie and his men skirmished with a group of Indians near Rock Creek (19 miles east of Tulia on Highway 86) and rode into Tule Canyon and set up a supply camp. His scouts reported a large body of Indians camped in Palo Duro Canyon farther north. Three days later (September 28th) MacKenzie's forces attacked the camp of Comanche, Kiowa, and Cheyennes by surprise. The Indians scattered to places of safety throughout the canyons. MacKenzie ordered the camp and supplies destroyed. The evening of the same day he rounded up the Indian horses and mules and drove them back upon the canyon rim and then south into Tule Canyon, Swisher County. They arrived at 1 o'clock the following morning. The Indian stock, 1,450 head, was shot. This action, on the Rogers Ranch 13 miles east of Tulia, is referred to today as "MacKenzie Battleground." MacKenzie greatly demoralized the Indians, and the Texas Panhandle had seen its last Indian War.

Tulia area had many buffalo in the early 1800's. Colonel Charles C. Goodnight was one of the first to help settle the Texas Panhandle, with many other Panhandle pioneer families close behind. In 1883 Goodnight brought the vast Tule Ranch into his already extensive JA Ranch holdings. The Tule contained some

170,000 acres. Headquarters were established on a part of Tule Canyon, some 12 miles east of the present site of Tulia. The first house in Swisher County was a log cabin, used as a JA cowboy line camp. Located near the cabin was a creek and "water hole" tank, of spring-fed water. Prehistoric man, Indians, Coronado, the famed Santa Fe expedition, trail drivers, Comancheros, MacKenzie, wagon trains, the famous and the infamous cowboys, outlaws, stage coaches, all watered their stock and themselves at this tree-lined water oasis of the plains, later called the JA tank. Goodnight fenced the Tule Ranch in 1884-45.

Early settlers built dugout type homes—dirt floors, walls and roof of sod. It was common to build one room dugouts, but there were also larger ones and some with wooden floors, also some frame houses were built from lumber hauled in or wood chopped in the canyons.

In the period of 1910-1920 Tulia was known as the "City of Windmills." Some city dwellers had as many as three windmills, one each for the house, garden, and stock. The "eclipse" windmill made the settlement of the plains possible.

One of the first irrigation wells was hand-dug on J. W. Vaughn's farm in 1912 (one mile south of Tulia).

Tulia's economy today depends basically on livestock, grain sorghum, wheat, cotton, and soybeans.

One of the things to see in the area is the MacKenzie Dam and Lake, located 19 miles east of Tulia. The dam is the tallest non-federally funded earthen dam in Texas. It is located in the beautiful, historically rich Tule Canyon. The length of the top of the dam is 2,300 feet. The lake has a 29 mile shoreline and contains 46,500 acre-feet of water.

TYLER

Tyler is known as the "City of Roses" and the "Rose Capital of the World." It is the county seat of Smith County and is situated near the western edge of the East Texas Pine Belt. It is 100 miles southeast of Dallas, 129 miles northeast of Waco, 200 miles north of Houston, and 78 miles west of the Texas-Louisiana state line. It can be reached by U.S. Highways 69 and 271, and State Highways 31, 64, 110, 155, and 323, and is about 5 miles south of Interstate 20.

Smith County was formed in 1846 by an Act of the Texas Legislature. A five-man commission, formed to establish a county government, picked a site near the geographic center of the county and named it "Tyler" for U.S. President John Tyler. A small log courthouse was built on the town square and, in 1848, the town was incorporated.

During the Civil War, Tyler served as headquarters for the Trans-Mississippi Department of the Confederacy. Camp Ford, the largest prisoner-of-war camp west of the Mississippi (holding some 6,000 Union troops), was located just northeast of Tyler; hence, Tyler has the only Union cemetery in Texas.

Shortly after the Civil War, nurserymen were attracted to the Tyler area because of the excellent soil and climate. Initially they specialized in fruit and nut trees; however, after many trees were destroyed by outbreaks of disease, they turned to roses and ornamental shrubs. As the demand for roses grew, more nurseries were established and more roses were cultivated.

The arrival of the railroad in the 1870's helped establish Tyler as a transportation center for agriculture as well as the nursery business. Another boost to population growth occurred in 1931 with the discovery of oil in the East Texas Oil Field. Tyler then became headquarters for major oil companies as well as for independent oilmen.

Tyler's population now is 84,500. Area nurseries produce 20 million rose bushes annually—more than one-third of the garden rose bushes produced in the United States. Tyler's Texas Rose Festival is an annual event in mid-October. Tyler has a mayor-council-city manager form of government.

In addition to the rose and nursery business, Tyler is an administrative and operations center for oil production; and is home to manufacturers and processors making tires, pipe, heating and cooling systems, refrigeration equipment, clothing, boxes, gas compressors and fertilizers. Area crops include blueberries, peaches, pecans, and vegetables. The nearby pine forests provide timber.

The Missouri-Pacific and the St. Louis Southwestern Railroads serve the city.

Texas College, the University of Texas at Tyler, Tyler Junior College, and the University of Texas Health Center are all located here. Tyler Junior College is home of the "Apache Belles," a well-known precision dance-drill team.

Of special interest in the area are the Caldwell Zoo, Hudnall

Planetarium (at Tyler Junior College), the Municipal Rose Garden (featuring 38,000 rose bushes representing 500 varieties), Tyler State Park, and the World of Wildlife Museum.

UNIVERSAL CITY

Universal City is located fourteen miles northeast of San Antonio. It is south of U.S. Highway 81 going to Austin, to the south on State Highway 218, it is just outside of Loop 1604.

The population of the city is 11,000. It was a development that started in 1930, as a residential area for officers and personnel based at Randolph Field. It is strictly a residential city. It has a very favorable tax structure.

The story about how Universal City was named is not certain. It is rumored that it is because Universal Studios of California were frequently shooting pictures at Randolph Air Force Base about the Air Force. The studios had their local headquarters and a number of trailers and a lot of equipment parked on a vacant area near Randolph Air Force Base. The local people came to refer to this as Universal City. When the town's citizens came to chosing a name for their new town, it was suggested that they call it Universal City, and consequently that name was selected.

UVALDE

Long before white men ever saw and described the country around Uvalde, roving bands of Plains Indians hunted on the prairies and gathered pecans along the mountain streams. Although the Spaniards knew of the region possibly as early as 1535, and later made frequent trips across it, only three attempts were made to settle here before the annexation of Texas to the United States.

The first of these was in 1762. Since the middle of the eighteenth century, the Apaches had been steadily pressed southward by the Comanche, Wichita, and Towkawa nations of the north. Enemy of both the whiteman and the Indian, the Apaches were the scourge of the Spanish, repeatedly attacking packtrains bound for San Antonio, or destroying the ranches near Laredo. With the hope of controlling these Indians, Captain Roboza and Father Ximenes were sent to found a mission and presidio on the Nueces River. On January 23, upon a site at present Camp Wood, Edward County, Father Ximenes and Father Banos formally founded

Mission San Lorenzo de la Santa Cruz. While 300 Indians joined in the ceremony and hundreds more looked on, Father Ximenes solemnly tolled the mission bell, which had been set up in a temporary shelter. The presidio was garrisoned with 20 soldiers, and the mission occupied by a band of Lipans under Chief Caberzon.

A few weeks later another mission, Nuestra Senora do la Candelaria, was founded for a band of Lipans under Chief Turnie, Mission Candelaria was four or five leagues down the Nueces and on the opposite side of the river from San Lorenzo, at the site of the present village of Montell, Uvalde County.

Each mission attracted more than 400 Lipan neophytes. Some of them were set to clearing land and planting corn, while others were given the task of making adobe bricks to build a church. By summer the church at San Lorenzo was completed, and the twelve bushels of corn which had been planted promised a good harvest. But the ambitious efforts of the missionaries failed. Long before the corn was ripe it was consumed by roving tribes of Indians. The neophytes were fickle and deserted the missions at will, returning chiefly to enjoy the protection afforded by the garrison from their enemies, the Comanches. The missionaries had other difficulties; officials in Mexico not only refused to aid these newly founded missions, but ignored their very existence. Often the priests were reduced to dire need.

All during the winter and spring of 1767, the Comanches harassed both missions relentlessly. Candelaria was abandoned after the Comanches massacred a large number of Lipans within sight of the mission; and though San Lorenzo continued a precarious existence for two more years, it, too, was eventually abandoned.

Having failed to convert the Indians, the Spaniards instituted a series of military campaigns to conquer them. Capt. Juan de Ugalde, Governor of Coahuila, partly solved the Apache problem by turning the Lipans against the Mescalero Apaches in a series of four campaigns between 1779 and 1783 in which he crossed the Rio Grande into the Chisos Mountains and sought the Mescaleros in their own haunts. In 1790, Ugalde united the Comanche, Taovayas, Wichita and Tawakoni tribes and led them to a decisive victory over the Apaches at Arroyo de la Boledad. The site of the battle was the west banks of the Sabinal River, four miles south of the present village of Utopia. The canyon became known as

Canon del Ugalde in commemoration of Ugalde's exploits. Corrupted, it became Uvalde, and gave a name to Uvalde County a century after the battle.

The town of Uvalde was to be called Uvalde in honor of Capt. Juan de Ugalde, Governor of Coahuila who helped to drive the Apaches from the Uvalde Area.

The men who were to bring organization to these frontier settlements and to build a city in the wilderness did not arrive until 1853.

Reading W. Black, son of a family of New Jersey Quakers, was but 22 years of age when he formed a partnership with Nathan L. Stratton to engage in livestock raising and trading in the Uvalde Region. With a capital of $9,500, the two men in March 1853 bought "an undivided leagur and labor" along the Leona River in Bexar Survey 71.

Although there were only 75 persons living within the present territorial limits of Uvalde County at that time, Black and Stratton could hardly have chosen a more apt location in Texas. In the fertile valley of the Leona, grass was abundant throughout the year, and further feeding of stock was rarely necessary. Their land, moreover, was near the main line of travel between San Antonio and Laredo, Fort Duncan and El Paso. The soldiers of Fort Inge and the Indians who frequently camped at two-mile water hole to the north traded with the partners.

To increase his cattle range, on June 12, 1854, Black added: just north of his original purchase, 646 acres fronting the Leona. At the end of his first two years on the Leona, however, stockraising had become merely one of his many enterprises. By this time he had opened a store, cleared land, set out an orchard, opened a lime kiln and two rock quarries. He had replaced the two-room house where he and Stratton first lived, with a sturdy stone building. A thousand head of sheep grazed his pastures and at his trading post on the Leona he was busy buying and selling horses, mules and general merchandise.

On April 5, 1855, Black cut the first street of present Uvalde. Then he selected William C. A. Thielepape, a German surveyor and lithographer, and later Reconstruction Mayor of San Antonio, to lay out a town which he proposed to call Encina. His choice was a fortunate one, for Thielepape was a talented artist. To him, perhaps rather than to Black, should be credited the intrinsic beauty of the town, whose streets and plazas cut through the forest of live oaks on the Leona. Thielepape divided the tract into 464 lots, four plazas (one of which was designated courthouse square) and laid off seven streets. On May 9, Black paid him $58 for his work.

Encina's first months were discouraging. Before the surveyor's work was completed the garrison at Fort Inge was moved to Fort Clark. After the withdrawal of federal troops, Lipan and Seminole Indians began raiding and plundering the region. When Capt. James H. Callahan and his rangers failed to defeat the Indians in a flight that led them into Mexico in October 1855, many families gave up their frontier holdings and moved back to San Antonio.

Undaunted, Black began to push a plan for organizing local government. When the legislature convened in 1855, he had ready a petition asking for the creation of a county embracing the territory now included in Maverick, Kinney and Uvalde Counties, to be called Uvalde, and with its county seat at Encina. The settlers on the Leona favored the plan, and it was also approved at Eagle Pass, Las Moras and at the Patterson Settlement. The petition bore 80 signatures, representing all sections of the territory to be organized except the upper Sabinal region. J. H. Cleveland, representative, introduced the bill on November 8, 1856 and it received a favorable committee report on December 10.

When passage seemed assured, Encina had its final real estate boom. Uvalde County organized its government units at a special election on April 21, 1856.

Encina was chosen the county seat. The name of the town, however, in accordance with the legislative act creating the county, was changed to Uvalde.

Uvalde is the county seat of Uvalde County. The city was first settled in 1853, and in 1855-56, and was known as Encina. It was once the domain of the notorious frontier sheriff and outlaw, J. King Fisher.

Uvalde today, has a population of 15,600. It is the retail center of an extensive cattle, sheep and goat ranching area.

The city is located at the intersection of two of the longest U.S. Highways in the southwest. They are Highways 90 and 83. State Highway 55 serves the city, as well as Farm-to-Market Roads 140, 481, 1049, 1023, 1435 and 2389.

Uvalde is located at the foot of the Balcones Fault. It has an elevation of 900 feet. The rainfall is 23.3 inches. North of the Balcones Fault are rolling limestone hills; below the Balcones Fault are a number of springs which feed the Sabinal, Frio, Leona and Nueces Rivers.

The city has several industries including vegetable-packing and processing plants, garment-making facilities; a large number of truck farmers operate in the area.

Uvalde has a number of points of interest. Some of these are:

GARNER MUSEUM—Memorial home of former Vice President John Nance Garner. Open Monday thru Saturday, 9:00 A.M.-12:00 Noon and 1-5:00 P.M.; located at 333 N. Park.

OPERA HOUSE—Recently restored; located on Uvalde's unique four square Plaza. Daily hours available, 9:00 A.M.-12:00 Noon and 1:00-5:00 P.M. Special events held frequently. Call 278-4082 for further information.

FORT INGE—Two miles south of Uvalde on Highway 140. This former army post established in 1849 is now operated as a county park and open to boating and fishing.

GARNER STATE PARK—Located 31 miles north of Uvalde, one of the state's most popular parks. Open year round—concessions only open in summer.

LOST MAPLES STATE NATURAL AREA—Popular hiking and picnic area, located four miles north of Vanderpool, the area is most beautiful when it dons its "Fall Colors."

In October the city of Uvalde turns out for Cactus Jack—the festival that celebrates the life of John Nance Garner, Vice President of the United States known affectionately as "Cactus Jack."

Uvalde also plays host to national soaring competition in August with over 70 pilots competing for the title of best in the nation. It is exhilarating to see the beautiful fiberglass sail planes circling overhead, climbing into the clouds on the power provided by nature.

VERNON

Vernon is the county seat of Wilbarger County in the Red River Valley of North Texas. It is located 50 miles northwest of Wichita Falls, 175 miles northeast of Lubbock, and 21 miles south of the Red River which forms the boundary between Texas and Oklahoma. It can be reached by U.S. Highway 283 and 287.

The area of present-day Vernon was the home of roving Comanche, Kiowa, and Wichita Indians until the arrival of white settlers. About 1880, Mr. W. B. Worsham of Henrietta established the R-2 Ranch in Wilbarger County, with headquarters at Big Springs (in what is now northwest Vernon). The ranch served as a gathering place for cowboys in the area to get news from their families back east. A trading post was soon established at Condon Springs (now the Hillcrest Country Club); and the growing community was called "Eagle Flat" because of the many eagles nesting in the area.

The U.S. Post Office Department later changed the name of the town to "Vernon" in honor of George Washington's home, Mount Vernon. Because there are no mountains in the area, the "mount" part of the name was dropped and the city was designated as just "Vernon."

Vernon was incorporated in 1889; that same year, an election was held to elect officers for the city.

Today, Vernon has a mayor-council-manager "home rule charter" type of municipal government, and is a commercial, agricultural, and oil center for a large area of Texas and Oklahoma. The city is served by the Burlington Northern Railroad.

Vernon State Hospital is located in the city. Local industries include agricultural supplies and processing, seed breeding, textiles, meat packing, and cottonseed and alfalfa milling. Cattle, hogs, and horses are raised in the surrounding area; and cotton, wheat, hay, guar, sorghums, and other grains are grown. The Waggoner Ranch is headquartered here.

Vernon's population is estimated at 14,029.

Of special interest in Vernon is the Red River Valley Museum located on the campus of Vernon Regional Junior College. The museum features a big game collection, Indian artifacts, and photographs and memorabilia of the ranching, farming, and oil industry in the county. There is also an exhibit of memorabilia of Jack Teagarden, the great jazz trombonist, who was born and reared in Vernon.

Also of interest in the area are Medicine Mound, an Indian camping ground; Ethel's Point, a rise near the Red River used for Indian rituals; and the home of Mr. and Mrs. Corwin Doan, built in 1881, at Doan's Crossing (one of the most famous of historic cattle crossings on the Red River) north of Vernon.

VICTORIA

Victoria is the county seat of Victoria County. It is situated on the Guadalupe River. It is 30 miles inland from the Gulf of Mexico and 125 miles southwest of Houston and 135 miles southeast of San Antonio. The average elevation is 105 ft. Within a 150 mile radius of Victoria, there are several of the fastest growing cities in the United States including Houston, San Antonio, Austin, and Corpus Christi. Victoria occupies an area of 89.3 square miles.

The population of Victoria is 61,000. It gained 22% in the decade between 1970 and 1980. In the last five years, it has had a population increase of 16.4%.

The Mexican government settled 41 Spanish families in the Victoria area in 1824.

Victoria was named in honor of General Guadalupe Victoria who was Mexico's first President.

Victoria is ideally served by good highways, railroads, air transportation and barge canals. U.S. Highways 59, 77 and 87 serve Victoria. The Union Pacific Railroad and the Southern Pacific Railroad serve the city. The Victoria Regional Airport, with a 9,100 ft. concrete runway, lighted with instrument landing systems, has six flights daily to Houston Intercontinental Airport. Other available airports are located in Corpus Christi, Houston, San Antonio and Austin. The Victoria Barge Canal is seven miles south of Victoria and runs 35 miles SE to the Gulf Intracoastal Waterway.

Victoria has a number of sizable employers. The largest of which, is the E. I. DuPont de Nemours & Company, which has a large petrochemical plant in the area and employs 1,320 people.

Victoria has the council-manager form of government. It has a police force of 111 men and a fire department with 76 firemen and 29 emergency medical personnel.

The tax structure at Victoria is reasonable and is as follows:

City Tax	$ .5900	per $100 Assessment
County	$ .3796	
School	$ .7900	
Total	$1.7596	which is an acceptable tax rate

(Anything over $1.75 is considered on the edge of being excessive in Texas.)

The educational facilities available to the citizens of Victoria are as follows:

Victoria Union College, which has 3,000 students per semester and the University of Houston-Victoria which has 1,200 students per semester.

Colleges and universities within a 125-mile radius of Victoria are:

San Antonio has ten colleges and universities of higher education, offering a variety of degree programs. Corpus Christi offers students two colleges offering degrees in business, science, the arts and education. Austin has ten colleges and universities offering a variety of degree programs. Houston has students enrolled in twenty-nine colleges, universities and institutes. Texas A & M at College Station offers many programs.

Victoria and Calhoun Counties are applying for a joint foreign trade zone. The zone will allow companies to bring in foreign goods and assemble products for export without having to pay U.S. customs duties on the foreign goods or raw materials. This should be a very decided advantage to increasing the industrial capacity of Victoria and area.

In 1530, only 38 short years after Columbus made his historic voyage, a Spanish expedition was shipwrecked in the Gulf of Mexico, and the survivors landed on the coast of Texas. Because of the abundance of stately pecan trees, the Guadalupe River was first named "The River of Nuts." The leader of the expedition was DeVaca. Fortuntely, of the four main Indian tribes which he encountered in the area, the Lipans and the Toncahuas were friendly and helped the Spanish castaways recover their health. The Comanches and the Karankawas were more warlike and unfriendly. Later the expedition, led by DeVaca, made its way to California and then returned to Spain. Indications are that Cabeza DeVaca was the first white man to ever set foot in Texas.

A tiny fort was established by Robert de LaSalle and named for his King—Fort St. Louis. Hostile Indians and disease forced LaSalle to abandon the fort, but not before the news of this French foothold had reached Spain. This caused much consternation at the Spanish court, and word was sent to Mexico. "Locate and get rid of the French." This was more easily said than done, however. It took four attempts before an expedition led by Captain Alonzo DeLeon got through to this area, rediscovered the river, and named it for the patron saint of Mexico, Our Lady of Guadalupe, in 1698. Robert de La Salle was killed by his men as he preached at Navasota. A monument to him is in the town square at Navasota, Texas.

In 1722 the Spanish established a mission and a fort for its protection on the site of old Fort St. Louis, thus reclaiming the soil for Spain. But Indians and disease were too much for the Spanish, and both the mission and the fort were moved to a valley on the Guadalupe River where there was some irrigation and cattle raising. This area is known today as Mission Valley and is located just northwest of Victoria. Later the mission and fort were moved to a place on the San Antonio River, the site of today's city of Goliad. Permanent buildings were erected and visitors to Goliad can visit the mission which was recently completely restored to its original state. The chapel was also restored, and services are conducted regularly. This mission, called LaBahia, played a prominent part in the Texas Revolution.

Neither the French or Spanish settlements made a permanent impression on the area, and it was left to Martin DeLeon to change forever this vast and virgin countryside. The year was 1805 and many things were happening. The United States had won its freedom from England, the French monarchy had been overthrown, and Spain's most important colony of Mexico had thrown off the Spanish yoke in 1821. Permission to establish a settlement with the official name of Nuestra De Guadalupe De Victoria was granted, but following Texas Independence the name was shortened to Victoria.

The boundaries of DeLeon's colony included parts of Jackson, Calhoun, DeWitt and Victoria counties, located roughly between the lower Guadalupe River and the Lavaca River. In 1824 the seat of government was located on the banks of the Guadalupe River on a 640-acre grant, and the original city plot was one of the first in Texas to show a site for a school. There were eight Anglo-American families of good standing and of the Catholic faith. Each colonist received one league of land and a town lot, and the colony prospered. In 1829 DeLeon obtained a contract to bring one hundred and fifty more families. His death and a cholera epidemic in 1833 prevented this.

DeLeon's first task was to plan his city, which was laid out in accordance with his knowledge of the European and Mexican cities. Of prime importance was the market square used by itinerant traders and local settlers. Today Victoria's City Hall stands on the old market square. It was not until after the Texas Revolution that Victoria started taking on its Anglo-American characteristics. Under the Republic of Texas, Victoria County was created on May 17, 1836 with the city of Victoria being the county seat.

There are many points of interest and recreational facilities in the Victoria area. Riverside Park has 562 acres of woodland and is bordered by four and one-half miles of the Guadalupe River. Two hundred picnic areas are provided with tables, barbecue pits and benches. Memorial Square is located at 400 E. Commercial St. at Wheeler. An old steam engine that once belonged to the Southern Pacific Railroad is on display.

Memorial Square is the oldest cemetery in Victoria and contains graves of some of the pioneer families of the city.

The old Dutch grist mill contains two grinding stones brought from Germany through Indianola to Goliad before 1860 by the Rudolph Witte family. Later, Louis Albrecht moved the mill to Coleto Creek near Raisin. In 1870, Fred Meiss, Sr., bought the mill and installed the original stones in the present mill, which he built at Spring Creek. In 1935, the Meiss grandchildren deeded the mill to the Morning Study Club, which moved it to its present site.

The Nave Museum and McNamara House are very interesting. The Nave Museum presents changing fine art exhibitions. The museum owns a permanent collection of paintings by Royston Nave, in whose memory the museum was built. The McNamara House, located at 502 N. Liberty, contains period rooms and local history exhibits, with a back gallery featuring changing exhibitions of local arts and crafts.

The Texas Zoo established in 1976, is young and growing. This zoo's collection consists exclusively of animals indigenous to Texas and offers the only opportunity for many people to observe native Texas wildlife at close range.

The region around Victoria offers many recreational facilities, including three 18-hole golf courses, 48 tennis courts, a public swimming pool, 12 city parks and the Texas Zoo.

Other recreational sites are Lake Texana, a 11,000 acre resevoir; Saxet Lake: swimming, fishing, and picnicking; Coleto Creek Resevoir: fishing, camping, boating and picnicking.

Abundant fishing and hunting are available 30 miles away in the vicinity of the Gulf of Mexico; the Arkansas National Wildlife Refuge is hour's drive from Victoria.

The Victoria Public Library holds over 100,000 books.

VIDOR

Vidor is located in Southeast Texas, east of the Neches River in Orange County. It is seven miles northeast of Beaumont and 21 miles east of Orange and the Texas-Louisiana boundary, and can be reached by Interstate 10 and Farm-to-Market Road 105.

About 1600, the site of present-day Vidor was inhabited by Attacapas Indians who fished and hunted the area. However, most of them died from diseases (such as measles) after contact with the first Europeans.

As early as 1719, French traders were trapping animals in the area and sending pelts to New Orleans. Then about 1800, the Spanish arrived. The Old Spanish Trail, a main route for westward travelers, still runs through the southern part of present-day Vidor.

In the early days, the area, with its abundant grass and virgin timber, attracted many residents. Homesteaders arrived in 1865 after the Civil War to raise cattle. Then, after 1900, C. S. Vidor (father of Hollywood director, "King" Vidor) of Galveston established the Vidor Lumber Company. Vidor owned most of the timber rights and sawmill sites in the area; he owned the rail (tram) line to carry timber to the sawmill; and he operated sawmills and employed logging crews.

During the logging boom, several settlements of temporary workers were established. One of them was called "Duncan Woods" and is now part of south Vidor. Another settlement named "Diana" was located on the Kansas City Railroad line running through what is now downtown Vidor. A third, named "Terry," was in the far southeastern corner of Vidor. Terry was a Japanese settlement of rice farmers which began in 1907.

In 1910, these three small communities were united into one community named "Vidor" in honor of C. S. Vidor who started the lumber boom in the county.

Until 1925, when a new highway was completed west to Beaumont, travelers had to rely upon a ferry to cross the Neches River. The highway bridge greatly facilitated travel to and from Vidor.

Today, Vidor's population is 11,834. Forest products, including Christmas trees, are still an important part of local industry. Rice, soybeans, and nursery stock are raised in the area. The Kansas City Southern Railroad runs through the Vidor area.

WACO

Waco is beautiful city located in central Texas on the banks of the Brazos River in the heart of rich, blackland farming country. It is the county seat of McLennan Counnty. It is one of Texas' most important cities.

The city has a population of 114,000 people. It is the trading and distribution center for the farming area to the north and east and the ranching country to the west.

Baylor University is located in Waco. It is endowed and supported by the Southern Baptist Convention. Baylor has an enrollment of approximately 12,000. Waco is a sizeable center of higher education. Besides Baylor University, Paul Quinn College, McLennan Community College, and the Texas State Technical Institute are located in the city. The Veterans Administration has a large hospital located in the city, and their regional office is located there.

The city is located on a web of state and federal highways. US 35, 81 and 77 run south to north through the city. US Highway 84 runs from the southwest to the northwest through the city.

The city is served by the AT and SF and MKT railroads. The city has a well equipped municipal airport.

When the Mexican government made a land grant to Stephen F. Austin, he selected the rich farmland between the Colorado and Brazos Rivers. Waco was the northern limit of the land in Austin's Colony.

WAXAHACHIE

Waxahachie is located on Interstate 35 East and U.S. Highway 287, 28 miles south of Dallas. It is the county seat of Ellis County.

The earliest inhabitants of the area of present-day Waxahachie were Tonkawa, Kickapoo, Bidai, Anadarko, and Waco Indians. The famed Shawnee Trail ran through what is now the center of Waxahachie. Nearby Waxahachie Creek was used as a watering place for cattle on the trail drives from South Texas to Kansas City.

The first white settler in the area, Emory W. Rogers, arrived in 1846. The land was then gently-rolling open prairie.

Ellis County was created by an Act of the Texas Legislature in 1849. Rogers donated 62 acres of land for a townsite for a county seat for the new county. The city of Waxahachie was officially organized on the banks of Waxahachie Creek, from which the city took its name, in 1851. The name "Waxahachie" (pronounced "Wawks uh hatchie") is derived from an Indian word meaning "Buffalo Creek" or "Cow Creek." In 1871, the town was incorporated.

From its beginnings, Waxahachie and Ellis County relied almost entirely on agriculture and cattle. Around the turn of the century, Ellis County was known as the "Banner Cotton County of the World." Although Ellis County is still a leading cotton-producing area, the economy of the city and the county are no longer so completely dependent upon agriculture and cattle. In the early 1930's, Waxahachie expanded into retailing and light industry. Today, the city is home to such industrial firms as International Extrusion, Chevron/Spirolite, Southwest Foam Molding, Owens-Corning Fiberglas, Larkin Division of Copper Industries, Tyler Refrigeration, Flexsteel Industries, Foster-Forbes Glass Company, Dart Container Corporation, The Lofland Company, and Burleson Honey.

Waxahachie's population has grown steadily from 1,354 residents in 1880 to an estimated 20,000 today. A number of residents commute to the Dallas Metroplex area for employment. The city has a city manager form of government with a mayor and four councilmen. Three railroads serve the city—the Southern Pacific, the Burlington-Rock Island, and the Missouri-Kansas-Texas.

Southwestern Assemblies of God College, a fully-accredited junior college with an enrollment of 650 students, is located in Waxahachie, as is a branch of Navarro Junior College.

Of special interest in the city are the Ellis County Historical Museum and Art Gallery; the Ellis County Courthouse built in 1895 of red sandstone and granite; the Mahoney-Thompson Home with authentic furnishings of its era; and the Waxahachie Chautauqua Auditorium in Getzendaner Park built in 1902. The Auditorium is an octagonal amphitheater, the only one of its kind in Texas and one of only three remaining in the United States. It was built for the Chautauqua circuit which brought live talent for religious and cultural events to rural areas. The park itself was donated to the city by its first mayor, Captain W. H. Getzendaner, and became a tent city for two weeks each July when families came from all over Texas to hear such American greats as William Jennings Bryan, Will Rogers, and the U.S Marine Band.

Waxahachie hosts the "Gingerbread Trail," including a tour of homes, the first weekend of June each year. "Gingerbread," of course, refers to the intricate, detailed wood ornamentation once so popular for homes.

WEATHERFORD

Weatherford was originated in 1850, when selected as the seat of Parker County. It was named after Jefferson Weatherford, a member of the Texas Senate, when the county was created in early years. The town was the last settlement on the western frontier on the route of the wagon trains operating between Fort Worth and Fort Belt Nap. The southwest area of the town boasts many Victorian-style residences built in the late 1800's.

Industries include oil field equipment, silicone and plastic products. The city is the home of the Weatherford Junior College established in 1869. It is the oldest continuing two-year college in the Southwest.

Evolving from a trading day, held when court was in session on the first Monday of each month, farmers and ranchers bring produce and livestock to town to sell. The sales now feature a variety of produce and some livestock sales.

Weatherford has a population of 14,500. Weatherford is the county seat of Parker County. Weatherford is located where two U.S. Highways merge—U.S. Highway 80 and U.S. Highway 20. State Highway 171 runs north and south through the city. The city is well served by a number of farm-to-market roads, which fan out in all directions from Weatherford.

The city is served by the Union Pacific and Burlington Northwest Railroad.

The city has an altitude of approximately 900 feet. It has an annual rainfall of 32.4 inches. The city serves a large farming area. The county has an annual income of $41 million, 80% of which comes from the raising of beef, dairy cattle, hogs and horses. The crops are chiefly peanuts, peaches, melons, and hay.

The city has some industry. It has plants that makes plastic and rubber products, and oil field equipment.

Weatherford College is located in the city.

Weatherford is 30 miles west of Fort Worth. Weatherford has a number of interesting tourist attractions, including Highland Lake Park and Oliver Lovings grave. Known as the "dean of the Texas cattle drivers," Lovings came to Parker County from Kentucky about 1856. He was wounded by the Indians during a drive with Charles Goodnight. He died at Ft. Sumner in 1867, after traveling in secret without food for five days. Lovings' son and Goodnight returned his body over 600 miles by wagon, for burial in Weatherford. The Parker County Courthouse is a historic building. It was designed by Architect Wesley Clarke Dotson of Waco, who designed nine other Texas Courthouses. The Victorian building is constructed of limestone quarried locally at a cost of $55,555. The Peter Pan Statue is a bronze statue sculptured by Artist Robert Thomason, which honors Weatherford's native, Mary Martin, who created the role Peter Pan on Broadway. The Santa Fe Depot was restored in 1909. This all-brick structure was one of the first in the area to be built with concrete floors. It now houses the Chamber of Commerce Office and Visitors Center.

WELLINGTON

Wellington is the county seat of Collingsworth County. The town is located 11 miles west of the east boundary of the Texas Panhandle and is 95 miles east of Amarillo. It was named for the Duke of Wellington.

Before 1890 it was one of the estates of the Rocking Chair Ranch, that was known to Texas Cowboys as "Nobility Ranch," because of ownership by the British nobleman, The Baron of Tweedmouth.

The city is located south of the Salt Fork of the Red River. U.S. Highway 83 runs north and south through the town. It is served by State Highways 203, and FM 338, 1035, 1056, and 339.

The Burlington Northern Railroad serves the town.

The altitude is 2050 feet above sea level. The annual rainfall is 22.0 inches. Wellington has a population of 3,100.

The terrain in the vicinity of Wellington is rolling country with sandy and loam soils. It is mostly prairie land.

The crops raised are cotton and milo maize. There are 10,000 acres of land irrigated in the county. There are several large feed lots in the vicinity of Wellington. The Ogallala Aquifer does not extend into Collingsworth County, except in one small area.

The town is the retail center for the farms and ranches in the area.

WESLACO

Weslaco is located in Hidalgo County in the heart of the lush Rio Grande Valley of South Texas. It is located about halfway between Harlingen and McAllen on U.S. Highway 83 and Farm-to-Market Road 88, about 10 miles north of the Texas-Mexico border.

Weslaco is situated on the former Llano Grande Land Grant, formerly an area of dwarf trees and thorny shrubs, and overrun by Mexican bandits.

Weslaco was named for the W. E. Stewart Land Company, owned by Walter Edgar Stewart. The city was incorporated in 1919; and the first post office opened in 1920.

Although W. E. Stewart owned the Weslaco townsite at one time and often visited the area, he never established residence here. In 1909, he came to the Rio Grande Valley and established four banks (at Mission, McAllen, Donna, and LaFeria); then in 1913, he sold his banks to raise money to buy land in the Valley. After constructing irrigation canals, he became involved in land sales.

Weslaco today has a population of 22,683 and is a center for agriculture, food processing, clothing manufacture, and tourism. Many northern visitors spend their winters in Weslaco. The Rio Grande Valley is famed as a citrus, vegetable and cotton producing area. Weslaco is home to the world's largest grapefruit juice canning plant. The Missouri Pacific Railroad serves the city.

An annual event is the sugar cane festival held in February.

Of special interest in Weslaco are the City Hall, a Texas Historical Site of Spanish Moorish architecture and design, built in 1928; Bicultural Museum; Tower Theatre, a theatre-in-the-round, built from a water storage tank; Nature Park, 5½ acres maintained by the Audubon Society; and Harlon Block Memorial Park, in honor of a local Marine who was one of those at the famed flag-raising at Iwo Jima.

WEST COLUMBIA

West Columbia was initially known as Columbia. The city was founded by Josiah H. Bell in the early 1800's. His first settlement, Marion, was 1½ miles east on the banks of the Brazos River. Columbia was a settlement on the west bank of the Brazos. As time went by, Columbia grew larger and an area newspaper began calling it West Columbia, and Marion, East Columbia. These names have stuck and so they are called today.

The population of West Columbia is approximately 4,500 people. The city has the aldermanic form of city government with a city manager.

West Columbia is located approximately 55 miles southwest of Houston on Highways 35 and 36. It is located thirteen miles west of Angleton, which is the county seat of Brazoria County.

State Highways 35 and 46 meet in West Columbia. The city is located eight miles west of Highway 288 which connects Freeport with Houston.

There are no railways at West Columbia, but the Union Pacific is available in Angleton and in Brazoria. The nearest commercial air service is available at Hobby Airport in Houston, which is approximately 60 miles to the northeast.

The major industries in this area are rice growing, cotton and cattle ranching. The petro-chemical industry is a major source of employment in the area also.

The first duly elected Congress of the Republic of Texas met at Columbia, the new capital, October 3, 1836. The provisional government had been forced to move many times after the Texans declared their independence from Mexico on March 2, 1836 at Washington-on-the-Brazos. The temporary capital was first established at Harrisburg on March 22, but in less than a month the officials were forced to leave to escape Santa Anna's troops. The government fled to Galveston just one day before Santa Anna arrived at Harrisburg to burn it down, and in a few weeks they moved again, this time to Velasco. Facilities in both places were inadequate, so in July, President David G. Burnett called for a general election and ratification on the constitution, and decreed that the first duly elected legislature of the Republic of Texas would convene at Columbia on the first Monday in October 1836.

Columbia was chosen as the capital for two principal reasons—there were greater facilities available than in any other town at that time (with the possible exception of Nacogdoches)—and the early newspapers the *Telegraph* and *Texas Register* were there. Columbia had served as a seat of justice for the municipality of Columbia under Mexico, and boasted a number of permanent buildings built while it was the seat of the courts, including a large hotel, offices and a few dwelling houses and log cabins.

Two buildings served to house the Texas Congress and the principal offices of the government, and some officials and committees used adjacent log cabins. One of the buildings used by Congress was built by Capt. Henry S. Brown in 1832, serving as his family residence until his death in 1834. This was a two-story building containing two rooms below and two above, separated by a large hallway, with an ell to the back. After Capt. Brown's death, this building was used by the firm of Knight and White. It stood on the south side of Brazos Avenue until it was destroyed in 1888.

Texas historians generally agreed that this first congress accomplished much. They ratified the constitution, appointed committees, provided for the army and navy, protection from Indians, created a judiciary, a postal department, a land office and established a financial system.

One of the most interesting historic places is the Hogg Family Plantation. In 1901 the former Texas Governor, James S. Hogg bought the property from the Varner Family. Initially he made the purchase as an investment, but Hogg soon came to think fondly of the plantation as a second home for his scattered, motherless family of four children. Hogg was also convinced that oil in quantities equal to Spindletop lay beneath the property, and before his death in 1906 he drilled several wells trying to find it. Fourteen years later his belief was vindicated when the West Columbia field was brought in. It soon became the cornerstone of the Hogg family wealth.

That same year, 1920, Hogg's children—Will, Ima, Mike and Tom—remodeled the plantation house as a weekend retreat. They replaced the second-floor rear gallery with a two-story portico supported by six columns, reorienting the house to face the West

Columbia road rather than Varner Creek. They enlarged the kitchen building substantially to include kitchen, butler's pantry, storeroom and dining room and built a covered walkway to connect it to the main house. Finally, they replaced the heavy stucco on all exterior walls with a lighter plaster.

As one of the Old Three Hundred of Austin's Colony and as a veteran of the Texas Revolution, Martin Varner holds a secure place in Texas history. His land grant from the Mexican government was the 12th of 300 issued under Stephen F. Austin's first colonization contract. Varner was in North Texas along the Red River as early as 1816. After marrying Betsy English, he and his bride settled near Independence in Washington County. They then moved in 1824 to Varner's league grant (4,605 acres) on the Brazos River in present Brazoria County. This is the land that former Texas Governor James Hogg bought to form the Hogg Plantation. The home that is now on the Hogg Plantation is a beautiful building and is a major tourist attraction.

WHARTON

Wharton is located on the east side of the Colorado River in southeast Texas. It is the county seat of Wharton County and is 59 miles southwest of Houston and 66 miles northeast of Victoria. It can be reached by U.S. Highway 59 and State Highway 60.

William Kincheloe had received a grant of land on the bank of the Colorado River in 1824; in 1847, after the creation and organization of Wharton County, he laid out a townsite for a community also to be called "Wharton" in honor of John Austin Wharton and William Harris Wharton. The Wharton brothers were descendants of Lord Wharton, His Majesty's Governor of Ireland in 1640. Members of the Wharton family had emigrated to Virginia and fought in the American Revolution. John and William were born in Virginia, but came to Texas in 1827 at the outbreak of the Texas Revolution. William was first appointed Commissioner to the United States to secure aid for Texas; and, later, when Sam Houston was President of the Republic of Texas, he was appointed Minister to the United States. John was Adjutant General of the Texas Army at the Battle of San Jacinto.

Today, the city of Wharton has a population of 9,443. Its plants process minerals, rice, hides, pipe, and farm equipment; the city, however, is primarily an agricultural center. Crops grown in the area include rice, sorghum, cotton, peaches, and soybeans; in fact, Wharton County is the state's leading rice producer. Also, beef cattle, hogs, and poultry are raised; and oil, gas, and sulphur are produced in the county.

Wharton County Junior College and the Gulf Coast Medical Center are located in the city of Wharton.

Of special interest are the Wharton County Museum housed in the old jail, which details the heritage and economic background of the county; the Veterans Memorial Monument downtown, bearing the names of all servicemen who died in combat; and the Dickson Monument honoring popular Sheriff Hamilton B. Dickson who was killed in 1894.

The founder of Wharton, William Kincheloe, and his brother-in-law, Jacobe Betts, are buried in the old Wharton city cemetery.

WHITE SETTLEMENT

The City of White Settlement is in Tarrant County. It has a population of 17,500. It is 37 miles west of Dallas and ten minutes west of downtown Fort Worth. It is on Belt Highway 920, which circles Fort Worth. It is six miles south of Lake Worth. White Settlement is adjacent to a huge airplane manufacturing plant and next to Carswell Air Force Base. The city has a council-manager form of city government.

The city can be considered as one of the "bedroom" type cities of Fort Worth. It is primarily a residential area and enjoys an excellent taxation base. The total taxation is $1.41 per $100.00 of assessed value.

There are a number of colleges and universities in a reasonable distance. They are as follows:

Tarrant Junior College	Fort Worth (24,959 students)
Texas Christian University	Fort Worth (7,105 students)
Texas Wesleyan College	Fort Worth (1,505 students)
University of Texas	Arlington (22,760 students

The government installations are:

Installation	Employment
Carswell Air Force Base	1,764
General Dynamics, manufactures aircraft	27,000

Transportation: Dallas/Fort Worth International Airport is located 20 miles east of White Settlement. It is served by 44 domestic and foreign airlines that fly national and international routes with regularly scheduled passenger and freight service. Nine railroad companies provide passenger/freight service in and out of Fort Worth.

One of the main assets of White Settlement is being located in the vicinity of a large progressive city like Fort Worth. They enjoy all of the benefits of living in Fort Worth.

WICHITA FALLS

Although Wichita Falls is the county seat of Wichita County in North Central Texas, the city also is located partly in Archer and Clay Counties. It is 115 miles northwest of Fort Worth, 143 miles northeast of Abilene, and approximately fifteen miles south of the Red River and the Texas-Oklahoma state line. It can be reached by Interstate 44; U.S. Highways 82, 277, 281, and 287; and State Highways 79 and 240.

The first settlers in the area of present-day Wichita Falls were the Wichita Indians who lived near the waterfalls of what is now called the Wichita River. When John A. Scott surveyed the townsite in 1876, he decided to name the future town "Wichita Falls"—after the Indians and the waterfalls.

By 1882, the Fort Worth & Denver Railroad Company had bought land to lay tracks through the new settlement. The first train reached the community on September 27, 1882; that marked the official beginning of Wichita Falls as an agricultural and trade center.

Wichita Falls then became headquarters for petroleum production, service, and manufacturing with the discovery of oil in the early 1900's.

The early 1940's marked a period of tremendous growth for the city with the construction of Sheppard Air Force Base, the expansion of medical facilities, and commercial air transportation offered by Continental Airlines.

When the oil industry began to decline in 1960, industrial development was begun. Since 1970, fifteen major national manufacturers have relocated to Wichita Falls. Among other products, fiberglass products, clothing, electric components, mechanical parts, and aircraft turbine components are manufactured. Some of the city's major industries are A/C Spark Plug, CertainTeed Corporation, Cryovac, Levi Strauss, and PPG Industries.

Wichita Falls was named an "All-American City" in 1980-81. Today, the city's population is 98,899. It is a regional center for agriculture, commerce, medical and educational services, and oil. Midwestern State University, a four-year liberal arts school, is located here. The Burlington Northern and the Missouri-Kansas-Texas Railroads serve the city.

The principal crops grown in Wichita County are wheat, cotton, alfalfa, and grain sorghum. Over 22,000 acres are irrigated for cotton and coastal bermuda pastures. Hereford and Angus cattle are raised in the county.

The original waterfalls of Wichita Falls were washed away by a flood in 1886. However, the 54-foot falls were re-created in 1987 as part of a trail system winding through Lucy Park and along the banks of the Wichita River.

Of interest in the area are the Kell House, home of Frank Kell, a local business and community leader, with its original 19th century furnishings; and the Wichita Falls Fire & Police Museum.

Lakes Arrowhead, Diversion, Kemp, Kickapoo, and Wichita are all nearby for water sports.

WILLS POINT

Wills Point is located in Van Zandt County, which is in north-east Texas. The city is 48 miles due east of Dallas on U.S. Highway 80. State Highway 64 runs to the southeast from Wills Point. Farm-to-Market Highways 47, 751 and 2565 serve the city, as well as several well paved county roads.

The city has a population of 3,100. It has a mayor and five councilmen. The altitude of the city is 530 ft. above sea level. The area of the city is only one and a half square miles, which shows that this is a small town.

Wills Point was originally settled in 1873 as Iola. The coming of the railroad and postal service plus the discovery of another Iola elsewhere in the state, persuaded it to name it in honor of William Wills, pioneer settler, who lived at the "point" of timber jutting out into the prairie near his home. The original Wills home, incidentally, "built of logs on two sides," has been preserved as an historic landmark by the Business & Professional Women's Club of Wills Point and can be seen today near the original site.

The city has a population of 3,100. There are 30,000 in its trade area. The city is located in a rich agricultural area.

The city is served by the Missouri and Pacific Railroad which runs due east and west through the city.

Lake Tawakoni, with its 250 miles of shoreline, with well equipped marinas and other business facilities, has beautiful residential additions and home sites, make it ideal for lake living, fishing, boating, skiing, and all other water sports. Lake Tawakoni is only nine miles from Wills Point and the south side of the lake is served by Wills Point mail routes.

Wills Point has several industrial plants which make clothing, and other products.

WIMBERLEY

Wimberley is located on the Blanco River in Hays County in the hills and valleys of Central Texas. It is fifteen miles northwest of San Marcos, 40 miles southwest of Austin, and 60 miles northeast of San Antonio. It can be reached by Farm-to-Market Roads 12, 2325, and 3237.

By 1850, 8-10 families had settled along Cypress Creek (then called Jacob's Well Creek) and the Blanco River (then known as the Rio Blanco) in the area of present-day Wimberley. They called their community "Glendale."

William C. Winters, a veteran of the Battle of San Jacinto, moved to the community in the early 1850's and established a mill to service the area. Because of the mill, the site soon became known as "Winters' Mill." Then, in 1864, upon Winters' death, his son-in-law, John Cude, took over the mill; and the town became known as "Cude's Mill."

About this time, Pleasant Wimberley, a North Carolina native, was settled at Llano with his family. Indian raids had decimated his herds of horses and livestock so, at the urging of his wife, Amanda, Pleasant set out to find a safer place to settle his family. After visiting Cude's mill, he bought the property for $8,000 in gold, moved his family to the community, and the town soon became known as "Wimberley's Mill."

In 1880, an application was made to the U.S. postal authorities for a post office for the community. There is some question as to whether the name of "Wimberley's Mill" or "Wimberleyville" was submitted; in any event, the post office shortened the name to "Wimberley"—and it has been "Wimberley" ever since.

Cedar grows so thick and profusely in the area that, at one

time, cutting and selling fence posts was Wimberley's main industry. Today, cedar posts are still sold; and goats, sheep, and longhorn cattle still graze in rocky pastures.

Wimberley now has a population of 3,065 and is an unincorporated village run primarily by volunteers. The "town square" is lined with art galleries, boutiques, and antique stores. The area around Wimberley is very picturesque with its hills and valleys, spring-fed streams, canyons, and caves. Visitors stop at Wimberley to shop and browse, bird watch, search for fossils, swim, camp, fish, and hunt. The city is a major tourist and recreation center as well as retirement area. Many artists live in Wimberley.

The town's namesake, Pleasant Wimberley, and his wife, Amanda, are buried in the Wimberley Cemetery.

Just south of Wimberley is a re-created Pioneer Town, an Old West village of 1800's buildings with wood sidewalks, an opera house, an emporium, a fort lookout, a narrow-gauge train, and a house built entirely of soft drink bottles.

WINNIE

The city of Winnie is located in the extreme northeastern corner of Chambers County. It is 1.3 miles south of Interstate 10 on State Highway 124. It is 64 miles east of Houston and 24 miles southwest of Beaumont. There is no city government; Winnie is unincorporated.

In 1895, the Gulf and Interstate Railway (now the Santa Fe Railroad) built a railroad through Winnie to Port Bolivar. The railroad engineer in charge of the survey for the right-of-way was Fox Winnie. A railroad station was located at the site of what is now Winnie. The settlement that grew at this location was named Winnie in honor of the engineer who built the railroad through the area.

At that time, the state of Texas was offering settlers a grant of 640 acres of land if they would live on the land continuously for three years and pay the State $1,200 in order to prove their claim. This offer brought some settlers. Some of them proved their claims, but others did not like pioneering with its hardships and diseases. Mosquitoes were plentiful and many people died of yellow fever and other diseases. Anthrax killed their cattle, and then came the big snow of 1895, which dealt a devastating blow to the area. However, most of the pioneers stuck it out.

In 1899, the Devers Canal was started and a good trade area was opened. The first rice crop was grown in 1900 without benefit of any irrigation. The canal was completed in 1901 and thereafter provided many acres with irrigation.

In 1900 a gulf hurricane did a vast amount of damage to the crops and cattle in the area, and high tides and water washed out the railroad as far north from the gulf as Seabreeze. The railroad was rebuilt in two weeks. Again, in 1915, another hurricane occurred that destroyed or wrecked many buildings in Winnie. The rice crop was a total loss.

The farmers in the area, besides raising rice, planted pecan trees, vegetables, and figs to supply the growing market for these products.

Today, the economy is supported by oil production and the raising of rice, cattle, and crawfish. The economy is healthy.

Winnie has a population of 4,600. The town has built a new school building; a new bank was built in 1966; and a new hospital and shopping center have been built. Winnie is the home of the Texas Rice Festival held the first weekend in October each year.

WINNSBORO

Winnsboro is located in northeast Texas, primarily in northern Wood County but extending into southern Franklin County. It is approximately 100 miles east of Dallas, 100 miles southwest of Texarkana (and the Texas-Arkansas state line), and 73 miles south of the Texas-Oklahoma state line. It is located at the intersection of State Highways 11 and 37, 18 miles south of Interstate 30.

In the early days, the Mount Pleasant and Belzora Landing Road (running generally east and west) intersected with the Gilmer and Greenville Road (running generally north and south) at the site of present-day Winnsboro. The roads were heavily traveled by freight wagons and settlers heading west. The surrounding area was an undulating unbroken slope covered with red oak, post oak, and hickory trees and with waist-high grass. Wild turkey and deer were plentiful.

In 1854, John Elliott Winn and his stepson, William Rile McMillan, former residents of Rusk County to the southeast, were searching for a new place to settle on the frontier. When they came to the crossroads, they were so impressed with the area and the business prospects at the intersection, they decided to buy property in the area. They were able to purchase 361 acres from the William G. Logan Estate, with the crossroads being near the center of their new land.

Winn and McMillan each built a home, opened a store, and laid out business lots for their new town of "Crossroads." Because of its strategic location for business, the new town began to flourish almost immediately.

When a post office was established the following year, 1855, William McMillan changed the name of "Crossroads" to "Winn's Borough" in honor of his beloved stepfather.

About 1878, a Mr. Hays started the town's first newspaper. However, after investing his money in a press, type, ink, and paper, he did not have enough money left to buy head type for the full name of his paper, *Winn's Borough Sentinel*. He therefore shortened the town's name to "Winsboro." The post office, however, kept the original spelling of "Winn" but dropped the last three letters of "borough."

Winnsboro has a city manager and mayor-council form of government.

Today, Winnsboro has a population of 3,666. One of the major industries in Winnsboro is oil and gas. Various manufacturing companies employ several hundred people in Winnsboro. Dairy and beef cattle and hogs are raised in the area; watermelons, sweet potatoes, other vegetables, hay, corn, and small grains are also grown here. Some Christmas trees are grown and the timber sold.

Many people visit Winnsboro every fall to see the foliage in the area. An annual event, every weekend in October, is Winnsboro's Autumn Trails, in April is Spring Trails, in July is Summer Trails, and in December, is Christmas Winter Trails.

Lake Winnsboro, southwest of town, Lake Fork, Lake Cyprus Springs, Lake Bob Sandlid, Lake Monticello are within 20 miles of Winnsboro and are popular spots for camping, swimming, fishing, boating, and other water sports.

WINTERS

Winters is located in Runnels County in Central West Texas. It is 41 miles south of Abilene, 52 miles northeast of San Angelo, and 215 miles northwest of Austin. It can be reached by U.S. Highway 83 and Farm-to-Market Roads 53 and 1770.

The area around present-day Winters is fertile farming country. As early as 1880, two families moved into the area, about a mile southeast of the present town. They called their settlement "Bluff Creek Valley." The first settlers were then joined by eight additional families in 1886. Three years later, J. H. Winters, rancher and land agent, donated land for a school house. At the time the school was built, it was the only public building in the town. In 1890, the residents met and agreed the town should be named for Mr. Winters. The town of Winters is unique in that it never had a designated townsite.

Until a post office was established in 1891, residents had to travel to the courthouse at Runnels City for their mail.

The town began to grow about 1900—a bumper cotton crop came in and the local gin ran day and night. Stores and homes were built. Main Street was the public road from Ballinger to Abilene. Population had increased to 163.

By 1904, the town had five churches, three doctors, and a community band. Shortly thereafter, it also had a hotel, a bank, ten cotton gins, running water, and a railroad. With the coming of the railroad in 1909, Winters was incorporated; land values jumped to $7 an acre; the city got its first major industry, Winters Cotton Oil Mill, and population increased to 600.

The Winters Chapter of the Future Farmers of America was the first chapter in Texas to receive a state charter (in 1930).

In 1949, the first oil well in the area came in; soon, several hundred wells were in operation. Oil-related businesses continue to be important to Winters' economy, as is agriculture. Cotton, sorghum, and wheat are grown; and cattle, sheep, and poultry are raised.

Today, Winters is a commercial and distribution center. Its population is 3,145. The area is served by the Missouri Pacific Railroad.

The Z. I. Hale Museum in Winters features exhibits and memorabilia of area history.

WOODVILLE

Woodville is the county seat of Tyler County in East Texas. It is 54 miles north-northwest of Beaumont, 109 miles northeast of Houston, and 62 miles west of the Texas-Louisiana state line. It can be reached by U.S. Highways 69, 190, and 287.

When a post office was established in 1847, the community was named for Senator George T. Wood, who became the second Governor of Texas.

Woodville's estimated population in 1989 was 3,250. Woodville today is a commercial center for lumbering and forest products; in fact, 90% of Tyler County is forested. Tourists are attracted to the area for its scenic beauty—the area is one of rolling hills, springs and streams, thousands of wild flowers, and 250 species of trees.

Agriculture in the area includes raising cattle, hogs, poultry, and goats; and growing vegetables and soybeans.

Of special interest in Woodville is the Shivers Library and Museum, a restored Victorian home presented to the people of Woodville by former Governor Allan Shivers, and his wife.

Nearby are the Alabama-Coushatta Indian Reservation (created in the 1850's largely through the efforts of Sam Houston); Big Thicket National Preserve (approximately 84,000 acres of dense woods, swamps, and streams); Heritage Garden (featuring a log cabin built in 1866, other buildings, shops, homes, and vehicles, as well as pictures, historical documents, and maps from pioneer days through the 1920's); and the John Henry Kirby State Forest. Heritage Garden also features the Pickett House where people come from miles around to eat.

Woodville will be opening a 1,000-bed minimum-security prison facility "The Gib Lewis Unit" in March, 1990.

WYLIE

Wylie is located in the southern part of Collin County, about 20 miles northeast of downtown Dallas. Wylie is located ten miles east of Plano on FM-544 East and is located 110 miles north of Garland on Hwy. 78 North.

In the 1850's, a community on the site of present-day Wylie was known as "Nickleville." Then, in 1886, Colonel W. D. Wylie, surveyor for the Santa Fe Railroad, met with the local residents to select a name for a new town. The Colonel stated that if the town would be named for him, he would do something for the town. The name of "Wylie" thereupon was chosen and approved. That summer, Col. Wylie bought 100 acres of land and platted it; and then, in October, almost the entire population of the whole area was on hand to welcome the first train into town. Townsite lots were sold, and a band and free beer contributed to the festivities.

Wylie, a sleepy farm town a few years ago, is becoming a suburb of Dallas. Its 1989 population was estimated to be 3,500. Beef cattle and horses are raised in the county; sorghum, wheat, hay, and cotton are also grown. The Atchison, Topeka & Santa Fe Railroad still serves the city.

Wylie has a city-manager/council form of government. The population of Wylie is 8,900.

Lavon Lake is northeast of the city and Lake Ray Hubbard is southeast—both are popular spots for fishing, boating, and other water sports. Seven miles west is the Southfork Ranch, the Wylie Opry is located in downtown Wylie.

ZAPATA

Zapata is the county seat of Zapata County. It is located in South Texas on the northern tip of Falcon Lake, just a few miles from the Texas-Mexico border. It is 49 miles south-southeast of Laredo and 151 miles southwest of Corpus Christi, and can be reached by U.S. Highway 83 and State Highway 16.

One of the early ranchers in the area was Colonel Antonio Zapata, a native of old Guererro. Col. Zapata attempted a coup on Mexican General Santa Anna in 1839, was captured, tried, and executed. Both the city of Zapata and the county of Zapata are named for him.

The town of Zapata was originally called "Carrizo" (Spanish for "cane" which grows along the river and was often used to thatch roofs); the name was changed to "Bellville" in 1858, then back to "Carrizo" in 1875. Because another town in Texas is named "Carrizo Springs," mail was often misdelivered.

A flood in 1898 caused the community to relocate to higher ground, and the new site was called "Zapata." When that site on the banks of the Rio Grande was flooded by Falcon Reservoir, new Zapata was built on U.S. Highway 83.

One of Col. Zapata's friends was Henry Redmond. Redmond owned a general store in old Zapata, and he donated land for the first courthouse in the town. Redmond's ranch was used temporarily as headquarters for United States infantry troops during skirmishes along the border. Juan Cortina, a well-known border bandit, at one time launched a raid on Redmond's ranch.

The battle at Mier, where the well-known "black bean" incident took place, was planned in Zapata.

Six flags have flown over Texas—those of France, Spain, the Republic of Texas, Mexico, the Confederacy, and the United States—but Zapata County can boast of a seventh—that of the short-lived Republic of the Rio Grande.

Today, Zapata is still unincorporated. Its population is approximately 3,500. The city's economy is based on oil and gas production, cattle, farming (sorghum, citrus fruits and vegetables), Falcon Lake activities, and tourism. Many northern visitors spend the winter in Zapata each year.

Of special interest in the city is the La Paz Museum. It is located in a 200-year-old Mexican home and features photos, furniture, equipment, and memorabilia of the early days in the area.

Zapata County is rich in mineral resources, mainly oil and gas. Much of the county is unimproved ranchland with mesquite and ebony trees, prickly pear cactus, and native grasses.

White bass, black bass, hybrid bass, stripers, and catfish abound in Falcon Lake. Falcon State Recreation Park covers 572.6 acres on the shores of Falcon Reservoir.